Contents

STUDIES IN THE DEAD SEA SCROLLS AND RELATED LITERATURE

Peter W. Flint and Martin G. Abegg Jr., General Editors

The Dead Sea Scrolls have been the object of intense interest in recent years, not least because of the release of previously unpublished texts from Qumran Cave 4 since the fall of 1991. With the wealth of new documents that have come to light, the field of Qumran studies has undergone a renaissance. Scholars have begun to question the established conclusions of the last generation; some widely held beliefs have withstood scrutiny, but others have required revision or even dismissal. New proposals and competing hypotheses, many of them of an uncritical and sensational nature, vie for attention. Idiosyncratic and misleading views of the Scrolls still abound, especially in the popular press, while the results of solid scholarship have yet to make their full impact. At the same time, the scholarly task of establishing reliable critical editions of the texts is nearing completion. The opportunity is ripe, therefore, for directing renewed attention to the task of analysis and interpretation.

STUDIES IN THE DEAD SEA SCROLLS AND RELATED LITERATURE is a new series designed to address this need. In particular, the series aims to make the latest and best Dead Sea Scrolls scholarship accessible to scholars, students, and the thinking public. The volumes that are projected — both monographs and collected essays — will seek to clarify how the Scrolls revise and help shape our understanding of the formation of the Bible and the historical development of Judaism and Christianity. Various offerings in the series will explore the reciprocally illuminating relationships of several disciplines related to the Scrolls, including the canon and text of the Hebrew Bible, the richly varied forms of Second Temple Judaism, and the New Testament. While the Dead Sea Scrolls constitute the main focus, several of these studies will also include perspectives on the Old and New Testaments and other ancient writings — hence the title of the series. It is hoped that these volumes will contribute to a deeper appreciation of the world of early Judaism and Christianity and of their continuing legacy today.

PETER W. FLINT
MARTIN G. ABEGG JR.

The Dead Sea Scrolls and Christian Origins

JOSEPH A. FITZMYER, S.J.

WILLIAM B. EERDMANS PUBLISHING COMPANY
GRAND RAPIDS, MICHIGAN / CAMBRIDGE, U.K.

© 2000 Wm. B. Eerdmans Publishing Co.
255 Jefferson Ave. S.E., Grand Rapids, Michigan 49503 /
P.O. Box 163, Cambridge CB3 9PU U.K.

Printed in the United States of America

05 04 03 02 01 00   7 6 5 4 3 2

Library of Congress Cataloging-in-Publication Data

Fitzmyer, Joseph A.
The Dead Sea scrolls and Christian origins / Joseph A. Fitzmyer.
p.   cm.   — (Studies in the Dead Sea scrolls and related literature)
Includes bibliographical references and indexes.
ISBN 0-8028-4650-5 paper
1. Dead Sea scrolls — Criticism, interpretation, etc.
2. Dead Sea scrolls — Relation to the New Testament.
I. Title.   II. Series.

BM487.F545   2000
296.1′55 — dc21   99-059276

Preface

Over the years since the Dead Sea Scrolls were first published in the early 1950s, I have been studying them and have published a number of books and articles devoted to them. Already published are two books that pertain to the study of the Scrolls. The first was *The Dead Sea Scrolls: Major Publications and Tools for Study* (SBLRBS 20; rev. ed.; Atlanta: Scholars Press, 1990). This was mainly a bibliographical work, which sought to guide students to the many scattered places where scrolls and fragments found in the eleven caves of Qumran and other places in the Judean Desert had been published. That book is out of date today, and almost out of print. The second was intended for a more general audience, *Responses to 101 Questions on the Dead Sea Scrolls* (New York/Mahwah, N.J.: Paulist Press, 1992). It sought to answer many of the questions that I have been asked about the Dead Sea Scrolls over the decades ever since they became newsworthy. Some of them deal with Qumran texts themselves, others with the impact that the discovery of these Scrolls have made on the study of the Bible or the New Testament and early Christianity.

I have also written a number of articles on various aspects of the Dead Sea Scrolls, a few of them for scholarly discussion, but many others for more general readers. Some of the articles were lectures that I have given, which have surveyed the impact of the Scrolls on different aspects of the Bible and especially on New Testament study. Twelve of these studies are now brought together here in one volume. Some of the articles have appeared in periodicals and books that are not easily accessible. For this reason I have tried to gather the more important of such publications into this volume. All of these articles have been published before except one (Chapter 5, "Qumran Messianism"), which now appears here for the first time. All of the others have been reworked or slightly revised. In two instances (Chapter 3, "The Aramaic "Son of God" Text from Qumran Cave 4 [4Q246]" and Chapter 8, "The Significance of the Qumran Tobit Texts for the Study of Tobit") two earlier articles on the given topic have been combined. Consequently, the presentation in these cases now takes a new form in this volume. In all the articles I have sought to update the matter, taking into account more recent discussions of it by others. All of the articles are timely, and it is to be hoped that some of them will contribute to the ongoing debate about the Scrolls.

In some cases I have changed the title of the article slightly, and the reader will find in the following list of acknowledgments the title under which the study originally appeared and the place of earlier publication. I am grateful to the editors and publishers of the works in which they originally appeared for their permission to reproduce them here in a revised form.

I am also grateful to Michael Thomson, Daniel Harlow, and their colleagues at Eerdmans Publishing Co. for their generous cooperation and help in making my manuscript into a proper book.

Joseph A. Fitzmyer, S.J.
Professor Emeritus, Biblical Studies
The Catholic University of America
Washington, D.C. 20064
Resident at: Jesuit Community
Georgetown University
P.O. Box 571200
Washington, D.C. 20057-1200

Acknowledgments

Thanks are hereby expressed to the editors and publishers who have granted permission for the reprinting of the following articles:

Chapter 1, "The Dead Sea Scrolls and Christian Origins: General Methodological Considerations," appeared under the same title originally in *The Dead Sea Scrolls and Christian Faith: In Celebration of the Jubilee Year of the Discovery of Qumran Cave I* (ed. J. H. Charlesworth and W. P. Weaver; Harrisburg, Penn.: Trinity Press International, 1998) 1-19 and is used with the permission of the publisher.

Chapter 2, "The Dead Sea Scrolls and Early Christianity," appeared under the same title in *Theology Digest* 42/4 (1995) 303-19 (the 39th Annual Bellarmine Lecture, Saint Louis University), used with the permission of the editor.

Chapter 3, "The Aramaic 'Son of God' Text from Qumran Cave 4 (4Q246)," is a combination of two articles, "4Q246: The 'Son of God' Document from Qumran," *Biblica* 74 (1993) 153-74, used with permission of Editrice Pontificio Istituto Biblico, and "The Aramaic 'Son of God' Text from Qumran Cave 4," in *Methods of Investigation of the Dead Sea Scrolls and the Khirbet Qumran Site: Present Realities and Future Prospects* (Annals of the New York Academy of Sciences 722; ed. M. O. Wise et al.; New York: New York Academy of Sciences, 1994) 163-78, used with the permission of the editor of the Annals.

Chapter 4, "The Background of 'Son of God' as a Title for Jesus," appeared under the title, "The Palestinian Background of 'Son of God' as a Title for Jesus," in *Texts and Contexts: Biblical Texts in Their Textual and Situational Contexts: Essays in Honor of Lars Hartman* (ed. T. Fornberg and D. Hellholm; Oslo/Boston: Scandinavian University Press, 1995) 567-77 and is used with the permission of the publisher.

Chapter 5, "Qumran Messianism," is now published for the first time.

Chapter 6, "A Palestinian Jewish Collection of Beatitudes," appeared under the same title in *The Four Gospels 1992: Festschrift Frans Neirynck* (BETL 100; ed. F. van Segbroeck et al.; Louvain: Leuven University Press/Uitgeverij Peeters, 1992) 509-15 and is used with the permission of Leuven University Press.

Chapter 7, "Aramaic Evidence Affecting the Interpretation of *Hōsanna* in the New Testament," appeared under the same title in *Tradition and Interpretation in the New Testament: Essays in Honor of E. Earle Ellis for His Sixtieth Birthday* (ed. G. F. Hawthorne with O. Betz; Grand Rapids: Eerdmans, 1987) 110-18 and is used with the permission of the publisher.

Chapter 8, "The Significance of the Qumran Tobit Texts for the Study of Tobit," is a combination of two articles, "The Aramaic and Hebrew Fragments of Tobit from Qumran Cave 4," *CBQ* 57 (1995) 655-75, used with the permission of the Executive Secretary of the Catholic Biblical Association, and "The Significance of the Qumran Tobit Texts for the Study of Tobit," which appeared under the title, "The Significance of the Hebrew and Aramaic Texts of Tobit from Qumran for the Study of Tobit," in *The Dead Sea Scrolls Fifty Years after Their Discovery: Major Issues and New Approaches* (ed. L. H. Schiffman et al.; Jerusalem: Israel Exploration Society, 2000), used with the permission of the Israel Exploration Society.

Chapter 9, "The Qumran Texts of Tobit," appeared under the title "Tobit," in *Qumran Cave 4: XIV. Parabiblical Texts, Part 2* (DJD 19; ed. M. Broshi et al.; Oxford: Clarendon, 1995) 1-76 (+ pls. I-X), (Text © Oxford University Press) and is used with the permission of Oxford University Press.

Chapter 10, "The Aramaic Levi Document," appeared under the same title in *The Provo International Conference on the Dead Sea Scrolls: Technological Innovations, New Texts, and Reformulated Issues* (STDJ 30; ed. D. W. Parry and E. C. Ulrich; Leiden: Brill, 1999) 453-64 and is used with the permission of the publisher.

Chapter 11, "The Qumran Community: Essene or Sadducean?" appeared under the same title in *Heythrop Journal* 36 (1995) 467-76 and is used with the permission of Blackwell Publishers of Oxford.

Chapter 12, "The Gathering In of the Teacher of the Community," appeared under the title, "The Gathering In of the Community's Teacher," in *Maarav* 8 (1992) 223-38 and is used with the permission of Western Academic Press, Rolling Hills Estates, Calif.

Abbreviations

General Abbreviations

AASOR	Annual of the American Schools of Oriental Research
AB	Anchor Bible
ABD	D. N. Freedman et al., eds., *The Anchor Bible Dictionary* (6 vols.; New York: Doubleday, 1992)
AbhDOG	Abhandlungen der deutschen Orient-Gesellschaft
ABRL	Anchor Bible Reference Library
AbrN	*Abr-Nahrain*
AbrNSup	Supplement to *AbrN*
AcOr	*Acta orientalia* (Copenhagen)
AD	G. R. Driver, *Aramaic Documents of the Fifth Century* B.C.: *Abridged and Revised Edition* (Oxford: Clarendon, 1957)
AGAJU	Arbeiten zur Geschichte des antiken Judentums und des Urchristentums
AHW	W. von Soden, *Akkadisches Handwörterbuch* (3 vols.; Wiesbaden: Harrassowitz, 1965, 1972, 1981)
AJT	*American Journal of Theology*
AnBib	Analecta Biblica
Ant.	Josephus, *Antiquities of the Jews*
AP	A. E. Cowley, *Aramaic Papyri of the Fifth Century* B.C. (Oxford: Clarendon, 1923; reprint, Osnabrück: Zeller, 1967)
APOT	R. H. Charles, *The Apocrypha and Pseudepigrapha of the Old Testament* (2 vols.; Oxford: Clarendon, 1913)
AsSeign	*Assemblées du Seigneur*

ATANT	Abhandlungen zur Theologie des Alten und Neuen Testaments
Aug	*Augustinianum*
b.	*Babylonian Talmud* (prefixed to the name of a tractate)
BA	*Biblical Archaeologist*
BAC	Biblioteca de autores cristianos
BARev	*Biblical Archaeology Review*
BASOR	*Bulletin of the American Schools of Oriental Research*
BDB	F. Brown, S. R. Driver, and C. A. Briggs, *The New Brown-Driver-Briggs-Gesenius Hebrew and English Lexicon with an Appendix Containing the Biblical Aramaic* (Peabody, Mass.: Hendrickson, 1979)
BETL	Bibliotheca ephemeridum theologicarum lovaniensium
BH	*Buried History*
Bib	*Biblica*
BibOr	Biblica et orientalia
BMAP	E. G. Kraeling, *The Brooklyn Museum Aramaic Papyri* (New Haven, Conn.: Yale University, 1953)
BO	*Bibliotheca orientalis*
BRev	*Bible Review*
BSac	*Bibliotheca sacra*
BZ	*Biblische Zeitschrift*
BZAW	Beihefte zur *ZAW*
BZNW	Beihefte zur *ZNW*
CB	*Cultura bíblica*
CBQ	*Catholic Biblical Quarterly*
ChrC	*Christian Century*
CivCatt	*Civiltà cattolica*
CJT	*Canadian Journal of Theology*
CRINT	Compendia rerum iudaicarum ad Novum Testamentum
CSEL	Corpus scriptorum ecclesiasticorum latinorum
DBSup	H. Cazelles and A. Feuillet, eds., *Supplément au Dictionnaire de la Bible* (Paris: Letouzey et Ané, 1928-)
DCH	D. J. A. Clines, ed., *The Dictionary of Classical Hebrew* (8 vols.; Sheffield, U.K.: Sheffield Academic Press, 1993-)
DJD	Discoveries in the Judaean Desert (of Jordan)
DNWSI	J. Hoftijzer and K. Jongeling, eds., *Dictionary of the North-West Semitic Inscriptions* (2 vols.; Leiden: Brill, 1995)
DSD	*Dead Sea Discoveries*
DSSMPTS	J. A. Fitzmyer, *The Dead Sea Scrolls: Major Publications and Tools for Study* (rev. ed.; SBLRBS 20; Atlanta: Scholars Press, 1990)

EDNT   H. Balz and G. Schneider, eds., *Exegetical Dictionary of the New Testament* (3 vols.; Grand Rapids: Eerdmans, 1990-93)
EHAT   Exegetisches Handbuch zum Alten Testament
ErIsr   Eretz Israel
ESBNT   J. A. Fitzmyer, *Essays on the Semitic Background of the New Testament* (London: Chapman, 1971; Missoula, Mont.: Scholars Press, 1974 [see *SBNT*])
EstBíb   *Estudios bíblicos*
EstEcl   *Estudios eclesiásticos*
ExpTim   *Expository Times*
FilNeot   *Filología neotestamentaria*
FRLANT   Forschungen zur Religion und Literatur des Alten und Neuen Testaments
GBH   P. Joüon, *A Grammar of Biblical Hebrew Translated and Revised* (trans. T. Muraoka; Subsidia biblica 14/1-2; Rome: Biblical Institute, 1991)
GesR   W. Gesenius, *Hebräisches und aramäisches Handwörterbuch über das Alte Testament* (18th ed.; ed. U. Rüterswörden et al.; Berlin/New York: Springer-V., 1987-)
GKC   *Gesenius' Hebrew Grammar as Edited and Enlarged by the Late E. Kautzsch: Second English Edition . . . by A. E. Cowley* (Oxford: Clarendon, 1910)
HALAT   W. Baumgartner, *Hebräisches und aramäisches Lexikon zum Alten Testament* (6 vols.; Leiden: Brill, 1967-96)
HAR   *Hebrew Annual Review*
HdO   Handbuch der Orientalistik
HeyJ   *Heythrop Journal*
HSS   Harvard Semitic Series
HTR   *Harvard Theological Review*
HUCA   *Hebrew Union College Annual*
ICC   International Critical Commentary
IDB   G. A. Buttrick, ed., *The Interpreter's Dictionary of the Bible* (4 vols.; New York/Nashville: Abingdon, 1962)
IEJ   *Israel Exploration Journal*
JAOS   *Journal of the American Oriental Society*
JBL   *Journal of Biblical Literature*
JBTh   *Jahrbuch für biblische Theologie*
JJS   *Journal of Jewish Studies*
JNES   *Journal of Near Eastern Studies*
JQR   *Jewish Quarterly Review*

JRAS	*Journal of the Royal Asiatic Society*
JSOT	*Journal for the Study of the Old Testament*
JSOTSup	Supplements to *JSOT*
JSP	*Journal for the Study of the Pseudepigrapha*
JSPSup	Supplements to *JSP*
JSS	*Journal of Semitic Studies*
JTS	*Journal of Theological Studies*
J.W.	Josephus, *Jewish War*
KJV	*King James Version* (of the Bible)
KlT	Kleine Texte
La	VL (used only in chap. 9)
LCL	Loeb Classical Library
LXX	Septuagint
m.	*Mishnah* (prefixed to the name of a tractate)
MGWJ	*Monatsschrift für Geschichte und Wissenschaft des Judentums*
MT	Masoretic Text
NAB	*New American Bible*
NEB	*New English Bible*
NIV	*New International Version* (of the Bible)
NJBC	R. E. Brown et al., eds., *The New Jerome Biblical Commentary* (Englewood Cliffs, N.J.: Prentice Hall, 1990)
NJV	*New Jewish Version* (of the Bible)
NovT	*Novum Testamentum*
NovTSup	Supplements to *NovT*
NRSV	*New Revised Standard Version* (of the Bible)
NTS	*New Testament Studies*
NTTS	New Testament Tools and Studies
OBO	Orbis biblicus et orientalis
OLZ	*Orientalistische Literaturzeitung*
OrAnt	*Oriens antiquus*
OTS	*Oudtestamentische Studiën*
PEQ	*Palestine Exploration Quarterly*
PL	J. Migne, *Patrologia latina*
PVTG	Pseudepigrapha Veteris Testamenti graece
PW	*Paulys Realencyclopädie der classischen Altertumswissenschaft* (Neue Bearbeitung von G. Wissowa; Stuttgart: Metzler, 1905-78)
QC	*Qumran Chronicle*
RB	*Revue biblique*
RBén	*Revue bénédictine*

RechBib	Recherches bibliques
REJ	*Revue des études juives*
ResQ	*Restoration Quarterly*
RevExp	*Review and Expositor*
RevQ	*Revue de Qumran*
RevSém	*Revue sémitique*
RSO	*Rivista degli studi orientali*
RSV	*Revised Standard Version* (of the Bible)
RTL	*Revue théologique de Louvain*
RTP	*Revue de théologie et de philosophie*
SANT	Studien zum Alten und Neuen Testament
SBL	Society of Biblical Literature
SBLEJL	SBL Early Judaism and Its Literature
SBLMS	SBL Monograph Series
SBLRBS	SBL Resources for Biblical Study
SBLSCS	SBL Septuagint and Cognate Studies
SBNT	J. A. Fitzmyer, *The Semitic Background of the New Testament: Combined Edition of Essays on the Semitic Background of the New Testament and A Wandering Aramean: Collected Aramaic Essays* (Grand Rapids: Eerdmans; Livonia, Mich.: Dove Booksellers, 1997 [see *ESBNT* and *WA*])
SBS	Stuttgarter Biblische Studien
SBT	Studies in Biblical Theology
SC	Sources chrétiennes
ScrBull	*Scripture Bulletin*
ScrHier	Scripta hierosolymitana
Sef	*Sefarad*
SE IV	*Studia evangelica IV* (= TU 102 [1968])
Sem	*Semitica*
SJLA	Studies in Judaism in Late Antiquity
SNTSMS	Studiorum Novi Testamenti Societas Monograph Series
SPB	Studia postbiblica
ST	*Studia theologica*
STDJ	Studies on the Texts of the Desert of Judah
SVTP	Studia in Veteris Testamenti pseudepigrapha
TAG	J. A. Fitzmyer, *To Advance the Gospel: New Testament Studies* (New York: Crossroad, 1981); 2d ed., Biblical Resource Series; Grand Rapids: Eerdmans; Livonia, Mich.: Dove Booksellers, 1998)
TBT	*The Bible Today*

TD	*Theology Digest*
TDNT	G. Kittel, ed., *Theological Dictionary of the New Testament* (10 vols.; Grand Rapids: Eerdmans, 1964-76)
TDOT	J. Botterweck and H. Ringgren, eds., *Theological Dictionary of the Old Testament* (10 vols. to date; Grand Rapids: Eerdmans, 1977-)
Tg.	*Targum*
TGl	*Theologie und Glaube*
TLZ	*Theologische Literaturzeitung*
TQ	*Theologische Quartalschrift*
TQTA	J. Carmignac and P. Guilbert, eds., *Les textes de Qumran traduits et annotés* (2 vols.; Paris: Letouzey et Ané, 1961-63)
TS	*Theological Studies*
TSAJ	Texte und Studien zum antiken Judentum
TSK	*Theologische Studien und Kritiken*
TU	Texte und Untersuchungen
TYDWJ	J. T. Milik, *Ten Years of Discovery in the Wilderness of Judaea* (SBT 26; London: SCM; Naperville, Ill.: Allenson, 1959)
TynBull	*Tyndale Bulletin*
Vg	Vulgate (Vulgata latina)
VL	Vetus Latina (Old Latin version of the Bible)
VT	*Vetus Testamentum*
VTSup	Supplements to *VT*
WA	J. A. Fitzmyer, *A Wandering Aramean: Collected Aramaic Essays* (SBLMS 25; Missoula, Mont.: Scholars Press, 1979; reprinted in *SBNT*)
WUNT	Wissenschaftliche Untersuchungen zum Neuen Testament
ZAW	*Zeitschrift für die alttestamentliche Wissenschaft*
ZKT	*Zeitschrift für katholische Theologie*
ZNW	*Zeitschrift für die neutestamentliche Wissenschaft*
ZWT	*Zeitschrift für wissenschaftliche Theologie*

Abbreviations of the Dead Sea Scrolls and Related Texts

(N.B. Superscript letters at the end of abbreviations denote copies of text)

1QapGen	*Genesis Apocryphon* from Qumran Cave 1
1QH	*Hôdāyôt* (Thanksgiving Psalms) from Qumran Cave 1
1QM	*Milḥāmāh* (War Scroll) from Qumran Cave 1

1QpHab	*Pēšer* (Commentary) on Habakkuk from Qumran Cave 1
1QS	*Serek* (Rule Book) from Qumran Cave 1
1QSa	First appendix to 1QS (= 1Q28a)
3Q15	Text 15 (= Copper Scroll) from Qumran Cave 3
4QAh A	Aharon A (Aaronic text) from Qumran Cave 4
4QapMoses	Apocryphon of Moses from Qumran Cave 4
4QBeat	The Beatitudes (= 4Q525) from Qumran Cave 4
4QD	*Damascus Document* from Qumran Cave 4
4QEn	Enoch texts from Qumran Cave 4
4QEnGiants	Giants texts related to 4QEn
4QFlor	Florilegium (4Q175) from Qumran Cave 4
4QMMT	*Miqṣāt maʿăśê hattôrāh* (Some Deeds of the Law) from Qumran Cave 4
4Qpap paraKgs	Paraphrase of Kings written on papyrus from Qumran Cave 4
4QpGen	*Pēšer* (Commentary) on Genesis from Qumran Cave 4
4QpIsa	*Pēšer* (Commentary) on Isaiah from Qumran Cave 4
4QpNah	*Pēšer* (Commentary) on Nahum from Qumran Cave 4
4QSap	Sapiential text from Qumran Cave 4
4QTestim	Testimonia text from Qumran Cave 4
4QTob	(Aramaic and Hebrew) texts of Tobit from Qumran Cave 4
4QTJud ar	Testament of Judah from Qumran Cave 4 in Aramaic
4QVisAmram	Vision of Amram from Qumran Cave 4
6QD	*Damascus Document* from Qumran Cave 6
7Q4, 7Q5	Texts 4 and 5 from Qumran Cave 7
11QMelch	Melchizedek text from Qumran Cave 11
11QtgJob	*Targum of Job* from Qumran Cave 11
CD	*Damascus Document* from the Cairo Genizah
As. Mos.	*Assumption of Moses*
1 Enoch	*Enoch* in the Ethiopic translation; also extant in Greek fragments
Ps. Sol.	*Psalms of Solomon* (in modern editions of the LXX)
Sib. Orac.	*Sibylline Oracles*

N.B. A dot above a letter in an Aramaic or Hebrew text means that the letter is only possible or probable; consult the photograph of the text.

CHAPTER 1

The Dead Sea Scrolls and Christian Origins: General Methodological Considerations

More than fifty years have passed since scrolls and fragments were first discovered by a Bedouin in 1947 in a cave close to the northwest shore of the Dead Sea, in what was then the British Mandate of Palestine. Since that time, especially during the course of the subsequent decade (1947-1956), ten other caves of the same area of the Jordanian-controlled West Bank near the Wadi Qumran yielded written materials of incredible value dating from the end of the third century B.C. up to the Roman destruction of Jerusalem in A.D. 70.

In a way that no one would have expected, these discoveries have shed light on four different areas of the ancient history of Judaism. They have given us firsthand knowledge about the form of the languages, Aramaic, Greek, and Hebrew, that Jews spoke and wrote at that time in ancient Judea. They have borne eloquent testimony to the shape of the text of the Old Testament or the Hebrew Scriptures that those Jews were reading. They have shed new light on diverse forms of ancient Palestinian Judaism itself in that period. And they have provided much information about the Palestinian Jewish matrix from which early Christianity emerged.

This chapter and the next one will concentrate on the last mentioned of these areas in order to bring out in a brief way the contribution that such discoveries have made to the beginnings of Christianity. First of all, however, some general methodological considerations have to be made. They are important because of the way the Dead Sea Scrolls have been presented at times

1

in the popular press, and some confusion has resulted. My comments about methodology will fall into three categories: the different senses of the title "Dead Sea Scrolls"; the privileged character of this newly acquired Judean literature for New Testament study; and some of the risks that this sort of study runs.

Different Senses of the Title "Dead Sea Scrolls"

At the outset, one has to be clear about what is meant by "Dead Sea Scrolls," since the term has been used at times in different ways.

In a broad sense, it embraces scrolls and fragmentary documents found at eight or nine different locations in the Judean Desert to the west of the Jordan River. This broad usage stems in part from the way popularizers, and sometimes even scholars, refer to such documents. The official series of publication of many of the texts is even called "Discoveries in the Judaean Desert" (Clarendon Press of Oxford).[1] In the list of such locations one would have to include the following:

1. the eleven Qumran caves, that is, caves in the vicinity of the torrent bed called Wadi Qumran;
2. remains of the ancient fortress of Masada;
3. four or five caves of the Wadi Murabba'at;
4. caves of Naḥal Ḥever (Wadi Khabra);
5. the cave of Naḥal Ṣe'elim (Wadi Seiyal);
6. the cave of Naḥal Mišmar (Wadi Mahras);
7. the remains of the Greek monastery at Khirbet Mird (ancient Hyrcania);
8. the Genizah of the Synagogue of Ezra in Old Cairo;
9. according to some scholars, even the cave of Wadi ed-Daliyeh (the Samaritan papyri).

In a narrow sense, the term denotes the scrolls and fragments recovered from the eleven caves in the vicinity of Khirbet Qumran, the stone ruins close to the Wadi Qumran, and the texts related to them, found either at Masada or in

---

1. To which title the phrase "of Jordan" has sometimes been added, because many of the texts recovered after the discovery of Qumran Cave 1 were found in the Jordanian-controlled West Bank (1952-1956). It became part of the State of Israel at the time of the Six-Day War (1967).

the Cairo Genizah. In the case of the last-mentioned locality, the Cairo Genizah, one must restrict the discussion to the texts recovered there that have some relation to those of Qumran, such as the *Damascus Document* or the *Testament of Levi*.[2] The texts found at Masada include some that are copies of Qumran texts, and others that even seem to have been copied by the same scribes as some Qumran texts. It may be, then, that texts copied at Qumran made their way to Masada, when members of the Qumran community joined the Jews who were making their last stand against the Romans at Masada in A.D. 73.[3]

Among the documents from other localities mentioned above under the broad sense of "Dead Sea Scrolls," some would have only a remote connection with the study of early Christianity.[4] For instance, the letters of Bar Kochba from the time of the Second Revolt of Palestinian Jews against Rome (A.D. 132-35) supply us with new and important evidence about aspects of that revolt put down by the Romans in the early second Christian century, but there is little, if anything, in them that pertains to Christians or the Christian church of that time. Those documents, however, bear witness to the languages, Aramaic, Greek, and Hebrew, that were in contemporary usage in Judea at the beginning of the second century.[5]

Similarly, the Samaritan papyri of the Wadi ed-Daliyeh are also of only remote interest. They come from a postexilic period of Judah and shed light on a little-known time of ancient Jewish history, in alluding to some historical figures[6] and revealing the kind of Aramaic then being

2. Actually, thousands of documents were retrieved from the Cairo Genizah, and most of them have no relation to the Qumran Scrolls. However, one should perhaps also include the Cairo Genizah Wisdom text, which may have some connection to the sapiential literature of Qumran Cave 4, which is only now being published. See K. Berger, *Die Weisheitsschrift aus der Kairoer Geniza: Erstedition, Kommentar und Übersetzung* (Texte und Arbeiten zum neutestamentlichen Zeitalter 1; Tübingen: Francke, 1989). Cf. K. Berger, "Die Bedeutung der wiederentdeckten Weisheitsschrift aus der Kairoer Geniza für das Neue Testament," *NTS* 36 (1990) 415-30.

3. For the Masada texts, see J. A. Fitzmyer, *DSSMPTS*, 77-78.

4. For a list of such texts, see ibid., 79-90.

5. See "The Bar Cochba Period," in J. A. Fitzmyer, *ESBNT* or *SBNT,* 305-54. Cf. S. Applebaum, "The Second Jewish Revolt (A.D. 131-35)," *PEQ* 116 (1984) 35-41; A. Oppenheimer, "The Bar Kokhba Revolt," *Immanuel* 14 (1982) 58-76; B. Isaac, A. Oppenheimer, and M. O. Wise, "Bar Kokhba," *ABD,* 1:598-606.

6. See F. M. Cross, "The Papyri and Their Historical Implications," in *Discoveries in the Wâdî ed-Dâliyeh* (ed. P. W. Lapp and N. L. Lapp; AASOR 41; Cambridge, Mass.: American Schools of Oriental Research, 1974) 17-29 (+ pls. 59-64); idem, "Samaria Papyrus 1: An Aramaic Slave Conveyance of 335 B.C.E. Found in the Wâdî ed-Dâliyeh," in *Nahman Avigad Volume* (ErIsr 18; Jerusalem: Israel Exploration Society, 1985) 7*-17* (+ pl. II); idem, "A Reconstruction of the Judean Restoration," *JBL* 94 (1975) 4-18.

used.[7] They are, however, mostly legal documents dealing with the sale or transfer of slaves and have nothing to do with the study of either the Qumran texts or early Christianity. One may wonder, then, why I am including them in the list even in the broad sense of the term. The reason is that texts from Wadi ed-Daliyeh are to be published in a coming volume of DJD, the same Clarendon Press series in which many of the Qumran texts have been or are to be published in definitive form. They have also been officially listed in the Dead Sea Scrolls Inventory.[8]

In a similar way, one might wonder why texts from Khirbet Mird are being included, since most of them date from the fifth to the tenth centuries A.D.[9] In this case, it is because of the early association of these documents with the Qumran texts in popular discussions,[10] since the site had been discovered more or less about the time that the first Qumran cave was found. Initially, the Khirbet Mird texts were thought to be related to the Qumran texts, but subsequently it became apparent that they are wholly unrelated.

The upshot of this discussion is that for the study of early Christianity it is "Dead Sea Scrolls" in the narrow or restricted sense on which one must concentrate, that is, on the Qumran Scrolls and on those texts from Masada and the Cairo Genizah that are related to them.

The Privileged Character of This Newly Acquired Judean Literature for New Testament Study

If I have restricted "Dead Sea Scrolls" to its narrow sense, there is still another general methodological consideration that has to be made. The Qumran texts, fragmentary though many of them are, supply us with firsthand information about the Palestinian Jewish matrix out of which early Christianity and its canonical writings emerged. Even though most of the Greek writings

---

7. See D. Gropp, "The Language of the Samaria Papyri: A Preliminary Study," in *Sopher Mahir: Northwest Studies Presented to Stanislav Segert* (= *Maarav* 5-6; ed. E. M. Cook; Winona Lake, Ind.: Eisenbrauns, 1990) 169-87.

8. See S. A. Reed, *Dead Sea Scroll Inventory Project: Lists of Documents, Photographs and Museum Plates: Fascicle 12, Wadi ed Daliyeh* (Claremont, Calif.: Ancient Biblical Manuscript Center, 1991). Also M. J. Winn Leith, *Wadi Daliyeh I: The Wadi Daliyeh Seal Impressions* (DJD 24; Oxford: Clarendon, 1997).

9. See J. A. Fitzmyer, *DSSMPTS*, 91.

10. See J. T. Milik, *TYDWJ*, 15, 19, 46, 130, 132, 137, 139; F. M. Cross, *The Ancient Library of Qumran and Modern Biblical Studies* (Garden City, N.Y.: Doubleday, 1958) 2, 21 n. 36; idem, *The Ancient Library of Qumran* (3d ed.; Sheffield: Sheffield Academic Press; Minneapolis: Fortress, 1995) 1, 35 n. 2.

of the New Testament stem from extra-Palestinian or extra-Judean prove-niences, a good number of them manifest their connection with that Palestin-ian Jewish matrix.[11] The Gospels and Acts depict for us the life and ministry of a first-century Palestinian Jew, Jesus of Nazareth, and the early stages of the first Jewish Christian church in Jerusalem and Judea, before the Christian message spread abroad "to the end of the earth" (Acts 1:8).

Before the discovery of Qumran Cave 1 in 1947, the amount of first-hand information about Palestinian Judaism was limited indeed. It con-sisted mostly of sparse inscriptions in Aramaic, Greek, and Hebrew.[12] There was also the information that the Jewish historian Flavius Josephus (A.D. 37/38-100?) had included in his Greek writings, which, being composed at roughly the same time as many of the New Testament writings, have shed important light on the same Jewish matrix of early Christianity. Though some scholars have at times questioned Josephus's reliability as a historian, his testimony, coming from a Palestinian Jew, has been without equal for the period concerned.[13] Although the writings of Philo Judaeus of Alexan-dria (30 B.C.–A.D. 45) have sometimes been important for interpreting cer-tain parts of the New Testament, they do not always reflect the desirable Palestinian background. Because the writings of Philo are cast in a philo-sophical mold and indulge in Alexandrian allegorical interpretation of the Old Testament, they are not so useful for historical information about Judean Judaism or for the understanding of early Christianity and the in-terpretation of the New Testament.[14]

Given this situation of meager information about first-century Pales-tine, one realizes the overall importance of the Qumran texts as a reflection of the Palestinian Judaism immediately prior to and contemporary with the life

---

11. It may be that all twenty-seven books of the New Testament come from localities of the eastern Mediterranean area outside ancient Palestine, but some scholars have toyed with the idea that at least two of the books were possibly composed in Judea itself, James and 1 Peter. See J. N. Sevenster, *Do You Know Greek? How Much Greek Could the First Jewish Christians Have Known?* (NovTSup 19; Leiden: Brill, 1968) 3-4, 11-13.

12. See my article, "The Languages of Palestine in the First Century A.D.," *CBQ* 32 (1970) 501-31; reprinted in slightly revised form in *WA* or *SBNT,* 29-56.

13. For a well-written survey of the relation of Josephus's writings to the study of the New Testament, see S. Mason, *Josephus and the New Testament* (Peabody, Mass.: Hendrickson, 1992). See also H. St. J. Thackeray and L. H. Feldman, *Josephus with an En-glish Translation* (LCL; 9 vols.; Cambridge, Mass.: Harvard University Press, 1926-65).

14. Since Philo predates Josephus, his writings would be a better reflection of Juda-ism contemporary with Jesus of Nazareth, but they do not necessarily reflect *Palestinian* Judaism. See F. H. Colson et al., *Philo with an English Translation* (LCL; 12 vols.; Cam-bridge, Mass.: Harvard University Press, 1929-53).

and ministry of Jesus of Nazareth and with the emergence of early Christianity. In general, the Qumran texts date from the end of the third century B.C. to a short time before the destruction of the community center in the summer of A.D. 68 at what is called today Khirbet Qumran. They have all been dated paleographically, that is, according to the handwriting in which they have been written. Various scholars have devoted their time and skill to this endeavor.[15] Moreover, these paleographic datings have recently been supported in an unexpected way by radiocarbon datings, carried out in Zurich in 1991 and in Tucson, Arizona, in 1994. Unfortunately, not all the texts have been submitted to the Accelerator Mass Spectometry or radiocarbon analysis, but the general confirmation that has come from it for the paleographic dating is, by and large, significant and noteworthy.[16] It certainly puts to rest the outlandish claims made by some students of the Qumran scrolls who questioned or ignored the paleographic datings.[17] Such a dating of the Qumran texts

15. See especially F. M. Cross, "Palaeography and the Dead Sea Scrolls," in *The Dead Sea Scrolls after Fifty Years: A Comprehensive Assessment* (2 vols.; ed. P. W. Flint and J. C. VanderKam; Leiden: Brill, 1998) 1:379-402; compare his earlier treatment, "The Development of the Jewish Scripts," in *The Bible and the Ancient Near East: Essays in Honor of William Foxwell Albright* (ed. G. E. Wright; Garden City, N.Y.: Doubleday, 1965) 170-264. See also N. Avigad, "The Palaeography of the Dead Sea Scrolls and Related Documents," in *Aspects of the Dead Sea Scrolls* (ScrHier 4; Jerusalem: Magnes, 1958) 56-87; S. A. Birnbaum, "The Dates of the Cave Scrolls," *BASOR* 115 (1949) 20-22; idem, "How Old Are the Cave Manuscripts? A Palaeographical Discussion," *VT* 1 (1951) 91-109; idem, "Notes on the Internal and Archaeological Evidence concerning the Cave Scrolls," *JBL* 70 (1951) 227-32. Cf. J. A. Fitzmyer, *DSSMPTS*, 152.

16. See G. Bonani et al., "Radiocarbon Dating of the Dead Sea Scrolls," *'Atiqot* 20 (1991) 27-32; "Radiocarbon Dating of Fourteen Dead Sea Scrolls," *Radiocarbon* 34/3 (1992) 843-49; A. J. Timothy Lull et al., "Radiocarbon Dating of Scrolls and Linen Fragments from the Judean Desert," *Radiocarbon* 37 (1995) 11-19; G. A. Rodley, "An Assessment of the Radiocarbon Dating of the Dead Sea Scrolls," *Radiocarbon* 35 (1993) 335-38; G. Doudna, "Dating the Scrolls on the Basis of Radiocarbon Analysis," in Flint and VanderKam, eds., *The Dead Sea Scrolls after Fifty Years,* 1:430-65.

Cf. S. Goranson, "Radiocarbon Dating the Dead Sea Scrolls," *BA* 54 (1991) 39-42; H. Shanks, "Carbon-14 Tests Substantiate Scroll Dates," *BARev* 17/6 (1991) 72; Z. J. Kapera, "AMS Carbon-14 Dating of the Scrolls," *QC* 2/1 (1992) 39-42; G. R. Stone, "C-14 Confirms Dead Sea Scroll Dates," *BH* 28/1 (1992) 20-22; idem, "Setting the Record Straight: A Correction and More on the Dead Sea Scroll Datings," *BH* 28/4 (1992) 109-22.

17. E.g., B. E. Thiering, *Redating the Teacher of Righteousness* (Australian and New Zealand Studies in Theology and Religion 1; Sydney: Theological Explorations, 1979) 34-49; eadem, *The Gospels and Qumran: A New Hypothesis* (Sydney: Theological Explorations, 1981) 4-8; eadem, *The Qumran Origins of the Christian Church* (Sydney: Theological Explorations, 1983) 12-14; eadem, *Jesus and the Riddle of the Dead Sea Scrolls: Unlocking the Secrets of His Life Story* (San Francisco: HarperSanFrancisco, 1992) 14-19. Also R. H.

gives these documents a status that is privileged for the study of early Christianity.

It is also necessary, however, to make some further distinctions, for the Qumran scrolls and fragments fall today into three generic categories, and they are not all of equal value for the study of the New Testament. First, there are the "biblical" texts, which are copies of books of the Hebrew Scriptures or the Old Testament. Although these are precious documents for the text-critical study of the Hebrew Scriptures, they bear only indirectly on the study of the New Testament, for example, when a New Testament author quotes an Old Testament passage. Then the Qumran biblical texts may bear witness to the Hebrew substratum of the Greek Old Testament, the Septuagint or LXX, which was normally used by New Testament writers or was closely related to their text. Sometimes that Hebrew substratum of the Greek Old Testament differs from the medieval Masoretic text (MT) presented in modern critical editions of the Hebrew Scriptures, but agrees with what one reads in the Greek New Testament.[18] The Qumran biblical texts thus show that the Greek translation in the LXX was not carelessly done but represents a different text tradition, which is now known.

Second, there are the *sectarian* texts, which are Hebrew documents that were composed by members of the Qumran community and destined for use by them. These would include such writings as the *Manual of Discipline*, the *Damascus Document*, the *Thanksgiving Psalms*, the *War Scroll*, various pĕšārîm (commentaries on biblical books), and numerous other fragmentary liturgical or cultic texts that display the theology and tenets that we have come

---

Eisenman, *Maccabees, Zadokites, Christians and Qumran: A New Hypothesis of Qumran Origins* (SPB 34; Leiden: Brill, 1983); idem, *James the Just in the Habakkuk Pesher* (SPB 35; Leiden: Brill, 1986).

18. An example of how such Qumran biblical texts help in the interpretation of the New Testament can be found in Acts 7:14, which counts the number of people who went down with Jacob to Egypt as "seventy-five persons." The Hebrew MT speaks rather of "seventy persons" (Gen 46:27; cf. Exod 1:5; Deut 10:22), whereas the LXX of the first two of these passages reads "seventy-five." So now do 4QGen-Exod[a] 17–18:2 and 4QExod[b] 1:5 (DJD 12:18, 84). Another instance is found in Acts 13:41, where Hab 1:5 is quoted according to the LXX, "Look, you scoffers, gaze well and be astounded," whereas the Hebrew MT reads, "Look at the nations and see." The *Pesher on Habakkuk* from Qumran Cave 1 (1QpHab 2:1-2) reads habbôgĕdîm, "scoffers," instead of baggôyîm, "at the nations," of the MT. Thus, Qumran texts reveal that there were indeed in pre-Christian Palestine Hebrew texts of Genesis, Exodus, and Habakkuk that read the same number and name as the Greek LXX, and that the latter version was not erroneous or tendentious. See further L. J. Greenspoon, "The Dead Sea Scrolls and the Greek Bible," in Flint and VanderKam, eds., *The Dead Sea Scrolls after Fifty Years*, 1:101-27.

to associate with the sect of Jews who formed the community.[19] Whether any of the Qumran Aramaic texts belong to this category is at the moment debatable, because so few of them seem to contain any of the distinctively sectarian tenets. Most of the Aramaic texts seem rather to have been composed elsewhere and been imported for use by members of the Qumran community, which seems to have restored Hebrew as the "sacred language" *(lĕšôn haqqōdeš)* for their normal community usage.

Third, there is the so-called *intertestamental* literature, a (Christian) misnomer. This would include all the extrabiblical and parabiblical Jewish writings that are not clearly sectarian: texts like *Enoch* and *Jubilees;* various Semitic forerunners of the Greek *Testaments of the Twelve Patriarchs;* and much other sapiential, hymnic, and liturgical literature that has come to light for the first time. Again, such writings seem to stem rather from a larger Jewish environment and may simply have been used by members of the Qumran community, even though they were not composed by them.

For the study of early Christianity and its New Testament writings, the sectarian texts and the so-called intertestamental documents from Qumran are clearly of great importance. Unfortunately, many of them are fragmentary, but even so, they have supplied *firsthand* information about a form of Palestinian Judaism of the first centuries B.C. and A.D., which was known earlier only from reports of Josephus, Philo, and other writers, namely, Essene Judaism.[20] Such information about the Essene community of Qumran has illumined in an unexpected way *part* of the Jewish matrix of early Christianity. Early Christians would have been influenced also by contemporary Pharisees and Sadducees, but unfortunately very little, if any, written material can be ascribed with certainty to these non-Essene Jewish contemporaries. Hence the value of the Qumran information about contemporary Essenes.

Still another aspect of the Qumran Scrolls has to be considered. Prior to 1947 and the first discovery of Qumran texts, because of the relative paucity

19. The Temple Scroll from Cave 11 (11QTemple) is a problematic text. Does it represent a sectarian text, as Y. Yadin seemed to think, or a pre-Essene document, as others have maintained?

20. For me the best identification of the Qumran sect is still the Essene. The attempt of L. H. Schiffman (*Reclaiming the Dead Sea Scrolls: The History of Judaism, the Background of Christianity, the Lost Library of Qumran* [Philadelphia/Jerusalem: Jewish Publication Society, 1994; reprinted in ABRL; New York: Doubleday, 1995] xxii) and others to relate the Qumran community to "a band of pious Sadducees" is, in my opinion, simply misguided. See further Chapter 11 below.

See G. Vermes and M. D. Goodman, *The Essenes according to the Classical Sources* (Oxford Centre Textbooks 1; Sheffield: JSOT Press, 1989); A. Adam, *Antike Berichte über die Essener* (KlT 182; 2d ed.; Berlin/New York: de Gruyter, 1972).

of Judean Jewish documentation that might be pertinent (such as that mentioned above in the second paragraph of this section), interpreters of the New Testament often had recourse to rabbinic literature to explain Jewish elements of the New Testament.[21] *Faute de mieux,* that rabbinic literature was used, but not always with requisite caution. Unfortunately, in some quarters today its use continues without due recognition that it was not written down until about A.D. 200; but it is treated as though it could shed light on first-century Palestinian Judaism, especially of the period prior to the destruction of Jerusalem in A.D. 70.[22]

On the one hand, examples of interpretative writing, which are related to discussions in the later rabbinic writings, have been recovered in Qumran texts.[23] Such Qumran "halakhic" writings may now show that some issues discussed in rabbinic writings were already alive in the first century B.C. or A.D. These Qumran texts, then, would provide the needed control for the correct use of rabbinic material to illustrate or explain New Testament writings. This Qumran halakhic material would, then, join the data from Josephus and Philo, who also on occasion witness to the early existence of legal traditions treated in rabbinic texts.

21. The classic in this endeavor has been the German commentary on the New Testament based on rabbinic literature by (H. Strack and) P. Billerbeck, *Kommentar zum Neuen Testament aus Talmud und Midrasch* (6 vols.; Munich: Beck, 1926-63).

22. Good examples of the misuse of late rabbinic writings can be found in the articles of S. Safrai ("Hebrew and Aramaic Sources") and Z. W. Falk ("Jewish Private Law") in *The Jewish People in the First Century: Historical Geography, Political History, Social, Cultural and Religious Life and Institutions* (CRINT 1/1; Assen: Van Gorcum; Philadelphia: Fortress, 1974) 1-18, 504-34. Safrai discusses "the problem of dating" (pp. 4-6), but he naively thinks that one can identify "earlier collections in the framework of a later redaction" and claims that form criticism helps. Form criticism may help, indeed, to tell which of three passages dealing with the same topic is the earliest, but it does not enable anyone to ascribe such a passage to "the first century" (as the title of the book claims). At length, Safrai admits that "Talmudic literature aimed at transmitting Halakhah and Haggadah, not historical tradition" (p. 12). If so, why limit the Hebrew and Aramaic *sources* of information about the Jewish people in the first century to later rabbinic writings and scarcely mention the Qumran material? Similarly, in the treatment of Jewish law, almost all of Falk's references are to rabbinic writings that date from long after "the first century."

23. See L. H. Schiffman, *The Halakhah at Qumran* (SJLA 16; Leiden: Brill, 1975); idem, ed., *Archaeology and History in the Dead Sea Scrolls: The New York University Conference in Memory of Yigael Yadin* (JSPSup 8; Sheffield: JSOT Press, 1990) passim; idem, "Qumran and Rabbinic Halakhah," in *Jewish Civilization in the Hellenistic-Roman Period* (ed. S. Talmon; Philadelphia: Trinity Press International, 1991) 138-46; J. M. Baumgarten, "Recent Qumran Discoveries and Halakhah in the Hellenistic-Roman Period," ibid., 147-58.

On the other hand, the Qumran texts have brought to light aspects of Palestinian Judaism that differ at times from the rabbinic material. This difference comes from the kind of Judaism that the Qumran texts represent, the Essene, whereas the rabbinic tradition is derived mainly from the Pharisaic. For this reason, the dating of the Qumran material gives to these texts a privileged status that must be correctly estimated in the study of the Palestinian matrix of early Christianity. Consequently, in general Qumran literature is to be preferred to the later rabbinic literature.[24]

To cite a few examples of the advantage that the Qumran material has had over the later rabbinic material in illustrating New Testament issues, I refer to my own comparative study of the use of isolated Old Testament quotations in Qumran literature and in the New Testament.[25] In the New Testament there are many instances where an Old Testament text is explicitly quoted and introduced with a formula, using the verbs either "to say" or "to write." One finds the same device in Qumran texts, especially in the sectarian writings. One also finds the same in the Mishnah, which was codified under the direction of Rabbi Judah the Prince ca. A.D. 200. Here too one finds 'āmar, "he said," and kātab, "he wrote," used in similar fashion.[26] There are, of

24. By "later rabbinic literature" I mean the Mishnah, the Tannaitic Midrashim, and the Palestinian Talmud. The use of most of the other rabbinic literature, for example, the Babylonian Talmud and the Midrash Rabbah, is even more problematic, the former because of its provenience (Babylonia) and normal lack of relevance to Palestine, and the latter because of its date. The same would have to be said of all Amoraic, Geonic, and later Jewish material.

In this connection, one has to ask further to what extent something that appears in this "later" Jewish literature is a reflection of controversy with Christianity. Simply because it is written in a Semitic language, Aramaic or Hebrew, does not mean that it reflects a tradition earlier than or prior to the Greek New Testament. Moreover, even in the case of the earliest of the rabbinic writings, the Mishnah and Tannaitic Midrashim, the attribution of sayings to a rabbi who may have lived in the first century A.D. does not necessarily mean that the tradition so ascribed goes back to him. At least some Christians have come to realize that not everything put on the lips of Jesus in the Gospels was necessarily uttered by him in the form preserved. Now it is necessary to get Christian scholars who use Jewish rabbinic material to make similar adjustments in their use of that material.

25. J. A. Fitzmyer, "The Use of Explicit Old Testament Quotations in Qumran Literature and in the New Testament," NTS 7 (1960-61) 297-333; reprinted in slightly revised form in ESBNT or SBNT, 3-58. Compare F. L. Horton, Jr., "Formulas of Introduction in the Qumran Literature," RevQ 7 (1969-71) 505-14.

26. See B. M. Metzger, "The Formulas Introducing Quotations of Scripture in the NT and the Mishnah," JBL 70 (1951) 297-307; reprinted in slightly revised form in his Historical and Literary Studies: Pagan, Jewish, and Christian (NTTS 8; Leiden: Brill, 1968) 52-63.

course, some general parallels, but the differences between the specific Mishnaic and Qumran formulas are striking and more numerous than the similarities. There is not one example involving *'āmar* or *kātab* in the Mishnah that is identical with the Qumran examples, and yet the New Testament formulas are often literal Greek translations of many of the Qumran introductory formulas. In other words, the New Testament introductory formulas reflect the first-century Palestinian Jewish usage, attested in the earlier or contemporary sectarian Qumran texts, whereas the Mishnaic formulas manifest a rabbinic development beyond that of the first-century Qumran usage.[27] This shows that the Mishnaic material is often not really adequate for comparison with the New Testament formulas.

In a similar way, one can point to certain Pauline phrases and terminology that one has always suspected of being derived from his Jewish background, but that had no counterparts in the Old Testament or in later rabbinic literature, but have now turned up in a striking way in Qumran literature. A brief indication of some of these will be given below in Chapter 2.[28] Many other examples of this Palestinian Jewish background for New Testament expressions could be cited.[29]

Some Risks That This Study Runs

The first risk that this study runs is the temptation to disregard the related archaeological data, the paleographic and radiocarbon dating of the texts, and the contents of the Qumran literature itself. The archaeological data reveal that the eleven caves of Qumran were related to the community center at what is called today Khirbet Qumran. That center was the desert retreat for Jews who lived there in the last century and a half B.C. and the first

27. See further J. M. Baumgarten, "A 'Scriptural' Citation in 4Q Fragments of the Damascus Document," *JJS* 43 (1992) 95-98; G. Vermes, "Biblical Proof-Texts in Qumran Literature," *JSS* 34 (1989) 493-508; M. Fishbane, *Biblical Interpretation in Ancient Israel* (Oxford: Clarendon, 1985) 213-20.

28. Cf. J. A. Fitzmyer, "Paul's Jewish Background and the Deeds of the Law," in *According to Paul: Studies in the Theology of the Apostle* (New York/Mahwah, N.J.: Paulist Press, 1993) 18-35.

29. For an early survey and discussion of such material, see H. Braun, *Qumran und das Neue Testament* (2 vols.; Tübingen: Mohr Siebeck, 1966). This book needs to be updated. Cf. J. Murphy-O'Connor and J. H. Charlesworth, eds., *Paul and the Dead Sea Scrolls* (New York: Crossroad, 1990); J. H. Charlesworth, ed., *John and the Dead Sea Scrolls* (New York: Crossroad, 1990). These two books appeared originally in 1968 and 1972 and therefore do not cope with the more recently published fragments that would be pertinent.

A.D.[30] The contents of the Scrolls, biblical, intertestamental, and sectarian, reveal that they come from people of Judea who were thoroughly Jewish. The Scrolls were not written by Christians, and they have to be accorded their proper place in Jewish history.

Chaim Potok in his foreword to Lawrence H. Schiffman's book *Reclaiming the Dead Sea Scrolls* complains about the popular notion "that the scrolls were relevant only to the study of nascent Christianity. Very few conceived of them as a window onto early rabbinic Judaism."[31] In his book, Schiffman himself has rightly sought to reclaim the genuine Jewish heritage for the Qumran Scrolls. His book "aims to correct a fundamental misreading of the Dead Sea Scrolls," because not enough of their contribution to the "history of Judaism" has been considered.[32] Consequently, anyone who fails to recognize this fundamental character of the Scrolls is making a big mistake. It is the mistake of those who have attempted to interpret the texts as Christian or Jewish Christian.[33] For these scrolls fill in details about the history of Palestinian Judaism between the Hasmonean dynasty and the time of Rabbi Judah the Prince, the codifier of the Mishnah. Schiffman calls the Scrolls "documents of various groups of Second Temple Jews whose writings were assembled by a particular sect inhabiting the Qumran settlement during the Hasmonean and Herodian periods, about 135 B.C.E.–68 C.E."[34] With such a description one cannot cavil; nor can one find fault with much of what Schiffman has written about how the Qumran scrolls fit into the history of Judaism of those periods, but the further question of "the Background of Christianity" and the contribution that the Scrolls make to it is still a legitimate question, which should not be ignored. Chapter 2 will briefly survey that contribution.

Part of the reason why Schiffman writes as he does is that so many of the early publications of the Scrolls were entrusted to Christian scholars: three of the seven major texts of Qumran Cave 1; all the other fragments of

30. See R. de Vaux, *Archaeology and the Dead Sea Scrolls* (Schweich Lectures of the British Academy 1959; London: Oxford University, 1973). This was unfortunately only a preliminary report, and de Vaux died before he could publish the definitive report. The report is now being published; see J.-B. Humbert and A. Chambon, *Fouilles de Khirbet Qumrân et de Aïn Feshkha I* (Novum Testamentum et Orbis Antiquus, series archaeologica 1; Fribourg: Editions Universitaires; Göttingen: Vandenhoeck & Ruprecht, 1994). Cf. E.-M. Laperrousaz, *Qoumrân: L'Etablissement essénien des bords de la Mer Morte: Histoire et archéologie du site* (Paris: Picard, 1976).

31. Schiffman, *Reclaiming the Dead Sea Scrolls*, xi.

32. Ibid., xiii.

33. E.g., Barbara Thiering and Robert H. Eisenman; see n. 17 above.

34. Schiffman, *Reclaiming the Dead Sea Scrolls*, xiii.

Cave 1; volumes 1-7, 9, and 12-13 in the DJD series; and the Enoch fragments of Cave 4. These Christian scholars were not always acquainted with or suffi- ciently attuned to the later rabbinic literature to make the requisite compari- sons or to show the connections.

It must be recalled, however, that a political situation was largely re- sponsible for the initial assignment of the texts. Cave 1 was discovered in 1947, in what was then the British Mandate of Palestine. The Mandate came to an end in May 1948, and shortly thereafter the Arab-Jewish War erupted. The State of Israel came into being, and when a truce was finally negotiated, the so-called West Bank came under the control of the Hashemite Kingdom of Jordan (1949-1967). When further caves (2-11) were discovered between 1952 and 1956, the Scrolls and fragments were discovered in the Jordanian- controlled West Bank, and not in Israel. The fragments, especially of Qumran Cave 4, were brought to the Palestine Archaeological Museum in East Jerusa- lem for study, where the great jigsaw puzzle was assembled between 1953 and 1960, from which ultimately came about 820 fragmentary texts. From 1949 to 1967 it was impossible for any Jew to come to East Jerusalem, where the Mu- seum was. So no Jewish scholar could become a member of the international and interconfessional team that was set up to handle the jigsaw puzzle. East Jerusalem was cut off from West Jerusalem and from Israel by a mined no- man's-land and high stone walls. That is why Christian scholars, who could read Hebrew and Aramaic, came to dominate the study and publication of the Qumran Cave 4 fragments.[35] In addition to the glory that that work brought them, they have had to shoulder the ignominy of the incredible delay they caused in the publication of this important material.

Now in more recent times Jewish scholars, among them Schiffman him- self, have been brought into the study and publication of the remaining frag- ments of Qumran Cave 4. Now one can finally get the necessary directives for the proper understanding of the relation of the Scrolls to rabbinic literature of the third and later centuries. One must not, however, think that the Scrolls are part of rabbinic literature. There is no rabbinic literature that comes to us from the last pre-Christian century or from the first two Christian centu- ries,[36] or that is needed for the proper understanding of the Scrolls of this pe- riod of Judaism. Moreover, the Qumran Scrolls come from a form of Judaism

---

35. I myself worked in the Scrollery of the Palestine Archaeological Museum from July 1957 to July 1958 and began the concordance of nonbiblical texts of Cave 4. The con- cordance work was later continued by R. E. Brown (1958-59) and W. G. Oxtoby (1959-60).

36. With the possible exception that a form of the *Megillat Ta'anit* comes from the early second century, ca. A.D. 100.

that is different from that of the rabbinic tradition, a difference that must be respected.

Even when full recognition is given to the Scrolls as Jewish writings, however, there is still plenty of room for recognizing the pertinence that they have to nascent Christianity. This is an aspect of the discovery of the Scrolls that cannot be neglected either. Hence one must not ignore the wholly Jewish nature of the Scrolls and also their pertinence to nascent Christianity. For they provide new light on the Judean matrix of the New Testament, a light that was not available before 1947.

In this regard, I must cite some of the writings of Geza Vermes about Jesus of Nazareth.[37] He has often used the Qumran Scrolls and fragments in his writings on Jesus, but he has also extrapolated information from the rabbinic literature of later centuries in a questionable fashion.

Another pitfall to avoid is that of Norman Golb of the University of Chicago, who denies the identification of Khirbet Qumran with any Jewish community center (let alone an Essene one) and believes that the site represents rather the remains of a (Herodian) fort. He further maintains that the Scrolls and fragments found in the various Qumran caves were actually deposits of books brought from various libraries in Jerusalem, possibly from the Temple itself.[38] He even claims that his interpretation of the Scrolls depends on evidence from the so-called *Copper Scroll* of Qumran Cave 3, which mentions the hiding of *sĕpārîm*, "books, writings."[39]

That some of the Scrolls and fragments discovered in the Qumran caves were copied by Jewish scribes outside of the Qumran scriptorium creates no

37. See his *Jesus the Jew: A Historian's Reading of the Gospels* (London: Collins, 1973); idem, *Jesus and the World of Judaism* (London: SCM, 1983); and especially his article "Jewish Studies and New Testament Interpretation," *JJS* 31 (1980) 1-17. Cf. J. A. Fitzmyer, "Problems of the Semitic Background of the New Testament," in *The Yahweh/Baal Confrontation and Other Studies in Biblical Literature and Archaeology: Essays in Honour of Emmett Willard Hamrick* (ed. J. M. O'Brien and F. L. Horton, Jr.; Studies in the Bible and Early Christianity 35; Lewiston: Mellen Biblical Press, 1995) 80-93.

38. See N. Golb, *Who Wrote the Dead Sea Scrolls? The Search for the Secret of Qumran* (New York: Scribner, 1995). Cf. his earlier articles: "Dead Sea Scrolls: A New Perspective," *American Scholar* 58 (1989) 177-207; idem, "Khirbet Qumran and the Manuscripts of the Judaean Wilderness: Observations on the Logic of Their Investigation," *JNES* 49 (1990) 103-14; idem, "The Freeing of the Scrolls and Its Aftermath," *QC* 2/1 (1992) 3-25; idem, "The Qumran-Essene Hypothesis: A Fiction of Scholarship," *ChrC* 109 (1992) 1138-43; idem, "The Major Anomalies in the Qumran-Sectarian Theory and Their Resolution," *QC* 2/3 (1993) 161-82.

39. See 3Q15 8:3. Cf. M. Baillet, J. T. Milik, and R. de Vaux, *Les 'Petites Grottes' de Qumrân* (DJD 3; Oxford: Clarendon, 1962) 292.

problem. After all, some of the biblical texts and much of the intertestamental Jewish literature could well have been copied elsewhere and brought to Qumran by Essenes who would merely have read and studied them there. The non-Qumran provenience of some Scrolls does not constitute a major obstacle to the identification of the Qumran community as Essene or of Khirbet Qumran as an Essene community center. What was copied at Qumran itself would have been mainly the sectarian literature of the Essenes, even if they did at times also copy other material, biblical or intertestamental. Emanuel Tov has detected a Qumran system of writing, copying, and orthography, which must not be ignored either.[40] The evidence seems to show that trained scribes were indeed copying texts according to a definite method, and the copying was undoubtedly done at the scriptorium of Qumran, which Roland de Vaux identified in his excavation of Khirbet Qumran. What bearing the Golb thesis would have on the study of early Christianity and of the New Testament might still have to be discussed, even if one were to accord his thesis any validity, which I do not.[41]

A different problem is posed by the Greek texts of Qumran Cave 7. From that cave came no fragments in Hebrew or Aramaic, but nineteen tiny fragments written in Greek. Scholars are aware of the attempt of the Spanish Jesuit José O'Callaghan to interpret 7Q4-10 as fragmentary copies of New Testament texts.[42] Although most New Testament interpreters have been reluctant to agree with O'Callaghan, the German scholar Carsten P. Thiede has supported him, especially in the identification of 7Q5 as a fragmentary copy of the Gospel of Mark.[43] This question will be treated more fully in Chapter 2,

40. See E. Tov, "Scribal Practices Reflected in the Texts from the Judaean Desert," in Flint and VanderKam, eds., *The Dead Sea Scrolls after Fifty Years*, 1:403-29; and his earlier article, "Hebrew Biblical Manuscripts from the Judaean Desert: Their Contribution to Textual Criticism," *JJS* 39 (1988) 5-37; reprinted in slightly revised form in *Jewish Civilization in the Hellenistic-Roman Period* (ed. S. Talmon; Philadelphia: Trinity Press International, 1991) 107-37.

41. See my dissent in "Scroll Origins: An Exchange on the Qumran Hypothesis," *ChrC* 110/10 (March 24-31, 1993) 326-29.

42. Beginning with "¿Papiros neotestamentarios en la cueva 7 de Qumran?" *Bib* 53 (1972) 91-100; translated into English by W. L. Holladay, supplement to *JBL* 91/2 (1972) 1-14. Cf. J. A. Fitzmyer, *DSSMPTS*, 168-72.

43. See C. P. Thiede, *The Earliest Gospel Manuscript? The Qumran Papyrus 7Q5 and Its Significance for New Testament Studies* (Carlisle, Cumbria: Paternoster, 1992); idem, "7Q — Eine Rückkehr zu den neutestamentlichen Papyrusfragmenten in der siebenten Höhle von Qumran," *Bib* 65 (1984) 538-59; idem, *Jésus selon Matthieu: La nouvelle datation du papyrus Magdalen d'Oxford et l'origine des Evangiles: Examen et discussion des dernières objections scientifiques* (Paris: François-Xavier de Guibert, 1996), esp. chap. 8.

but if there were any truth in such a claim, what would one have to say about the relation of Qumran Cave 7 fragments to early Christianity? At the moment, this issue is among the perils of considering Qumran fragments as containing New Testament writings.

These, then, are some of the risks that one must be aware of when studying the relation of the Dead Sea Scrolls to early Christianity. All of them affect the methodology that one employs in the study of the Scrolls.

CHAPTER 2

The Dead Sea Scrolls
and Early Christianity

In the first chapter I called attention to the book of Lawrence H. Schiffman, *Reclaiming the Dead Sea Scrolls,*[1] in which he "aims to correct a fundamental misreading of the Dead Sea Scrolls," because not enough of the contribution of the scrolls to the "history of Judaism" has been considered.[2] The subtitle of Schiffman's book mentions "the Background of Christianity," but apart from scattered references to items in the Scrolls that impinge on Christianity or certain Christian tenets, he has devoted no formal discussion to that background. This, then, is the topic to which I now turn. I do this, not because I want to play down the contribution that the discovery of the Scrolls and fragments have made to the study of ancient Judaism and its history. The Scrolls are tremendously important for that history, and we are constantly learning more about it as fragments continue to be published and interpreted, especially as they reveal the antecedents of the rabbinic form of Judaism and help fill in a gap that has long existed in our knowledge between the end of the Old Testament and the beginning of rabbinic literature, roughly between the time of the early Hasmonean kings and Rabbi Judah the Prince, the compiler of the Mishnah (ca. A.D. 200).

There is still room, however, for the study of the impact that these im-

---

1. L. H. Schiffman, *Reclaiming the Dead Sea Scrolls: The History of Judaism, the Background of Christianity, the Lost Library of Qumran* (Philadelphia/Jerusalem: Jewish Publication Society, 1994; reprinted in ABRL; New York: Doubleday, 1995). See the review of Schiffman's book by J. J. Collins, *DSD* 2 (1995) 244-47.

2. Schiffman, *Reclaiming the Dead Sea Scrolls,* xiii.

portant documents have made on our knowledge of the Palestinian Jewish matrix of early Christianity, which began in that same area of ancient Judea. This, then, is the topic that I should like to survey here briefly. I shall make my further remarks under three headings: John the Baptist, Jesus of Nazareth, and the writings of the New Testament.

John the Baptist

In none of the roughly 820 fragmentary or complete manuscripts from the eleven Qumran caves is there mention of the ancient Palestinian Jew about whom we have learned from the New Testament, John the Baptist.[3] The Jewish historian Flavius Josephus, who lived during the time that the New Testament was being written, also tells us about "John called the Baptist." Josephus knew of John as a preacher who urged people "to join in baptism" and whom Herod Antipas, the tetrarch of Galilee, "sent as a prisoner to Machaerus" and had "put to death."[4] Yet there is nothing about this Jewish precursor of Jesus in the Dead Sea Scrolls, at least so far.

3. This question has been discussed before, but not always with apposite arguments. See, e.g., O. Betz, "Was John the Baptist an Essene?" *BRev* 6/6 (1990) 18-25. Cf. H. Burgmann, "John the Baptist Was an Essene!" in *Mogilany 1989: Papers on the Dead Sea Scrolls Offered in Memory of Jean Carmignac: Part I. General Research on the Dead Sea Scrolls, Qumran and the New Testament, the Present State of Qumranology* (ed. Z. J. Kapera; Cracow: Enigma, 1993) 131-37; H. Lichtenberger, "Johannes der Täufer und die Texte von Qumran," ibid., 139-52; idem, "Reflections on the History of John the Baptist's Communities," *Folia orientalia* 25 (1988) 45-49; H. Stegemann, *Die Essener, Qumran, Johannes der Täufer und Jesus: Ein Sachbuch* (Freiburg im Breisgau: Herder, 1993) 292-313, available in English as *The Library of Qumran: On the Essenes, Qumran, John the Baptist, and Jesus* (Grand Rapids: Eerdmans, 1998) 211-27; J. E. Taylor, "John the Baptist and the Essenes," *JJS* 47 (1996) 356-85; eadem, *The Immerser: John the Baptist within Second Temple Judaism* (Grand Rapids: Eerdmans, 1997) 15-48.

4. *Ant.* 18.5.2 §116-19. Josephus's text reads:

Some of the Jews thought that Herod's army had been destroyed by God and that he had been justly punished because of the execution of John called the Baptist. For Herod put to death this good man, who was exhorting Jews to live upright lives, in dealing justly with one another and submitting devoutly to God, and to join in baptism *(baptismō synienai)*. Indeed, it seemed to John that even this washing would not be acceptable as a pardon for sins, but only as a purification for the body, unless the soul had previously been cleansed through upright conduct. When still others joined the crowds around him, because they were quite enthusiastic in listening to his words, Herod became frightened that such persuasiveness with the people might lead to some uprising; for it seemed that they might go to any length on his

The question, however, always rises: Could John have spent some of his youth as a candidate for membership in or as a member of the Essene community of Qumran? My answer to that question is yes, as a plausible hypothesis, one that I cannot prove, and one that cannot be disproved.

Reasons for considering it a plausible hypothesis are the following seven:

1. The Gospel of Luke depicts John as a child born of elderly parents, "who lived out in the desert until the day that he was manifested to Israel" (1:80). Luke also says that a "message came from God to John, the son of Zechariah, in the desert" (3:2), and that message has to be understood as the turning point in his career, no matter what he had been doing before it. In my view, John then broke off from the Essenes of Qumran, with whom he had been living for some time, to go forth and preach a "baptism of repentance for the forgiveness of sins" (3:3). Part of the reason for interpreting the Lucan text in this way is that John, though born into a priestly family, is never portrayed in any of the Gospels as serving in the Jerusalem Temple, as did his father Zechariah (Luke 1:5). After the death of his elderly parents, John might have been adopted by the Essenes, who according to Josephus were wont to take "other men's children, while yet pliable and docile . . . and mold them according to their own ways."[5]

2. Josephus tells that he himself had spent time as a youth among the Essenes.[6] John's connection with the Essenes of Qumran would have likewise been temporary, until he was called by God to another task.

3. In all four Gospels, Isa 40:3, "the voice of one crying out in the wilderness," is used to explain why John is in the desert (Mark 1:3; Matt 3:3; Luke 3:3-6; John 1:23). Yet that very text of Isaiah is used in an Essene rule book, the *Manual of Discipline*, to explain why the community is in the desert: ". . . to go into the desert to prepare there the way of HIM, as it is written, 'Make ready in the desert the way of .... [four dots = Yahweh]; make straight in the wilderness a path for our God.' This means the study of the Law" (1QS 8:12-16). The way to be prepared for God's coming is different: for the Essenes it meant the study of the Law; for John it was a preparation for his

---

advice. So before any new incident might stem from him, Herod considered it far better to seize John in advance and do away with him, rather than wait for an upheaval, become involved in a difficult situation, and regret it. As a result of this suspicion of Herod, John was sent as a prisoner to Machaerus . . . and there was put to death. This made the Jews believe that the destruction of Herod's army was a vindication of this man by God who saw fit to punish Herod.

5. *J.W.* 2.8.2 §120.
6. *Life* 2 §10-11.

ministry of baptizing for the forgiveness of sins. The common use of Isa 40:3, explaining why both the Essenes and John were in the desert, could of course be a sheer coincidence, but when it is considered with the other factors, it becomes significant.

4. Before the discovery of the Dead Sea Scrolls, John's baptism was often explained as a ritual washing derived from the baptism of proselytes among the Jews.[7] That explanation, however, often raised more problems than it solved, mainly because there is so little evidence for the existence of proselyte baptism in the first century of the Christian era. John's baptism, however, is now better explained as a development of the ritual washings of the Essene community. The excavated remains of the Qumran community center have several cisterns and a few *miqwā'ôt,* "baths," for the ritual washing of community members. The Essene *Manual of Discipline,* when it refers to ritual washing, speaks of it as a way of entering the covenanted life of the community. "To enter the Covenant" is to turn from one's sin, to "enter into water," and thus become a member. "One shall not enter the water to partake of the pure meal of holy men, for they shall not be cleansed unless they repent of their wickedness; for unclean are all who transgress His word" (1QS 5:13-14).[8] Such Essene washings were not unique, initiatory, or not-to-be-repeated (as Christian baptism eventually came to be described), but neither was John's baptism. He apparently would administer his baptism for the forgiveness of sins to any Jew who would come to him, and as often as one would come.

5. When John preached his baptism, he spoke of it as a baptism of water, but referred to another, coming baptism of "spirit and fire" (Luke 3:16). The mention of water, fire, and spirit also has a remarkable parallel in the Essene *Manual of Discipline,* which speaks of God "purging by His truth all the deeds of human beings, refining [i.e., by fire] for Himself some of mankind to remove every spirit from their flesh, to cleanse them with a holy Spirit, and sprinkle them with a Spirit of truth like purifying water" (1QS 4:20-21). Here one finds "water," "holy Spirit," "Spirit of truth," and "refining" as elements of God's activity as He purges this community. This sounds very much like ele-

---

7. See H. H. Rowley, "Jewish Proselyte Baptism and the Baptism of John," *HUCA* 15 (1940) 313-34. Cf. T. M. Taylor, "The Beginnings of Jewish Proselyte Baptism," *NTS* 2 (1955-56) 193-98; D. C. Smith, "Jewish Proselyte Baptism and the Baptism of John," *ResQ* 25 (1982) 13-32; K. Pusey, "Jewish Proselyte Baptism," *ExpTim* 95 (1983-84) 141-45.

8. See also 1QS 3:3-5: "He shall not be counted among the perfect; he shall neither be purified by expiation nor cleansed by purifying waters: Unclean, unclean shall he be, as long as he despises the precepts of God, without being instructed in the community of His counsel."

ments of John's preaching about his own baptism and that of the coming "more powerful" one (Jesus).

6. Still another Essene rule book, the *Damascus Document*, says, "He made known to them his holy Spirit through his Messiah(s)" (CD 2:12). This text provides a Palestinian background for John speaking of Jesus, the Messiah, as the bearer of the Spirit (especially in the Lucan Gospel).

7. Finally, for what it is worth, an ancient tradition about John baptizing along the banks of the Jordan River points to a spot that was within walking distance of Khirbet Qumran, the Essene community site.[9]

These are, then, reasons that have made interpreters of the Qumran Scrolls think that John, the son of the priest Zechariah, may well have spent some of his youth among the Essenes of Qumran. None of the reasons is so cogent that it convinces absolutely, but the ensemble of them makes it at least a plausible hypothesis that he did so. Not even John's descent from a priestly family, which served according to what the Qumran Essenes considered a tainted temple service,[10] militates against the hypothesis that John had been adopted by Essenes of Qumran and had lived among them for a time.

Jesus of Nazareth

If one can thus make out a plausible case for John the Baptist, what about Jesus of Nazareth, the founder of Christianity? One realizes today that Jesus himself was not a Christian, in the sense in which that term came to be used later on. He was a Jew, a native of Palestine, but did he have any connection with the Qumran community? So far he is not mentioned in any of the 820 fragmentary texts, just as the Baptist is not. One reason for the lack of mention of either of them is that most of the Qumran texts were composed and even copied in the last two pre-Christian centuries,[11] well before John or Jesus was born.

Moreover, in the case of Jesus there are simply no reasons similar to those just presented for John the Baptist and his connection with the Essenes of Qumran. Jesus, a Palestinian Jew, began his ministry on the heels of John,

9. See C. Kopp, *The Holy Places of the Gospels* (New York: Herder and Herder, 1963) 99-105; D. Baldi, *Enchiridion locorum sanctorum: Documenta s. Evangelii loca respicientia* (Jerusalem: Franciscan Press, 1955) 169-88.

10. See 1QpHab 9:4-10 for a criticism of the Jewish priests serving the Temple in Jerusalem.

11. See Chapter 1 above, p. 6 for the paleographic and radiocarbon dating of the Qumran fragments.

but nothing similar can be lined up to establish a connection of him with the Essene community of Qumran.

Did Jesus know of the Qumran Essenes? Presumably he did, but strangely enough the Gospel tradition presents him in debate or controversy with Pharisees and Sadducees, but never with Essenes, who are, moreover, never mentioned in the New Testament. Some interpreters have suggested that one or other saying of Jesus may refer to Essenes. For instance, in the Sermon on the Mount Jesus says, "You have heard that it was said [to your ancestors], 'You shall love your neighbor and hate your enemy'" (Matt 5:43). To love one's neighbor is found in Lev 19:18, but one looks in vain in the Old Testament for the hatred of one's enemy. To what would the latter part of Jesus' saying have referred? Now in the *Manual of Discipline,* one reads that Qumran community members were "to love all sons of light . . . and hate all the sons of darkness" (1QS 1:9-10). "Sons of light" was a designation of the members of the community; all other Jews and outsiders were "sons of darkness," and so to be hated. Or again, Jesus' saying about "those who have made themselves eunuchs for the sake of the kingdom" (Matt 19:12) has been interpreted as an allusion to the celibate Essenes of Qumran, about whom both Josephus and Pliny the Elder have reported.[12] Moreover, Jesus' prohibition of divorce may also echo the Essene prohibition of it.[13] Such sayings of Jesus may reflect, indeed, Essene practices or tenets, but there is no way of being certain that these sayings actually referred to the Essenes of Qumran, and there is no evidence that Jesus ever visited the Qumran community center or spent time there.

This lack of evidence has to be emphasized in light of the allegations of Barbara Thiering, an Australian interpreter of the Scrolls, who claims that the Essene mode of interpreting Scripture found in some Scrolls supplies the key to decoding the New Testament itself. According to her, John the Baptist was the community's "Teacher of Righteousness," and Jesus the "Wicked Priest," titles used in sectarian Qumran writings for the leader of the community and the chief of its opponents. In her latest book, *Jesus and the Riddle of the Dead Sea Scrolls: Unlocking the Secrets of His Life Story,*[14] Thiering goes so far as to maintain that Jesus was born at Qumran, crucified at Qumran, secretly revived at the Dead Sea, and eventually wed to a woman bishop, from whom he

---

12. See Josephus, *J.W.* 2.8.2 §120 (but cf. 2.8.13 §160-61); Pliny, *Naturalis Historia* 5.15.73.

13. See my article, "The Matthean Divorce Texts and Some New Palestinian Evidence," *TS* 37 (1976) 197-226; reprinted in slightly revised form in *TAG,* 79-111.

14. (San Francisco: HarperSanFrancisco, 1992).

had children and with whom he lived to a ripe old age. All of which is sheer "hokum" — to borrow the word that *Time* magazine used of her thesis.[15]

Writings of the New Testament

Although the Qumran Scrolls provide information that may help to explain the background of John the Baptist but practically nothing about Jesus and his background or ministry, interpreters have nevertheless discovered many striking details in the Scrolls that shed light on the New Testament writings. All of its twenty-seven books were composed in Greek, and almost all of them in places outside of Palestine; yet many items in those Greek writings have been illumined by these new Hebrew and Aramaic scrolls discovered at Qumran. Even though none of them refers to anything Christian or mentions any Christians, they do give us firsthand evidence of the Palestinian Jewish matrix from which ideas and phrases found in these Christian writings emerged and to which they are related.

After all, Jesus of Nazareth, a Palestinian Jew, taught and preached in Aramaic, and probably spoke some Greek.[16] Christianity, the movement that is traced back to him, is rooted in his Palestinian ministry. What is recorded in the Greek New Testament represents various forms of a recollection of his words and his deeds, along with an early Christian interpretation of them and of his meaning for humanity. So the Scrolls, in bringing to light contemporary evidence of such Palestinian Jewish ideas and phrases, have had a remarkable impact on our understanding of the record compiled about Jesus in the New Testament and on the interpretation of him there.

Before I descend to details, I must mention two issues that have surfaced at times, but that are merely distractions. The first of these concerns Qumran Cave 7, from which nineteen Greek fragments were recovered, and

15. For reactions to this book of Thiering, see D. Peterson, "The Dead Sea Scrolls Again," *BH* 28/3 (1992) 87-90; cf. O. Betz, "Peschermethode und Jesusroman," *QC* 5/1 (1995) 23-30; D. M. Paton, "An Evaluation of the Hypothesis of Barbara Thiering concerning Jesus and the Dead Sea Scrolls," ibid., 31-45; G. O'Collins, *Tablet* 246/2 (26 September 1992) 1184-86; W. Wink, *Critical Review of Books in Religion* 6 (1993) 298-301; R. A. Burridge, *Sewanee Theological Review* 36 (1993) 435-39; H. Shanks, *BARev* 18/5 (1992) 69-70; G. F. Snyder, *Chicago Theological Seminary Register* 83 (1993) 69-70. See also J. H. Charlesworth, ed., *Jesus and the Dead Sea Scrolls* (New York: Doubleday, 1992).

16. See my article, "Did Jesus Speak Greek?" *BARev* 18/5 (1992) 58-63, 76-77; reprinted in *Approaches to the Bible: The Best of Bible Review. Volume I: Composition, Transmission and Language* (ed. H. Minkoff; Washington, D.C.: Biblical Archaeology Society, 1994) 253-64, 343-46.

none in Hebrew or Aramaic. I have already alluded to it briefly above in Chapter 1, but more has to be said about it. Two of the fragments of Cave 7 were identified as Old Testament texts in Greek: Exod 28:4-7 and a variant of the Epistle of Jeremiah 43-44.[17] The other seventeen fragments, however, proved at first to be unidentifiable. In 1972 a Spanish Jesuit named José O'Callaghan claimed that some of these were fragments of New Testament passages: specifically 7Q4 a copy of 1 Tim 3:16–4:3 and 7Q5 a copy of Mark 6:52-53. In the latter case O'Callaghan maintained that the fragment showed that Mark's Gospel was already in existence about A.D. 50.[18] Yet apart from a handful of followers, especially the German scholar Carsten P. Thiede, the identification of O'Callaghan has fallen on deaf scholarly ears.[19] The trouble is that the fragments are so tiny and contain so few Greek letters that they can be identified with almost anything. Computers and special photographing techniques have been employed, and all the pros and cons have been gathered in a German book entitled *Christen und Christliches in Qumran?*[20] The most interesting item in this publication is the enlarged photograph produced by the Division of Identification and Forensic Science of the Investigations Department of the Israeli National Police on 12 April 1992.[21] At first sight, it seemed to confirm O'Callaghan's reading of a word on line 2 of the fragment as *autōn,* with traces of a final *N,* which scholars had earlier contested. Consequently, as might have been expected,

17. This is actually vv. 43-44 of chap. 6 of the deuterocanonical book of Baruch. For both Greek texts, see M. Baillet et al., *Les 'petites grottes' de Qumrân* (DJD 3; Oxford: Clarendon, 1962) 142-43.

18. See J. O'Callaghan, "¿Papiros neotestamentarios en la cueva 7 de Qumrān?" *Bib* 53 (1972) 91-100; translated by W. L. Holladay as "New Testament Papyri in Qumrān Cave 7?" Supplement to *JBL* 91/2 (1972) 1-14. Cf. J. O'Callaghan, *Los papiros griegos de la cueva 7 de Qumrân* (BAC 353; Madrid: Editorial Católica, 1974).

19. See C. P. Thiede, *The Earliest Gospel Manuscript? The Qumran Papyrus 7Q5 and Its Significance for New Testament Studies* (Exeter: Paternoster, 1992). For further bibliography on the topic, see *DSSMPTS,* 168-72.

20. See B. Mayer, ed., *Christen und Christliches in Qumran?* (Eichstätter Studien n.s. 32; Regensburg: Pustet, 1992). Cf. L. Stuckenbruck, *QC* 2/3 (1993) 195-97; K. Backhaus, "Qumran und die Urchristen: Zu einem neueren Diskussionsbeitrag," *TGl* 83 (1993) 364-68.

21. Mayer, ed., *Christen und Christliches,* 243. See also the explanatory article of C. P. Thiede, "Bericht über die kriminaltechnische Untersuchung des Fragments 7Q5 in Jerusalem," ibid., 239-45. Thiede speaks of a letter (of 12 December 1990) received from A. R. Millard in Liverpool, England, who reported that O'Callaghan's reading of the combination of letters on the five lines, when searched out electronically on a computer using the entire corpus of Greek literature, resulted in identifying "für 7Q5 *nur* Mk 6,52-53" (ibid., 240 [his italics]).

O'Callaghan has reiterated his contention,[22] and Thiede has pursued the matter still further.[23] The scholarly world, however, remains unconvinced.[24] The last word has not yet been uttered on the identification of 7Q5, and so it is at the moment a distracting item.

If this confirmed reading were to prove acceptable, and if a fragment of Mark was indeed found in Qumran Cave 7, what does that say about all the rest of the fragments of that cave? In itself, the identification of 7Q5 as Marcan would not be impossible, because many scholars have held that the Marcan Gospel was composed as early as A.D. 65, that is, a short time prior to the destruction of Jerusalem. If a copy of that Gospel had been brought from Rome or Italy, where many think the Marcan Gospel was composed, to Christians in Jerusalem in a year or so thereafter, it could have become the property of Jerusalem Christians who may have wanted to store it for safekeeping in a cave used by Essene friends, when they realized the coming of the siege of Jerusalem by the Romans.

It is usually thought that the Essene community's center at Khirbet Qumran was destroyed in the summer of A.D. 68, and one usually judges that the caves would have contained their deposits by that time. That would mean

22. See J. O'Callaghan, "Sobre el papiro de Marcos en Qumran," *FilNeot* 5 (1992) 191-97; idem, "L'Ipotético papiro di Marco a Qumrân," *CivCatt* 143/2 (1992) 464-73; idem, *Los primeros testimonios del Nuevo Testamento: Papirología neotestamentaria* (Córdoba: Ediciones el Almendro, 1995) 95-145.

23. See now C. P. Thiede, "Greek Qumran Fragment 7Q5: Possibilities and Impossibilities," *Bib* 75 (1994) 394-98; idem, *Jésus selon Matthieu: La nouvelle datation du papyrus Magdalen d'Oxford et l'origine des Evangiles: Examen et discussion des dernières objections scientifiques* (Paris: François-Xavier de Guibert, 1996) 101-18.

24. Part of the trouble is that Thiede has now joined to his campaign for 7Q5 as a Marcan fragment another claim about an alleged first-century fragment of Matthew's Gospel. Two parts of it are found in the Library of Magdalen College, Oxford, and in Barcelona. This claim, too, scholars are again quite reluctant to admit, because those fragments of Matthew have always been dated to the late second century A.D. See now G. N. Stanton, *Gospel Truth? New Light on Jesus and the Gospels* (Valley Forge, Penn.: Trinity Press International, 1995) 11-48.

See the more recent criticism of M.-E. Boismard, "A propos de 7Q5 et Mc 6,52-53," *RB* 102 (1995) 585-88; P. Grelot, "Note sur les propositions du Pr Carsten Peter Thiede," *RB* 102 (1995) 589-91; E. Puech, "Des fragments grecs de la grotte 7 et le Nouveau Testament? 7Q4 et 7Q5, et le Papyrus Magdalen grec 17 = P[64]," *RB* 102 (1995) 570-84. It now appears that several of these Greek fragments are part of a translation of *1 Enoch* in Greek; see E. Puech, "Notes sur les fragments grecs du manuscrit 7Q4 = 1 Hénoch 103 et 105," *RB* 103 (1996) 592-600; E. A. Muro, Jr., "The Greek Fragments of Enoch from Qumran Cave 7 (*7Q4, 7Q8, & 7Q12 = 7QEn gr = Enoch* 103:3-4, 7-8)," *RevQ* 18 (1997) 307-12; E. Puech, "Sept fragments grecs de la *Lettre d'Hénoch* (*1 Hén* 100, 103 et 105) dans la grotte 7 de Qumrân (= *7QHéngr*)," *RevQ* 18 (1997) 313-23.

that sometime between A.D. 65 and the summer of A.D. 68 a copy of the Marcan Gospel came to Cave 7.[25] How did it get there? Was it brought by Jerusalem Christians to their Essene neighbors' cave near Khirbet Qumran? Or was it brought by Essenes from Jerusalem? Who knows? The problem would become even more acute if one were to insist on the date of the composition of the Marcan Gospel as A.D. 70, as many do, or later! One realizes today how hypothetical this problem of identification really is.

If one could admit that 7Q5 were indeed a fragment of the Gospel according to Mark, what must be said about 7Q4, which O'Callaghan has identified as 1 Tim 3:16; 4:1, 3?[26] That a copy of a Pastoral Epistle should be found in a Qumran Cave prior to A.D. 68 is problematic indeed!

What evidence is there, however, that would negate or gainsay a deposit of Christian scrolls in Cave 7 at a period later than A.D. 68? The so-called *Copper Scroll* (3Q15) is a case in point. Its text mentions sixty-four hiding places where treasures have been buried, and it was written in a form of Hebrew that is not the same as that of most of the Qumran Hebrew texts, especially the sectarian writings. It has been dated by its chief editor, J. T. Milik, to ca. A.D. 100.[27] So the question has been asked whether it might have been deposited in Cave 3 sometime after A.D. 70. If so, then why could not Christian texts have been deposited in Cave 7 after A.D. 68?

The other distracting issue is the interpretation of Qumran texts as Jewish Christian. This interpretation has been proposed by Robert H. Eisenman of California State University at Riverside, who in more recent times has had access to a previously unknown collection of official photographs of Qumran Cave 4 texts. Eventually, Eisenman became one of the editors of *A Facsimile Edition of the Dead Sea Scrolls*,[28] a photographic reproduction of 1,785 plates of fragmentary texts from Qumran Cave 4. Eisenman then claimed that among this newly released material was a fragment that "refers to the execution of a Messianic leader" and that this text has to do "with Christian origins

---

25. It should be noted that Cave 7 was hollowed out in antiquity in the southern edge of the plateau on which the community center, Khirbet Qumran, was located. Unfortunately, even more of it has crumbled into the wadi below since its discovery in 1952, and today one can only see where the cave once was. So little remains of that area that all recent calls for a fresh reexamination of the cave or further excavation of it seem doomed to failure. I visited the site in June 1993.

26. See C. P. Thiede, "Bericht," 241 (with an enlarged photograph of the fragment).

27. See Baillet et al., *Les 'petites grottes' de Qumrân*, 217: "l'écriture . . . 'hérodienne évoluée' . . . entre 30 et 130 après J.-C., en chiffres ronds, avec préférence pour la seconde moitié de cette période."

28. *Prepared with an Introduction and Index*, with J. M. Robinson (2 vols.; Washington, D.C.: Biblical Archaeology Society, 1991).

in Palestine."[29] Newspaper reports said that he had found a "Jesus-like messiah . . . in scrolls."[30] This claim, however, turned out to be only another misinterpreted text, suiting a pattern of several years of Eisenman's publications, in which he has been maintaining that the Qumran Teacher of Righteousness was James, who is called "the brother of the Lord" (Gal 1:19); that the Wicked Priest was Ananos, the son of the high priest Annas, who put James to death; and that the "Man of the Lie" was the Apostle Paul. Still more recently, Eisenman has published (along with Michael O. Wise) a book entitled, *The Dead Sea Scrolls Uncovered: The First Complete Translation and Interpretation of 50 Key Documents Withheld for over 35 Years.*[31] This book too made headlines, for, despite its subtitle, close to twenty-five of the fifty texts had been published earlier, and some were based on questionable sources (e.g., handouts at scholarly meetings, along with their noteworthy errors), or what has been called "the 'unethical appropriation' of others' research," especially in transcribing and reconstructing the texts.[32] The claim that the Scrolls are Jewish *Christian* documents, closely related to early stages of Christian history, is highly exaggerated and simply wrong. They are Jewish texts, and the teachings in them are Jewish to the hilt. Now that the dust has settled on this issue, one sees that Eisenman's claim has proved to be only a distraction. As a result, the claims of Thiering and Eisenman cannot be taken seriously, even when one studies the impact of this important discovery on the study of the New Testament.

29. See *California State University, Long Beach, News Release,* 1 November 1991, p. 1; cf. *New York Times,* 8 November 1991, p. A8.

30. The text to which the sensational headlines referred was 4Q285, about which Eisenman subsequently published an article, "A War Prayer," *BARev* 17/6 (1991) 65. See, however, G. Vermes, "The 'Pierced Messiah' Text — An Interpretation Evaporates," *BARev* 18/2 (1992) 80-82; idem, "The Oxford Forum for Qumran Research: Seminar on the Rule of War from Cave 4 (4Q285)," *JJS* 43 (1992) 85-90. Cf. M. G. Abegg, Jr., "Messianic Hope and 4Q285: A Reassessment," *JBL* 113 (1994) 81-91; M. Bockmuehl, "A 'Slain Messiah' in 4Q Serekh Milḥamah (4Q285)?" *TynBull* 43 (1992) 155-69; J. D. Tabor, "A Pierced or Piercing Messiah? — The Verdict Is Still Out," *BARev* 18/6 (1992) 58-59.

31. (Rockport, Mass.: Element Books, 1992).

32. See *New York Times,* 13 December 1992 (International Section, p. 28). Cf. J. N. Wilford, "New Access to Scrolls Fuels Scholars' Warfare," *New York Times,* Science Section, Tuesday, 22 December 1992, C1; "Scroll Scholars Resolve Dispute," *New York Times,* Friday, 18 December 1992, A15. This book has evoked severe criticism; see the reviews by G. Vermes, *Times Literary Supplement* (4 December 1992) 6-7; J. C. Greenfield, *Jerusalem Post Magazine* (19 February 1993) 26; P. S. Alexander, *JJS* 44 (1993) 139-40; D. J. Harrington and J. Strugnell, "Qumran Cave 4 Texts: A New Publication," *JBL* 112 (1993) 491-99; F. García Martínez, *RevQ* 16 (1993-95) 123-50; A. S. van der Woude, *JSJ* 24 (1993) 298-99. See also G. Vermes, "A Regrettable Public Squabble over the Scrolls," *JJS* 44 (1993) 116-17.

If there is nothing in the Qumran Scrolls about Jesus or Christians and no New Testament writing among them, why, then, are the Scrolls so important for the understanding of early Christianity? I shall try to answer that question by citing four kinds of material found in the Scrolls that reveal the Palestinian background to (1) important Pauline teachings; (2) christological titles used in the New Testament; (3) select Gospel passages, and (4) light shed on Melchizedek in the Epistle to the Hebrews.

First, even though the uncontested letters of the convert Diaspora Jew Paul of Tarsus were written in eastern Mediterranean areas outside of Palestine between A.D. 51 and 58, they contain ideas and phrases that show that his teaching was rooted, indeed, in a Palestinian Jewish matrix.

For instance, Paul speaks at times of a divine attribute, "the righteousness of God" (*dikaiosynē theou*, Rom 1:17; 3:5, 21, 22; 10:3), and the phrase sounds like a frequently used slogan. Yet it is never found *verbatim* in the Old Testament, which otherwise often calls God "righteous" and speaks of his "righteousness."[33] It has now, however, turned up verbatim in the Dead Sea Scrolls, either as *ṣedeq 'ēl* (1QM 4:6) or as *ṣidqat 'ēl* (1QS 10:25; 11:12). Clearly, then, Paul was echoing a phrase current in the Judaism of his day.

Related to that phrase is Paul's teaching on justification by grace through faith. "Justification" is derived, of course, from the Hebrew Scriptures, which taught Jews of old that they could achieve a righteous status in God's sight by observing the Mosaic Law, by doing "the works of the Law." In contrast, Paul insisted that that status of righteousness in God's sight was something that Christ Jesus had attained for humanity by his vicarious death and resurrection. For Paul such righteousness was a grace bestowed by God on people of faith. Two aspects of Essene teaching now found in the Scrolls shed light on this Pauline teaching, for the Essenes of Qumran also insisted on the justification of human beings by God's "mercy" and "grace." In fact,

---

33. See Deut 32:4; Ps 119:137; 129:4; Job 34:17 for *ṣaddîq* said of God; Job 36:3; Hos 2:21; Ps 36:7; 71:19 for *ṣedeq* or *ṣĕdāqāh* used of Him.

The closest one comes to a Hebrew equivalent of the Pauline Greek phrase in the Old Testament is found in Deut 33:21, *ṣidqat YHWH*, which the RSV translates, "just decrees of the Lord"; the NRSV, "what the Lord deemed right"; and what the LXX rendered as *dikaiosynēn Kyrios epoiēsen*, "The Lord has wrought righteousness." Or again in Judg 5:11, *ṣidqôt YHWH*, which the RSV translates, "the triumphs of the Lord," the NRSV, "the victories of the Lord," and what the LXX rendered as *ekei dōsousin dikaiosynas Kyriō*, "there they will grant the Lord righteous acts." These different modes of translating the same phrase show that it is scarcely the same as the Pauline phrase.

L. Alonso Schökel, however, thinks that I have not done justice to the Old Testament data in this matter; see his "Tres notas de hermenéutica," *EstBíb* 53 (1997) 73-87, esp. 79-83; and my response, "Alonso Schökel and *Dikaiosynē Theou*," *EstBíb* 54 (1998) 107-9.

their teaching forms an interesting transition between the Old Testament teaching about righteousness and the Pauline. The hymn with which the community rule book, the *Manual of Discipline*, ends has this striking paragraph:

> As for me, I belong to wicked humanity, to the assembly of perverse flesh; my iniquities, my transgressions, my sins together with the wickedness of my heart belong to the assembly doomed to worms and walking in darkness. [No] human being sets his own path or directs his own steps, for to God alone belongs the judgment (of him), and from His hand comes perfection of way. . . . And I, if I stagger, God's grace *(ḥasdê ʾēl)* is my salvation forever. (1QS 11:9-12)

Similarly, the author of the sectarian *Thanksgiving Psalms* proclaims:

> As for me, I know that righteousness belongs not to a human being, nor perfection of way to a son of man. To God Most High belong all the deeds of righteousness, whereas the path of a human is not set firm. . . . I have based myself on Your grace and on the abundance of Your mercy. For You expiate iniquity to clean[se a human be]ing from guilt by Your righteousness. (1QH 4:30-38)

In a very similar way, Paul insisted that all human beings "have sinned and fall short of the glory of God" (Rom 3:23), that is, because of their sins they fail to attain the glorious destiny planned by God for them. The one big difference between the Essene teaching on justification and the Pauline is that the Apostle insists that human beings appropriate this status of righteousness and acquittal in God's sight through faith in Christ Jesus. For Paul, the vicarious death and the resurrection of Jesus of Nazareth have made a difference, and the important difference is "faith" *(pistis)* in Christ, by which one appropriates that status of righteousness. Nevertheless, the Qumran tenet in this matter is clearly transitional, for it shows how the Old Testament teaching about righteousness could develop and be used by a Christian writer like Paul.

Moreover, the Qumran Scrolls have shed light on Paul's use of "the works of the Law." Paul insisted that "a human being is justified by faith apart from works of the law" (Rom 3:28; cf. Gal 2:16). *Erga nomou* is used by Paul so frequently that it too sounds like a well-known Jewish slogan, and yet its equivalent is never found in the Hebrew of either the Old Testament or the rabbinic literature of later periods. It has, however, turned up in Qumran texts as *maʿăśê hattôrāh*, "deeds of the law" (4QFlor [4Q174] 1-2 i 7; 4QMMT C 27). In these writings it clearly means things prescribed by the Mosaic Law,

and in the latter passage it occurs in a context that speaks of "righteousness."
It runs thus:

> Moreover, we have written to you (about) some of the deeds of the law,
> which we consider for your welfare and that of your people, because w[e
> recognize] (that) you have prudence and knowledge of the Law. Be wise in
> all these (things) and seek from Him your good counsel that He may keep
> far from you evil plots and the scheming of Belial, so that you may rejoice at
> the end of time, as you find that some of our words (are) right. It will be
> reckoned to you as righteousness,[34] as you do what is upright and good be-
> fore Him for your welfare and (that) of Israel. (4QMMT C 25-32)[35]

This text shows again that Paul, in relating "works of the Law" to the pursuit
of "righteousness," knew whereof he was speaking. It manifests how he was
coping with current Palestinian Jewish ways of thinking about God and the
human condition.[36] Such examples, which could be multiplied, reveal how
the Scrolls have helped us to a better comprehension of Pauline teaching.

A second area in which the Scrolls have made an impact in New Testament interpretation is that of christological titles. Such titles as "Lord," "Son
of God," "Messiah," and "Son of Man" are applied to Jesus in the New Testament, but there has always been a debate about whence early Christians derived such titles and the background out of which they have come.

Apropos of "Lord," Rudolf Bultmann once maintained that the unmodified *(ho) Kyrios,* "(the) Lord," could not have been part of the primitive Jewish Christian proclamation about Jesus, because Jews themselves would never
have used such a title of God. In his renowned *Theology of the New Testament,*
Bultmann wrote:

> At the very outset the unmodified expression "the Lord" is unthinkable in
> Jewish usage. "Lord" used of God is always given some modifier; we read:
> "the Lord of heaven and earth," "our Lord" and similar expressions.[37]

34. This phrase is probably an echo of Ps 106:31, which refers to the Phineas incident of Num 25:1-8.

35. See E. Qimron and J. Strugnell, *Qumran Cave 4: V. Miqṣat maʿaśe ha-torah* (DJD
10; Oxford: Clarendon, 1994) 62 + pl. VIII (4Q398 14 ii 2-8). The epilogue of this document, quoted above, is addressed to adversaries of the Qumran community (probably
Pharisees), whom the writers are trying to convert to the community's way of understanding righteous conduct.

36. See further M. Abegg, "Paul, 'Works of the Law,' and MMT," *BARev* 20/6 (1994)
52-55, 82.

37. R. Bultmann, *Theology of the New Testament* (2 vols.; London: SCM, 1952-55)
1:51.

Hence early Jewish Christians of Palestine could not have taken over such a title allegedly used of Yahweh in Jewish circles and applied it to the risen Christ. Rather, Bultmann alleged, "the Kyrios-cult [of Jesus] originated on Hellenistic soil."[38] Accordingly, the title *Kyrios* would have been picked up by Christian missionaries as they carried the message about Christ from Palestine into the contemporary Greco-Roman world, where gods, emperors, and other illustrious persons were sometimes called *Kyrios*. Bultmann had derived that idea about the origin of the *Kyrios*-title from Wilhelm Bousset, and many New Testament interpreters have followed him in so understanding this christological title.

All that, however, has changed since the discovery of the Qumran Scrolls. In the fragmentary Aramaic translation of Job, recovered from Qumran Cave 11, a clear example of an unmodified *mārê*', "Lord," is used as a title for God. In the original Hebrew of his poetic discourse, Elihu says to Job, "Indeed, God will not act wickedly; the Almighty will not pervert justice" (34:12). That statement becomes a question in the Aramaic targum, "Now will God really prove faithless, and [will] the Lord [distort judgment]?" (11Qtg-Job 24:6-7).[39] Here *mārê*', "Lord," stands in parallelism with *'ĕlāhā*', "God." It shows clearly that it was not unthinkable for a Palestinian Jew of the first century B.C. to refer to God simply as "Lord." Another clear example of *maryā*', "the Lord," has turned up in the 4QEn[b] 1 iv 5.[40] The upshot of this is that *Kyrios*, "Lord," used so often of the risen Christ in the New Testament, was fully at home in the earliest stratum of Palestinian Christian teaching, at least as a confessional title, if not also as a kerygmatic title.

An even more important christological title is "Son of God." Given its Old Testament background, where it is used sometimes of corporate Israel, or of the king on the Davidic throne, or of angels, or even of an individual Jew,[41] most New Testament commentators have been reluctant to claim that its use for Jesus in the New Testament was derived from contemporary Hellenistic or Greco-Roman usage. And yet, W. Bousset once wrote:

38. Ibid.

39. See J. P. M. van der Ploeg and A. S. van der Woude, *Le targum de Job de la grotte xi de Qumrân édité et traduit* (Koninklijke nederlandse Akademie van Wetenschappen; Leiden: Brill, 1971) 58.

40. See J. T. Milik, *The Books of Enoch: Aramaic Fragments of Qumrân Cave 4* (Oxford: Clarendon, 1976) 175. Moreover, there is an instance of Hebrew *'ādôn*, "Lord," in the Hebrew form of Psalm 151 recovered from Cave 11 (11QPs[a] 28:7-8) and in 4Q403 1 i 28, not to mention the often overlooked instance of *'ādôn* in the canonical psalter itself (Ps 114:7). See further my article, "The Semitic Background of New Testament *Kyrios*-Title," in *WA* or *SBNT*, 115-42.

41. See Chapter 4 below.

May we, without further ado, assume that already the first community of Jesus' disciples had taken the daring step and had creatively formed the title "the Son of God," which the Old Testament and the messianic faith of late Judaism did not know, out of Old Testament beginnings (Ps 2:7) and the tradition about Jesus' baptism and transfiguration? Or did this title ultimately develop first on Greek soil, in the Greek language?[42]

Although Bousset expressed his hesitation about the relation of the New Testament title to what he called "Jewish messianology"[43] and believed that the title came to undisputed dominance in "the area of popular conceptions in the Gentile Christian church and in that of the Pauline-Johannine Christology,"[44] he did not go as far as Adolf Deissmann had, who maintained that the title's "'Old Testament presuppositions' were not extant" among Gentile Christians, for whom rather its connection with the imperial cult and the well-known formula *divi filius (theou huios)* would have been the way they understood it.[45] A number of other writers have similarly related "Son of God" to a Hellenistic origin, including G. P. Wetter[46] and W. G. Kümmel.[47] In this instance it would, of course, be foolhardy to deny that contemporary Hellenistic usage of "Son of God" for demigods or heroes born of gods and goddesses, or even for *theioi andres,* may have exerted some influence on early Christians in their use of such a title for the risen Christ.

No one would have expected that a striking instance of the title would turn up in a Palestinian Jewish text copied at the turn of the era. Among the last fragments of Qumran Cave 4 acquired from the Bedouin in July 1958, there was found an Aramaic text in which this title occurs. Unfortunately, the text is fragmentary, broken vertically down the center of a column, which makes it impossible to say who the person was to whom the title is applied.

42. W. Bousset, *Kyrios Christos: A History of the Belief in Christ from the Beginnings of Christianity to Irenaeus* (Nashville: Abingdon, 1970) 95-96. Although this translation was only published in 1970, its German original dates from 1913. I shall return to this matter below, pp. 64-65.

43. Ibid., 207.

44. Ibid., 97.

45. G. A. Deissmann, *Bible Studies: Contributions Chiefly from Papyri and Inscriptions to the History of the Language, the Literature, and the Religion of Hellenistic Judaism and Primitive Christianity* (2d ed.; Edinburgh: Clark, 1909) 166-67; cf. idem, *Light from the Ancient East: The New Testament Illustrated by Recently Discovered Texts of the Graeco-Roman World* (rev. ed.; London: Hodder and Stoughton; New York: Doran, 1927) 346-47.

46. G. P. Wetter, *Der Sohn Gottes* (FRLANT 26; Göttingen: Vandenhoeck & Ruprecht, 1916).

47. W. G. Kümmel, *The Theology of the New Testament according to Its Major Witnesses: Jesus — Paul — John* (Nashville: Abingdon, 1973) 76.

That person will long be debated, and the debate has only begun, because the text was fully published only in 1992. It will be fully discussed below in Chapter 3, but the crucial part of it may be cited now. It reads:

> [X shall be gr]eat upon the earth. All peoples sha]ll make [peace with him]; they shall all serve [him. For] he shall be called [the holy one of] the [G]reat [God], and by His name shall he be named. (Col. 2) He shall be hailed son of God, and they shall call him son of the Most High. Like the comets you saw (in your vision), for (some) years they shall rule over the land, and shall trample on all: one people shall trample upon another, and one province on an[o]ther, *(vacat)* until there arises the people of God, and everyone rests from the sword *(vacat)*. (4Q246 1:8–2:4)[48]

No one who reads that text fails to see its importance. It not only shows that the title *běrēh dî 'ēl*, "Son of God," was current in Palestinian Judaism, but it uses the same titles, "Son of God" and "Son of the Most High," as are found in the Lucan infancy narrative, when Gabriel informs Mary about the birth of Jesus: "He will be great and will be called Son of the Most High" (1:32); "therefore the child to be born will be called holy, the Son of God" (1:35). One cannot contend that Luke knew of this Palestinian Jewish text and borrowed from it such titles for Jesus. It may be sheer coincidence that he uses them, but this Aramaic text shows that such titles were in current use in contemporary Judaism and at home on Palestinian soil. Hence there is little reason to seek to explain the New Testament usage as derived from Greco-Roman or Hellenistic sources.

The titular use of "Messiah" for the risen Christ is another instance of how the Scrolls have aided our understanding of a christological title. For the Qumran material reveals that Judaism had, indeed, developed at least by the end of the second century B.C. a clear belief in a coming Messiah or Messiahs. Jewish scholars sometimes ascribe the emergence of messianism among Jews to the Roman period.[49] The only place in the Old Testament where Hebrew *māšîaḥ* has the connotation of an expected or awaited anointed figure of Davidic descent is found in Dan 9:25: *'ad māšîaḥ nāgîd*, "to the coming of an anointed one, a prince" *(RSV)*. There in the book of Daniel one may debate

---

48. See E. Puech, "Fragment d'une apocalypse en araméen (4Q246 = pseudo-Dan[d]) et le 'royaume de Dieu,'" *RB* 99 (1992) 98-131. Puech has also published the *editio princeps* in "246. 4QApocryphe de Daniel ar," *Qumran Cave 4: XVII. Parabiblical Texts, Part 3* (DJD 22; ed. G. Brooke et al.; Oxford: Clarendon, 1996) 165-84.

49. See H. L. Ginsberg, "Messiah," *Encyclopaedia Judaica* (16 vols.; New York: Macmillan; Jerusalem: Keter, 1971) 11:1407-8.

whether one should translate the Hebrew word *māšîaḥ* as "anointed one" or as "messiah," but Qumran texts that date from only a short time after the final redaction of the book of Daniel (ca. 165 B.C.) now make it clear, as they build on that Danielic passage, that Palestinian Jews had developed a belief in the coming of a "Messiah" (with a capital M) or even "Messiahs" (in the plural).[50]

The Christian belief that Jesus of Nazareth was God's "Messiah" was a still further development of that Jewish tenet. In fact, even though the Greek *christos*, "anointed one," is used on occasion as a title of Jesus (e.g., Rom 9:5), it has in most instances already become his second name, Jesus Christ.

The titular use of "Son of Man," such as one finds for Jesus in the New Testament, is still without a parallel in the Qumran texts, even though there are instances of the Aramaic phrase *bar 'ĕnāš* used both in a generic sense, "human being" (11QtgJob 9:9; 26:2-3), and in an indefinite sense, "someone" (or, in a negative clause, "no one," 1QapGen 21:13).[51] Little light, then, is shed from the Qumran evidence on this phrase as a christological *title* in the New Testament. So much for the Qumran background of titles used for Christ.

In still a third way, striking parallels have been found in the Qumran Scrolls for some Gospel passages. In a recently published Cave 4 text, a collection of beatitudes resembling the collections in the Matthean and Lucan Gospels has come to light. The beatitude is a literary form often found in the Old Testament, and there are even paired beatitudes in the Old Testament. One looks in vain, however, for a *collection of beatitudes* such as Matt 5:3-11 (eight or nine beatitudes, depending on how one counts) or in Luke 6:20-22 (four beatitudes, paralleled by four woes). Such a collection of beatitudes is now found in a fragmentary Hebrew text from Cave 4. It will be discussed at greater length in Chapter 6, but part of its translation can be given here for the sake of this survey:

[Blessed is the one who speaks truth] [1]with a pure heart and slanders not with his tongue. Blessed are those who cling to her statutes and cling not [2]to paths of iniquity. Bles[s]ed are those who rejoice in her and babble not about paths of foolishness. Blessed are those who search for her [3]with clean hands and seek not after her with a deceitful heart. Blessed is the man who has attained wisdom and walks [4]by the law of the Most High and fixes his

---

50. See further Chapter 5 below. Compare J. H. Charlesworth, ed., *The Messiah: Developments in Earliest Judaism and Christianity* (Minneapolis: Fortress, 1992); F. García Martínez, "Messianische Erwartungen in den Qumranschriften," *JBTh* 8 (1993) 171-208. Cf. J. J. Collins, *The Scepter and the Star: The Messiahs of the Dead Sea Scrolls and Other Ancient Literature* (ABRL; New York: Doubleday, 1995).

51. See J. A. Fitzmyer, *WA* or *SBNT*, 143-60.

heart on her ways, gives heed to her admonishments, delights con[stant]ly in her chastisements, ⁵and forsakes her not in the stress of [his] trou[bles]; (who) in time of distress abandons her not and forgets her not [in days of] fear, ⁶and in the affliction of his soul rejects [her] not. For on her he meditates constantly, and in his anguish he ponders [the law]; and in [al]l ⁷his existence [he considers] her [and puts her] before his eyes, so as not to walk in the paths of [   ]. (4QBeat [4Q525] 0-7)⁵²

In this Qumran sapiential text five beatitudes appear together. Since the text is fragmentary, we do not know how many beatitudes it may originally have had, especially at the beginning of the fragment. The feminine pronoun or pronominal suffix used throughout the fragment refers to "wisdom" (*ḥokmāh*) or to "the Law" (*tôrāh*), both feminine nouns in Hebrew. For the Essene community of Qumran the Mosaic Law was the embodiment of wisdom, and this collection of beatitudes extols the observance of the Law and exhorts members of the community to the wise practice of such observance. Jesus' beatitudes might also seem to have been a form of sapiential teaching, but they are more markedly eschatological. In any case, the evangelists who gathered Jesus' beatitudes into a collection of eight or four were undoubtedly aware of and perhaps influenced by a similar Palestinian Jewish literary form of collected beatitudes now made known to us by this Qumran fragment.

Furthermore, at times the New Testament refers to Christians as "sons of light" (Luke 16:8; John 12:36; 1 Thess 5:5; Eph 5:8). Although "sons of darkness" is not found in the New Testament, an equivalent phrase occurs in "sons of disobedience" (Eph 2:2; 5:6) and in "son of perdition" (John 17:12; 2 Thess 2:3).⁵³ At any rate, the phrase recalls the dualistic pair, light and darkness, well known from the Old Testament as a symbol of good and evil (e.g., Isa 45:7; Job 24:14). In fact, it is almost a natural figure, found in many ancient literatures, including Greek.⁵⁴ There are, however, distinctive aspects of the Qumran dualistic pair that are not found elsewhere: *běnê ʾôr*, "sons of light," and *běnê ḥôšek*, "sons of darkness," make use of a Semitic expression,

52. See E. Puech, "Un hymne essénien en partie retrouvé et les béatitudes: 1QH v 12–vi 18 (= col. xiii-xiv 7) et *4QBéat.*," *RevQ* 13 (Mémorial Jean Carmignac, 1988) 59-88; idem, "4Q525 et les péricopes des Béatitudes en Ben Sira et Matthieu," *RB* 98 (1991) 80-106.

53. Compare the Qumran equivalent phrases: *běnê ʿāwel*, "sons of wickedness" (1QS 3:21); *běnê ʿawlāh*, "sons of wickedness" (1QH 5:8); [*běnê*] *rišʿāh*, "sons of evil" (1QH 6:29-30); *běnê ʾašmāh*, "sons of guilt" (1QH 5:7; 6:30; 7:11); *běnê haššaḥat*, "sons of the Pit" (CD 6:15). The last mentioned is not far from the New Testament phrase, "son of perdition."

54. See Plato, *Republic* 507e-509b.

"sons of," which denotes groups or guilds, for example, "sons of the prophets" (1 Kgs 20:35); "sons of rebellion" (Num 17:25). Moreover, this dualistic pair with such Semitic phraseology divides all humanity into two distinct groups, "sons of light" and "sons of darkness," a division never found in the Old Testament or in later rabbinic literature. As far as I can see, this formulation and this division are unique to the Qumran Scrolls. The division is implied in the New Testament, but it now finds its full and original expression in Qumran literature. The first line of the sectarian *War Scroll* speaks of an eschatological war that is to take place between "the sons of light" and "the sons of darkness" (1QM 1:1; cf. also 1QS 1:9-10, quoted above). This pair is found not only in Hebrew sectarian literature of Qumran, but even in some Aramaic texts, so that it was well at home as a designation for the Essene community of Qumran. Early Christians seem, then, to have borrowed this expression, "sons of light," from such a Palestinian Jewish literary tradition to designate themselves.

Still another interesting Qumran fragment that sheds light on a New Testament passage is one that mentions the deeds of God's Messiah (4Q521). It too will be discussed further, in Chapter 5, but part of the translation of its fragmentary text[55] can be given or the sake of this survey:

> *Frg. 2, Col. ii*
> 1 [the hea]vens and the earth will listen to His Messiah,
> 2 [and all th]at is in them will not swerve from the commandments of holy ones.
> 3 Be strengthened in His service, all you who seek the Lord!
> 4 Shall you not find the Lord in this, all those (= you) who hope in their hearts?
> 5 For the Lord will visit pious ones, and righteous ones He will call by name.
> 6 Over afflicted ones will His Spirit hover, and faithful ones He will renew with His power.
> 7 He will honor (the) pious ones on a throne of eternal kingship,
> 8 freeing prisoners, giving sight to the blind, straightening up those be[nt over].
> 9 For[ev]er shall I cling [to tho]se who hope, and in His steadfast love He will recompense;
> 10 and the frui[t of a] good [dee]d will be delayed for no one.

55. See E. Puech, "Une apocalypse messianique *(4Q521)*," *RevQ* 15 (1991-92) 475-522 (+ 3 pls.).

11 Wond<r>ous things, such as have never been (before), the Lord will do, as He s[aid].

12 For He will heal (the) wounded, revive the dead, (and) proclaim good news to the afflicted;

13 (the) [po]or He will satiate, (the) uprooted He will guide, and on (the) hungry He will bestow riches;

14 and (the) intel[ligent   ], and all of them (will be) like hol[y ones]

Here we have in a historic Jewish text a clear description of what Jews of Palestine expected God would accomplish when His expected Messiah would arrive on the scene. Because the text is fragmentary it is not possible to interpret with certainty the role of "the Lord" and the role of "His Messiah," and or be certain about who are called *qĕdôšîm*, "holy ones" (lines 2, [14]). The original editor of the text, Emile Puech, called it a "messianic apocalypse." That it is messianic is clear, but that it is apocalyptic is not. The use of the future tense in it may rather be intended in a hortatory sense, in that it urges its Jewish readers to perseverance and fidelity. The wondrous things that are to be accomplished, the freeing of prisoners, restoring of sight to the blind, and so forth, are all ascribed to "the Lord," that is, to God. Possibly, however, the text means that "the Lord" will bring about all such things through "His messiah," even though that is not explicitly said. In any case, the text echoes phrases known from Isaiah and some Psalms.[56] Lawrence H. Schiffman has also noted parallels to it in the ancient Jewish prayers *Shemoneh 'Esre* and *Amidah*.[57] He rightly explains that the Messiah mentioned has "ultimate authority over the heavens and earth and calls upon those who seek God to observe the Torah even more vigilantly"; they are "enjoined to concentrate on God's service." He also complains about the effort of some interpreters "to render a Christianized reading of this material . . . to suggest that the messiah, not God, will revive the dead." In this complaint he is right: "that interpretation . . . is difficult to defend."[58] The text, when correctly read, is wholly Jewish, expressive of important Jewish messianic tenets current among the Essenes of Qumran.

This text provides, however, an interesting Palestinian Jewish background for the description of Jesus' activity in some of the Gospels. No Christian who reads this thoroughly Jewish text can fail to note the echoes of its

56. See below, pp. 93-95.
57. Schiffman, *Reclaiming the Dead Sea Scrolls*, 348.
58. Ibid.

phraseology in passages that record Jesus' answer to be given to the imprisoned John the Baptist in Luke 7:22 or Matt 11:5: "the blind receive their sight, the lame walk, lepers are cleansed, the deaf hear, the dead are raised, and the poor have the good news preached to them."

Lastly, I cite the new light that has been shed on the interpretation of the Epistle to the Hebrews by an important fragmentary text from Qumran Cave 11. It is 11QMelch, and it depicts Melchizedek, the king mentioned in Gen 14:18-20, in a way that was unknown before. The text may well be sectarian, because it uses some of the specific terminology of the Qumran sect of Jews, such as "for all the sons of [light] and men [of the l]ot of Melchizedek." Moreover, it is composed in the form of a *pēšer* (commentary) on a number of Old Testament texts (Lev 25:13; Deut 15:2; Lev 25:10; Pss 82:1; 7:8-9; 82:2; Isa 52:7; Lev 25:9), or what the editor, A. S. van der Woude, called an "eschatological midrash." The quotations from Leviticus 25 run through the fragmentary text, which is not easy to read and interpret, but they unite its commentary. It tells of the tenth or last jubilee year, which is given an eschatological interpretation as the year when Melchizedek will bring about release for the sons of light and the men of his lot by expiating their sins. The text portrays Melchizedek not as an earthly king (as in Genesis), but as a heavenly figure, performing a priestly act of expiation. It gives him the title *'Elôhîm* and depicts him as taking his stand "in the as[sembly of 'El]" and "in the midst of gods *('lwhym)*," by whom are undoubtedly meant the angelic court of heaven, and "giving judgment." It applies to him the words of Ps 82:2 and says further: "And Melchizedek shall exact the ven[ge]ance of the jud[g]ments of God *('El)* [from the hand of Be]lial and from the hand(s) of all [the spirits of] his [lot]." The expiation that Melchizedek is to bring about is related, moreover, to "the Da[y of Atone]ment" during the tenth jubilee.

What is noteworthy here is the depiction of Melchizedek as *'elôhîm*, which literally means "god," and of him standing "in the midst of gods" (= angels). It thus makes of him a heavenly redemption figure. This way of regarding Melchizedek is not found in the Old Testament (in Gen 14:18-20 or in Ps 110:4) and perhaps prefigures some of the ways in which he is regarded in later literature, both Jewish and Christian. The exaltation of Melchizedek, however, which sounds like an apotheosis of him, helps to understand why Christ in the Epistle to the Hebrews is said to be *hiereus kata tēn taxin Melchisedek*, "a priest according to the order of Melchizedek" (6:6). In Hebrew 7, a midrash is composed on Gen 14:18-20, explaining the various titles given to the Canaanite king of Salem, but it adds the striking admission about him, that he is "without father or mother or genealogy, and has neither beginning of days nor end of life, but resembling the Son of God he continues a priest for ever" (Heb 7:3). The reason why Melchizedek is said to be "without father or mother or genealogy" is that Jews puzzled over him, because in Genesis 14 he is to have been *kōhēn lĕ'ēl 'elyôn,* "a priest of God Most High," and they wondered how someone could be called a priest of God without a genealogy. The explanation of that puzzling question comes from the rootless character of verses 18-20 in Genesis 14, where they have been secondarily inserted in the story of the return of Abram from the defeat of the kings and his meeting with the king of Sodom. Those three verses introduce a secondary meeting of Abram with the king of Salem (= Jerusalem) and call that king a priest of God Most High even though he has no genealogy, because not even Psalm 110, the only other place in the Old Testament in which he is mentioned, supplies such information about this priest. Now because Melchizedek is depicted in the Qumran fragment as a heavenly redemption figure, called *'elôhîm,* this is why he can be said to "resemble the Son of God" and to have "neither beginning of days nor end of life," and so to continue as "a priest for ever." If we had not recovered this text about Melchizedek so portrayed, would we ever have understood correctly what was meant by Heb 7:3 and its affirmation about him? If Melchizedek were indeed thought of by pre-Christian Jews as a heavenly redemption figure who performed a priestly function (expiation) for the men of his lot, then one can see how the author of the Epistle to the Hebrews could depict Christ, the "Son of God," and "without beginning of days or end of life," as a "priest according to the order of Melchizedek." This example, then, shows us what an important text has been recovered from Qumran Cave 11 for the interpretation of the Epistle to the Hebrews.[59]

Some of these Qumran texts will be discussed more fully in succeeding chapters, but this brief survey of features of Qumran Scrolls serves to show how many Jewish ideas and expressions, which have been recovered from the Palestinian writings of Qumran, have shaped the early form of the Christian message.

The Christian message itself, however, has found no parallel in those Scrolls. There is nothing about Jesus of Nazareth or his story or the interpretation of him, nothing about the Christian church, nothing about the vicarious and salvific character of what Jesus accomplished for humanity in his passion, death, and resurrection. I am not saying this in a defensive or apologetic way; it is simply a statement of fact. For all the light that the Scrolls have shed on the Palestinian Jewish matrix of Christianity and on ways that early

---

59. See further my articles, "'Now This Melchizedek . . . (Heb 7:1)" and "Further Light on Melchizedek from Qumran Cave 11," in *ESBNT* or *SBNT,* 2212-43, 245-67.

Christians borrowed ideas and phrases in order to formulate their kerygmatic proclamation of the Christian message, there is nothing in the Scrolls that undermines or is detrimental to that message. Despite allegations made at times, nothing in the Scrolls militates against the "uniqueness" of Jesus.

Edmund Wilson once claimed,

> The monastery [of Qumran] . . . is, perhaps, more than Bethlehem or Nazareth, the cradle of Christianity. . . . These new documents have thus loomed as a menace to a variety of rooted assumptions, from matters of tradition and dogma to hypotheses that are exploits of scholarship. . . . It would seem an immense advantage for cultural and social intercourse — that is, for civilization — that the rise of Christianity should, at last, be generally understood as simply an episode of human history rather than propagated as dogma and divine revelation. The study of the Dead Sea scrolls — with the direction it is now taking — cannot fail, one would think, to conduce to this.[60]

Wilson wrote those words in the 1950s, but, alas, he did not prove to be a prophet, and more sober assessments have been recorded about the significance of the Qumran discoveries in the meantime. More recently, however, his words have been picked up and echoed by equally tendentious interpreters of the Qumran Scrolls and their impact on Christianity. Michael Baigent and Richard Leigh, in their book *The Dead Sea Scrolls Deception*,[61] have reiterated the same nonsense.

In contrast to Wilson and Baigent and Leigh, *Time* magazine summed up the matter very well in 1957:

> The only Christians whose faith the scrolls can jolt are those who have failed to see the paradox that the churches have always taught: that Jesus Christ was a man as well as God — a man of a particular time and place, speaking a specific language, revealing his way in terms of a specific cultural and religious tradition. For Christians who want to know more of that matrix in which their faith was born, the People of the Scrolls are reaching a hand across the centuries.[62]

60. E. Wilson, *The Scrolls from the Dead Sea* (New York: Oxford University, 1955) 97-98, 100, 108. Wilson's position becomes more nuanced in the later edition, entitled *The Dead Sea Scrolls, 1947-1969* (New York: Oxford University, 1969) 275-92.

61. M. Baigent and R. Leigh, *The Dead Sea Scrolls Deception* (London: Jonathan Cape; New York: Summit Books, 1991) 41-44.

62. *Time*, 15 April 1957, 43.

CHAPTER 3

The Aramaic "Son of God" Text from Qumran Cave 4 (4Q246)

The Aramaic text, which was discovered in Qumran Cave 4 in 1952 and employs the titles "Son of God" and "Son of the Most High," figures in the account of a notorious book by Michael Baigent and Richard Leigh, *The Dead Sea Scrolls Deception,* which I mentioned at the end of the preceding chapter.[1] They based their account of that text on the brief article that Hershel Shanks, the editor of the *Biblical Archaeology Review,* wrote, having heard me lecture on the Dead Sea Scrolls at the Johns Hopkins University in Baltimore in 1989. Shanks quoted some lines of the text,[2] which I had published fifteen years before,[3] after J. T. Milik had publicly lectured on it at Harvard University in 1972 and it was judged to be in the public domain. According to Baigent and Leigh, an "unnamed scholar, whose conscience was troubling him," had leaked the text to the *Biblical Archaeology Review* only in 1990!

Worse still, Baigent and Leigh thought that this was the document to which John M. Allegro had alluded in one of his letters to Roland de Vaux, the excavator of Khirbet Qumran and director of the scroll team that was working on the Cave 4 fragments, which Allegro had written in September 1956.

---

1. Michael Baigent and Richard Leigh, *The Dead Sea Scrolls Deception* (London: Jonathan Cape; New York: Summit Books, 1991) 66.

2. Anonymous, "An Unpublished Dead Sea Scroll Text Parallels Luke's Infancy Narrative," *BARev* 16/2 (1990) 24.

3. J. A. Fitzmyer, "The Contribution of Qumran Aramaic to the Study of the New Testament," *NTS* 20 (1974) 382-407, esp. 391-94; reprinted in a slightly revised form in *WA* or *SBNT,* 85-113, esp. 92-93.

There Allegro spoke of the Essene belief in their Davidic Messiah as "a 'son of God', 'begotten' of God. . . ."[4] Baigent and Leigh were ignorant, of course, of a passage in Appendix A of the *Manual of Discipline* from Qumran Cave 1, which, according to Allegro and some other scholars, speaks of God's "begetting the Messiah." From it Allegro had concluded that there was an Essene belief in a Davidic Messiah as Son of God. This Cave 1 text had been published only shortly before, in 1955,[5] and Allegro was really referring to it, and not to the "Son of God" text of Cave 4.

Moreover, Baigent and Leigh were also ignorant of the fact that the Aramaic "Son of God" text had not yet even been acquired by the Palestine Archaeological Museum in 1956, when Allegro wrote to de Vaux. It was, in fact, among the last eight pieces of Cave 4 material that were bought from Kando on 9 July 1958,[6] on the day before I left Jerusalem to return to the U.S.A., after the first year of work on the concordance of nonbiblical texts of Qumran Cave 4, eventually exploited by Ben Zion Wacholder and Martin G. Abegg.[7]

4. Baigent and Leigh, *The Dead Sea Scrolls Deception*, 56.

5. See D. Barthélemy and J. T. Milik, *Qumran Cave 1* (DJD 1; Oxford: Clarendon, 1955) 110, 117: 1QSa (1Q28a) 2:11-12. The pertinent part of this text reads: אם יוליד [אל] [ת]א[ל] המשיח אתם, a contested reading, which Barthélemy originally translated as "au cas où *Dieu mènerait* le Messie avec eux." He preferred to interpret יוליד as יוליך, believing with Milik that יוליד, "the practically certain . . . reading," was actually "a faulty reading of the scribe." Allegro, in his first publication of part of 4QFlorilegium (*JBL* 75 [1956] 174-187, esp. 177), referred to this text and said that the "implication of 'sonship' of the Messiah has obvious NT parallels, and has, perhaps, to be connected with the יוליד of 1QSa." Allegro also noted that "a special infra-red photograph taken then [Summer of 1955] leaves no doubt as to the correctness of the editor's reading" (n. 28), i.e., of יוליד. So Allegro certainly understood the mention of "the Messiah" in 1QSa as implying divine sonship. Why we never heard more from him in this regard once the contents of 4Q246 became known is a mystery. In his later book, *The Dead Scrolls and the Christian Myth* (Devon: Newton Abbot; Buffalo: Prometheus, 1979), he makes no mention of it, tinder though it would have been for his thesis.

6. This date is now officially confirmed by the editor in the *editio princeps*; see E. Puech, "**246**. 4QApocryphe de Daniel ar," in *Qumran Cave 4: XVII. Parabiblical Texts, Part 3* (DJD 22; ed. G. Brooke et al.; Oxford: Clarendon, 1996) 165 n. 1.

7. "Bootleg" is the word used for their work in *New York Times*, 5 September 1991, p. A1. See B. Z. Wacholder and M. G. Abegg, *A Preliminary Edition of the Unpublished Dead Sea Scrolls: The Hebrew and Aramaic Texts from Cave Four: Fascicle One* (Washington, D.C.: Biblical Archaeology Society, 1991); *Fascicle Two* (1992); *Fascicle Three* (1995); *Fascicle Four* (1996).

P. R. Davies has objected to my conduct with regard to this "Son of God" text; see "The Qumran Affair: 1947-1993," *QC* 5/2 (1995) 133-42, esp. 138, 139. I can only smile at his would-be omniscient exposure of my involvement in the publication of a few lines of this text in 1974. For the sake of the record I have to say: I was not "in the audience" when

So the "Son of God" text could not have been the one to which Allegro was referring in his letter of 1956 sent to de Vaux.

Such misinformation about this Aramaic text is only a token of the larger pattern of errors and misinformed statements that make the Baigent and Leigh book itself *the deception par excellence* about the Dead Sea Scrolls![8]

The "Son of God" text was entrusted to J. T. Milik for publication in 1958, and although he lectured on it at Harvard University in 1972, he never published it. He has referred to it in two of his other writings.[9] On the basis of my preliminary publication of seven lines of the text, a number of other studies appeared, chiefly those of David Flusser and Florentino García Martínez.[10] More recently, with Milik's approval, Emile Puech has at long last published the text in full,[11] and further discussions of it have since appeared.[12] Now we can discuss it further, since more has still to be said about it.

Milik delivered the lecture on 4Q246 at Harvard in 1972 (not "in the 1960s," as Davies would have it). I was then several hundred miles away from Cambridge, teaching in the theology department of Fordham University in the Bronx, N.Y. After Milik's lecture, during which he apparently displayed on a screen the Aramaic text and gave out an English translation of the text that he was interpreting, I received in the mail a copy of the full text (and his translation) from two different persons who had copied it and sent it on. Subsequently I learned that the text had been the subject of a seminar at Harvard University; then, that it was considered to be in the public domain.

8. See further my review of their book in "The Dead Sea Scrolls: The Latest Form of Catholic-Bashing," *America* 166/5 (15 February 1992) 119-22.

9. See J. T. Milik, *The Books of Enoch: Aramaic Fragments of Qumran Cave 4* (Oxford: Clarendon, 1976) 60, 213, 261; and idem, "Les modèles araméens du livre d'Esther dans la grotte 4 de Qumran," *RevQ* 15 (1991-92) 321-99, esp. 383-84.

10. D. Flusser, "The Hubris of the Antichrist in a Fragment from Qumran," *Immanuel* 10 (1980) 31-37; reprinted in *Judaism and the Origins of Christianity* (Jerusalem: Magnes, 1988) 207-13. F. García Martínez, "4Q246: ¿Tipo del Anticristo o Libertador escatológico?" in *El misterio de la Palabra: Homenaje a L. Alonso Schökel* (ed. V. Collado and E. Zurro; Madrid: Ediciones Cristiandad, 1983) 229-44; in English: "The Eschatological Figure of 4Q246," in *Qumran and Apocalyptic: Studies on the Aramaic Texts from Qumran* (STDJ 9; Leiden: Brill, 1992) 162-79.

11. E. Puech, "Fragment d'une apocalypse en araméen (4Q246 = pseudo-Dan[d]) et le 'royaume de Dieu,'" *RB* 99 (1992) 98-131. This was only a preliminary publication, but Puech has published the *editio princeps* as "246. 4QApocryphe de Daniel ar," in *Qumran Cave 4: XVII. Parabiblical Texts, Part 3* (ed. G. Brooke et al.; Oxford: Clarendon, 1996) 165-84.

12. See J. J. Collins, "The *Son of God* Text from Qumran," in *From Jesus to John: Essays on Jesus and Christology in Honour of Marinus de Jonge* (JSNTSup 84; ed. M. de Boer; Sheffield: JSOT Press, 1993) 65-82; J. A. Fitzmyer, "4Q246: The 'Son of God' Document from Qumran," *Bib* 74 (1993) 153-74 [reproduced here along with my treatment of the

Text

Column 1

1 [ ] וכדי דחלה רבה ע[לוהי שרת נפל קדם כרסיא

2 [ואמר לה חיי מ]לכא [ל]עלמא אתה רגז ושנוך

3 [זיוך ואפשר מל]כא חזוך וכלא אתה עד עלמא

4 [ארי ביד מלכין ר]ברבין עקה תתא על ארעא

5 [להוה קרב בעממיא]ונחשירין רב ב‍מ‍דינתא

6 [ולקצת יומיא יאבדון]מלך אתור[ום]צרין

7 [אדין יקום מלך והוא] רב להוה על א‍רעא

8 [כל עממיא שלם עמה י]ע‍בדון וכלא ישמ‍שון

9 [לה והוא קדיש אל ר]בא יתקרא ובשמה יתכנה

Col. 2

1 ברה די אל יתאמר ובר עליון יקרונה כזיקיא

2 די חזו‍תא כן מלכותהן תהוה שני[ן] ימלכון על

3 ארעא וכלא ידשון עם לעם ידוש ומדינה למדי[נ]ה

4 (vacat) עד יקום עם אל וכלא ינוח מן חרב (vacat)

5 מלכותה מלכות עלם וכל ארחתה בקשוט ידי[ן]

6 ארעא בקשט וכלא יעבד שלם חרב מן ארעא י‍סף

7 וכל מדינתא לה יסגדון אל רבא באילה

8 הוא י‍עבד לה קרב עממין ינתן בידה וכלהן

9 ירמה קדמוהי שלטנה שלטן עלם וכל תהומי

text in "The Aramaic 'Son of God' Text from Qumran Cave 4," in *Methods of Investigation of the Dead Sea Scrolls and the Khirbet Qumran Site: Present Realities and Future Prospects* (Annals of the New York Academy of Sciences 722; ed. M. O. Wise et al.; New York: New York Academy of Sciences, 1994) 163-78]; E. Puech, "Notes sur le fragment d'apocalypse 4Q246 — 'Le Fils de Dieu,'" *RB* 101 (1994) 533-58; F. M. Cross, "Notes on the Doctrine of the Two Messiahs at Qumran and the Extracanonical *Daniel Apocalypse* (4Q246)," in *Current Research and Technological Developments on the Dead Sea Scrolls: Conference on the Texts from the Judean Desert, Jerusalem, 30 April 1995* (STDJ 20; ed. D. W. Parry and S. D. Ricks; Leiden: Brill, 1996) 1-13.

Translation

Col. 1

1 [When great awe] settled [u]pon him, he fell down before the throne
2 [and said to him, "Live,] O King, forever! You are distressed, and changed is
3 [your complexion. I shall interpret, O Ki]ng, your vision, and all that is coming in the future.
4 [For by the hand of m]ighty [kings] shall distress come upon the land;
5 [there shall be war among the peoples] and great carnage in the provinces.
6 [At the end of days] the king of Assyria [and E]gypt [will perish].
7 [Then shall arise a king, and he shall be] great upon the earth.
8 [All peoples sh]all make [peace with him]; they shall all serve
9 [him. For] he shall be called [the holy one of] the [G]reat [God], and by His name shall he be named.

Col. 2

1 He shall be hailed Son of God, and they shall call him Son of the Most High. Like the comets
2 that you saw (in your vision), so shall their reign be. For (some) years they shall rule over
3 the land, and they shall trample on all: one people shall trample upon another, and one province upon an[o]ther,
4 *(vacat)* until there arises the people of God, and everyone rests from the sword. *(vacat)*
5 His kingdom (shall be) an everlasting kingdom, and all his ways (shall be) in truth. He shall jud[ge]
6 the land with truth, and all shall make peace. The sword shall cease from the land,
7 and all the provinces shall pay him homage. The Great God is Himself his might.
8 He shall make war for him; peoples shall He put in his power, and all of them
9 He shall cast down before him. His dominion (shall be) an everlasting dominion, and none of the abysses of
10 [the earth shall prevail against it]!

Notes

Col. 1

1. וכדי דחלה רבה עלוהי שרת. "When great awe settled upon him." This description probably refers to a seer who falls before the enthroned king. Milik had originally restored רוחה, "his Spirit," thinking that God's throne was involved, as in *1 Enoch* 14:24.[13] It is clear, however, that the enthroned person is human; so some other restoration is needed. What is used here depends on Dan 10:7, אבל הרדה גדלה נפלה עליהם, "but great fear fell upon them," as Milik eventually rightly saw. שרת is 3d sg. fem. of שרי, "settle, abide." This restoration is also used by Puech, who discusses other less likely possibilities, some of them with רוחא די נבואה, "the spirit of prophecy."

נפל קדם כרסיא. "He fell down before the throne." This characteristic phrase for prostration before an enthroned person refers to the one who addresses the king, probably a seer who will interpret a vision that the king has seen. Compare Dan 7:20 (נפל מן קדם), and even better καὶ ἔπεσαν ἐνώπιον τοῦ θρόνου (Rev 7:11; cf. 4:10; 11:16; 14:3; 19:4). Puech regards the noun כרסיא as fully written; it is rather the normal writing of the emphatic state, "the throne."

2. ואמר לה. "And said to him." Puech inserted in the lacuna here the name of Daniel. Even though this might be a pseudo-Danielic text, it is not certain that Daniel is the seer involved, given its fragmentary state. That, however, is not an impossible interpretation. Milik also thought of Enoch or some other visionary of sacred history, such as Levi, Moses, or Elijah.[14] I am now following the suggested reconstruction of F. M. Cross.[15]

חיי מלכא לעלמא. "Live, O King, forever!" The reading is problematic. [מ]לכא creates no problem, but it is followed by a dot, possibly the bottom of an initial *lamedh:* hence לעלמא. Puech so reads the text but thinks that it has been corrected; but that correction is not clear. For parallel sayings, see Dan 2:4 (מלכא לעלמין חיי); 3:9; 5:10; 6:7, 22. Though the word order differs, the greeting is the same. This greeting must refer to some Jewish king, not a Seleucid.

אתה רגז. "You are distressed." Because of the broken state of the text, the reason for the king's distress is unknown, but there seems to have been mention of a vision that the king had seen, which has terrified him. A dot of

---

13. See Milik, *The Books of Enoch*, 60.
14. Ibid.
15. Cross, "Notes on the Doctrine," 5, 8.

ink appears between ג and ז, which might suggest the reading רגיז, the passive participle, but it is too tiny to be certain that it is a letter. Hence the active participle רגז is preferred.

ושנוך זיוך. "And changed is your complexion." Both Milik and Puech understood the last word in line 2, ושניך, to mean "your years." Although it is possible, it does not fit with what precedes. Compare Dan 5:6, זיווהי שנוהי, "and his complexion was changed," an idiomatic expression used in a similar context where emotion is mentioned. I am now following the reading of Cross, which is similar to what I originally proposed, but better.

3. ואפשר מלכא חזוך. "I shall interpret, O King, your vision." Cross has shown that Puech's reconstruction (בדחלה הן אש[רא or בדחלה הן אק[רא) is not suitable and that my earlier suggestion "leaves the dream interpretation without an introduction."[16] So I have followed him in understanding חזוך as "your vision." This meaning is found in Dan 2:19, 28; 4:2, 7, 10; 7:2, 7, 13. The *peal* and *pael* of פשר שר are used similarly in Dan 5:16, 12 (respectively); cf. 4QEnGiants[b] 2:14.

וכלא אתה עד עלמא. "And all that is coming in the future," literally, forever. Again I am following the suggestion of Cross to take this clause as the continuation of the interpretation that the seer will give, but correcting his anomalous Hebrew עולם to the Aramaic עלמא, which is clear in the photograph. Puech takes עד עלמא with an improbable reconstruction חיי ארו, "Toi, à jamais [vis! Voici."

4. ארי ביד מלכין רברבין עקה תתא על ארעא. "For by the hand of mighty kings shall distress come upon the land." One could rather read ארו. Thus begins the seer's interpretation of the king's vision about things to come. For similar apocalyptic statements, see Dan 12:1 (והיתה עת צרה) or Mark 13:19 (ἔσονται γὰρ αἱ ἡμέραι ἐκεῖναι θλῖψις οἵα οὐ γέγονεν τοιαύτη ἀπ' ἀρχῆς κτίσεως). Cross prefers to restore the beginning of this line with [חזיתא די ישפלון ר]ברבין, "[You saw in your vision that the] might[y shall be humbled]," appealing to Dan 2:45; 4:17 for the restoration of the first two words. That seems possible, but the rest of the restoration is less likely. My suggestion seeks rather to explain whence the distress comes.

5. להוה קרב בעממיא ונחשירין רב במדינתא. "There shall be war among the peoples and great carnage in the provinces." This line describes in detail the "distress" of line 4. Though J. Carmignac once tried to explain נחשיר, "carnage," as a form derived from חשר,[17] it is now recognized as a

---

16. Ibid., 8.
17. J. Carmignac, "Précisions apportées au vocabulaire de l'hébreu biblique par la Guerre des Fils de Lumière contre les Fils de Ténèbres," *VT* 5 (1955) 345-65, esp. 363-64.

Persian word (<*naḥčīr*).[18] The word is also found in 1QM 1:9, 10, [13]. For Puech the singular adjective רב demands the reading נחשירון (so read also by Cross), but there is no difference in the shape of the two *yodhs*. The form is rather the absolute plural, a plural of intensification (see GKC §124g), which can be modified by a singular adjective (cf. Isa 19:4, אדנים קשה). Moreover, Puech's reading introduces a questionable Hebraic form (in ון-). Compare נחשירותא of the Bodleian text of Cairo *Testament of Levi* (a3). Elsewhere נחשיר stands in parallelism to קרב; hence the restoration here.

6. ולקצת יומיא יאבדון מלך אתור ומצרין. "At the end of days the king of Assyria and Egypt will perish." Again I am following the suggestion of Cross for the restoration of the beginning of this line; he compares Dan 4:31 for the first two words. The mention of Assyria and Egypt is similar to that in 1QM 1:2, 4, which may be a symbolic way of referring to enemy nations to the east and the west of Israel, or may be a way of referring to the Seleucids and Ptolemies, as Cross has understood the names. Milik understands מלך אתור to mean historically "roi de Syrie," that is, one of the Seleucid kings.[19] The form אתור, instead of אשור which is still used in 1QapGen 17:8, is to be noted; it is also found in *Aḥiqar* 3-5, 8, 10-14, etc. It has been called a Persian pronunciation.[20] Compare Sinaiticus of Tob 14:4 (Ἀθούρ).

7. אדין יקום מלך והוא רב להוה על ארעא. "Then shall arise a king, and he shall be great upon the earth." This restoration is inspired in part by that of Puech, who reads at the beginning of the line [יקום מלך אחרן והוא], "[Se lèvera un autre/dernier roi, et lui]." Cross reads rather [ויקום בר אנש מלך], "[And there shall arise a son of man]. He shall be a great [king] over the [whole] earth." Cross compares Ps 48:3 (מלך רב) and Dan 2:10 (כל מלך רב). One can also compare Luke 1:32, οὗτος ἔσται μέγας, said of Jesus, or Luke 1:15, ἔσται γὰρ μέγας ἐνώπιον [τοῦ] Κυρίου, said of John the Baptist.

I still think that the "king" mentioned could be the son of the king seated on the throne, a Jewish king, who has had the vision of what is to come. I too think that this apocalyptic text is related to Daniel and shares "linguistic and literary traits" found in that biblical writing, but I do not see why the king *has to be* presumably "Nebuchadnezzar, Darius, Belshazzar, or Cyrus," even though such kings are addressed in the Daniel literature, as

18. See J. P. de Menasce, "Iranian naxčīr," *VT* 6 (1956) 213-14; J. P. Asmussen, "Das iranische Lehnwort *naḥšir* in der Kriegsrolle von Qumrān (1QM)," *AcOr* (Copenhagen) 26 (1961-62) 3-20.

19. Milik, "Modèles araméens," 383.

20. F. Altheim and R. Stiehl, *Die aramäische Sprache unter den Achaimeniden* (Frankfurt am M.: V. Klostermann, 1963) 1:184.

Cross argues. Why could not a Jewish seer seek to console a Jewish king who has had a disturbing vision?

8. כל עממיא שלם עמה יעבדון וכלא ישמשון / לה. "All peoples shall make peace with him; they shall all serve him." My restoration follows that of Puech, save for the added כל. His alternate reading מלכיא, "kings," is not impossible, but less likely than כל עממיא, a phrase found in Dan 3:7(bis), 31. Cross reads rather [וכל אנש לה י]עבדון וכלא ישמשון / [לה], "[And all mankind] shall serve [him], And all shall minister / [to him]." He rightly notes the bicolon character of this line and compares Dan 7:10, where the same verb שמש is used, but he strangely translates the verb עבד as "serve," a meaning otherwise unknown in Aramaic. Flusser similarly introduced this Hebraism in translating it "worship." Compare 2:6 below.

9. והוא קדיש אל רבא יתקרא. "For he shall be called the holy one of the Great God." This lacuna is the most difficult one to restore. Milik once suggested [בר מלכא ר]בא, "son of the great king," taking it as a reference to Alexander Balas, pretended son of Antiochus IV Epiphanes, the Seleucid dynast from 150-145 B.C., who had the same name as the conqueror, Alexander the Great. Later on Milik used חלפת instead of בר, but that would mean "succession," and not successor. He also understood the verb יתקרא as middle, "il se proclamera Fils de Dieu et (qu')on appelera Fils du Très Haut."[21]

Puech used rather [בר מרא ר]בא, "le fils du Grand Souverain," appealing to 4QEn[b] 1 iii 14. The Enoch text, only partially preserved, reads אנתא] [הוא] מרנא רבא [הו]א מרא עלמא, "[You are] our great Lord, the Lord of eternity."[22] There the emphatic רבא modifies a suffixal form, which is correct, but Puech's combination of the absolute מרא with the emphatic רבא creates an anomaly; one would have to write מריא. I have used והוא בר אל רבא as the restoration, because אל רבא is found in 2:7. It suits the context here, especially in light of the following clauses.

Flusser regards my emendation as repetitious of what is said in the immediate context; he would rather restore [אל ר]בא, "Great [God] he shall be called." That may suit better Flusser's understanding of the text as a whole, but his interpretation is not without its difficulties. Moreover, that restoration would be too short for the lacuna, as Puech has also noted.

ובשמה יתכנה. "And by His name shall he be named." That is, by God's name. The form יתכנה is probably *ithpaal*.

---

21. Milik, "Modèles araméens," 383.
22. See Milik, *The Books of Enoch*, 171.

Column 2

1. ברה די אל יתאמר. "He shall be hailed Son of God." Noteworthy is the use of this title "Son of God" in a pre-Christian Jewish extrabiblical text for the king who is to come. The use is probably inspired by 2 Sam 7:14, where Nathan's oracle says of David, "I will be a father to him, and he shall be my son." Cf. T. de Kruijf, *Der Sohn des lebendigen Gottes* (AnBib 16; Rome: Biblical Institute, 1962) 10-24.

Note also the use of אל as "God" in an Aramaic text. Though not found in Biblical Aramaic, it occurs again in 2:4, 7. So there is no doubt about its use in Aramaic. See also 1QapGen 12:17; 19:[8]; 20:12, 16; 21:2, 20; 22:15, 16 (bis), 21; 11QJN 14:1. This may solve the problem about whether ἠλί, "my God," in Matt 27:46 (ἠλὶ ἠλὶ λέμα σαβαχθάνι) could be wholly Aramaic, and not a mixture of Hebrew and Aramaic, as it has some-times been explained.

This clause has a Greek counterpart in Luke 1:35, κληθήσεται υἱὸς Θεοῦ. Note too the similar use of אמר in the Hebrew of Isa 4:3, "will be called holy."

ובר עליון יקרונה. "And they shall call him son of the Most High." The text now uses another title to emphasize the character of the coming king, a striking collocation with "Son of God" and in close proximity to his being "great upon the earth" (1:7). This combination is parallel to the Christian counterpart in Luke 1:32, οὗτος ἔσται μέγας καὶ υἱὸς ὑψίστου κληθήσεται.

עליון is employed as a divine name in the Old Testament by non-Jews: by the Canaanite priest Melchizedek (Gen 14:18-20) and by Balaam (Num 24:16); cf. Isa 14:14. Both אל and עליון are found as a pair of gods in the eighth-century-B.C. Aramaic inscription of Sefire (I A 11).[23]

עליון is also utilized for the God of Israel (Deut 32:8; Isa 14:14); the two names אל and עליון appear in parallelism in Ps 73:11; 107:11, and in Ps 91:9 יהוה and עליון are also parallel. The combination אל עליון occurs in 1QapGen 22:15, 16, rendering Hebrew of Gen 14:18, 20. It thus differs from the usual Biblical Aramaic title, אלהא עליא (Dan 3:26, 32; 5:18, 21).

The use of ὕψιστος, "most high," in the LXX (e.g., Gen 14:18, 20) and the New Testament reflects the widespread Jewish use of this Greek title (see Philo, *In Flaccum* 7 §46; *Ad Gaium* 36 §278; 40 §317; Josephus, *Ant.* 16.6.2 §163), but it was undoubtedly affected by the use of this epithet in the Greek-speaking world: for Zeus (e.g., Sophocles, *Philoctetes* 1289: Ζηνὸς ὑψίστου;

---

23. See my book, *The Aramaic Inscriptions of Sefire* (rev. ed.; BibOr 19A; Rome: Bib-lical Institite, 1995) 42, 75.

Pindar, *Nemean Odes* 1.60; 11.2; Aeschylus, *Eumenides* 28); and for other gods (Γῆ, Ἥλιος).[24]

כזיקיא די חזותא כן מלכותהן תהוה. "Like the comets that you saw (in your vision), so shall their reign be," that is, like comets that appear to the eye momentarily as they speed across the heavens. The comparison stresses the fleeting and ephemeral character of the reigns to be mentioned. Cf. *1 Enoch* 41:3 ("there my eyes saw the secrets of the flashes of lightning"); 43:1. Also Luke 17:24, ὥσπερ γὰρ ἡ ἀστραπὴ ἀστράπουσα ἐκ τῆς ὑπὸ τὸν οὐρανὸν εἰς τὴν ὑπ' οὐρανὸν λάμπει οὕτως ἔσται ὁ υἱὸς τοῦ ἀνθρώπου [ἐν τῇ ἡμέρᾳ].

2. שני[ן] ימלכון על ארעא. "For (some) years they shall rule over the land." Fleeting though the reigns will be, they may last for years.

3. ה. וכלא ידשׁון עם לעם ידושׁ ומדינה למד[ין]. "And they shall trample on all: one people shall trample upon another, and one province upon an[o]ther." So shall be the war and carnage mentioned in 1:5. The verb דושׁ is used in an apocalyptic context in Dan 7:23. A commonplace of apocalyptic writing is employed: see Isa 19:2; Mark 13:8; Matt 24:7; Luke 21:10; *4 Ezra* 13:31 *(gens ad gentem et regnum aduersus regnum); Or. Sib.* 3.635-36.

4. עד יקום עם אל. "Until there arises the people of God." So the success of the Jewish people is described, the people over whom the enthroned king rules. At its rising, it will bring to an end the hostile reign of enemy kingdoms. Cf. Dan 7:17-18. The clause describes the advent of the end-time, introduced by the eschatological עד with the imperfect. Compare Luke 21:24, ἄχρι οὗ πληρωθῶσιν καιροὶ ἐθνῶν. Sometimes the infinitive construct is used instead of the imperfect, as in 4QPBless 1 i 3-4, עד בוא משׁיח הצדק, "until the coming of the righteous Messiah"; 1QS 9:11; CD 5:5. Puech notes that the verb might be read as the causative יקים, "until he causes the people of God to arise." Though possible, that reading is less likely because of the syntax of the following clause, in which כלא is subject, as it is in line 6. Moreover, it is hardly likely that "God" is the subject of יקים, since He is mentioned in the phrase עם אל, "people of God."

עם אל does not appear in the Old Testament, where one does find עם יהוה (Num 11:29; 17:6; Judg 5:11) or עם אלהים (Judg 20:2; 2 Sam 14:13); also "my people" (Hos 2:25; Isa 22:4; Jer 51:45; cf. Lev 26:12). The phrase itself occurs in similar eschatological usage in 1QM 1:5; 3:13. Its Greek equivalent

24. See C. Roberts, T. C. Skeat, and A. D. Nock, "The Gild of Zeus Hypsistos," *HTR* 29 (1936) 39-88, esp. 55-72; F. Cumont, "Ὕψιστος," *PW* 9/1 (1914) 444-450; C. Colpe, "Hypsistos," in *Der kleine Pauly* (5 vols.; Stuttgart: Druckenmüller, 1964-75) 2:1291-92; G. Bertram, *"Hypsistos," TDNT*, 8:614-20.

λαὸς Θεοῦ is known in the New Testament: 1 Pet 2:10; with articles in Heb 4:9; 11:25.[25]

וכלא ינוח מן חרב. "And everyone rests from the sword." Compare Esth 9:16, 22: "rest from one's enemies"; Isa 2:4; Mic 4:3; Jer 14:13, 15; 4QEn[c] 5 ii 21-22; 4QEn[g] 1 ii 16 (ותנוח אר[עא מן חרב]). See Note on 2:6 below.

5. מלכותה מלכות עלם. "His kingdom (shall be) an everlasting kingdom." This statement stands in contrast to the fleeting reigns of the enemy kings (2:2). It is borrowed from Dan 3:33 or 7:27. Compare Luke 1:34, καὶ τῆς βασιλείας αὐτοῦ οὐκ ἔσται τέλος. The possessive suffix could possibly refer to God or even to God's people: "its kingdom (shall be) an everlasting kingdom." Since the king to come will be part of that people, the change in meaning is insignificant. "His," however, referring to the coming king, is preferred because of the following clauses, and especially because of the second one, "he shall judge the land with truth."

וכל ארחתה בקשוט. "And all his ways (shall be) in truth," or "in righteousness." So the conduct of the coming king is described. Cf. Dan 4:34, וכל כי כל דרכיו משפט, Rev 15:3, δίκαιαι מעבדוהי קשט וארחתה דין; Deut 32:4, καὶ ἀληθιναὶ αἱ ὁδοί σου. Here קשוט is written fully, as in 4QVisAmram[f] (4Q548) 1 ii 12; contrast the form in the next clause.

ידין ארעא בקשט. "He shall judge the land with truth," or "with righteousness," a characteristic of the rule of the coming king. Cf. *Ps. Sol.* 17:29, κρινεῖ λαοὺς καὶ ἔθνη ἐν σοφίᾳ δικαιοσύνης, "he will judge peoples and nations with righteous wisdom." Also Ps 72:1-2, where such judgment is to be given to the king.

6. וכלא יעבד שלם. "And all shall make peace." This is another general characteristic of the reign of the coming king: all peoples will be at peace. Cf. Isa 17:5. One is reminded here of the famous *pax Augusta* of a later date in the Roman world.

חרב מן ארעא יספ. "The sword shall cease from the land." This simply repeats 2:4. יספ is defectively written, equaling יסוף. It could conceivably equal *aphel* יסיפ, but then, who would be the subject of "cause to cease"? God? The coming king? The people? Compare 1 Macc 9:73, καὶ κατέπαυσεν ῥομφαία ἐξ Ἰσραήλ. This parallel would argue in favor of the imperfect peal. See Note on 2:4 above.

7. וכל מדינתא לה יסגדון. "And all the provinces shall pay him hom-

---

25. See N. A. Dahl, *Das Volk Gottes: Eine Untersuchung zum Kirchenbewusstsein des Urchristentums* (Darmstadt: Wissenschaftliche Buchgesellschaft, 1963).

age," that is, will bow down before him. For the verb סגד, see Dan 2:46; 3:5, 7, 10, 12, 14, 15, 18; 4QTJud ar 1 a 4.[26]

אל רבא באילה הוא. "The Great God is Himself his might." When the coming king has to do battle, he will have the "Great God" for his support. The preposition ב is probably an instance of *bet essentiae*. הוא may be simply the copula, but it could also serve as an emphatic pronoun. Cf. Sir 5:1, יש לאל ידי.

Aramaic אל רבא is not found in the Old Testament, where אלה רב or אלהא רבא rather appears (Ezra 5:8; Dan 2:45). It is the equivalent of Hebrew אל גדול (Deut 7:21; 10:17; Ps 77:14; 95:3; Jer 32:18; Dan 9:4; Neh 1:5; 9:32; 1QM 10:1). Compare קדישא רבא, "the Great Holy One" (1QapGen 12:17; 4QEnGiants[b] [4Q530] 7 ii 17). A Greek form of the title is found on a Caesarean inscription: ΘΕΩΙ ΜΕΓΑΛΩΙ ΔΕ[σπότῃ].[27] In Nabatean inscriptions a combined form רבאל is used.[28]

8. הוא יעבד לה קרב. "He shall make war for him." If occasion arises, God will be in battle on the coming king's side. Cf. Deut 7:21-22; 1QM 1:9-10; 13:13-14. The idiom קרב עבד also occurs in 1QapGen 21:25, 31; 4QEnGiants[c] 2:4.[29]

עממין ינתן בידה. "Peoples shall He put in his power," literally, "in his hand." This probably expresses the extent of the coming king's rule.

וכלהן / ירמה קדמוהי. "And of them He shall cast down before him." Another expression of the universality of the king's rule. Cf. *Ps. Sol.* 17:30, καὶ ἕξει λαοὺς ἐθνῶν δουλεύειν αὐτῷ ὑπὸ τὸν ζυγὸν αὐτοῦ, "he will have peoples of the nations to serve him under his yoke."

9. שלטנה שלטן עלם. "His dominion (shall be) an everlasting dominion." The duration of the rule of the coming king is guaranteed to be long. The clause is derived from Dan 4:31 or 7:14.

וכל תהומי. "And none of the abysses of the earth shall prevail against it!" The cosmic scope of the dominion is stressed; nothing that opposes the

---

26. See J. T. Milik, "Ecrits préesséniens de Qumrân: D'Hénoch à Amram," in *Qumrân: Sa piété, sa théologie et son milieu* (BETL 46; ed. M. Delcor; Gembloux/Paris: Duculot, 1978) 91-106, esp. 97. Milik uses an unconventional siglum for the text, 4QAJu, which should not be repeated.

27. B. Lifshitz, "Inscriptions de Césarée," *RB* 74 (1967) 50-59.

28. See G. A. Cooke, *A Text-Book of North Semitic Inscriptions* (Oxford: Clarendon, 1903) §95.3; §97 iii 3; §101.9; J. Teixidor, "Bulletin d'épigraphie sémitique 1970," *Syria* 47 (1970) 357-89, esp. 366.

29. See Milik, *The Books of Enoch*, 307; cf. his "Turfan et Qumran: Livre des Géants juif et manichéen," in *Tradition und Glaube: Das frühe Christentum in seiner Umwelt: Festgabe für Karl Georg Kuhn* . . . (ed. G. Jeremias et al.; Göttingen: Vandenhoeck & Ruprecht, 1971) 118-27, esp. 124.

dominion of that king shall succeed. In Ps 71:20 תהומי הארץ is used in the sense of Sheol. Perhaps one could restore the line thus: ארעא לא יתקפון מנה. Compare וכול צבו לא תקפתכה, "and nothing is stronger than you" (4QEnGiants[a] 9:4); or [דאנו]ן תקיפין מני, "they are more powerful than I" (4QEnGiants[c] 2:6-7).[30] Also Matt 16:18, καὶ πύλαι ᾅδου οὐ κατισχύσουσιν αὐτῆς. תהום occurs in 11QtgJob 38:8. Puech restores: וכל תהומי [ארעא ישמעון לה or ישמשון לה, "et tous les abîmes de [la terre(?) lui obéiront]."

Commentary

The text is written in a fine Herodian script, easily decipherable. Milik dated the text to the last third of the first century B.C., and Puech agrees: between 4QSam[a] and 1QIsa[b] or 1QM — hence ca. 25 B.C. There is no reason to contest this paleographic dating of the copy. It thus gives us precious firsthand information about pre-Christian Palestinian Jewish beliefs.

The importance of this text for the tenets and theology of the Qumran community cannot be underestimated. Its language reveals it to be apocalyptic: it speaks of distress that will come upon the land and of the disastrous reign of enemies, which is to be, however, short-lived; that reign will last only "until there arises the people of God, and everyone rests from the sword." The text promises the appearance of some figure, called "Son of God" and "Son of the Most High," who will rule in peace and with everlasting prosperity. The apocalyptic stage props are clear.

There is little difficulty in reading and interpreting column 2. The problem is the reconstruction of the beginning of the nine lines of column 1. I have given above my attempt to reconstruct them and the justification of the attempt.

The broken text begins with a fragmentary narrative sentence: When something happened, someone, probably a seer, fell before a throne. The prostrate person addresses an enthroned human king with the second singular independent pronoun and pronominal suffix (-k). The enthroned king is depicted as shaken by the evils seen in a vision. He has been made to realize that they are coming in his time, evils that are described in lines 4-6. Among them are war, carnage, and trouble from the "king of Assyria and Egypt." On line 7 the seer begins to explain the nature of what is to ensue: A figure will arise who will be great, be served by all, and be given lofty titles and guarantees of divine favor.

30. See Milik, *The Books of Enoch*, 316-17, 307-8.

In column 2, which is completely preserved, line 1 continues the titles. Line 2 tells of the short-lived duration of the enemy's reign (with plural suffixes and plural verbs that clearly refer to persons or peoples other than the one who bears the titles "Son of God" and "Son of the Most High." Their reign will last "until there arises the people of God" (line 4). His rule, or possibly its rule, is then extolled: respite from war, everlasting kingship, and paths of truth and peace with all provinces in submission. For the Great God will be with him (or it), and He will subject all enemies to him (or it).

The difficulty of interpreting the text is sixfold: (i) Who is the speaker and whom does he address? (ii) Are the references to the "king of Assyria and Egypt" and the plurals being used allusions to historical figures, or are they symbolic names for enemies? (iii) If they are to be taken in an apocalyptic sense rather than in a historical sense, can one say to whom they refer? (iv) Who is X, the person who will arise and to whom the titles are applied? (v) Is X to be understood in a positive or a negative sense, as a Jewish king or as an enemy who arrogates to himself such titles? (vi) To whom does the third singular masculine in 2:5-9 refer? Is it X, the expected figure of 1:9, or the "people of God" (2:4)?

At least six different interpretations have been given to the document.

1. J. T. Milik was originally of the opinion that God, seated upon a divine throne, was being addressed, but now thinks that the text refers rather to a historical king of Syria (מלך אתור, 1:6), whose reign would be disastrous (for Israel) and whose supreme blasphemy would be to proclaim himself Son of God; he would be called Son of the Most High by his followers.[31] This would refer to the last Seleucid king, whose reign would be followed, according to this text, by the rule of the people of God. Because Alexander Balas (150-145 B.C.), the pretended son of Antiochus IV Epiphanes, who became king of Syria on the death of Demetrios I Soter, used the Greek title Θεοπάτωρ on coins of his realm,[32] the titles "Son of God" and "Son of the Most High" in this Qumran text would refer to him. So X would be understood in a negative sense.

This interpretation is problematic, first, because one wonders why such a Palestinian text of clearly Jewish provenience would tolerate such a laudatory appellation of a pagan king with titles "Son of God" and "Son of the Most High."[33] Second, would a Jewish writer of Judea refer to a Seleucid king

31. Milik, "Modèles araméens," 383.

32. See F. Imhoof-Blumer, *Monnaies grecques* (Koninklijke Nederlandse Akademie van Wetenschappen, Afdeeling Letterkunde, Verhandelingen 14; Amsterdam: J. Muller, 1883) 433-34 (§102, pl. H 13).

33. Cross also argues against Milik's interpretation of the epithets as belonging to the Seleucid king Alexander Balas ("Notes on the Doctrine," 5).

as מלך אתור, "king of Assyria"? Third, how would one then account for the mention of "Egypt" in this situation? Fourth, no matter who the speaker is, he is addressing a human king who needs reassurance about the continuation of his reign, about who will succeed him and who is related to "the people of God." Whether that person be his son, as I once understood the text, or some other human successor may be debated. In any case, this seems to be the message that the prostrate seer is trying to give the enthroned king, as he also tells of the disasters that are to come upon the land before that reign of peace is established. Fifth, as Florentino García Martínez has pointed out, through Alexander Balas's intervention Jonathan became the Hasmonean high priest.[34] Would he then be regarded as an enemy of Israel, arrogating to himself such titles, as Milik's interpretation would presuppose? Hardly.

2. David Flusser regards the document as apocalyptic, but thinks that it speaks of a coming Antichrist.[35] For Flusser, the *vacat* with which 2:4 begins starts a new topic: the rise of God's people. Hence, what precedes the *vacat* would describe "the king or the leader of this horrible kingdom" who will bring all the distress. It also tells of those who worship and serve him and of the way they regard him. The first part of the text would refer, then, not to a historical enemy, but to an Antichrist, an idea which Flusser maintains "is surely Jewish and pre-Christian," that is, a "human exponent of the Satanic forces of evil." He compares 2 Thess 2:1-12, with its description of "the man of lawlessness," and three other apocalyptic texts: (a) *Ascension of Isaiah* 4:2-16, which tells of an incarnation of Beliar, "a lawless king and a matricide," in whom all people of the world will believe: "they will sacrifice to him and serve him";[36] (b) *Oracle of Hystaspes*, which describes a king who will arise from Syria, "a destroyer of the human race . . . a prophet of lies" who "will constitute and call himself God and will order himself to be worshipped as the Son of God";[37] and (c) *Assumption of Moses* 8, which tells of a "man who rules with great power," who will persecute the Jewish people.[38] Hence in this Qumran text, too, one would read of the same sort of "hubris of the Antichrist."

34. See Josephus, *Ant.* 13.2.2 §45. Cf. García Martínez, "4Q246: ¿Tipo del Anticristo," 235; idem, "The Eschatological Figure," 169.

35. Flusser, "The Hubris of the Antichrist." Cf. his article, "D. Hystaspes and John of Patmos," in *Irano-Judaica: Studies Relating to Jewish Contacts with Persian Culture throughout the Ages* (ed. S. Shaked; Jerusalem: Ben-Zvi Institute, 1982) 12-75; reprinted in his *Judaism*, 390-453.

36. See H. F. D. Sparks, ed., *The Apocryphal Old Testament* (Oxford: Clarendon, 1984) 791.

37. See Lactantius, *Divinae Institutiones* 7.17.2-4; CSEL 19:638-39.

38. See Sparks, ed., *The Apocryphal Old Testament*, 611-12.

Although the parallels are striking, much of Flusser's interpretation depends on his questionable understanding of the Aramaic verb יעבדון (1:8) as a Hebraism meaning "they will worship." Moreover, even though he insists that the idea of Antichrist is "Jewish and pre-Christian," all the evidence he uses comes from Christian texts, as García Martínez has also noted. That Qumran texts envision some eschatological opponent of Melchizedek or even of a Messiah might be admitted, but that does not make the opponent an Antichrist. Ἀντίχριστος first emerges in Greek literature in 1 John 2:18, 22; 4:3; 2 John 7; cf. Polycarp, *Phil.* 7:1. This title obviously means someone who is "an opponent of Christ," which presupposes the emergence of Χριστός as a name in the Christian world. To say that it means "Antimessiah" and that it could be used of a "Jewish and pre-Christian" figure would be an extrapolation that goes beyond the evidence.[39] Finally, it is not obvious that all that precedes the *vacat* (2:4) is to be understood in a negative sense, since one may be encountering here the kind of repetitious treatment of a topic characteristic of apocalyptic writing.

3. Florentino García Martínez also understands the text as apocalyptic, but thinks that the mysterious personage is an eschatological savior of angelic or heavenly character.[40] He would be someone "designated in other texts [11QMelchizedek; 4QVisAmram, 4Q175] as Michael, Melchizedek, Prince of Light (*1QM* XIII 10) and proclaimed in this text as 'Son of God' and 'Son of the Most High,'" whose intervention would usher in the end time. García Martínez finds an intelligible context for this text in what is said in 1QM 17:5-8, where Michael is promised to come in the end time to bring low the Prince of the dominion of wickedness.

That there are such heavenly figures in Qumran texts is clear and that

---

39. See R. E. Brown, *The Epistles of John: Translated with Introduction, Notes, and Commentary* (AB 30; Garden City, N.Y.: Doubleday, 1982) 332-33. Brown notes the use of ἀντίθεος, "opposed to God," in Philo, *De Fuga* 25 §140; of ἀντίδικος, "opposed to δίκη, "justice" (Luke 18:3), and applied to the devil in 1 Pet 5:8.

Compare J. R. Hinnells, "The Zoroastrian Doctrine of Salvation in the Roman World: A Study of the Oracle of Hystaspes," in *Man and His Salvation: Studies in Memory of S. G. F. Brandon* (ed. E. J. Sharpe and J. R. Hinnells; Totowa, N.J.: Rowman and Littlefield, 1973) 125-48. Collins notes that Hinnells defends the Persian origin of the *Oracle* but does not include the cited passage of Lactantius among the fragments of it. Cf. also G. C. Jenks, *Origin and Early Development of the Antichrist Myth* (BZNW 59; Berlin: de Gruyter, 1991) 30-32, 41-43, who mentions that among the earliest patristic writers who discuss the Antichrist myth Hippolytus of Rome traces it to Daniel, especially chaps. 10-12, without, of course, using the term. Otherwise all the witnesses to the myth that Jenks discusses are Christian.

40. García Martínez, "Eschatological Figure," 172-79.

they form part of the Qumran community's eschatological tenets is also correct, but that they supply the key to the interpretation of this text and to the identification of the mysterious figure called "Son of God" and "Son of the Most High" is the problem. For such titles are never used elsewhere of such heavenly figures. As John J. Collins has noted,[41] this text depicts God as "the might" or source of strength of the mysterious figure. Would that be said of a heavenly figure? The thrust of the text, however, is such that one would expect these titles to be ascribed to a human being. García Martínez called my earlier attribution of the titles to a successor or son of the king gratuitous, but that can be said with much more reason of the heavenly eschatological savior that he has proposed.

4. Martin Hengel has suggested that the titles should be interpreted collectively "of the Jewish people, like the Son of Man in Dan. 7,13."[42] This suggestion exploits the unclarity of the third person singular reference in some of the sentences of column 2. Though not impossible, it is unlikely, given the parallels to those sentences in other writings that point rather to an individual person.

5. Emile Puech has also questioned some of these interpretations and has proposed instead a messianic reading of this Aramaic document.[43] For him the text is apocalyptic, and the titles are to be ascribed to an expected "Messiah." In this he has followed H.-W. Kuhn,[44] and is supported by J. J. Collins,[45] S. Kim,[46] and F. M. Cross.[47] This sort of interpretation was also mentioned by authors who had not even seen the text.[48]

41. Collins, "The *Son of God* Text" (n. 12 above).

42. M. Hengel, *The Son of God: The Origin of Christology and the History of Jewish-Hellenistic Religion* (Philadelphia: Fortress, 1976) 45.

43. See Puech, "Fragment," 125-30; cf. his publication of the *editio princeps*. Puech did toy with the interpretation of the text in a negative sense, that the mysterious person could be a Seleucid ruler, either Alexander Balas, as Milik interpreted it, or Antiochus IV Epiphanes ("Fragment," 127-30). Because Puech was allowed by Milik to publish this text in full, he did not want to reject outright Milik's interpretation, but his otherwise wide-ranging discussion of the document in a messianic sense reveals where his preference lies.

44. H.-W. Kuhn, "Rom 1,3f und der davidische Messias als Gottessohn in den Qumrantexten," in *Lesezeichen für Annelies Findeiss* . . . (ed. C. Burchard and G. Theissen; Heidelberg, 1984) 103-13 [non vidi].

45. Collins, "The *Son of God* Text." He considers "Son of God" to be an "early interpretation of the 'one like a son of man' in Daniel 7, who also stands in parallelism to the people," without, however, being "simply an exposition of Daniel 7."

46. S. Kim, *"The 'Son of Man'" as the Son of God* (WUNT 30; Tübingen: Mohr Siebeck, 1983) 20-22, esp. n. 33.

47. Cross, "Notes on the Doctrine," 11-13.

48. E.g., A. D. Nock, in a review of H.-J. Schoeps, *Paulus: Die Theologie des Apostels*

I find the messianic interpretation of this Aramaic text questionable. That there was, indeed, a lively messianic expectation in the Qumran community is beyond doubt; that it was dyarchic or bipolar, expecting both a Davidic and a priestly messiah, is also accurate,[49] and Cross has recently done well to insist on all of this.[50] Such an interpretation of this text, however, encounters several problems:

(a) The word מׁשיח does not occur in the text, and to import it is gratuitous.

(b) Would the titles "Son of God" and "Son of the Most High" be understood without further ado as "messianic" in pre-Christian Judaism? Both of these titles have a distinct background in the Old Testament, and there one does not denote the other. Moreover, there is no clear passage in the Old Testament where either of these titles is used of a figure called מׁשיח.[51] Although the king on the Davidic throne is often said to be God's son (e.g., 2 Sam 7:14; Ps 2:7-8), this title is never used there of the king as an awaited "messianic" figure.[52] In the New Testament these titles are used of him who is for Christians the Messiah (e.g., John 11:27), but that is an entirely different matter. *Per se,* the title "Son of God" does not connote "Messiah" in the Old Testament; nor does it do so in any of the Qumran texts. Only a naive interpretation, stemming more from a traditional understanding than from critical thinking, would espouse that connotation.

(c) Puech's messianic interpretation of this Aramaic text depends on his reading of certain Old Testament passages as speaking of "un messie roi du judaïsme."[53] But by what right does one call 2 Sam 7:12-16 and 23:5, Gen 49:10-12, Psalms 2, 89, and 110, Isaiah 9–11, and Zech 3:8 and 6:12 "messi-

---

im Lichte der jüdischen Religionsgeschichte (Tübingen: Mohr Siebeck, 1959) in *Gnomon* 33 (1961) 581-90, esp. 584; A. J. B. Higgins, "The Old Testament and Some Aspects of New Testament Christology," *CJT* 6 (1960) 200-210, esp. 202 n. 12.

49. See 1QS 9:11 and my discussion of this passage in Chapter 5 below. For secondary literature on Qumran messianism, see *DSSMPTS,* 164-67.

50. Cross, "Notes on the Doctrine."

51. See E. Lohse, "Huios," *TDNT,* 8:361: "Thus far there is no clear instance to support the view that in pre-Christian times Judaism used the title 'son of God' for the Messiah. The Messiah is 'my son' in Eth. En. 105:2, but this v. was added later, since it is not in Gr. En. and has thus to be disregarded." Cf. J. A. Fitzmyer, *Paul and His Theology: A Brief Sketch* (2d ed.; Englewood Cliffs, N.J.: Prentice Hall, 1989) §PT 49-50.

52. It should be needless to point out that, although Ps 2:2 uses מׁשיחו, it cannot be translated there "his Messiah." The KJV, RSV, NRSV, NAB, NJV, NEB, REB, and NIV all translate it properly as "his anointed (One, king)," because the psalm refers to one who already sits on the Davidic throne, not an *awaited* anointed agent of God.

53. Puech, "Fragment," 88; cf. 127.

anic" within pre-Christian Jewish tradition?[54] I shall discuss further in Chapter 5 the Old Testament passages that use מָשִׁיחַ.[55]

Some Old Testament passages, especially 1 Sam 2:10, 35 and Ps 132:17, refer to the dynasty that develops as Davidic, but they must be understood *generically* as indicative of a divine guarantee for the future of the Davidic household or dynasty, or of what has been called "restorative monarchism."[56] The person mentioned as "anointed" may be part of the continuation or even restoration of the monarchy of old. In other words, such passages express eschatological hopes, but *not directly eschatological messianism*. Often they refer to persons who have been "anointed" in the past or were anointed agents whom God *has* appointed, but they are not Messiahs (with a capital M), that is, future or awaited anointed figures *to be raised up* by God for the good or the salvation of His people. Hence, in none of these instances is the adjective "messianic" truly applicable.

Consequently, I continue to question the correctness of importing messianism into the interpretation of this pre-Christian Aramaic Son of God text. When one opts for a messianic interpretation of this text, one is introducing the same kind of eisegetical "messianic" interpretation of the "Son of Man" figure in Dan 7:13, which was common for many centuries, but which even Collins admits "has fallen into disfavor in recent times."[57]

6. I rather consider this apocalyptic text to be speaking positively of a coming Jewish ruler, who may be a successor to the Davidic throne, but who is not envisaged as a Messiah. The text should be understood as a sectarian affirmation of belief in God's provision and guarantee of a royal dynasty for Israel. Just as not every king of old who sat on David's throne was given the title

---

54. That some of these passages were understood in a messianic sense in later Judaism is clear. For the rabbinic period, see S. H. Levey, *The Messiah: An Aramaic Interpretation: The Messianic Exegesis of the Targum* (Cincinnati: Hebrew Union College–Jewish Institute of Religion, 1974). Most of the passages are conveniently listed here, but note the reviews of this book in *Bib* 56 (1975) 421-24; *JBL* 94 (1975) 473-77.

Puech contests my denial of a messianic understanding of Psalm 2 in pre-Christian Judaism ("Fragment," 127 n. 60), appealing for proof to *Psalms of Solomon* 17 and 1QSa 2:11, as if these passages showed that that psalm were indeed understood there as messianic. He also appeals to a popular, non-critical article by R. Tournay, "Le Psaume *(Ps 2):* Le Roi-Messie," *AsSeign* 88 (1966) 46-63. However, to see that I am not alone, cf. J. Becker, *Messianic Expectation in the Old Testament* (Philadelphia: Fortress, 1980) 28 n. 8, 68; G. Cooke, "The Israelite King as Son of God," *ZAW* 73 (1961) 202-225, esp. 205; M. Treves, "Two Acrostic Psalms," *VT* 15 (1965) 81-90, esp. 85.

55. See pp. 76-82 below.

56. See Becker, *Messianic Expectation*, 54-57.

57. Collins, "The *Son of God* Text," 81.

משיח, even in a historical sense, so too it is not clear that the successor to the enthroned king in this text will necessarily be an expected Messiah, even though the text hails him as "Son of God" and "Son of the Most High." Because the Aramaic text uses a good number of phrases and words from the book of Daniel, its dependence on that writing is clear. However, it is noteworthy that neither David nor the Davidic dynasty finds any mention in that book. So the "Son of God" text may well be continuing the thinking of the book of Daniel, but without any reference to a future Davidic king.

However one wants to interpret the unnamed character of this apocalyptic Qumran writing, the text at least makes it clear that such titles as "Son of God" and "Son of the Most High" were "not completely alien to Palestinian Judaism."[58]

In my earlier discussion of this text I called attention to the pertinence it has for the interpretation of the Lucan infancy narrative, and especially to the Palestinian Jewish background that it provides for the words of the angel Gabriel to Mary in the annunciation scene.[59] Here I shall only list the pertinent parallels:

οὗτος ἔσται μέγας (1:32)	compare 4Q246 1:7
υἱὸς ὑψίστου κληθήσεται (1:32)	compare 4Q246 2:1
κληθήσεται υἱὸς θεοῦ (1:35)	compare 4Q246 2:1
βασιλεύσει . . . εἰς τοὺς αἰῶνας (1:33)	compare 4Q246 2:5

A problem remains, however, since we cannot say whether this is perchance a coincidental use by Luke of Palestinian Jewish titles known to him or whether "Luke is dependent in some way, whether directly or indirectly, on this long lost text from Qumran."[60] In any case, the debate over this important sectarian Qumran text is far from over.

58. Hengel, *The Son of God*, 45.
59. Fitzmyer, "The Contribution of Qumran Aramaic," 394; *WA* or *SBNT*, 93; *The Gospel according to Luke* (AB 28, 28A; Garden City, N.Y.: Doubleday, 1981, 1985) 205-7, 347-48.
60. Collins, "The *Son of God* Text," 66.

CHAPTER 4

The Background of "Son of God" as a Title for Jesus

The designation of Jesus in the New Testament as "Son of God" is widespread, and no other title of his can claim as much significance for later theological development than it. If the title "Son of Man" outstrips it in enigma, it certainly does not in implication. Whether the title is used in the anarthrous form, υἱὸς θεοῦ, or the arthrous form, ὁ υἱὸς τοῦ θεοῦ, or is uttered by a heavenly voice as υἱός μου, "my Son," or used as a description of Jesus by some New Testament writer as υἱὸς αὐτοῦ or υἱὸς ἑαυτοῦ, "his Son," its meaning is clear. It expresses the distinctive relationship of Jesus to the God of Israel, Yahweh, who is his heavenly Father.

My further remarks on the background of this title will be made under four headings: the problem; Old Testament data bearing on the title "Son of God"; the new Palestinian Jewish material; and implications of the new material for various New Testament passages.

The Problem

The title "Son of God" occurs in the Synoptic Gospels: Mark 1:1, 11; 3:11; 5:7; 15:39; Matt 2:15; 3:17; 4:3, 6; 8:29; 14:33; 16:16; 17:5; 26:63; 27:40, 43, 54; Luke 1:32, 35; 3:22; 4:3, 9, 41; 8:28; 9:35; 22:70. It is also found in the Johannine Gospel: 1:18, 34, 49; 3:18; 5:25; (9:35);[1] 10:36; 11:4, 27; 19:7; 20:31.

1. Consult the Greek *apparatus criticus* on this passage.

Likewise in Acts: 8:37; 9:20; 13:33; in the uncontested Pauline letters: Rom 1:3-4, 9; 5:10; 8:3, 29, 32; 1 Cor 1:9; 2 Cor 1:19; Gal 1:16; 2:20; 4:4, 6; 1 Thess 1:10; in the Deutero-Pauline Eph 4:13; in the Epistle to the Hebrews: 1:5; 4:14; 5:5; 6:6; 7:3; 10:29; in the Johannine Epistles: 1 John 1:3, 7, 8; 3:23; 4:9, 10, 15; 5:5, 9, 10, 11, 12, 13, 20; 2 John 3; in the book of Revelation: 2:18; and in 2 Peter: 1:17. Moreover, it not only occurs in some Pauline passages that are often regarded as fragments of the primitive kerygma (1 Thess 1:10; Rom 1:3-4), but it even develops within the New Testament itself so that it becomes merely "the Son," an absolute form of the title, used either by Jesus of himself (Mark 13:32; Matt 24:36) or by Paul (1 Cor 15:28).

This usage suggests a certain parallelism with the title *Kyrios*, which is likewise employed in an absolute form along with modified expressions.[2] New Testament interpreters, aware of the various nuances of the use of *ben* or *huios*, "son," in the Old Testament to designate a special relationship of someone to God, have often sought the background of the Son of God title in the Old Testament itself, but some have noted that it is "a long way" from such simple usage in the Old Testament to the solemn and lofty title, "the Son of God," such as one finds in the New Testament, especially for Jesus. Years ago Wilhelm Bousset posed the question whether this title did not rather first develop on Greek soil and in the Greek language.[3] Bousset expressed hesitation about the connection of the New Testament title with what he called "Jewish messianology" and thought that the title came to undisputed dominance in the popular conceptions of the Gentile Christian church. He did not, however, go so far as Adolf Deissmann had, who saw a close "connection with the imperial cult and the well-known formula" *divi filius (theou huios)*.[4] For Bousset, the New Testament title "Son of God" was not so clearly of Hellenistic and pagan origin as *Kyrios*, "Lord," was alleged to be. As is well known, several interpreters have sought blatantly to relate the latter as a title for Jesus to such an origin,[5] but a few writers have related ὁ υἱὸς τοῦ θεοῦ to a similar Hellenistic background: G. P. Wetter, W. G. Kümmel (with varying nuances).[6]

---

2. Compare the uses of *Kyrios* that I gathered in "The Semitic Background of the New Testament *Kyrios*-Title," in *WA* or *SBNT,* 115-42, esp. 127-30.

3. See the quotations from Bousset, *Kyrios Christos,* 95-96 and 207 on p. 32 above.

4. G. A. Deissmann, *Bible Studies: Contributions Chiefly from Papyri and Inscriptions to the History of the Language, the Literature, and the Religion of Hellenistic Judaism and Primitive Christianity* (2d ed.; Edinburgh: Clark, 1909) 166-67.

5. See J. A. Fitzmyer, "The Semitic Background," 116.

6. See G. P. Wetter, *Der Sohn Gottes* (FRLANT 26; Göttingen: Vandenhoeck & Ruprecht, 1916); W. G. Kümmel, *The Theology of the New Testament according to Its Major Witnesses: Jesus — Paul — John* (Nashville: Abingdon, 1973).

The opinion of Rudolf Bultmann, however, was more complicated. Although he thought that "Hellenistic-Jewish Christians had brought along the *title* 'Son of God' embedded in their missionary message, for the earliest Church had already called Jesus so,"[7] he maintained that the connotation of the title as indicative of "divine origin" or of being "filled with divine 'power'" (and not merely messiahship) was related to a Gentile or Hellenistic setting. For him the title was associated with the role of Jesus as θεῖος ἀνήρ,[8] and its real content was thus of Hellenistic imprint.

Obviously, it would be foolhardy to deny that such a Hellenistic or Roman use of the title for emperors, demigods, or heroes born of gods and goddesses, or even for *theioi andres* in the contemporary world had somewhat influenced early Christians in their use of the title for Jesus. This might be especially true of its use in the writings of Paul or John, which stem from settings in the Greco-Roman world of the eastern Mediterranean area, but the problem really is to trace that "long way" from the Old Testament data, which many New Testament interpreters still think were at the root of the title for Jesus, to the solemn title itself. No little part of the problem is the rare occurrence of the title as such (in the singular) in late Old Testament writings despite numerous allusions to figures in the Old Testament who are called "son" or "sons," yet scarcely with the connotations that the title has for Jesus in the New Testament. So the problem is posed. New light has been shed on the Palestinian Jewish background of the title from the recent publication of the Qumran "Son of God" text discussed in the preceding chapter. In order to appreciate the significance of this new text and the place that it holds in the debate about the New Testament problem, one has to consider again the Old Testament data which bear on the title.

Old Testament Data Bearing on the Title "Son of God"

The plural expressions in Hebrew, *běnê hā'ělōhîm*, "sons of God" (Gen 6:2, 4; Job 1:6; 2:1; 38:7), *běnê 'ēlîm*, "sons of God" (Ps 29:1; 89:6), and *běnê 'elyôn*, "sons of the Most High" (Ps 82:6) are found in the Old Testament as names for angelic beings in the heavenly court of Yahweh.[9] The plural expression, either as in *běnê 'ēl ḥay*, "sons of the living God" (Hos 2:1), or simply some form of *bānîm*, "sons, children" (Deut 14:1; Isa 1:2; 30:1; Jer 3:22), is sometimes put on

---

7. R. Bultmann, *Theology of the New Testament* (2 vols.; London: SCM, 1952) 1:128.
8. Ibid., 1:130.
9. In Ps 82:6 the phrase may refer to "judges" according to some commentators.

God's lips and used of the Israelites. On occasion collective Israel is spoken of in the singular as *běnî*, "my son" (Exod 4:22; Hos 11:1). The closest one comes to the singular usage in the Old Testament, resembling the New Testament title, is found not in Hebrew, but in Aramaic and Greek. Thus the (angelic) figure who appears with Shadrach, Meshach, and Abednego walking about freely in the fiery furnace is described as *dāmēh lěbar 'ělāhîn*, "(one) resembling a son of God" (Dan 3:25). Again, Israel itself is referred to in the singular as *theou huion*, "God's son" (Wis 18:13). Yet neither of these expressions implies a physical father-son relationship between Yahweh and the person(s) so designated. Neither the descriptive title for the angel in Daniel nor the collective title for the people of Israel in Wisdom provides the intelligible background or an adequate explanation for the New Testament title used of Jesus of Nazareth. For this reason Bousset rightly spoke of the "long way" from the simple Old Testament usage to the solemn New Testament title.

"Son" is also used at times of individuals in the Old Testament tradition. Thus, though he is never formally or explicitly called "Son of God," the king who sits on the Davidic throne is twice related to Yahweh as "son" and once as the "first-born": 2 Sam 7:14; Ps 2:7; cf. Ps 89:26-27. These texts, however, call for further scrutiny.

Psalm 2:7 uses of the Davidic king the graphic expression *yělidtîkā*, "I have begotten you." Commentators are usually hesitant to assert that this implies a physical divine sonship for the king, such as might be the connotation of similar expressions in the ancient myths of the eastern Mediterranean world.[10] Rather, the father-son relationship so expressed connotes divine sponsorship, support, or assistance for the king, and by implication for his dynasty. That is the meaning of the begetting of the king in Ps 2:7. It is also the implication of Nathan's oracle in 2 Sam 7:14, and the legitimation of the dynastic rule is further described in the poetic language of Ps 89:3-4, 19-37. Indeed, it may have been played out in a coronation ritual.[11]

In the deuterocanonical writings of Ben Sira and Wisdom, however, one finds "son" used also of a righteous or upright individual Israelite: "Be like a father to the fatherless and help a widow as a husband would; and God will call you 'son,' show you his favor, and save you from the pit" (Sir 4:10).[12]

---

10. C. J. Gadd, *Ideas of Divine Rule in the Ancient East* (Schweich Lectures of the British Academy, 1945; London: Cumberlege/Oxford University Press, 1948) 45-50.

11. G. von Rad, "Das jüdische Krönungsritual," *TLZ* 72 (1947) 211-16; K.-H. Rengstorf, "Old and New Testament Traces of a Formula of the Judaean Royal Ritual," *NovT* 5 (1962) 229-44.

12. In Hebrew, ואל יקראך בן ויחנך ויצילך משחת, but the LXX reads: καὶ ἔσῃ ὡς υἱὸς ὑψίστου.

Again, "If the righteous man is God's son (υἱὸς θεοῦ), He will help him" (Wis 2:18).

Thus in a few instances in Old Testament writings we find a background for the expression "Son of God": in dynastic sayings about the Davidic king and in four instances even the formal singular expression itself, used once of an angel, once of collective Israel, and twice of a righteous individual Israelite. The connotations may vary, but they are all figurative usages. Because some of these instances occur in deuterocanonical writings, they may not have been used by Bousset in his way of thinking about the Old Testament.

Psalm 2, however, is the source of the tendency of some biblical interpreters to regard the title "Son of God" as messianic. Since this adjective is properly understood of such Old Testament figures as were "anointed," the title "Son of God" does not express that idea either precisely or per se. And yet, the question whether "Son of God" connoted a Messiah or an Anointed One in pre-Christian Palestinian Judaism is constantly raised and debated. The root of the problem is verse 2, where the king on the Davidic throne is called "His [i.e., the Lord's] anointed" (מְשִׁיחוֹ), and verse 7 says, "You are my son; today I have begotten you" (בְּנִי אַתָּה אֲנִי הַיּוֹם יְלִדְתִּיךָ, or υἱός μου εἶ σύ, ἐγὼ σήμερον γεγέννηκά σε). In verse 2, however, the phrase "his anointed" is used of an unnamed historical king, one who was sitting upon the Davidic throne and at whose enthronement was "anointed," and even called by God "my son." However, this phrase is not used there of a future, ideal David who is awaited, of whom Jer 30:9 once spoke: "they shall serve the Lord their God and David their king, whom I will raise up for them."[13] Hence despite the connection of "anointed one" and "son" in Psalm 2, where they occur together, albeit several verses apart, neither in pre-Christian Palestinian Judaism nor in the Judaism of the Diaspora have we any clear evidence that Psalm 2 was being understood "messianically," that is, of an expected or coming anointed figure, a Messiah in the strict sense.[14] Nor have we a clearly attested instance of the title "Son of God" being applied to an awaited "Messiah" in pre-Christian Jewish literature.

13. See further Chapter 5, pp. 76-82 below.

14. P. Billerbeck, in his comment on "concerning His Son" (Rom 1:3), cites under the heading "Der Messias," only the problematic passages, *1 Enoch* 105:2 and *4 Ezra* 7:28-29; 13:32, 37, 52; 14:9, and concludes, surprisingly, "Überall ist hier der Ausdruck 'mein Sohn' in Gottes Mund eine Messiasbezeichnung synonym mit Χριστός oder מָשִׁיחַ" ("the expression 'my Son' in God's mouth is in every case a description of the Messiah synonymous with *Christos* or *Mašiaḥ*") (Str-B, 3:17). That, of course, is an unsubstantiated comment. When Ps 2:7 is mentioned by Billerbeck, it is listed under the heading, "Der König Israels" (3:15), with nary a hint that it might have a "messianic" connotation.

The New Palestinian Jewish Material

Now over against such an Old Testament background one has to consider the new Palestinian Aramaic text from Qumran, 4Q246, which has been discussed at length above in Chapter 3. The translation of part of it is repeated here for the sake of the further discussion.

Column 1

    7 [Then shall arise a king, and he shall be] great upon the earth.
    8 [All peoples sh]all make [peace with him]; they shall all serve
    9 [him. For] he shall be called [the holy one of] the [G]reat [God], and by His name shall he be named.

Column 2

    1 He shall be hailed son of God, and they shall call him son of the Most High. Like the comets
    2 that you saw (in your vision), so shall their reign be. For (some) years they shall rule over
    3 the land, and they shall trample on all: one people shall trample upon another, and one province upon an[o]ther,
    4 (vacat) until there arises the people of God, and everyone rests from the sword. (vacat)
    5 His kingdom (shall be) an everlasting kingdom, and all his ways (shall be) in truth. He shall jud[ge]
    6 the land with truth, and all shall make peace. The sword shall cease from the land,
    7 and all the provinces shall pay him homage. The Great God is Himself his might.
    8 He shall make war for him; peoples shall He put in his power, and all of them
    9 He shall cast down before him. His dominion (shall be) an everlasting dominion, . . .

This fragmentary copy of the Son of God text has been dated paleographically to the last third of the first century B.C.; so it clearly comes from a pre-Christian period of Palestinian Judaism. Whether this is the autograph of the text or the only surviving copy of it from among many that may have been produced, no one can say. Moreover, the fragmentary nature of the text unfortunately does not permit one to determine who the person is to whom the titles "Son of God" and "Son of the Most High" are attributed.

In the preceding chapter I set forth in some detail the six different attempts to identify the person concerned: (1) the Seleucid king, Alexander Balas, whose blasphemous reign would be followed by the eschatological rule of the people of God; (2) an Antichrist, an incarnation of Beliar, who would be unseated and followed by the rule of God's people; (3) an eschatological savior "of angelic nature," someone like the heavenly Melchizedek, Michael, or the Prince of Light mentioned in other Qumran texts; (4) the Jewish people collectively, as the title "Son of Man" is used in Dan 7:13; (5) a Davidic Messiah, who is awaited; and (6) a coming Jewish king, who is not called or regarded as a Messiah (in the strict sense).

No matter what interpretation may eventually win out and become commonly accepted, the titles *bĕrēh dî 'ēl*, "Son of God," and *bar 'elyôn*, "Son of the Most High," are clearly being attributed to an expected human being who will rule over the people of God in some Palestinian Jewish context. When the text was originally composed, members of the Hasmonean dynasty were undoubtedly still ruling. Since the text is written in Aramaic and this language was in common use in Syria at the time, one might think that it could be of Syrian or even of Seleucid origin. It seems hardly likely, however, that a Jew in Palestine would have copied such a non-Jewish writing, or that it would have been used among the Essenes of Qumran, if that were its origin, because the Seleucid dynasty was fundamentally Hellenistic and pagan. So it is unlikely that such titles would have emerged from such a context. Moreover, the titles are almost certainly intended to describe the coming one who will be ruling over "the people of God," which seems to mean the Jewish people. The tone of the text suggests that it at least fed the aspirations and expectations of the Qumran community, if it was not actually composed by someone in that community. Its presence in Qumran Cave 4 is, consequently, the best indication of its use to foster eschatological beliefs of Qumran Essenes, even if it otherwise contains none of the characteristic sectarian tenets or phrases. It may be difficult to maintain that it was actually composed by a member of the Qumran community, and because the text is composed in Aramaic and lacks anything that closely identifies it with the Qumran community, it seems to reveal expectations of Palestinian Jews of a broader circle than the Essenes of Qumran. Whether, then, the coming king would be a member of the Hasmonean dynasty or a member of the restored Davidic dynasty might be debated. Given the Qumran community's attitude toward certain kings of the Hasmonean dynasty, one might hesitate to think that it refers to a successor of that line, and so prefer a Davidic king, but see below.

Implications of the New Material for New Testament Passages

First, the titles "Son of God" and "Son of the Most High" are clearly related to an apocalyptic setting in this document of Palestinian Judaism. The apocalyptic character of the text is clear in its reference to occupying forces, which in God's good time will be overcome with His aid and assistance. This part of the message is being revealed and passed on as consolation directly to the enthroned king, but indirectly to Palestinian Jews, just as the apocalyptic message of the book of Revelation in the New Testament is meant to console and strengthen Christians in a period of persecution and distress. Other apocalyptic stage props are also used: a vision of distress, war, and carnage; an interpreting seer; a promise of peace and an end of the sword.

Second, "Son of God" and "Son of the Most High" are used in this text in a *titular* sense in this pre-Christian Palestinian context. This is shown by the Aramaic verbs that accompany them: יתאמר, "he shall be hailed," and יכנונה, "they shall call him." In the given text there are also other verbs of "calling" or "naming" that leave no doubt about the appellative sense in which the phrases are being used.

Third, these titles are not applied to anyone who is directly called "messiah" (משיחא); at least this term is not found in any part of the extant text. Thus, even this text bears out the contention that Bousset once made that there is no direct connection between the title "Son of God" and "Jewish messianology."[15] However, another of Bousset's contentions can now be modified. He wrote, "The whole of later Jewish apocalypticism was unacquainted with the messianic title 'Son of God.'" This text now reveals that Jewish apocalypticism was not unacquainted with the title "Son of God," even if it is still not applied to a messianic figure or used with a messianic nuance. Since the titles are associated in this Aramaic text with someone who will rule, possibly even a son of the enthroned king, this further makes unlikely the suggestion of W. Grundmann that "Son of God" was the title for the *priestly* messiahship of Jesus.[16] The titles are used for a kingly figure whose dominion and reign will be everlasting.

15. W. Bousset, *Kyrios Christos: A History of the Belief in Christ from the Beginnings of Christianity to Irenaeus* (Nashville: Abingdon, 1970; German original, 1913) 207.
16. See W. Grundmann, "Sohn Gottes," *ZNW* 47 (1956) 113-33.

Fourth, if there is no connection of the title "Son of God" with messianic expectations of Palestinian Jews (and specifically with the messianism of the Qumran community), there is even less connection of it with miracles or with a θεῖος ἀνήρ setting, not to mention an association of it with gnostic redeemer myths.[17]

The context of the use of the title in this Qumran text is one of political strife, and the "Son of God" figure is hailed apocalyptically as a harbinger of peace and everlasting dominion, as a bearer of those things that might be associated even with the restoration of Davidic kingship, although the Davidic connection is not stated in the text. The text, indeed, borrows phrases found in the canonical book of Daniel and reflects the kind of thinking which that late biblical writing represents, in which David is not mentioned.

Fifth, I have already called attention to the strikingly similar use of the same titles in the Lucan infancy narrative.[18] This is not the first time that an Aramaic parallel to an expression in the Lucan infancy narrative has turned up in Qumran literature.[19] So it raises a question about the long-standing debate about the sources that Luke used in that part of his Gospel. Because it is a narrative written in a more semitized Greek than the rest of the Gospel, the suspicion has been that the evangelist may have been dependent on some Semitic source. In reality, however, the Semitic character of the infancy narrative is largely owing to Luke's use of Septuagintisms. Attempts to relate the infancy narrative to a Semitic source have usually postulated a Hebrew rather than an Aramaic source.[20] In my opinion, the parallels of this Qumran text to the Lucan infancy narrative scarcely show that Luke was dependent on it. Rather, he may have been aware of an Aramaic tradition that made use of such phrases. If I am right in agreeing with the ecclesiastical tradition that the author of the Third Gospel was Luke, a Syrian, possibly from Antioch, then he would have been a native Aramaic speaker as an *incola* of that region, but

---

17. Contrast what R. Bultmann wrote in his *Theology of the New Testament,* 1:130.

18. See p. 61 above.

19. See J. A. Fitzmyer, "'Peace on Earth among Men of His Good Will' (Luke 2:14)," *TS* 19 (1958) 225-27; reprinted in *ESBNT* and *SBNT,* 101-4.

20. See G. H. Box, "The Gospel Narratives of the Nativity and the Alleged Influence of Heathen Ideas," *ZNW* 6 (1905) 80-101; H. Gunkel, *Zum religionsgeschichtlichen Verständnis des Neuen Testaments* (FRLANT 1; Göttingen: Vandenhoeck & Ruprecht, 1903); R. Laurentin, "Traces d'allusions étymologiques en Luc 1–2," *Bib* 37 (1956) 435-56; 38 (1957) 1-23; P. Winter, "Two Notes on Luke I, II with Regard to the Theory of 'Imitation Hebraisms,'" *ST* 7 (1953) 158-65. Cf. J. A. Fitzmyer, *The Gospel according to Luke* (2 vols.; AB 28, 28A; Garden City, N.Y.: Doubleday, 1981-85) 1:312.

one who also had a good Greek education, such as would have been usual in his day in such a Hellenized area.[21]

Sixth, the title בר עליון, "Son of the Most High," shows how a traditional Old Testament designation for God was being adapted in a title of filiation. The title is related to the compound divine name אל עליון (Gen 14:18-22), which has also turned up in the *Genesis Apocryphon* from Qumran Cave 1 (12:17; 20:12, 16; 21:2, 20; 22:15, 16 [bis], 21). The title, as used here, supplies a Palestinian Jewish background for the address of the Gerasene demoniac in Mark 5:7; Luke 8:28: υἱὲ τοῦ θεοῦ ὑψίστου, "Son of God Most High."

Seventh, the attestation of the title "Son of God" in this pre-Christian Qumran text makes it possible that it was used of Jesus in the primitive kerygma formulated by Jewish Christians in Palestine. In other words, such a title for him was not necessarily developed as the product of Christian missionary activity among Gentiles in the eastern Mediterranean world.

Lastly, although in Psalm 2 the term "son" is related to "begetting," the titles in this Aramaic text do not directly express such a relation. The kingly figure to whom the titles are attributed is not said to be divinely begotten. Hence, when this notion eventually enters the Christian tradition about Jesus, it may be partly dependent on the formulation of Ps 2:7, but may also be derived from a tradition that goes beyond the psalm and such titles as are found in this Qumran Aramaic text. The connotations with which the New Testament title "Son of God" for Jesus is fraught remain unexpressed in this text, such as the implication of preexistence, incarnation, or miraculous conception. It is scarcely to be expected that a Palestinian Jewish text mentioning "Son of God" would carry all the nuances or connotations that came to be associated with such a title for Jesus in the New Testament and in the later Christian theology.

This occurrence of such Palestinian titles is admittedly isolated. How much more frequently they would have been in pre-Christian Jewish use, and with what specific nuance, is hard to say. One can raise such questions about them, but until the titles turn up again in some future discovery there is no answer to them. Now, however, we see at least that there is an Old Testament background and evidence of a pre-Christian Jewish usage of the New Testament title "Son of God."

---

21. Fitzmyer, *The Gospel according to Luke,* 1:41-47. Cf. J. A. Fitzmyer, *Luke the Theologian: Aspects of His Teaching* (New York/Mahwah, N.J.: Paulist, 1989) 3.

CHAPTER 5

Qumran Messianism

The noun "messianism" and the adjective "messianic" have in recent years been given a rubber-band extension. They have been made at times to include all sorts of expected figures in Jewish and Christian history. To point up the issue, I cite the often-used *Dictionary of the Bible* of J. L. McKenzie:

> In general messianism includes those ideas which represent the Israel of the future as identical with the universal kingdom of Yahweh. It is not quite the same as eschatology, which deals with the end of history as accomplished by an intervention of Yahweh, although messianism is at least partly eschatological; nor is it quite the same as apocalyptic thought, which represents the end of history as a world catastrophe, although some forms of messianism contain apocalyptic elements. In spite of the derivation of the word, messianism does not always include the idea of a future king or deliverer; some scholars insist that the term should be so restricted in order to distinguish messianism from eschatology.[1]

I class myself among those scholars whom McKenzie mentions in the last half of the last sentence.

1. J. L. McKenzie, *Dictionary of the Bible* (Milwaukee: Bruce, 1965) 569. McKenzie makes use of the article of A. Gelin, "Messianisme," *DBSup* 5 (1957) 1165-1212. Cf. J. J. Collins, "Messiahs in Context: Method in the Study of Messianism in the Dead Sea Scrolls," *Methods of Investigation of the Dead Sea Scrolls and the Khirbet Qumran Site: Present Realities and Future Prospects* (Annals of the New York Academy of Sciences 722; ed. M. O. Wise et al.; New York: New York Academy of Sciences, 1994) 213-29, esp. 214. See now also J. J. Collins, *The Scepter and the Star: The Messiahs of the Dead Sea Scrolls and Other Ancient Literature* (ABRL; New York: Doubleday, 1995).

More recently, Lawrence H. Schiffman has taken up the matter in his book, *Reclaiming the Dead Sea Scrolls*.[2] In earlier chapters I have already agreed with much that Schiffman has said about reclaiming the Jewish character of the Scrolls and putting them in a proper place in Jewish history. In his discussion of Qumran messianism one will find many good interpretative points and proper emphases, but I hesitate to go along with his two types of messianism among Jews, the restorative and the utopian.[3] That such ideas became characteristic of Jewish messianism in eras prior to the twentieth century I would not deny; that one can find that distinction in pre-Christian Judaism or in the Qumran period is difficult to admit.

No little confusion has been introduced into the discussion of Qumran messianism by the failure to keep "messianism" distinct from other forms of Jewish expectation and other forms of Jewish eschatological belief. Moreover, there is the tendency at times to confuse "eschatological" and "apocalyptic" in this recent debate.[4]

Related to this question is the way christological titles are predicated of Jesus of Nazareth in the New Testament. "Prophet," "Son of God," "Son of Man," "Lord," and "Messiah" are used of him in various New Testament writings, where they are all attributed to one individual. In effect, such conflation in Christian thinking is the culmination and fulfillment of different or varied strands of Old Testament and extrabiblical Jewish teaching that have usually been discrete. They are conflated and attributed to him, who is for Christians the "Savior, Messiah, Lord" (Luke 2:11). Christians even speak of him as the "suffering Messiah," as Lucan theology has taught them (Luke 24:26; cf. Acts 3:18; 17:3; 26:23), but the problem has always been to explain whence Luke derived such a notion of a *suffering* Messiah, which is not found in the Old Testament.[5] Moreover, such New Testament conflation has made some Christian scholars claim at times that "Son of God" is a "messianic" title, even though no one can detect such a use of this title in pre-Christian Jewish his-

---

2. L. H. Schiffman, *Reclaiming the Dead Sea Scrolls: The History of Judaism, the Background of Christianity, The Lost Library of Qumran* (Philadelphia: Jewish Publication Society, 1994; reprinted in ABRL; New York: Doubleday, 1995) 317-50.

3. See also L. H. Schiffman, "The Concept of the Messiah in Second Temple and Rabbinic Literature," *RevExp* 84 (1987) 235-46. Cf. A. I. Baumgarten, "Rabbinic Literature as a Source for the History of Jewish Sectarianism in the Second Temple Period," *DSD* 2 (1995) 14-57.

4. Although McKenzie does not confuse them in the above quotation, he does relate them and hints at a definition of "apocalyptic" that is part of the problem.

5. *Pace* R. A. Rosenberg ("The Slain Messiah in the Old Testament," *ZAW* 99 [1987] 259-61), there is no slain messiah in the Old Testament.

tory. They are used together in John 11:27, σὺ εἶ ὁ Χριστὸς ὁ υἱὸς τοῦ θεοῦ, "You are the Messiah, the Son of God" (cf. 20:31), and that is what one would expect in such a Christian Gospel. Being found in the Gospel according to John, the last of the four Gospels to be written, it represents the culmination of the Christian conflation of titles attributed to Jesus.

Furthermore, the problem of conflation is not found only among Christians, because in Jewish usage, especially during the early Christian centuries, one also finds conflation, even if it is not the same as the Christian. For instance, the Isaian Servant becomes "My servant, the Messiah" (*Tg. Jonathan,* Isa 42:1 [in some copies]; 43:10; 52:13; 53:10).[6] This problem is compounded by the messianic interpretation of still other Old Testament passages, which in the Hebrew have no mention of משיח. Such interpretation is found in the classic targums (e.g., Gen 49:10; Num 24:17 in *Tg. Onqelos*).[7] This interpretation of Old Testament passages in the targums is also problematic, because the date of this targumic tradition does not certainly antedate the third century A.D. One wonders whether this identification of certain Old Testament figures with the Messiah is not a reaction to Christian teaching about Jesus of Nazareth, that he was God's Messiah. Since it surfaces only when Christianity is already well under way, it seems like a reaction to Christian doctrine as Jewish targumic translators sought to identify who in the Old Testament were Messiahs for the Jewish people.

The problem is further compounded by the fact that משיח is not always used in the same sense in the Old Testament itself, to which one has to trace the origin of both the title and the idea of messianism. Indeed, the same can be said of other christological titles in the New Testament. Yet because they all represent, in fact, outgrowths of strands of Old Testament teaching, which

6. See A. Sperber, *The Bible in Aramaic Based on Old Manuscripts and Printed Texts* (4 vols., vol. 4 in two parts; Leiden: Brill, 1959-73) 3:84, 87, 107, 108. Cf. J. F. Stenning, *The Targum of Isaiah Edited with a Translation* (Oxford: Clarendon, 1949) 141, 145, 179, 181; B. D. Chilton, *The Isaiah Targum: Introduction, Translation, Apparatus and Notes* (Aramaic Bible 11; Wilmington, Del.: Glazier, 1987) 80, 84, 103, 104.

Note also the insertion of משיחא in *Tg. Jonathan* of Isa 4:2; 9:5; 10:27; 11:1, 6; 14:29; 16:1, 5; 28:5. In all these instances there is no mention of משיח in the Hebrew text of Isaiah. In that prophetic book, the title is given only to Cyrus, the Persian king (Isa 45:1). Cf. R. A. Aytoun, "The Servant of the Lord in the Targum," *JTS* 23 (1921-22) 172-80; P. Humbert, "Le Messie dans le targum des prophètes," *RTP* 43 (1910) 420-27; 44 (1911) 5-46; A. S. van der Woude, *TDNT,* 9:524.

7. See further S. H. Levey, *The Messiah: An Aramaic Interpretation: The Messianic Exegesis of the Targum* (Cincinnati: Hebrew Union College, 1974); M. McNamara, *The New Testament and the Palestinian Targum to the Pentateuch* (AnBib 27; Rome: Biblical Institute, 1966) 238-52.

initially appear independently of one another, one should respect this independent emergence and not conflate or confuse either their denotations or the connotations associated with them, until they appear in history. Above all, one should allow for the development of each of them, which is part of their historical usage. When in the course of time they are conflated in certain texts, even in Jewish texts, then it is admissible to conflate the connotations of one title with another; but even then the denotation should remain distinct and should be respected. In doing this, one respects *the history of ideas,* for such titles did not all emerge at the same time in the history of Israel or even relate to one another at the same time.

I shall devote my further remarks on this topic to three headings: the Old Testament data that deal with משיח; the Qumran and related data; and implications of Qumran messianism for New Testament usage.

Old Testament Data Dealing with משיח

We must distinguish the noun משיח, *māšîăḥ,* "anointed one," from uses of the verb משח, "anoint." The verb "anoint" is used often enough, but hardly any of its occurrences has to do with an expected or eschatological figure; so they do not concern us now.[8]

In the Old Testament, the noun משיח occurs thirty-nine times in all. Once it may refer to Saul's shield (2 Sam 1:21), or perhaps to Saul himself. In two instances commentators debate whether the term is used of Israel as a whole or to its reigning king: Hab 3:13; Ps 28:8. Otherwise in the vast majority of occurrences it refers to a king (usually of Israel), contemporary or past. Its basic denotation is that such a historical ruler is or was an anointed agent of God designated for the guidance, governance, or deliverance of His people.

8. The verb משח occurs sixty-nine times in the MT. Almost half of the instances have to do with the anointing of Aaron and his sons, priests, the altar, or other cultic objects; the other half occur in passages mentioning the anointing of historical kings (Saul, David, Solomon, Absalom, Hazael, Jehu, Joash, Jehoahaz). There is never an instance of the verb that refers to a Messiah (in the strict sense of a future or expected anointed figure).

Cf. J. Becker, *Messianic Expectation in the Old Testament* (Philadelphia: Fortress, 1980); J. J. M. Roberts, "The Old Testament Contribution to Messianic Expectations," in *The Messiah: Developments in Earliest Judaism and Christianity* (The First Princeton Symposium on Judaism and Christian Origins; ed. J. H. Charlesworth et al.; Minneapolis: Fortress, 1992) 39-51; R. E. Clements, "The Messianic Hope in the Old Testament," *JSOT* 43 (1989) 3-19; J. L. Sicre, *De David al Mesías: Textos básicos de la esperanza mesiánica* (Colección 'El Mundo de la Biblia'; Estella: Editorial Verbo Divino, 1995).

In time, especially when the monarchy was no more, the title was applied to the high priest. In a few instances it may be attributed to prophets or patriarchs, but there the matter is disputed. The instances are as follows:

1. Kings
   a. A king in a generic sense or an unnamed king of the Davidic dynasty: 1 Sam 2:10, 35; 16:6; Ps 2:2; 20:7; 84:10; possibly 28:8 (see above)
   b. Saul: called משיח יהוה, "Yahweh's Anointed One," in 1 Sam 24:7, 7, 11; 26:9, 11, 16, 23; 2 Sam 1:14, 16; cf. 1 Sam 12:3, 5
   c. David (as a historical king): 2 Sam 19:22; 22:51; 23:1; Ps 18:51; 89:39, 52; 132:10, 17 (in some of the last-mentioned instances משיח is also extended to descendants of David)
   d. Solomon: 2 Chr 6:42
   e. Zedekiah: Lam 4:20 (cf. 2 Kgs 25:4-6)
   e. Cyrus, king of Persia: Isa 45:1
2. Priests
   הכהן המשיח, "the anointed priest": Lev 4:3, 5, 16; 6:15
3. Prophets/Patriarchs[9]
   1 Chr 16:22; Ps 105:15
4. Dan 9:25, 26 (to be discussed below)

What should be noted about these occurrences, first of all, is the books in which they occur. There is no reference to a king as משיח in the Pentateuch,[10] or to a king of Israel as such in any of the major prophets. King

9. See the commentators on these debated passages. Cf. J. Giblet, "Prophétisme et attente d'un messie prophète dans l'ancien judaïsme," in *L'Attente du Messie* (RechBib 1; Bruges: Desclée de Brouwer, 1958) 85-130. Note the anointing of prophets in 1 Kgs 19:16 and Isa 61:1.

10. This is undoubtedly the reason for the failure of the Samaritans to believe in a coming Messiah. Instead, they spoke of *hat-Tāhēb* (Hebrew) or *Tāhēbāh* (Aramaic), "the Returning One" (*Memar Marqah* 2:9; 4:11, 12), undoubtedly a development in Samaritan teaching of the prophet like Moses (Deut 18:15, 18). The name *Tāhēbāh* is sometimes translated as "Restorer," but rightly? See J. Macdonald, *Memar Marqah: The Teaching of Marqah* (2 vols.; BZAW 84; Berlin: Töpelmann, 1963) 1:44, 108, 110-11. Cf. A. Merx, *Der Messias oder Ta'eb der Samaritaner: Nach bisher unbekannten Quellen* (BZAW 17; Giessen: Töpelmann, 1909) 34-45; J. Macdonald, *The Theology of the Samaritans* (London: SCM, 1964) 362-71; J. A. Montgomery, *The Samaritans: The Earliest Jewish Sect: Their History, Theology and Literature* (1907; reprint, New York: Ktav, 1968) 246-51; R. J. Coggins, *Samaritans and Jews: The Origins of Samaritanism Reconsidered* (Atlanta: John Knox, 1975) 146.

Zedekiah is the sole instance in Lam 4:20, which in the Hebrew Scriptures is found among the "Writings." Cyrus, King of Persia, is the only one called מְשִׁיחוֹ, "his anointed One," in the book of Isaiah (45:1).[11]

Second, some of these passages, where מָשִׁיחַ may be used of David or his dynasty (1 Sam 2:10, 35; Ps 2:2; 132:17), celebrate the king's accession to the throne. In one or other of them one may detect the *seeds* of a teaching about a future or awaited king or his everlasting dynasty, but it is not yet messianism in the full-blown sense and does not use the term.

The origins of messianism are to be traced, indeed, to various divine promises in the Old Testament of a guaranteed and enduring succession of David's dynasty or of a future "David," but here one has to respect the vague or nebulous form of such promises.[12] Shortly before the destruction of Jerusalem in the early sixth century B.C., the prophet Jeremiah announced: "Therefore thus says the LORD concerning Jehoiakim, king of Judah, 'He shall have none to sit upon the throne of David; his dead body shall be cast out to the heat by day and the frost by night'" (36:30; cf. 22:30). Yet the same prophet also announced: "It shall come to pass in that day, says the LORD of hosts, that I will break the yoke off their necks and burst their bonds, and strangers shall no more make slaves of them. They shall serve the LORD, their God, and David, their king, whom I will raise up for them" (30:9).[13] Or again, Jeremiah announces: "Behold, days are coming, says the LORD, when I will raise up for David a righteous Scion (צֶמַח צַדִּיק);[14] he shall reign as king, deal wisely, and execute justice and righteousness in the land. In his days Judah shall be saved, and Israel shall live in safety" (23:5-6; cf. Jer 33:14-22; 22:4-5;

11. As J. J. Collins rightly notes, Cyrus is not one who would restore the Davidic kingship, but is rather "an agent of deliverance for the Jewish people" (*The Scepter and the Star*, 31).

12. Note how it is still formulated as late as 1 Macc 2:57: "David, because he was merciful, inherited a kingly throne (or: a throne of kingship) forever." David is not called "Messiah" in this passage, even though the writing comes from a late period in Judaism when the title in the full-blown sense is already attested.

13. A similar idea is found in Hos 3:5: "Afterward the children of Israel shall return and seek the LORD their God, and David their king." Some commentators think that the last phrase is a Judean addition of later date.

14. צֶמַח means "sprout, shoot, branch," but it can be used of a "descendant." This promise is echoed in Zech 3:8: "Behold, I am bringing my servant, the Scion." It is a clear reference to the same Davidic heir. Some commentators find it to be an echo of Isa 4:2, where צֶמַח יְהוָה occurs as well, and even of Isa 11:1, where צֶמַח does not occur but rather נֵצֶר, "a branch" from his (i.e., Jesse's) roots. Cf. Isa 9:6-7 (the one to sit "upon the throne of David" is described in terms that will later be used to describe the expected Messiah; but that seated one is *not yet so entitled* in Isaiah 9); cf. 32:1-5.

30:21). To these texts of Jeremiah one can add similar passages in Ezekiel, for example, 34:23-24 ("I will set up over them one shepherd, my servant David, and he shall feed them and be their shepherd. I, the Lord, will be their God, and my servant David shall be prince among them"[15]); 37:24-25; 17:3-4, 22-23. In none of these texts, which promise the coming of a future "David" or a "righteous Scion," is there mention of משיח, "anointed one," or of any anointing. Even though משיח has already been used of the historical David (in texts of an earlier date?), its absence in the context of these promises is not to be overlooked.[16] משיח as a future or expected "Messiah" has not yet entered the history of Jewish ideas.

Third, what is reflected in these passages is the growth of a tradition about David. That tradition grew up independently of Israel's ancient credo derived from earlier times: its belief in what Yahweh had done for it in constituting Israel as His people. With the passage of time, especially with the formation of the monarchy, the Davidic tradition grew, for instance, in the work of the Deuteronomist. Eventually the two traditions were fused, and then in the time of exilic and postexilic writers (Ezekiel, Second Isaiah, Haggai, Zechariah, Nehemiah) one begins to read of Yahweh's intervention on behalf of David and his dynasty as the continuation of His salvific deeds recalled in Israel's ancient credo.

John J. Collins admits that "we have very little evidence of messianism in Judaism in the period 500-200 BCE."[17] What he claims to be "messianic" before 500 is non-existent. Whenever משיח is applied to figures before 500 B.C., they are historical persons, and in no sense expected or eschatological figures.

Fourth, along with the promise of a future "David," who will reign as

15. Note how רעה, "shepherd," is used, not משיח.

16. For this reason I cannot agree with the analysis of the "biblical background" of messianism given by Schiffman (*Reclaiming the Dead Sea Scrolls,* 318-21), if by that term he means that a "Messiah" is already mentioned there. He considers such texts as the following to supply that background: 2 Samuel 7; 22:44-51 (= Ps 18:44-51); 23:1-3,5; references to the "Day of the Lord" in Amos; Zech 6:9-16; Sir 36:11-14. In none of these texts, which may well be eschatological, is there mention of משיח in the sense of a future, awaited Messiah. True, משיח occurs in 2 Sam 22:51 (= Ps 18:51), but that refers to the historical King David, on whom, as "His anointed," God has already bestowed "great victories." The mention there of "David and his offspring forever" makes of that verse the background for the development of messianism only in the sense that I have mentioned above; it supplies the "seeds" of the idea (a "David" of the future), but not the full-grown tree. In the texts cited by Schiffman one finds only a divine promise about the enduring and guaranteed character of the Davidic dynasty, but that is not yet "messianism."

17. Collins, *The Scepter and the Star,* 33; see also p. 40.

king and deal wisely and righteously with God's people, there eventually is formulated the coming of a משׁיח, "an anointed one," that is, a future anointed agent of Yahweh to be sent on behalf of His people. This we see in Dan 9:25-26:

מן מצא דבר להשׁיב ולבנות ירושׁלם עד משׁיח נגיד שׁבעים שׁבעה
ושׁבעים שׁשׁים ושׁנים תשׁוב ונבנתה רחוב וחרוץ ובצוק העתים
ואחרי השׁבעים שׁשׁים ושׁנים יכרת משׁיח ואין לו

> from the utterance of a word to restore and build Jerusalem until (the coming of) an anointed one, a prince, there shall be seven weeks. Then for sixty-two weeks it shall be built again with squares and moats, but in a time of trouble. And after the sixty-two weeks (the) anointed one shall be cut off and have nothing.

This passage in Daniel is part of the prophecy of seventy weeks about the rebuilding and restoration of Jerusalem, the explanation of an oracle once uttered by Jeremiah (25:11-12; 29:10). I have left the translation of משׁיח as "an anointed one," because one may debate whether "Messiah" would be proper in this case, just as one debates about the one to whom the coming prince (נגיד) refers. This is the only place in the Hebrew Scriptures, however, where one finds *māšîăḥ* used in a temporal phrase with the preposition *'ad*, implying a term of expectation and expressing a future or coming "anointed one." It thus contributes in its own way to the emergence of a real messianic expectation among the Jewish people. When Collins discusses this passage in Daniel 9, he speaks of it as "the Transformation of Messianism,"[18] whereas he should have spoken of it as the emergence of messianism, because up to this point in the history of the Jewish people there has not yet been messianism. So it is against this entire, complicated Old Testament background that one has to judge the teaching about expected anointed figures in the Qumran texts.

Fifth, from the foregoing survey it should be clear that I do not consider

---

18. Ibid., 34. On p. 37 he more correctly says, "Rather than messianic expectation, ... what we have in Daniel is a transformation of the royal mythology." That is what Collins should have been saying all along, because "there is no evidence for true messianism until the second century B.C." (Becker, *Messianic Expectation,* 50). I am not sure, however, that "there is no role here for a Davidic king" (*The Scepter and the Star,* 37); to my way of thinking, that is exactly what Dan 9:25 is talking about. On the contrary, Collins maintains that Dan 9:25-26 refers to High Priests (pp. 11, 143) or "historical High Priests" (p. 34): "Joshua the postexilic High Priest, who was one of the two 'sons of oil' in Zechariah" and Onias III (pp. 34-35).

such Old Testament passages that express various divine promises of a guaranteed perpetual succession of David's dynasty to be messianic in the proper sense: such as Gen 49:10; Num 24:15-19; 2 Sam 7:11-17; 22:44-51 (= Ps 18:44-51); 23:1-3, 5; Isa 11:1-9; Amos 9:11; Zech 3:8; 6:12-13. As Collins has well put it (in writing about 2 Sam 7:11-17), "The emphasis . . . is on the permanence of the Davidic line, not on an individual king."[19] When such passages speak of future figures or promise that the Davidic dynasty will last forever, those figures are not *eo ipso* anointed "messiahs" without further ado. Some of these Old Testament passages are associated in later times with messianic figures (e.g., in some Qumran texts or in the targums), but then that is part of the *further development.* Such passages then take on further connotations, which they did not have in their original formulation; they then become "messianic."

Sixth, before we proceed to the analysis of Qumran texts, we should note the way some modern Jewish scholars interpret messianism and its relation to their Hebrew Scriptures. As an example, I cite the article on the "Messiah" from the *Encyclopaedia Judaica,* which was written by H. L. Ginsberg, D. Flusser, and others. Ginsberg defines the Messiah as

a charismatically endowed descendant of David who the Jews of the Roman period believed would be raised up by God to break the yoke of the heathen and to reign over a restored kingdom of Israel to which all the Jews of the Exile would return. This is a strictly postbiblical concept. Even Haggai and Zechariah, who expected the Davidic kingdom to be renewed with a specific individual, Zerubbabel, at its head, thought of him only as a feature of the new age, not as the author or even agent of its establishment. One can, therefore, only speak of the biblical prehistory of messianism.[20]

Ginsberg then lays out the biblical material, in a way similar to what I have given above. In the continuation of that article, Flusser builds on what Ginsberg has already laid out.[21] Significantly, such modern Jewish scholars treat messianism as a phenomenon in Judaism that emerged in the Roman period.[22] I personally hesitate to date the emergence of messianism as late as Ginsberg does, because one usually reckons with 63 B.C. as the beginning of Roman rule in Judea. I should rather date it as emerging toward the end of

19. Collins, *The Scepter and the Star,* 23.

20. *Encyclopaedia Judaica* (Jerusalem: Keter; New York: Macmillan, 1971) 11:1407.

21. D. Flusser, "Messiah: Second Temple Period," ibid., 11:1408-10.

22. See also S. Talmon, "The Concepts of *Māšîaḥ* and Messianism in Early Judaism," in Charlesworth, ed., *The Messiah,* 79-115; L. H. Schiffman, "The Concept."

the Hellenistic period. If 165 B.C. is taken as the date of the final redaction of the book of Daniel, then messianism must have emerged not later than the second quarter of the second pre-Christian century, possibly even in its first quarter; at any rate, shortly before the Essenes of Qumran came on the scene.

Seventh, by contrast to such Jewish interpretations of messianism and its relation to the Hebrew Scriptures, I cite the recent interpretation of a Christian scholar, John Collins, who maintains that he is concerned "primarily with Jewish messianism,"[23] but who finds the term of the development about the Davidic dynasty already in its origins. He predicates "messiah" or "messianic" of figures in the Old Testament who are not yet so labeled and thus fails to reckon with the late date when "messianism" really emerges. He does not allow for the development of ideas in Judaism and thus rides roughshod over the history of ideas.

Qumran and Related Data

It is not easy to present the Qumran messianic material because there is still little consensus about the chronological order of the pertinent texts.[24] So I shall line up the Qumran texts as best I can and give an interpretation of what is important in them.

1. 1QS 9:11[25]

ונשפטו במשפטים הרשונים אשר החלו אנשי היחד ל<ה>תיסר בם
עד בוא נביא ומשיחי אהרון וישראל

... but they shall be governed by the first regulations, by which the men of the community began to be instructed, until the coming of a prophet and the Messiahs of Aaron and Israel.

23. Collins, *The Scepter and the Star*, 3.

24. For attempts to show development in Qumran messianic teaching, see J. Starcky, "Les quatres étapes du messianisme à Qumrân," *RB* 70 (1963) 481-505; but cf. R. E. Brown, "J. Starcky's Theory of Qumrân Messianic Development," *CBQ* 28 (1966) 51-57. See also G. J. Brooke, "The Messiah of Aaron in the *Damascus Document*," *RevQ* 15 (1991-92) 215-30; A. Caquot, "Le messianisme qumrânien," in *Qumran: Sa piété, sa théologie et son milieu* (BETL 46; ed. M. Delcor; Paris/Gembloux: Duculot; Louvain: Leuven University, 1978) 231-47.

25. See M. Burrows, *The Dead Sea Scrolls of St. Mark's Monastery: Volume II, Fascicle 2: Plates and Transcription of the Manual of Discipline* (New Haven, Conn.: American Schools of Oriental Research, 1951) pl. 9.

This passage from the *Serek hayyaḥad,* or *Manual of Discipline,* deals with the continuing validity of the "counsels of the Law," the primitive precepts in which members of the community were once instructed and which they were to continue to observe, apparently as a preparation for the coming of expected figures. Such a requirement also finds an echo in CD 6:11, but this passage clearly affirms the community's expectation of three coming figures: a *prophet* (undoubtedly a prophet like Moses, an allusion to Deut 18:15, 18),[26] a (priestly) *Messiah of Aaron,* and a (kingly or Davidic) *Messiah of Israel.* The imagery behind the last two terms can be found in "Israel" and "Aaron," as used in 1QS 8:5-9; 9:5-7.

The expectation of a Messiah of Israel is a natural development of the Old Testament promise of a future "David," and also of the משיח נגיד of Dan 9:25.

Even though משיח was applied in post-monarchical times to a historical priest in Leviticus 4, it is a surprise to see a priestly figure become part of the Qumran community's messianic expectations, because there is little in the Old Testament itself about a future "priest," unless Zech 6:13b is so understood. The Qumran formulation goes beyond Zech 6:13 in making such a priest a "Messiah of Aaron." If the primitive nucleus, however, of the Qumran community stemmed from priestly families, as many hold, then it is really not surprising that a priestly Messiah would join such expectations.[27]

The whole last clause of 1QS 9:11, however, is missing in 4QSᵉ (4Q259) 1 iii 6, the oldest copy of the *Serek,* which has 1QS 9:12 following directly on

---

26. This allusion is confirmed by the quotation in 4QTestim 1-8 of Deut 18:18-19, preceded by Deut 5:28-29, a combination already found in the Samaritan Pentateuch of Exod 20:21. See notes 76-77 below. There is no evidence that the Teacher of Righteousness was regarded as returning as this prophet like Moses, despite claims to the contrary. See further J. J. Collins, "Teacher and Messiah? The One Who Will Teach Righteousness at the End of Days," in *The Community of the Renewed Covenant: The Notre Dame Symposium on the Dead Sea Scrolls* (ed. E. Ulrich and J. VanderKam; Notre Dame: University of Notre Dame Press, 1994) 193-210, esp. 205-6 and n. 39. With this expectation, one should not confuse that of *Elias redivivus,* which is a development of Mal 3:1, "the messenger to prepare the way before me," eventually identified as "Elijah the prophet," who will come "before the great and awesome day of the LORD" (Eng. 4:5). See n. 66 below.

27. The expectation of a coming "new priest" is also mentioned in *T. Levi* 18:1 (τότε ἐγερεῖ κύριος ἱερέα καινόν), which is problematic, because this passage may be a Christian gloss. See M. de Jonge, "The Testaments of the Twelve Patriarchs," in *The Apocryphal Old Testament* (ed. H. F. D. Sparks; Oxford: Clarendon, 1984) 505-600, esp. 536. Cf. J. J. Collins, "Teacher and Messiah?" 207; J. VanderKam, "Messianism in the Scrolls," in Ulrich and VanderKam, eds., *The Community,* 211-34, esp. 220.

1QS 8:12.[28] It thus raises a question about the time when this expectation rose in the Qumran community and about the composite character of the *Manual of Discipline,* which apparently passed through different stages of composition or redaction.[29] As a result, this reference to two messiahs in 1QS 9:11 may be unique and has to be compared with statements in *Damascus Document* (see CD passages below).

2. 1QSa 2:11-12[30]

[אל] זה מו[שב אנשי השם [קריאי] מועד לעצת היחד אם יוליד
א[ת] המשיח אתם יבוא [ב]רואש כול עדת ישראל וכול א[חיו
בני] אהרון הכוהנים

[This is the as]sembly of the men of renown [summoned] to a meeting for the council of the community, when [God] will beget the Messiah among them. He will enter [at] the head of all the congregation of Israel and all [his] br[others, the sons] of Aaron, the priests.

This passage is controverted, because some think that the reading יוליד is not correct, but it is practically certain.[31] Noteworthy, however, is the men-

---

28. See J. T. Milik, *TYDWJ*, 124. Cf. J. H. Charlesworth et al., eds., *The Dead Sea Scrolls: Hebrew, Aramaic, and Greek Texts with English Translations: Volume 1, Rule of the Community and Related Documents* (Tübingen: Mohr Siebeck; Louisville: Westminster John Knox, 1994) 88-89; F. García Martínez, *The Dead Sea Scrolls Translated: The Qumran Texts in English* (trans. W. G. E. Watson; Leiden: Brill, 1994) 27.

29. J. VanderKam notes, however, that 4QS[e] may be "defective," or actually a classic case of haplography ("Messianism in the Scrolls," 213). Cf. J. Pouilly, *La règle de la communauté de Qumrân: Son évolution littéraire* (Cahiers de la *RB* 17; Paris: Gabalda, 1976) 15-34.

30. See D. Barthélemy and J. T. Milik, *Qumran Cave I* (DJD 1; Oxford: Clarendon, 1955) 110. The original editor called it "Règle de la Congrégation," which is certainly a better title than the misnomer, "Messianic Rule," used by G. Vermes, *The Dead Sea Scrolls in English* (3d ed.; London: Penguin, 1987) 100; cf. Collins, *The Scepter and the Star,* 75.

31. Barthélemy originally read יוליד, calling this reading "pratiquement certaine," but later accepted Milik's emendation of יוליך and translated the clause, "au cas où *Dieu* mènerait le Messie avec eux" (*Qumran Cave I,* 117 [his italics]). Other scholars, however, have insisted that the final letter is indeed a *dalet*. See F. M. Cross, *Die antike Bibliothek von Qumran und die moderne biblische Wissenschaft* (Neukirchen: Neukirchener Verlag, 1967) 94 n. 71: "Dalet ist nahezu sicher." Note also Cross's rejection of T. H. Gaster's attempt to read the text differently, in Cross, *The Ancient Library of Qumran* (3d ed.; Minneapolis: Fortress, 1995) 76 n. 3, where Cross, surprisingly, now toys with the possibility of reading יוליך, even while admitting that "the fifth letter, *dalet* is virtually certain . . . : *ywlyd.*" Cf. J. M. Allegro, "Further Messianic References in Qumran Literature," *JBL* 75 (1956) 174-87,

tion of only one Messiah (with the definite article). Although in the next two passages derived from the same context mention is made of the Messiah of Israel, "the priest" is given precedence over him in lines 19-21. Consequently המשיח here may possibly refer to the Messiah of Aaron, the priestly Messiah, who is then the likely subject of the following verb יבוא, "he will enter."

3. 1QSa 2:14-15[32]

ואחר י[שב מש]יח ישראל וישבו לפניו ראשי א[לפי ישראל אי]ש
לפי כבודו

And afterwards the [Mes]siah of Israel shall ta[ke his seat]. Then there will sit before him the heads of the th[ousands of Israel, ea]ch according to his dignity.

The crucial term is partly restored, but with certainty. The passage speaks of the Messiah of Israel, expected to join an assembly of the community "at the end of days." The word ואחר, "and afterward," comes after the mention of [הכוהן], "the priest" (restored with certainty), to whom the Messiah of Israel is subordinated.

4. 1QSa 2:20-21[33]

ואח[ר יש]לח משיח ישראל ידיו בלחם

And afterwards the Messiah of Israel will put forth his hands to the bread.

---

esp. 177 n. 28. Allegro states: ". . . a special infra-red photograph taken then [Summer of 1955] leaves no doubt as to the correctness of the editor's reading." P. W. Skehan, "Two Books on Qumrân Studies," *CBQ* 21 (1959) 71-78, esp. 74. H. N. Richardson, "Some Notes on 1QSa," *JBL* 76 (1957) 108-22, esp. 116-17 n. 53; E. Puech, "Fragment d'une apocalypse en araméen (4Q246 = pseudo-Dan[d]) et le 'royaume de Dieu,'" *RB* 99 (1992) 98-131, esp. 100 n. 6; VanderKam, "Messianism in the Scrolls," 221-24.

Cf. C. A. Evans, "A Note on the 'First-born Son' of 4Q369," *DSD* 2 (1995) 185-201, esp. 186-88; S. Talmon, "The Concepts," 110 n. 71; G. Vermes, *The Dead Sea Scrolls: Qumran in Perspective* (rev. ed.; Philadelphia: Fortress, 1977) 196; M. A. Knibb, *The Qumran Community* (Cambridge: Cambridge University Press, 1987) 153; M. Hengel, *The Son of God* (Philadelphia: Fortress, 1976) 44; P. Sigal, "Further Reflections on the 'Begotten' Messiah," *HAR* 7 (1983) 221-33; L. H. Schiffman, *The Eschatological Community of the Dead Sea Scrolls: A Study of the Rule of the Congregation* (SBLMS 38; Atlanta: Scholars, 1989) 53-54 (he follows the reading of J. Licht, יהודה מדבר ממגילות הסרכים מגילת: *The Rule Scroll* [Jerusalem: Bialik, 1965] 269-70).

32. See Barthélemy, *Qumran Cave I,* 110, 117-18.

33. Ibid., 111, 117-18.

In this case again the Messiah of Israel is preceded by הכוהן, "the priest" (2:19), who is to be the first to bless the bread and the new wine. It seems, then, that "the priest" (= the Messiah of Aaron?),[34] together with the Messiah of Israel, is expected to preside over a meal or a banquet באחרית הימים, "at the end of days." "The priest" (= the Messiah of Aaron?) and "the Messiah of Israel" in these two passages of 1QSa would thus agree with 1QS 9:11 and undoubtedly represent an explicit messianic development of שני בני היצהר, "the two sons of oil," of Zech 4:14.

5. 1QM 11:7-8[35]

וביד משיחיכה הוזי תעודות הגדתה לנו ק[צי] מלחמות ידיכה

And through your Anointed Ones, who discern (your) testimonies, you have told us about the ti[mes] of the battles of your hands. . . .

This passage is difficult to interpret, because it is a poetic composition that refers not to expected figures, but to figures of the past, probably ancient prophets of Israel. In the immediately preceding context, the author alludes to Num 24:17-19, so that Balaam might be considered among such anointed ones.

6. 1Q30 1:2[36]

[. . .]שיח הקודש[מ . . .]

. . . the holy [M]essiah (lit., the anointed one of holiness).

The context is lost, and it is impossible to say whether משיח is being used in a future sense or not. A parallel expression is found in CD 6:1 below.[37]

---

34. The text is so understood also by Collins (*The Scepter and the Star*, 76) and many others.

35. See E. L. Sukenik, אוצר המגילות הגנוזות שבידי האוניברסיטה העברית (Jerusalem: Bialik Institute and the Hebrew University, 1954) pl. 26.

36. See Barthélemy and Milik, *Qumran Cave I*, 132 (+ pl. XXX).

37. M. G. Abegg, Jr., "The Messiah at Qumran: Are We Still Seeing Double?" *DSD* 2 (1995) 125-44, esp. 134; he tries to relate this instance to 1QSa 2:11.

7. 4QpGen^a (4Q252) 1 v 3-4 (olim 4QPBless)[38]

‏[ואל]פי ישראל המה הדגלים *(vacat)* עד בוא משיח הצדק צמח /
‏דויד כי לו ולזרעו נתנה ברית מלכות עמו עד דורות עולם...

... and the thousands of Israel are "the standards" until the coming of the righteous Messiah (lit., the anointed one of righteousness), the Scion of David. For to him and to his offspring has been given the covenant of kingship over (lit., of) His people for everlasting generations.

In this passage the biblical term "Scion" is explicitly joined with "David" and related to a coming Messiah, to whom is now attributed the quality of "righteousness," as it was to the Scion in Jer 23:5 (‏והקמתי לדוד צמח צדיק, "I will raise up for David a righteous scion").

It occurs, moreover, in a comment on Gen 49:10,[39] which is significantly modified by the addition of ‏שליט, "a ruler." Instead of ‏לא יסור שבט מיהודה, "the scepter shall not depart from Judah," as Gen 49:10 reads, line 1 of column v has ‏[לו]א יסור שליט משבט יהודה, "A ruler shall not depart from the tribe of Judah." That person, a ruler, is further identified as ‏יושב כסא לדויד, "one sitting upon the throne of David," (line 2). This addition introduces a vague individual into the oracle of Genesis, which thus prepares for the mention of "the righteous Messiah, the Scion of David," in line 3. Here in this Qumran text one finds explicit reference to a kingly and Davidic Messiah, whose appearance will

---

38. G. Brooke, "252. 4QCommentary on Genesis A," in *Qumran Cave 4: XVII. Parabiblical Texts, Part 3* (DJD 22; ed. G. Brooke et al.; Oxford: Clarendon, 1996) 185-207, esp. 205-6. The text was partly published by J. M. Allegro, "Further Messianic References in Qumran Literature," *JBL* 75 (1956) 174-87, esp. 174-76 (+ pl. I). The six columns of fragment 1 are also found in B. Z. Wacholder and M. G. Abegg, *A Preliminary Edition of the Unpublished Dead Sea Scrolls: The Hebrew and Aramaic Texts from Cave Four* (4 fascicles; Washington, D.C.: Biblical Archaeology Society, 1991-96) 2:212-15, esp. 215. Cf. A. Steudel, "4QMidrEschat: 'A Midrash on Eschatology' (4Q174 + 4Q177)," in *The Madrid Qumran Congress: Proceedings of the International Congress on the Dead Sea Scrolls Madrid 18-21 March, 1991* (STDJ 11/1-2; ed. J. Trebolle Barrera and L. Vegas Montaner; Leiden: Brill, 1992) 2:531-41; eadem, *Der Midrasch zur Eschatologie aus der Qumrangemeinde (4QMidrEschat^{a.b})* (STDJ 13; Leiden: Brill, 1994); García Martínez, *The Dead Sea Scrolls Translated*, 215; R. H. Eisenman and M. Wise, *The Dead Sea Scrolls Uncovered: The First Complete Translation and Interpretation of 50 Key Documents Withheld for Over 35 Years* (Shaftesbury, Dorset: Element, 1992) 86-87; G. J. Brooke, "The Genre of 4Q252: From Poetry to Pesher," *DSD* 1 (1994) 160-79.

39. Gen 49:10b mentions ‏רגלים, "feet," a word that some have read in the Qumran commentary too, instead of "the standards," but the editor insists on the *dalet* as the correct reading in line 3, ‏הדגלים, "the standards," and not ‏הרגלים.

mark the eschaton. This Qumran passage is important because of the messianic interpretation that it finally gives to Gen 49:10, a passage which in itself makes no mention of a Messiah. It thus shows how the implicit thrust of the Old Testament thus finally comes to explicit formulation.

This instance, mentioning "the Scion of David," has to be related, moreover, to the person referred to in 4QFlor (4Q174) 1-2 i 11,[40] which speaks of God's establishing forever the royal throne of one to whom He will be father and whom He will regard as His son: הואה צמח דויד העומד עם דורש התורה אשר [. . .] בציון באחרית הימים, "He is the Scion of David who is to arise with the Interpreter of the Law, who [. . .] in Zion in the last days." Even though there is no mention of a "Messiah" in this case, the "Scion of David" clearly has to be understood as the same expected messianic figure as in 4QpGen[a] (4Q252). 4QpGen[a] is, then, a good example of how the biblical passages mentioning "Scion" are at length clearly related to משיח in a way they never were in the Old Testament itself — a significant development in the history of Jewish ideas. At this stage I have no difficulty in admitting that the "Scion of David" is the same as משיח ישראל, and that the "Interpreter of the Law" is undoubtedly the same as משיח אהרון, as Collins has maintained.[41]

8. 6QD (6Q15) 3:4[42]

ביד מש]ה וג]ם [במשיחי הקודש[

(They preached rebellion against the commandments of God given) [through Mo]ses and al]so by the holy anointed ones (lit., the anointed ones of holiness).

This text is supposed to correspond to CD 5:21–6:2 (see below). It seems to be related to the expression cited in the broken text of number 6

40. See J. M. Allegro, *Qumrân Cave 4: I (4Q158-4Q186)* (DJD 5; Oxford: Clarendon, 1968) 53-57; cf. *JBL* 75 (1956) 176-77; G. J. Brooke, *Exegesis at Qumran: 4QFlorilegium in Its Jewish Context* (JSOTSup 29; Sheffield: JSOT Press, 1985) 204. Brooke notes that this text preserves part of Deuteronomy 33, which in verse 10 says of the descendants of Levi, "they shall teach Jacob your ordinances and Israel your law." In 4QpIsa[a] 7-10 iii 22, צמח is restored (almost with certainty) to produce another instance of the Scion of David: [צמח] דויד העומד באח]רית הימים], "[the Scion of] David who arises at the en[d of days]."

41. See Collins, "Teacher and Messiah?" 207.

42. See M. Baillet, J. T. Milik, and R. de Vaux, *Les 'petites grottes' de Qumrân: Exploration de la falaise, Les grottes 2Q, 3Q, 5Q, 6Q, 7Q à 10Q; Le rouleau de cuivre* (DJD 3; 2 vols.; Oxford: Clarendon, 1962) 128-31, esp. 130. Cf. García Martínez, *The Dead Sea Scrolls Translated*, 71.

above (1Q30 1:2), where משיח is singular. Since it speaks of משיחי in the past, it is not a reference to expected Messiahs, but undoubtedly refers to prophets of old.

9. CD 2:12[43]

ויודיעם ביד משיחו רוח קדשו וחוזי אמת<ו>

And He instructed them through (those) anointed with His holy Spirit and those who perceive <His> fidelity (lit., through anointed ones of His holy Spirit).

In this passage one should most likely read the construct plural משיחי, as in 6QD 3:4 (text 8 above), instead of משיחו. A less likely interpretation is to translate it: "And He made known His Holy Spirit to them through His anointed ones," understanding משיחו as defective writing for משיחיו.[44] In any case, the phrase, used with a past verb, again undoubtedly refers to prophets of old.

10. CD 5:21–6:2[45]

כי דברו סרה על מצות אל ביד משה וגם במשיחו הקודש וינבאו
שקר להשיב את ישראל מאחר אל

For they preached rebellion against the commandments of God (given) through Moses and also by the holy Anointed Ones; and they prophesied deceit to make Israel turn from following God.

In this passage one should again read the construct plural משיחי, as in 6QD 3:4, instead of משיחו. Again, the reference is probably to prophets of old. A slightly different form of this text is found in 4QD[b] (4Q267) 2:5-7:

כי דברו עצה סרה על מצוות אל בנ[י]ד [מוש]ה וגם במשיחי הקודש

---

43. See M. Broshi, ed., *The Damascus Document Reconsidered* (Jerusalem: Israel Exploration Society and the Shrine of the Book, Israel Museum, 1992) 12-13. Cf. S. Schechter, *Documents of Jewish Sectaries* (2 vols.; Cambridge: Cambridge University Press, 1910; reprinted with a prolegomenon by J. A. Fitzmyer; New York: Ktav, 1970) 1:xxxiii; C. Rabin, *The Zadokite Documents* (Oxford: Clarendon, 1954) 8-9.

44. So G. Vermes has taken it (*Dead Sea Scrolls in English,* 84). But cf. García Martínez, *The Dead Sea Scrolls Translated,* 34: "And he taught them by the hand of the anointed ones through his holy spirit and through seers of the truth."

45. See Broshi, ed., *Damascus Document,* 18-21.

וינבאו שקר לה[ש]יב את [ישר]אל מאחרי אל, but the translation would be the same.[46]

11. CD 12:23–13:1[47]

המתהלכים באלה בקץ הרשעה עד עמוד משוח אהרן וישראל עד
עשרה אנשים . . .

Those who walk according to these (statutes) in the wicked end-time until the rising of the Messiah of Aaron and Israel; and (they shall form groups) of up to ten men. . . .

Here one should read משיח. One might be tempted to read the plural משיח<י>, as in 1QS 9:11, but the medieval copy clearly reads the singular. The change to the singular has been thought to reflect a later understanding. Whereas the Qumran community looked forward to the coming of two Messiahs, the later copyist of this tenth-century manuscript seems to have adapted the text to the medieval belief in the coming of one Messiah.[48] However, the following text, especially in its 4Q form, reveals that the singular was already used at Qumran. So it raises the question of whether the Qumran community thought of one or two Messiahs throughout all the stages of its existence.[49]

12. CD 14:18–19[50]

וזה פרוש המשפטים אשר [ישפטו בהם בקץ הרשעה עד עמוד
משי[ח אהרן וישראל ויכפר עונם

---

46. See J. M. Baumgarten, *Qumran Cave 4: XIII. The Damascus Document (4Q266-273)* (DJD 18; Oxford: Clarendon, 1996) 97. The text can also be found in Wacholder and Abegg, *Preliminary Edition*, 1:28. The third word עצה, "counsel," is not found in CD 5:21, but that omission does not change the meaning. Cf. 4QD^d (4Q269) 4 i 2-3, which has preserved some of the same text, but not the crucial words משיחי הקודש. Cf. García Martínez, *The Dead Sea Scrolls Translated*, 60, 68.

47. See Broshi, ed., *Damascus Document*, 32-35.

48. See K. G. Kuhn, "The Two Messiahs of Aaron and Israel," in *The Scrolls and the New Testament* (ed. K. Stendahl with J. H. Charlesworth; New York: Crossroad, 1992 [originally 1957]) 54-64, esp. 59.

49. One would also have to reckon with the possibly distributive sense of the *nomen regens* in the construct chain; see S. Talmon, "The Concepts," in Charlesworth, ed., *The Messiah*, 105 n. 64; cf. Abegg, "The Messiah at Qumran," 129-30.

50. See Broshi, *Damascus Document*, 36-37.

This is the exact interpretation of the regulations [by] which [they will be judged in the wicked end-time, until the rising of the Mess]iah of Aaron and Israel, and he will expiate their iniquity.

Again the singular משיח appears, the first part of which is restored with certainty; note the singular verb that follows. A form of this text is found in 4QD^a (4Q266) 10 i 11-13:

וזה פרוש [המשפטים אשר יש]פטו בם עד {מ}<ע>מוד משיח אהרון
וישראל [ויכפר עונם]

Also possibly in the badly preserved 4QD^d (4Q269) 11 i 1-2: עד עמוד משיח]
א[הרון וישראל.⁵¹ Here the Messiah is to perform a notably priestly function (of expiation).

13. CD 19:10⁵²

והנשארים ימסרו לחרב בבוא משיח אהרן וישראל

And those who are left will be given over to the sword at the coming of the Messiah of Aaron and Israel.

Again, the singular Messiah appears, who is of both Aaron and Israel; his appearance marks the time of eschatological visitation.

14. CD 19:35–20:1⁵³

... מיום האסף {יור מורה} {מיום} מורה היחיד עד עמוד משיח
מאהרן ומישראל

... from the day of the gathering in {erasures} of the Teacher of the Community until the rising of a Messiah from Aaron and from Israel.

Instead of היחיד one should read היחד. It seems clear that the medieval copyist did not understand the meaning of יחד, "community," and so changed it to the better known יחיד. More interesting is the expectation of

---

51. See Baumgarten, *Qumran Cave 4: XIII*, 72, 134. Cf. Wacholder and Abegg, *Preliminary Edition*, 1:53; García Martínez, *The Dead Sea Scrolls Translated*, 69.

52. See Broshi, *Damascus Document*, 42-43.

53. Ibid., 44-47.

the rising of a Messiah, again a singular one, from both Aaron and Israel,[54] marking the arrival of the end time.

15. 4QD^e (4Q270) 2 ii 13-14[55]

[או] אשר יגלה את רז עמו לגואים או יקלל א[ת עמו או ידבר]
סרה על משיחי רוח הקדש ותועה ב[חוזי אמתו בהמרותו]
את פי אל ...

[or anyone] who will disclose a secret of his people to the Gentiles or will curse [his people or preach] rebellion against those anointed by the holy Spirit or leads astray [the seers of His truth in rebelling against] God's word. . . .

This passage, which has no counterpart in the medieval CD, seems to be related, at least in some of its formulation, to CD 2:12 and 5:21–6:2 (texts 9 and 10 above). Whereas those passages clearly dealt with the past, this one seems to be related to the present or future; but does the phrase משיחי רוח הקדש refer to coming Messiahs as such? It is a puzzling passage.

16. 11QMelch 18[56]

והמבשר הו[אה מ[שוח הרו[ח] אשר אמר דנ[יאל בו ...]

. . . the herald i[s] the (agent) [a]nointed of the Spir[it], [about] whom Dan[iel] spoke . . .

In this instance a different figure, a מבשר, "herald," is regarded as anointed by the holy Spirit. Possibly this instance should not be booked here, since, though the editor A. S. van der Woude originally read משיח, it was subsequently corrected by Yigael Yadin to the participle משוח.[57] The phrase, however, is problematic and may be related to that used in CD 2:12 above. If it merits inclusion, then it associates with those figures expected in the

54. On the meaning of האסף, see Chapter 12 below, pp. 261-65.
55. See Baumgarten, *Qumran Cave 4: XIII,* 144. Cf. Wacholder and Abegg, *Preliminary Edition,* 1:41; García Martínez, *The Dead Sea Scrolls Translated,* 64.
56. See A. S. van der Woude, "Melchisedek als himmlische Erlösergestalt in den neugefundenen eschatologischen Midraschim aus Qumran Höhle XI," *OTS* 14 (1965) 354-73. Cf. M. de Jonge and A. S. van der Woude, "11Q Melchizedek and the New Testament," *NTS* 12 (1965-66) 301-26; J. A. Fitzmyer, *ESBNT* or *SBNT,* 221-67.
57. See Y. Yadin, "A Note on Melchizedek and Qumran," *IEJ* 15 (1965) 152-54.

Qumran community a coming "anointed herald," a development possibly from Isa 61:1. Van der Woude already suggested that the Anointed One was meant to be more of a prophetic than a political figure.[58]

17. 4Q521 2 ii + 4[59]

1 [כי הש]מים והארץ ישמעו למשיחו

2 [וכל א]שר בם לוא יסוג ממצות קדושים

3 התאמצו מבקשי אדני בעבדתו

4 הלוא בזאת תמצאו את אדני כל המיחלים בלבם

5 כי אדני חסידים יבקר וצדיקים בשם יקרא

6 ועל ענוים רוחו תרחף ואמונים יחליף בכחו

7 כי יכבד את חסידים על כסא מלכות עד

8 מתיר אסורים פוקח עורים זוקף כפ[ופים]

9 ול[ע]לם אדבק [במ]יחלים ובחסדו י[שלם](?)]

10 ופר[י מעש]ה טוב לאיש לוא יתאחר

11 ונכ<ב>דות שלוא היו ישעה אדני כאשר ד[בר]

12 כי ירפא חללים ומתים יחיה ענוים יבשר

13 ו[דלי]ם ישב[יע] נתושים ינהל ורעבים יעשר

14 ונב[ונים   [וכלם כקד[ושים](?)]

1 [for the hea]vens and the earth will listen to His Messiah,

2 [and all th]at is in them will not swerve from the commandments of holy ones.

3 Be strengthened in His service, all you who seek the Lord!

4 Shall you not find the Lord in this, all those (= you) who hope in their hearts?

5 For the Lord will seek out pious ones, and righteous ones He will call by name.

6 Over afflicted ones will His Spirit hover, and faithful ones He will renew with His power.

7 He will honor (the) pious ones on a throne of eternal kingship,

---

58. See van der Woude, "Melchisedek," 367.

59. See E. Puech, "Une apocalypse messianique *(4Q521),*" *RevQ* 15 (1991-92) 475-522. The text of this fragment can also be found in Eisenman and Wise, *The Dead Sea Scrolls Uncovered,* 19-23, but it is to be used with caution; the readings do not always agree with the preliminary publication of Puech. Cf. R. H. Eisenman, "A Messianic Vision," *BARev* 17/6 (1991) 65. Cf. J. J. Collins, "The Works of the Messiah," *DSD* 1 (1994) 98-112; F. García Martínez, "Los Mesías de Qumrán: Problemas de un traductor," *Sef* 53 (1993) 345-60, esp. 347-52.

8 freeing prisoners, giving sight to the blind, straightening up those be[nt over].

9 For[ev]er shall I cling [to tho]se who hope, and in His steadfast love He will [recompense];

10 the frui[t of a] good [dee]d will be delayed for no one.

11 Wond<r>ous things, such as have never been (before), will the Lord do, just as He s[aid].

12 For He will heal (the) wounded, revive the dead, (and) proclaim good news to the afflicted;

13 (the) [po]or He will satiate, (the) uprooted He will guide, and on (the) hungry He will bestow riches;

14 and (the) intel[ligent   ], and all of them (shall be) like hol[y ones]

This text differs considerably from the others that refer to the future and mention משיח, but it agrees with some of them at least in its expectation of a coming messianic figure. In this case it is again the singular משיח, but fitted with a suffix, "His," that is, God's Messiah. When J. Starcky first spoke of this text, he wrote, "One fine manuscript mentions the Messiah, but the gracious work of eschatological salvation, spoken of in terms of *Is*. xl ff. and *Ps*. cxlvi, is attributed directly to the Lord, *Adonay*."[60] As used in this Qumran writing, Psalm 146, on which it heavily depends, is considerably modified by the introduction of "His messiah," a term not found in the psalm itself, where the bounties are ascribed to God. Some echoes of Ps 146 are found in this fragment: 6b (כל אשר בם), 7 (מתיר אסורים), 8 (זקף כפופים . . . פקח עורים); as also echoes of Isa 34:1 (תשמע הארץ); 35:5 (תפקחנה עיני עורים); 61:1 (לבשר ענוים).

The editor, Emile Puech, has called this text a "messianic apocalypse," but what has been preserved in the fragment reveals "none of the formal marks of apocalyptic revelation," as Collins has rightly noted.[61] Collins is also right in describing this coming Messiah as a prophetic type rather than a kingly type. In this regard the treatment of the Messiah in 4Q521 is again a development beyond what one finds in the Old Testament itself, even though it resembles the way that the Qumran texts have often spoken of historical prophets as anointed agents of God.

As the fragment has been interpreted at times, however, the wondrous deeds of freeing prisoners, giving sight to the blind, healing the wounded, re-

60. See P. Benoit et al., "Editing the Manuscript Fragments from Qumran," *BA* 19 (1956) 75-96, esp. 96 (French original in *RB* 63 [1956] 49-67, esp. 66).

61. Collins, "The Works of the Messiah," 98.

viving the dead, and so forth have been ascribed to the Messiah, "as God's agent" or as "an eschatological prophet."[62] This, however, is far from clear, for the deeds seem rather to be those of "the Lord" (אדני), who is mentioned explicitly in lines 4, 5, 11.

Moreover, both the original editor and others have spoken unfortunately about this text as mentioning "resurrection."[63] The word "resurrection" evokes different images among readers, Jewish and Christian; so it is better avoided in the interpretation of this Jewish text.[64] For "resuscitation," which is the proper understanding of line 12 of this text, is something different from "resurrection," whether that of Jesus Christ or of the general resurrection of the dead (Dan 12:2).

In this connection one should consider still another line of 4Q521, which mentions no messiah, but speaks of יק[ם המחיה את מתי עמו, "(when) the vivifier will [rai]se up the dead of his people" (7+5 ii 6).[65] This is almost certainly a reference to God, hardly to a messianic figure.[66]

---

62. Ibid., 98-99; on p. 112, Collins goes so far as to speak of such "works" as indicative "of a prophetic messiah of the Elijah type rather than of the royal messiah." This means that Collins is now speaking even of "Elijah" as a kind of messiah! Cf. M. O. Wise and J. D. Tabor, "The Messiah at Qumran," *BARev* 18/6 (1992) 60-65, who read line 12 differently.

63. Puech, "Une Apocalypse messianique," 475 ("ce texte aux mentions irréfutables de la résurrection"); J. D. Tabor and M. O. Wise, "4Q521 'On Resurrection' and the Synoptic Gospel Tradition: A Preliminary Study," *JSP* 10 (1992) 149-62. Cf. G. Vermes, "Qumran Forum Miscellanea I," *JJS* 43 (1992) 299-305, esp. 303-4, who speaks of "The Resurrection fragment," but then adds the adjective "so-called." At the end he says, "Line 12 displays the most explicit evidence to date in the Scrolls concerning the doctrine of the resurrection from the dead (ומתים יחיה) . . ." (p. 304); cf. also Collins, "The Works of the Messiah," 98.

64. See the complaints of Schiffman, *Reclaiming the Dead Sea Scrolls,* 348. Recall the ancient Jewish prayer, *Šěmōneh 'Eśre* 2: "Lord, you are mighty forever, reviving the dead . . . making the dead alive out of great mercy . . . healing the sick, freeing the captives, and keeping your word to those who sleep in the dust. . . . You are faithful in making the dead alive. Blest are you, Lord, who make the dead alive."

65. Puech, "Une apocalypse messianique," 501. Puech reads the lines 7-8 as follows: ונ[ו]דה ונגידה לכם צד[ק]ות אדני אשר] [בנ]י תמ[ותה ופתח] קברות / לוחות [, which he translates, "Alors nous ren[d]rons grâce et nous vous annoncerons les actes de jus[ti]ce du Seigneur qui [a *délivré/ressucité?*] les fil[s de la m]ort et a ouvert [*leurs tombeaux/les tombeaux des (justes)/les tablettes*]." Cf. Ps 79:11; 102:21. Puech's restoration of קברות, "graves," is far from certain, even if it suits his thesis about "resurrection."

66. As Collins ("The Works of the Messiah," 101) agrees; see his critical note on J. Neusner (ibid., n. 12). That "the resurrection of the dead shall come through Elijah of blessed memory" (*m. Sotah* 9:15) is clearly a still further development in the Mishnah of the rabbinic period, a teaching that cannot be ascribed to the Qumran community without further ado. How legitimate is it to cite *Pesiqta de R. Kahana* 76a for the interpretation

18. 4Q521 8:9[67]

ה וכל משיחיה[   ]

[   ]H and all its (fem.) Anointed Ones (*or* Messiahs).

The text seems to deal with the Temple, but it is broken; so it is impossible to determine further the sense of משיח.[68]

19. 4Q521 9:3[69]

כה תעזוב ב[י]ד משיח[   ]

[   ] your [   ] you will abandon into the [ha]nd of (your?) Messiah (*or* Anointed One).

Again, because of the broken state of the text, the meaning is uncertain.

20. pap4QparaKings (4Q382) 16:2[70]

מ]שיח ישר[א]ל[. .]   [   ]

[M]essiah of Isr[a]el[   ].

The context is lost on this small fragment of four lines.

21. 4Q375 (4QapMos[a]) 1 i 9[71]

לפני / [ה]כוהן המשיח אשר יוצק על ר[ו]אשו שמן המשיחה

---

of a Qumran text? At the earliest, that text is dated to the fifth century A.D.; some have even dated it ca. A.D. 700 (H. L. Strack and G. Stemberger, *Introduction to the Talmud and Midrash* [Edinburgh: Clark, 1991] 321).

67. See Puech, "Une Apocalypse messianique," 508.

68. Puech (ibid.) restored ה[נ]כה before the phrase, translating it, "la prêtri]se et tous ses oints." Cf. Abegg, "The Messiah at Qumran," 142.

69. See Puech, "Une Apocalypse messianique," 509.

70. See S. Olyan, "4Qpap paraKings et al.," in H. Attridge et al., *Qumran Cave 4: VIII Parabiblical Texts, Part 1* (DJD 13; Oxford: Clarendon, 1994) 363-416, esp. 372.

71. See J. Strugnell, "375. 4QApocryphon of Moses[a]," in *Qumran Cave 4: XIV, Parabiblical Texts, Part 2* (DJD 19; Oxford: Clarendon, 1995) 111-19, esp. 113; cf. his article, "Moses-Pseudepigrapha at Qumran: 4Q375, 4Q376, and Similar Works," in *Archaeology and History in the Dead Sea Scrolls: The New York University Conference in Memory of Yigael Yadin* (JSPSup 8; ed. L. H. Schiffman; Sheffield: JSOT Press, 1990) 221-56.

. . . before the anointed priest, upon whose head will be poured the oil of anointing.

The context in which these words occur is fragmentary and uncertain, but it seems to be giving general prescriptions about what Israel is to do with a prophet accused of advocating apostasy, whom some try to defend. They are to come to a certain place that God will choose (probably the sanctuary) and appear before an "anointed priest." Nothing in the text is eschatological; so it scarcely has to do with the so-called Mosaic eschatological prophet. It uses the noun המשיח instead of the passive participle משוח, which one might expect. The words are actually a modified quotation of Lev 21:10, which reads והכהן הגדול מאחיו אשר יוצק על ראשו שמן המשחה, "the priest who is chief among his brethren, upon whose head the anointing oil is poured. . . ." In any case, המשיח is here an appositive to ה[כוהן], and it is hardly being used in the sense of "Messiah."

22. 4Q376 (4QapMos[b]) 1 i 1[72]

נ]י הכוהן המשיח   [   ] 1

[. . .].NY the anointed priest

This may be another copy of the same text, the preceding 4Q375, or one related to it. The four-lined fragment is too small to ascertain any real context.

23. 4Q381 15:7[73]

כי אתה]תפארת הדו ואני משיחך אתבננתי[

[For you are] the glory of (its) splendor, whereas for me, I have grown in understanding from your MŚYḤ.

Here the text is problematic. Eileen Schuller has probably translated the word משיחך correctly as "from Your discourse."[74] In doing so, she has preferred to relate it to the root *śyḥ*, "muse, talk," having considered the possibility of "Your anointed one." The fragment is broken, and the first half of the

---

72. See J. Strugnell, "**376.** 4QApocryphon of Moses[b]," in *Qumran Cave 4: XIV,* 122-36, esp. 123.

73. See E. M. Schuller, *Non-Canonical Psalms from Qumran: A Pseudepigraphic Collection* (HSS 28; Atlanta: Scholars Press, 1986) 94-97, 101-2.

74. Ibid., 97.

lines is missing; so there is no certainty about the context or the subject matter. It is mentioned here only for the sake of completeness of coverage.

To these instances one may eventually have to add consideration of three other texts where משיח occurs in a badly broken context: 4Q287 (4QBerakot[b]) 10:3; 4Q377 (4QapMos[c]); 4Q458 (4QNarrative).[75]

These, then, are the Qumran texts in which משיח occurs, many of which clearly express messianic expectations. Some, however, have at times been considered "messianic," but are only problematically so. Some, too, use the word to refer to prophets of old and so are not utilized in a truly messianic sense. Other problematic texts, however, have to be considered.

The first of such texts is 4QTestim (4Q175).[76] This testimonia list presents a number of biblical and nonbiblical passages written on a single sheet of skin: Deut 5:28-29 + 18:18-19; Num 24:15-17; Deut 33:8-11; and 4QPsalms of Joshua. The original editor, John M. Allegro, admitted that the last paragraph, the excerpt from 4QPsJosh, had no messianic import, but he and others have often understood the first three paragraphs as referring to the prophet and the Messiahs of Aaron and Israel mentioned in 1QS 9:11 (text 1 above).

The first paragraph in 4QTestim, which combines Deut 5:28-29 and 18:18-19 and promises a prophet like Moses, has no more "messianic" meaning than the last paragraph, but it is considered to have "messianic" connotation by extrinsic denomination. It contains the Deuteronomy passage to which the "prophet" in the expectations of 1QS 9:11 refers, which also mentions Messiahs.[77]

The second paragraph in 4QTestim is an excerpt from the Oracle of Balaam (Num 24:15-17), which has no more "messianic" connotation than the first. The "star that shall march forth from Jacob" and the "sceptre that shall arise from Israel" are, in the Old Testament, not yet references to a "Messiah" in this book of the Pentateuch. This pentateuchal passage enjoyed favor

75. See M. G. Abegg, Jr., "The Messiah at Qumran," 140-41.

76. See J. M. Allegro, *Qumrân Cave 4*, 57-60; cf. *JBL* 75 (1956) 174-87, esp. 182-87. Cf. J. A. Fitzmyer, *ESBNT* or *SBNT*, 59-89. This text has been regarded as messianic by Milik, *TYDWJ*, 124-25; A. Dupont-Sommer, *The Essene Writings from Qumran* (Oxford: Blackwell, 1961) 315-18; G. Vermes, *The Dead Sea Scrolls in English*, 295-96; and T. H. Gaster, *The Scriptures of the Dead Sea Sect* (London: Secker and Warburg, 1957) 353-59.

77. Years ago P. W. Skehan noted that "the passages named . . . are given as one single text, continuously, in one paragraph . . . [as] a citation from Ex 20,21b, according to the Samaritan recension of the Pentateuch, beginning as that text does with the introductory formula וידבר יהוה אל משה לאמר instead of with Dt's ויאמר יהוה אלי ("The Period of the Biblical Texts from Khirbet Qumrân," *CBQ* 19 [1957] 435-40, esp. 435). 4QTestim actually begins thus: וידבר .... אל מושה לאמור. Cf. J. A. Fitzmyer, *ESBNT* or *SBNT*, 83.

among the Qumran community, as can be seen from the use of it in 1QM 11:6 and in CD 7:18-21. In the latter instance, the star and the sceptre are interpreted as two figures: "the star is the Interpreter of the Law (דורש התורה), who will come to Damascus,"[78] and who is usually understood to be an eschatological priest. If he is meant to be the same as the Messiah of Aaron, it is only by indirection. "The sceptre is a Prince of the Whole Congregation (נשיא כל העדה)," of whom it is said that "when he rises, he will destroy all the children of Seth" (7:18-21).[79] The future or eschatological role predicated

78. Another passage in CD perhaps sheds some light on this דורש התורה: "God remembered the covenant of (the) first members and raised up from Aaron discerning ones and from Israel sages, and he made them listen. They dug the well: 'A well that the princes dug, that the nobles of the people delved with the staff' (Num 21:18). The 'well' is the Law, and those who dug it are the returnees of Israel, who went out from the land of Israel and sojourned in the land of Damascus. All of them God called princes because they sought Him, and their renown has not been diminished in anyone's mouth. The 'staff' is the Interpreter of the Law, of whom Isaiah said, 'He brings forth a tool for his work' (Isa 54:16). The 'nobles of the people' are those who come to dig the well with the staves, which the 'scepter' decreed: to walk according to them in all the age of wickedness, and without which they will not attain it (instruction), until there arises one who teaches righteousness at the end of time" (CD 6:2-11; on this text, see p. 103 below). From this passage it would seem clear that דורש התורה was not always understood as a coming, future figure, as he is in 4QFlor (4Q174) 1-2 i 11-12, but that it was a title sometimes given to a historical person in the community, a teacher who has already imparted an interpretation of the law (compare 1QS 6:6). He would have been someone like the historical מורה הצדק, "Teacher of Righteousness," not necessarily the same as the expected יורה הצדק, of whom CD 6:10-11 speaks. Note that in this text the דורש התורה is likewise distinct from the יורה הצדק.

79. Recall that נשיא העדה is also mentioned in (1) 4Q285 4:2: נ]שיא העדה עד [...הים הג]דול, "the [P]rince of the Congregation as far as the [Great] Sea" (if the final word is rightly restored?); (2) 4Q285 5:4 (on which see below); 6:6, 10; (3) 1QM 5:1 ("on the sh[ield] of the Prince of the Whole Congregation they shall write his name and the name of Israel, Levi, and Aaron and the names of the twelve tribes of Israel . . ."; this refers to the eschatological war, but it does not make "the Prince of the Whole congregation" an eschatological figure any more than the rest of those whose names are to be so inscribed; in fact, it suggests that he was indeed a historical figure); (4) 4QpIsaᵃ (4Q161) 5-6:3 (in a broken context); (5) 4Q376 1 iii 1 (נשיא כול העדה mentioned as being "in the camp"). (6) In 4QSapᵉ (4Q423) 5:3 a figure called נשיא עמכה appears, who has been taken to be the same as נשיא העדה. (7) Only in CD 7:20, copies of which are also found in 4QDᵃ (4Q266) 3 iii 21 and 4QDᵈ (4Q269) 5:4, is his "rising" mentioned. The title נשיא may well be derived from Ezek 34:24; 37:25, where it is used of the future "David"; this may explain why a figure with this title is given an eschatological role. The title, however, seems to have been used for a historical leader of the community as well as for an expected figure, who would duplicate the role of the historical leaders in an eschatological sense, just as the historical מורה הצדק did not exclude the expectation of one who would come to "teach righteousness" (CD 6:10-11). That the title has such a double function is not always reckoned with.

of the Prince may be meant to identify him as the Messiah of Israel, but again that is done only by indirection. Moreover, any messianic connotation given to both these pentateuchal figures is derived from Qumran interpretation; this does not mean that Num 24:15-17 had such a meaning in itself.

The third paragraph in 4QTestim, quoting Deut 33:8-11, is from the Blessing of Moses pronounced over Levi, whose task it was to teach Israel and minister at the altar in the Temple. It is thus clearly a priestly text, referring to an eschatological figure. Is he the Messiah of Aaron? If so, is he different from "the star that shall march forth from Jacob" mentioned in the second paragraph? In other words, the purpose of the composition of the so-called *Testimonia* from Qumran Cave 4 is badly in need of reassessment.[80] Its messianic character has simply been overstated.[81]

The second text that needs to be reconsidered is 1QSb, the second appendix of the *Manual of Discipline,* which formulates various blessings. J. T. Milik originally named it "Recueil des Bénédictions,"[82] and doubted that the blessings were ever used in a community liturgy, calling it rather "une composition livresque" (a bookish composition).[83] The phrase באחרית הימים, "at the end of days," never occurs in this text, and so the reason for regarding it as "bénédictions de la Congrégation *eschatologique*" (blessings of the eschatological congregation)[84] is far from clear. In it Milik distinguished a blessing for faithful members of the congregation (1-8 i 1-20), a blessing for the High Priest (1-8 i 21-iii 21), a blessing for the Sons of Zadok, the priests (1-8 iii 22-v 19), and a blessing for the Prince of the Congregation (1-8 v 20-29[?]). Geza Vermes concurred with Milik's messianic analysis.[85] Despite the reasons that Milik gives, however, nothing in the text indicates that the second blessing was intended for a high priest or for the Messiah of Aaron,[86] or that the last

---

80. Collins (*The Scepter and the Star,* 64) rightly calls this text "a collection of passages with eschatological significance"; but it is far from clear that "Balaam's oracle was widely understood in a messianic sense, and that 'Prince of the Congregation' was a messianic title" (ibid.). See further J. Lübbe, "A Reinterpretation of 4QTestimonia," *RevQ* 12 (1985-87) 187-97. Lübbe rightly questions the messianic interpretation of 4QTestim, but I am not sure that his alternative interpretation will convince many.

81. See further my article, "'4QTestimonia' and the New Testament," *ESBNT* or *SBNT,* 59-89, esp. 82-86, where I went along with the then-prevailing interpretation.

82. See Barthélemy and Milik, *Qumran Cave I,* 118-30.

83. Ibid., 120.

84. Ibid., 121: "bénédictions de la Congrégation *eschatologique*" (my emphasis).

85. See Vermes, *Dead Sea Scrolls in English,* 235.

86. Milik introduced into his translation of 1QSb 1-8 i 21 the phrase, "pour bénir *le Grand Prêtre . . .*" (to bless *the High Priest* [in brackets]), but nothing in the text itself mentions כוהן הרואש, a title for the High Priest that is otherwise used in the sectarian writings

blessing was for the Messiah of Israel. More likely the second blessing was to be uttered by the משכיל, "Instructor," over the priestly head of the Qumran community, whoever he might have been at a given time, and the last blessing over the Prince of the Congregation, some historical member of the community who enjoyed this title.[87] The blessings in this collection, which were influenced by Isaiah 11 and were to be recited by the Instructor, are florid in their poetic and rhetorical phrasing. They were undoubtedly to be used on liturgical occasions, when the Instructor uttered blessings over members of the community: ordinary members, the priestly leader, the sons of Zadok, and the Prince of the Congregation. Consequently, both the eschatological and the messianic nuances of this text are far from certain.

The third text that needs scrutiny is what some have called the Pierced Messiah text of Qumran Cave 4 (4Q285). It is related to the *War Scroll*, and according to Milik represents a portion that is now lost from the end of 1QM.[88] It has to be considered along with other texts of the *War Scroll* from Cave 4.[89] Fragment 5 of this text runs as follows:[90]

1 [   ] כאשר כתוב בספר [ישעיהו הנביא ונוקפ[ו]

2 [סבכי היער בברזל והלבנון באדיר י]פול ויצא חוטר מגזע ישי

3 [ונצר משרשיו יפרה   צמח דויד ונשפטו את [כול]

4 [חיל בליעל ועמד מלך הכתיים למשפט] והמיתו נשיא העדה צמ[ח]

5 [דויד   יצאו בתופי[ם ובמחוללות וצוה כוהן

6 [הרואש   לטהר את בשרם מדם ח[ללי]י כתיים [וכו[ל] העם]

(1QM 2:1; 15:4; 16:13; 18:5; 19:11; 4QM[d] 1 ii 4); or even הכוהן הגדול (11QTemple 15:15; 23:9; 25:16; 26:3; 58:18). Milik's interpretation has been queried as well by J. Licht (מגילת הסרכים, 274-75) and J. VanderKam ("Messianism in the Scrolls," 224-25).

87. See my comment on the diverse usage of this title in n. 79 above.

88. See Milik, "*Milkî-ṣedeq* et *Milkî-rešaʿ* dans les anciens écrits juifs et chrétiens," *JJS* 23 (1972) 95-144, esp. 143. Another copy of fragments 3-4 of 4Q285 is found in A. S. van der Woude, "Ein neuer Segensspruch aus Qumran (11 Q Ber)," in *Bibel und Qumran: Beiträge zur Erforschung der Beziehungen zwischen Bibel- und Qumranwissenschaft: Hans Bardtke zum 22.9.1966* (ed. S. Wagner; Berlin: Evangelische Haupt-Bibelgesellschaft, 1968) 253-58 (+ pl).

89. See 4QM[a-f] (4Q491-96), in M. Baillet, *Qumrân Grotte 4: III (4Q482-4Q520)* (DJD 7; Oxford: Clarendon, 1982) 12-68. Possibly 4Q285 should now be labeled 4QM[g], as F. García Martínez has suggested.

90. The text of 4Q285 can be found in Wacholder and Abegg, *Preliminary Edition*, 2:223-27 (fragment 5 on p. 225). Tentatively, I am following the form of fragment 5 given by M. G. Abegg, "Messianic Hope and 4Q285: A Reassessment," *JBL* 113 (1994) 81-91, esp. 87 (with a slight modification). Cf. García Martínez, *The Dead Sea Scrolls Translated*, 124.

[1][As is written in the book of] Isaiah the prophet, [2]"[And the thickets of the forest] shall be cut down [with an iron axe, and Lebanon with (its) splendor] shall fall. A shoot shall sprout from Jesse's stump, [3][and a bud shall blossom from his roots" (Isa 10:34–11:1)   ] the Scion of David. And they shall enter into judgment with [all [4]the army of Belial; the king of the Kittim shall stand for judgment], and the Prince of the Congregation, the Sci[on(?) of [5]David,] shall put him to death. [They shall go forth with timbrel]s and with dances. Then [6][the high] priest shall give an order [to cleanse their flesh of the blood of th]ose woun[ded by] the Kittim; [and al]l [the people . . .].[91]

In this unfortunately badly preserved text, צמח דויד may be in apposition to נשיא העדה (line 4), but one has to reckon with the broken condition of the text. First, דויד, "David," is wholly restored at the beginning of line 5. Second, the letter following ṣade in line 4 is not certainly a *mem;* it could just as well be a *bet* or a *kap.*[92] Yet even if one admits the correctness of the resto-

---

91. 1QIsa[a] 10:19 reads the singular ונקף along with the MT, but otherwise the text of Isaiah in this fragment agrees with the MT and 1QIsa[a]. The niphal of שפט is used in line 3 with the preposition את, as in Jer 2:35; Ezek 17:20; 20:35-36, in the sense of "entering into judgment *with.*" The text of this fragment should also be compared with 4QpIsa[a] (4Q161) 8-10:2-9, where parts of Isa 10:34–11:1 are preserved and interpreted in a pesher (see Allegro, *Qumrân Cave 4:I,* 13-15). The pertinent part reads:

[וניקפו] סבכי [היער] בברזל ולבנון באדיר / [יפול   פשרו על הכ]תיאים אש[ר]
יכת[ו] בית ישראל וענוי / [   ]כול הגואים וגבורים יחתו ונמס ל[בם /
[   ] רמי] הקומה גדועים המה גבורי כת[יאים] / [ואשר אמ]ר וניקפו
סובכי [ה]יער בברזל ה[מה] / [   ].ם למלחמת כתיאים ולבנון בא[דיר /
יפול   פשרו על ה]כתיאים אשר ינת[נו] ביד גדולו[ן   ] / [   ].ים בברחו
מלפני ל.[   ].[מ]   [

[2]"The thickets [of the forest] will be cut down with an iron axe, and by a majestic one [will] Lebanon [3][fall." The interpretation of it concerns the K]ittim, who will crush the house of Israel and the afflicted ones of[[4]   ]all the Gentiles and warriors will be dismayed; and their hea[rt(s)] will melt. [[5] "the great] in height will be hewn down": They are the warriors of the Kit[tim [6]   And as for what it sa]ys, "And the thickets of [the] forest will be cut down with an iron axe," th[ey [7]].M for the war of the Kittim. "And by a ma[jestic one will] Lebanon [8][fall," the interpretation of it concerns the] Kittim, who will be given over into the hand of His great one[ ]. [9][ ].YM in his flight from before L[ ].

This pesher on Isaiah, which clearly expresses a promise of eschatological victory over the Kittim, is pertinent to the understanding of 4Q285, because it gives an interpretation of Isa 10:34–11:1 by alluding to the Romans under that code name, but makes no mention of a messianic figure. Even the phrase ביד גדולו (line 8) is a studied circumlocution avoiding that.

92. Wacholder and Abegg read צב[א, as did the preliminary concordance of the

ration of line 4 and the application of צמח דויד to the Prince of the Congregation, his "messianic" character is not *eo ipso* evident. Third, I agree with those who have interpreted the text by making the Prince of the Congregation the subject of the verb והמיתו, against the interpretation of Robert Eisenman.[93] The phrases צמח דויד and נשיא העדה appear together here and may ascribe an eschatological role to the Prince of the Congregation in executing an enemy. That is the most one can say about this text. It only shows how complicated the interpretation of Isaiah was at Qumran in the development of the community's eschatological beliefs.

The fourth text that needs to be scrutinized is CD 6:10-11, which reads: וזולתם לא ישיגו עד עמד יורה הצדק באחרית הימים, "and without them they will not attain it (instruction) until there arises at the end of days one who teaches righteousness."[94] In the last clause יורה הצדק, "one who teaches righteousness," is a play on Hos 10:12, ועת לדרוש את יהוה עד יבוא וירה צדק לכם, "It is time to seek Yahweh that He may come and rain down upon [or: teach] you righteousness." The expression, "one who teaches righteousness," derived from Hosea, now becomes a way of referring to an expected figure. The awaited יורה הצדק may be a teacher like the historical Teacher of Righteousness, but he is not the same person; the text does not imply that the historical מורה הצדק is somehow to return to become "their resurrected Teacher who would lead the theocratic community of the New Israel in the Last Days."[95] The historical Teacher of Righteousness was a priest, but nothing in this text suggests that the expected יורה הצדק was to be the Messiah of Aaron.[96]

---

nonbiblical texts from Cave 4, compiled back in the late 1950s by myself, R. E. Brown, and W. G. Oxtoby.

93. Eisenman understood נשיא העדה as the object of the plural verb והמיתו, despite the absence of the sign of the accusative before those words, maintaining that the text "refers to the execution of a Messianic leader" (*California State University, Long Beach, News Release*, 1 November 1991, p. 1; cf. *New York Times*, 8 November 1991, p. A8). See further M. Bockmuehl, "A 'Slain Messiah' in 4Q Serekh Milḥamah (4Q285)?" *TynBull* 43 (1992) 155-69; G. Vermes, "The Oxford Forum for Qumran Research Seminar on the Rule of War from Cave 4 (4Q285)," *JJS* 43 (1992) 85-90, summarized in "The 'Pierced Messiah' Text — An Interpretation Evaporates," *BARev* 18/4 (1992) 80-82; R. Bauckham, "The Messianic Interpretation of Isa. 10:34 in the Dead Sea Scrolls, 2 Baruch and the Preaching of John the Baptist," *DSD* 2 (1995) 202-16, esp. 203, 206. Cf. M. O. Wise and J. D. Tabor, "The Messiah at Qumran," *BARev* 18/6 (1992) 60-63, 65; J. D. Tabor, "A Pierced or Piercing Messiah? — The Verdict Is Still Out," *BARev* 18/6 (1992) 58-59; VanderKam, "Messianism in the Scrolls," 217.

94. See Broshi, ed., *Damascus Document*, 20-21.

95. As J. M. Allegro once put it (*The Dead Sea Scrolls: A Reappraisal* (2d ed.; Harmondsworth, Middlesex: Penguin, 1964) 167.

96. See further Collins, "Teacher and Messiah?" 193-210; M. Knibb, "The Teacher of

The fifth text that needs to be reconsidered is 4Q246, which mentions the "Son of God" and "Son of the Most High," but which in my opinion is not messianic. I have treated this text above in Chapter 3 and shall simply refer here to that treatment.[97]

In any case, one sees in the differing Qumran texts that use the term משיח three main developments beyond the Old Testament usage itself. The first is the clear application of the title to prophets of old. If this was a debatable issue in the Old Testament itself, it is found clearly in texts 5 and 8-10 above, with a verb in the past tense, and doubtfully in text 15.

The second development is the clear use of משיח in the sense of an expected or future Messiah. Although some writers have thought it better to speak only of an "Anointed One,"[98] in my opinion the Qumran texts show that the term had already become titular in Judaism, referring to an expected or eschatological anointed agent of God to be sent for the good of His people. Many of these texts were written (or at least copied) shortly after the final redaction of the book of Daniel and speak of one or two expected figures, some of them using משיח in a future sense. This is a development beyond the future reference found in Dan 9:25, עד משיח נגיד. The thrust of Daniel 9 makes one hesitate to say that the translation "Messiah" (with a capital M) should be used there. This, however, is not the case with the Qumran texts cited above, where I have translated משיח as "Messiah" (texts 1, 2, 3, 4, 6, 7, 11, 12, 13, 14, 17). They show clearly the belief in the coming of a Messiah, or of two Messiahs, as prevalent among Essene Jews in Palestine of the last two pre-Christian centuries.[99]

The third development is the expectation of other figures along with the Messiahs of Aaron and Israel. One is the "prophet" like Moses; another is the "anointed herald"; another is "one who teaches righteousness at the end of days," and another is the "Prince of the (Whole) Congregation," who may or may not be the same as the Messiah of Israel.

This development of a clear messianic expectation and of other escha-

---

Righteousness — A Messianic Title?" in *A Tribute to Geza Vermes: Essays on Jewish and Christian Literature and History* (JSOTSup 100; ed. P. R. Davies and R. T. White; Sheffield: JSOT Press, 1990) 51-65. Both write against the interpretation given by P. R. Davies, "The Teacher of Righteousness and the 'End of Days,'" *RevQ* 13 (1988-89) 313-17.

97. See pp. 41-61 above.

98. See L. H. Silberman, "The Two 'Messiahs' of the Manual of Discipline," *VT* 5 (1955) 77-82. Cf. M. de Jonge, "The Use of the Word 'Anointed' in the Time of Jesus," *NovT* 8 (1966) 132-48.

99. See further L. H. Schiffman, "Messianic Figures and Ideas in the Qumran Scrolls," in Charlesworth, ed., *The Messiah*, 116-29.

tological expectations may be tied in with the Qumran community's understanding of itself as the "New Covenant" (1QpHab 2:3; CD 6:19; 8:21; 19:33-34; 20:12).

In any case, משיח as a title for a coming Messiah is not a Christian invention. It was in use among Palestinian Jews long before Jesus of Nazareth, and even before the period of Roman occupation. How widespread the use of that title was among Palestinian Jews in the last pre-Christian centuries is another question, one to which we have no answer at this time.

There are also passages in other intertestamental Jewish literature that have entered into the discussion of Messianism, on which I should comment, even though they have nothing to do directly with Qumran Messianism. For instance, in the early Enochic literature "Messiah" occurs twice in the so-called Similitudes (*1 Enoch* 48:10; 52:4): "His Anointed" or "His Messiah" (= the Lord's). It is a title used of the mysterious expected figure who is also called "Elect One," "Son of Man," and "Righteous One." These titles seem to refer to a coming ideal ruler of Israel, and they show how various titles were beginning to be conflated and attributed to one individual already in pre-Christian Judaism. The Enochic literature found at Qumran is not clearly sectarian, and undoubtedly it was used by many Jews other than the Qumran community. The title "Messiah" in *1 Enoch* undoubtedly fed into the development of Qumran Essene expectations, even if no part of the Similitudes has been found among the fragments of Enoch at Qumran.[100] A small fragment of 4QEn^c 5 i contains a word or two of *1 Enoch* 105,[101] but nothing that corresponds to the passage in 105:2 that is often thought to be "Messianic": "For I and my son will join ourselves with them for ever in the paths of uprightness during their lives, and you will have peace."[102] "My son" is often taken to be a designation of a messianic figure,[103] but rightly?

---

100. I consider it sheer chance that the so-called Similitudes have not turned up among the fragments of Qumran Cave 4. I do not share the conviction of J. T. Milik that they were a Christian substitute for the Enochic Book of Giants (*The Books of Enoch: Aramaic Fragments of Qumrân Cave 4* [Oxford: Clarendon, 1976] 89-107). See my article, "Implications of the New Enoch Literature from Qumran," *TS* 38 (1977) 332-45; cf. J. C. Greenfield and M. E. Stone, "The Enochic Pentateuch and the Date of the Similitudes," *HTR* 70 (1977) 51-65; "The Books of Enoch and the Traditions of Enoch," *Numen* 26 (1979) 89-103; M. Knibb, "The Date of the Parables of Enoch: A Critical Review," *NTS* 25 (1978-79) 345-59.

101. See Milik, *The Books of Enoch,* 207 (+ pl. XIV).

102. See M. A. Knibb, *The Ethiopic Book of Enoch* (2 vols.; Oxford: Clarendon, 1978) 2:243-44. Chap. 105 is not extant in Greek *Enoch,* and Knibb's interpretation of the chapter as a "Messianic reference" is unsubstantiated.

103. See the quotation from P. Billerbeck in Chapter 4, n. 14 above.

In the late first-century-B.C. writing *Psalms of Solomon* the Greek word *christos* occurs four times, but never in an absolute, unmodified form. Psalm 18 is entitled *epi tou Christou Kyriou,* "About the Anointed of the Lord" (or "the Anointed Lord"), and this form is also found in 17:32 and 18:7; but 18:5 has *Christou autou* (i.e., *Kyriou*). *Christos* refers not to a priestly Messiah, but to an awaited faithful descendant on David's throne, who will do God's will in Israel: *basileus dikaios didaktos hypo theou . . . hoti pantes hagioi, kai basileus autōn christos Kyriou,* "(he will be) a righteous king, taught by God . . . because they all (will be) saints, and their king the Messiah of the Lord" (17:32).[104] This may be the beginning of a restricted use of "Messiah" in the Davidic or kingly sense that one finds later on.

Here one might also consider *4 Ezra* 7:28-29; 12:32; 13:32, 37, 52; 14:9, if one could establish the text of these verses, which are badly transmitted (mainly in Latin).[105] The occurrence of a "Messiah" in 7:28-29 is questionable, because it speaks of *filius meus Jesus,* "my son Jesus," and *filius meus Christus,* "my son the Messiah (*or* Christ)," whereas 14:9 uses only *cum filio meo,* without any mention of an anointed figure.[106] The use of "my son" in this text is often called "messianic," as in the case of *1 Enoch* 105:2 (above).

There are also problematic passages in the Greek *Testaments of the Twelve Patriarchs. T. Levi* 8:13-14 possibly alludes to a priestly and a Davidic Messiah, but there Χριστός is used as a title for neither figure. *T. Reuben* 6:8 speaks of μέχρι τελειώσεως χρόνων ἀρχιερέως χριστοῦ, "the fulfillment of the

---

104. See M. de Jonge, *TDNT,* 9:513-14; cf. S. P. Brock, "The Psalms of Solomon," in Sparks, ed., *The Apocryphal Old Testament,* 649-82, esp. 678-79, 681; M. Knibb, "Messianism in the Pseudepigrapha in the Light of the Scrolls," *DSD* 2 (1995) 165-84.

105. *4 Ezra* is extant also in Syriac, Ethiopic, Arabic, Armenian, Sahidic, and Georgian, almost all of which are translations of a lost Greek text, which is occasionally quoted by patristic writers. It was written originally in a Semitic language by a Jew at the end of the first century A.D. M. E. Stone (*Fourth Ezra* [Hermeneia; Minneapolis: Fortress, 1990] 207-8) compares various versions that have rendered the verses, but he never uses the term "Messiah" or "Anointed One," and speaks only of a "redeemer figure." Cf. B. Violet, *Die Esra-Apokalypse (IV. Esra): Erster Teil. Die Überlieferung* (GCS 18; Leipzig: Hinrichs, 1910) 140-41.

106. The Syriac version of *4 Ezra* 7:28-29 has *běrî měšîḥā',* but that of 14:9 does not. Moreover, there is no mention of a "Messiah" in chap. 13, even though verses 32, 37, 52 speak of *filius meus* or in Syriac *běrî.* See further J. A. Robinson, ed., *Liber Esdrae Quartus* (Texts and Studies 3/2; text prepared by R. L. Bensley; Cambridge: Cambridge University Press, 1895) 27, 69. Cf. R. J. Bidawid, *4 Esdras* (The Old Testament in Syriac according to the Peshitta Version 4/3; Leiden: Brill, 1973) 16, 45; L. Gry, *Les dires prophétiques d'Esdras (IV. Esdras)* (2 vols.; Paris: Geuthner, 1938); S. Gero, "'My Son the Messiah': A Note on 4 Ezr 7,28-29," *ZNW* 66 (1975) 264-67; F. Zimmerman, "The Language, the Date, and the Portrayal of the Messiah in IV Ezra," *Hebrew Studies* 26 (1985) 203-18.

times of an anointed high priest."[107] *T. Simeon* 7:2 reads: ἀναστήσει γὰρ κύριος ἐκ τοῦ Λευὶ ὡς ἀρχιερέα, καὶ ἐκ τοῦ Ἰούδα ὡς βασιλέα, θεὸν καὶ ἄνθρωπον, "and the Lord will raise up from Levi as it were a high priest, and from Judah as it were a king, God and man." Still other passages in the *Testaments* speak of a coming kingdom or priesthood, but make no mention of an anointed figure or an anointing, so they may well be eschatological but are not "messianic" in any sense. The problem with these passages is obvious, because the *Testaments* have always been suspected of Christian interpolation in their Greek form, even though some of them are related to earlier Jewish writings.[108]

As for much later Judaism, "Messiah" is found in two places in the Mishnah: *m. Berakoth* 1:5 interprets the phrase "all the days of your life" (Deut 16:3) to "include the Days of the Messiah" (להביא לימות המשיח), which tells us little about the sense in which the title was used; and *m. Sotah* 9:15 speaks of "the footprints of the Messiah" as signs that herald his coming at the end of the time of exile.[109] Thus the rabbinic tradition by the beginning of the third century A.D. had formulated some different nuances of messianic belief, and to these should be added the instances of משיחא inserted in the classic targums of the third and later centuries, mentioned at the beginning of this paper.[110]

107. A footnote in M. de Jonge's translation reads: "Or 'of Christ, the high priest.'" See H. F. D. Sparks, *The Apocryphal Old Testament,* 520.

108. See M. de Jonge, *The Testaments of the Twelve Patriarchs: A Study of Their Text, Composition and Origin* (2d ed.; Assen: Van Gorcum, 1975); idem, *The Testaments of the Twelve Patriarchs: A Critical Edition of the Greek Text* (PVTG 1/2; Leiden: Brill, 1978). Cf. L. Rost, *Judaism outside the Hebrew Canon: An Introduction to the Documents* (Nashville: Abingdon, 1976) 140-46.

The only other pre-Christian text that might be considered is *The Sibylline Oracles,* Book 3, which Schiffman (*Reclaiming the Dead Sea Scrolls,* 320) has cited as a text that treats of messianism in the Second Temple Period. It speaks, indeed, of an expected "king," but the references are to an expected Egyptian (Ptolemaic) king. Even though the oracles may stem from second-century-B.C. Alexandrian Judaism, it hardly refers to a Messiah (in the strict sense). Collins, who translated the text of Book 3 in *The Old Testament Pseudepigrapha* (2 vols.; ed. J. H. Charlesworth; Garden City, N.Y.: Doubleday, 1983-85) 1:354-80, calls the king "a virtual messiah" (p. 355). That title for a non-Jewish king may be influenced by the use of משיח for the Persian King Cyrus in Isa 45:1, but it is not evidence for a Jewish Messiah.

109. So it is explained in H. Danby, *The Mishnah* (Oxford: Oxford University Press, 1933) 306 n. 9. Cf. A. S. van der Woude, *TDNT,* 9:522, who discusses reasons why Messianic expectations seem to have died out. Also Schiffman, "The Concept of the Messiah," 241-42.

110. See p. 75 above. Note also the way Hos 10:12 was eventually interpreted in

I have mentioned these non-Qumran passages in the preceding paragraphs only to state where I stand with reference to them, since they have often entered into the discussion of the Qumran texts. Some of them are of dubious value, but others manifest how the developing messianic tradition progressed among Jews and later among Christians.

Implications for New Testament Usage

Early disciples may have thought of Jesus as a "Messiah" during his public ministry, but apart from Mark 14:62a, where Jesus himself is depicted by an evangelist as admitting before the Sanhedrin that he was "the Messiah, the Son of the Blessed One," the Gospel tradition displays a reluctance to depict Jesus accepting that title during his ministry (see Matt 16:20; Luke 9:21; the reformulation of the Marcan Jesus' answer before the Sanhedrin in Matt 26:64b; cf. Luke 22:67-70). Even the confession of Peter, "You are the Messiah" (Mark 8:29), is immediately corrected by Jesus, who "charges" the disciples not to use that title (8:30; Luke 9:21) and rebukes Peter (Mark 8:32). The evangelist substitutes for that another title: "he began to teach them that the Son of Man must suffer" (8:31; Luke 9:22). That early Christians soon after Jesus' death began to refer to him as "the Messiah" or in Greek as ὁ Χριστός is the widespread message of New Testament writers. Only rarely in the New Testament, however, is Χριστός found as a *title* for Jesus, Rom 9:5 being one such instance. For Χριστός quickly became, as it were, Jesus' second name, Jesus Christ. Here one is dealing with a Christian development of messianism; it goes beyond the Palestinian Jewish data in its own way. Martin Hengel has rightly noted that "Auferweckung bzw. Entrückung zu Gott haben mit Messianität nichts zu tun."[111] Yet resurrection and heavenly exaltation are what New Testament writers have predicated of the Christian Messiah, especially Luke in Acts 2:36: "God has made him both Lord and Messiah, this Jesus whom you crucified" (cf. 2:32). This is what God has made of the crucified Jesus in the view of early Christians.

The title "Messiah" used of Jesus by later disciples may have to be related to the inscription that Pilate affixed to the cross on which Jesus died.

---

terms of a coming Elijah; see J. J. Collins, "Teacher and Messiah?" 206 n. 42, 210 n. 56. Cf. G. Molin, "Elijahu der Prophet und sein Weiterleben in den Hoffnungen des Judentums und der Christenheit," *Judaica* 8 (1951) 81.

111. See M. Hengel, "Jesus, der Messias Israels," in *Messiah and Christos: Studies in the Jewish Origins of Christianity Presented to David Flusser . . .* (ed. I. Gruenwald et al.; Tübingen: Mohr Siebeck, 1992) 155-76, esp. 158.

The inscription has come down to us in four different forms, but the substance of it identifies him as ὁ βασιλεὺς τῶν Ἰουδαίων (Mark 15:26; Matt 27:37; Luke 23:38; John 19:19). Pilate's inscription and the title he used undoubtedly became the catalyst for Jesus being recognized as ὁ Χριστός, as Nils A. Dahl has argued.[112] Christians would never have said that Jesus was "the king of the Jews," and the Johannine Gospel even records a Jewish objection to Pilate's use of the term (John 19:21). Pilate's use of "king," however, and the contemporary Jewish expectation of a kingly Messiah undoubtedly led Christians to call the crucified Jesus "the Messiah" (ὁ Χριστός), even if that does not explain all the nuances of the title.

In light of the above Qumran evidence, one should consider the Q passage in which Jesus is depicted answering the question put to him by the messengers sent by John the Baptist (Luke 7:18-23; Matt 11:2-6): "Go and inform John of what you have seen and heard: blind people recovering their sight, cripples walking, lepers being cleansed, deaf hearing again, dead being revived, and good news being preached to the poor" (Luke 7:22; cf. Matt 11:5). The Q passage conflates phrases that allude to Isa 35:5; 26:19; 61:1, without exact quotation.[113] This kind of conflation one finds in 4Q521 2 ii + 4:8,12, even if it is not identical. I have already noted the allusions to Ps 146:6-8 as well as to various Isaian passages in that Qumran text. In any case, Jesus' answer preserved in this Q passage implies that he is not a fiery reformer like Elijah, as the Baptist's question implied, "Are you the 'One who is to come,' or are we to look for someone else?" (Luke 7:19), where "One who is to come" is a title derived from Mal 3:1, which in that prophetic oracle was eventually understood of the fiery reformer, Elijah (Mal 3:23-24). Now that a Qumran text speaks of "His (i.e., God's) Messiah" to whom "heaven and earth will listen" and ascribes to God such wondrous deeds as those mentioned in the conflated phrases from Isaiah and Psalm 146 as characteristics of the time and coming of such a Messiah, one sees that Jesus' answer was making use of terminology that implied that he was not a fiery reformer like Elijah, but rather a messianic figure, as his followers would eventually recognize, and undoubtedly a messianic figure of prophetic type.

112. See N. A. Dahl, *The Crucified Messiah and Other Essays* (Minneapolis: Augsburg, 1974) 10-36; idem, "Messianic Ideas and the Crucifixion of Jesus," in Charlesworth, ed., *The Messiah,* 382-403.

113. Collins ("The Works of the Messiah," 107) limits the allusion to Isa 61:1, where one does not find any mention of reviving the dead. For a better interpretation of this Gospel passage, see J. A. T. Robinson, "Elijah, John and Jesus: An Essay in Detection," *NTS* 4 (1957-58) 263-81, reprinted in *Twelve New Testament Studies* (SBT 34; Naperville, Ill.: Allenson; London: SCM, 1962) 28-52.

This, then, is the contribution that Qumran texts have made to the study of messianism in Judaism in the last two pre-Christian centuries and the first of the Christian era. The Qumran texts show that one does not have to work with such a vague definition of "messiah" as Collins has proposed: "an agent of God in the end-time who is said somewhere in the literature to be anointed, but who is not necessarily called 'messiah' in every passage."[114] That is another instance of the "rubberband extension" of the term with which I began. "Somewhere in the literature" means that one can predicate "messiah" of every stage of the development of eschatological expectations without any regard for the history of ideas. That is what I question.[115]

114. J. J. Collins, "'He Shall not Judge by What His Eyes See': Messianic Authority in the Dead Sea Scrolls," *DSD* 2 (1995) 145-64.

115. See now J. Zimmermann, *Messianische Texte aus Qumran: Königliche, priesterliche und prophetische Messiasvorstellungen in den Schriftenfunden von Qumran* (WUNT 2/104; Tübingen: Mohr Siebeck, 1998).

CHAPTER 6

A Palestinian Jewish
Collection of Beatitudes

Beatitudes uttered by Jesus are preserved in two main places in the New Testament, a series of nine beatitudes in Matt 5:3-11 and a series of four in Luke 6:20-22. In the latter instance the beatitudes are paralleled by four woes, a distinctive feature of the Lucan Gospel. Other isolated beatitudes of Jesus are scattered throughout the various Gospels. The collection of nine or four beatitudes has always been considered unique. Yet the Gospel beatitudes are not the only ones found in New Testament writings.

In the New Testament one can count at least forty-one beatitudes introduced by μακάριος or μακάριοι, "blessed (is/are)": thirteen in Matthew's Gospel (5:3, 4, 5, 6, 7, 8, 9, 10, 11; 11:6; 13:16; 16:17; 24:46); fifteen in Luke's Gospel (1:45; 6:20, 21 [bis], 22; 7:23; 10:23; 11:27, 28; 12:37, 38, 43; 14:14, 15; 23:29); two in John's Gospel (13:17; 20:29); three in Romans (4:7, 8; 14:22); at least one in James (1:12; cf. 1:25); and seven in Revelation (1:3; 14:13; 16:15; 19:9; 20:6; 22:7, 14).

In most cases the adjective μακάριος is predicated of a substantivized adjective or participle, such as of οἱ πτωχοί, "the poor" (Matt 5:3), οἱ πενθοῦντες, "those mourning" (Matt 5:4), ἡ πιστεύσασα, "she who has believed" (Luke 1:45), or a relative clause, ὃς ἐάν, "whoever . . ." (Luke 7:23), ὅστις, "whoever . . ." (Luke 14:15), or ὧν, "of those who . . ." (Rom 4:7). Occasionally, parts of the body are the object of the macarism: οἱ ὀφθαλμοί, "eyes" (Luke 10:23), ἡ κοιλία, "the womb" (Luke 11:27). In a few instances a noun for a person appears, ἀνήρ, "(the) man" (Rom 4:8 [= Ps 32:2]; James 1:12).[1]

---

1. See G. Strecker, "Μακάριος," *EDNT,* 2:376-79. Also S. Agourides, "La tradition des

111

"Blessed" is the usual translation of the Greek μακάριος, the adjective used to express a "beatitude" or "macarism." Together with the Lucan woes, the beatitudes belong to a literary form called "ascription."[2] They consist of an exclamation in a nominal sentence, introduced with some word or phrase like "Blessed the one who. . . ." Counterparts of the New Testament beatitudes or macarisms have been found in Egyptian literature,[3] classical and Hellenistic Greek literature,[4] and the Old Testament.[5]

The immediate background for the New Testament beatitude as a literary form is usually regarded as the Greek Old Testament, where the adjective μακάριος is employed to translate Hebrew אשרי, a construct plural noun denoting concretely something like "the happiness of . . ." or "the fortunate things of. . . ." Thus in Psalm 1: אשרי האיש אשר לא הלך בעצת רשעים, "Blessed is the one who walks not according to the counsel of the wicked." This becomes in the LXX, μακάριος ἀνήρ, ὃς οὐκ ἐπορεύθη ἐν βουλῇ ἀσεβῶν. The beatitude form was especially used in the wisdom literature of the Old Testament and took on a religious sense as the expression of God's good favor toward human beings.[6]

---

béatitudes chez Matthieu et Luc," in *Mélanges bibliques en hommage au R. P. Béda Rigaux* (ed. A. Descamps and A. de Halleux; Gembloux: Duculot, 1970) 9-27; S. Bartina, "Los macarismos del Nuevo Testamento: Estudio de la forma," *EstEcl* 34 (1960) 57-88; J. Dupont, *Les Béatitudes* (3 vols.; Paris: Gabalda, 1969 [reprint of 1958 edition], 1973, esp. vol. 1, pp. 355-58 (bibliography on the beatitudes); A. George, "La 'forme' des béatitudes jusqu'à Jésus," in *Mélanges bibliques rédigés en l'honneur de André Robert* (Travaux de l'Institut Catholique de Paris 4; Paris: Bloud et Gay, 1957) 398-403; C. de Heer, *Makar, eudaimon, olbios, eutychēs: A Study of the Semantic Field Denoting Happiness in Ancient Greek to the End of the 5th Century B.C.* (Amsterdam: Hakkert, 1969); P. Humbert, *Recherches sur les sources égyptiennes de la littérature sapientiale d'Israël* (Mémoires de l'Université de Neuchâtel 7; Neuchâtel: Delachaux et Niestlé, 1929); K. Kohler, "Die ursprüngliche Form der Seligpreisungen," *TSK* 91 (1918) 157-82; G. Lejeune Dirichlet, *De veterum macarismis* (Religionsgeschichtliche Versuche und Vorarbeiten 14/4; Giessen: Töpelmann, 1914) 71; E. Lipiński, "Macarismes et psaumes de congratulation," *RB* 75 (1968) 321-67; G. Strecker, "Die Makarismen der Bergpredigt," *NTS* 17 (1970-71) 255-75; N. Walter, "Die Bearbeitung der Seligpreisungen durch Matthäus," in *SE IV* (TU 102; Berlin: Akademie, 1968) 246-58.

2. See T. Y. Mullins, "Ascription as a Literary Form," *NTS* 19 (1972-73) 194-205.

3. See J. Dupont, "Béatitudes égyptiennes," *Bib* 47 (1966) 185-222; P. Humbert, *Recherches*.

4. See F. Hauck, "Μακάριος," *TDNT* 4 (1967) 362-64; C. de Heer, *Makar*.

5. See G. Bertram, "Μακάριος," *TDNT* 4 (1967) 364-67; H. Cazelles, *TDOT* 1 (1974) 445-48. There are fifty such beatitudes in the Old Testament, or fifty-three, if one counts the paired beatitudes separately.

6. W. Janzen, "אשרי in the Old Testament," *HTR* 58 (1965) 215-26. Cf. C. Westermann, "Der Gebrauch von 'šry im Alten Testament," in *Forschung am Alten Testament: Gesammelte Studien II* (Theologische Bücherei 55; ed. R. Albertz and E. Ruprecht;

In the Greek world the gods were often considered to be supremely μάκαρες (e.g., Homer, *Odyssey* 5.7), but in the Jewish and Christian tradition the beatitude form is not used of God.[7] In the LXX, God is, indeed, said to be "blessed," that is, blest, praised, extolled, but this is not really a beatitude or macarism. For the term employed is then the adjective εὐλόγητος or the participle εὐλογημένος, both of which translate the Hebrew participle ברוך. Thus frequently in prayers, "Blest be God/Yahweh" (Exod 18:10; Gen 9:26; 24:27). The same Greek terms can also be used of human beings, but then they express the fact of being blessed (i.e., blest) by God, whereas μακάριος, "blessed," emphasizes rather the person's happy, prosperous, or fortunate condition as the result of such divine blessing.

In the Old Testament the beatitude form is never found in a legal text; it occurs only once in narrative texts (in the double beatitude uttered by the Queen of Sheba over the wives and servants of Solomon who were able to listen to his wisdom, recorded both in 1 Kgs 10:8 and 2 Chr 9:7), and once in a poetic text (Deut 33:29). It is found three times in prophetic texts (Isa 30:18; 32:20; 56:2). Otherwise it occurs frequently in the wisdom literature of the Old Testament, both of poetic and hortatory or eschatological types.[8]

Given this Old Testament usage, it is not surprising that the literary form has been found in Qumran literature. In 4Q185 1-2 ii 8 one reads, אשרי אדם נתנה לו מן א. [ ], "Blessed is the one to whom is given by G[od . . .]."[9] Again, in 4Q185 1-2 ii 13-14 one reads, אשרי אדם יעשנה ולא רגל עליה ו[ברו]ח[ן] מרמה לא יבקשנה ובחלקות לא יחזיקנה, "Blessed is the one who does it and utters no slander against [her or] with a deceitful spir[it] seeks her not out and lays hold of her with flatteries."[10] Again, in 1QH 6:13, Emile

Munich: Kaiser, 1974) 191-95; C. Keller, "Les 'béatitudes' de l'Ancien Testament," *Maqqél Shâqédh . . . Hommage à Wilhelm Vischer* (Montpellier: Causse, Graille, Castelnau, 1960) 88-100.

7. See 1 Tim 1:1, 11; 6:15 for a different use of μακάριος when applied to God.

8. See the varied use of אשרי in Deut 33:29; 1 Kgs 10:8; Isa 30:18; 32:20; 56:2; Ps 1:1; 2:12; 32:1-2; 33:12; 34:9; 40:5; 41:2; 65:5; 84:5, 6, 13; 89:16; 94:12; 106:3; 112:1; 119:1-2; 127:5; 128:1-2; 137:8-9; 144:15; 146:5; Job 5:17; Prov 3:13; 8:32, 34; 14:21; 16:20; 20:7; 28:14; 29:18; Qoh 10:17; Dan 12:12; 2 Chr 9:7. Cf. also the varied use of μακάριος in the LXX of Gen 30:13; Isa 31:9; Sir 14:1, 2, 20; 25:8, 9; 26:1; 28:19; 31:8; 34:15; 48:11; 50:28; Tob 13:16; Wis 3:13; Bar 4:4; 4 Macc 7:15; 18:9.

Cf. *Ps. Sol.* 6:1; 10:1; 17:44; 18:6; *Greek Enoch* 99:10; 103:5; *1 Enoch* 58:2; 81:4; 82:4; *As. Mos.* 10:8; *Sib. Orac.* 3:371.

9. See J. M. Allegro, *Qumran Cave 4:1 (4Q158-4Q186)* (DJD 5; Oxford: Clarendon, 1968) 85-86.

10. Ibid., 86. Cf. J. Strugnell, "Notes en marge du Volume V des 'Discoveries in the Judaean Desert of Jordan,'" *RevQ* 7 (1969-71) 163-276, esp. 271.

Puech has rightly restored the beatitude: אשרי] אנשי אמת ובחירי צ[דק דורש]י שכל ומבקשי בינה בונ[י] שלום, "[Blessed are] the people of truth and the righteous elect, those who seek after insight and look for understanding, the builders of peace."[11]

However, there is an aspect of the beatitudes in the Matthean and Lucan Gospels that is not wholly explained by the Old Testament background. In Matt 5:3-11 there are nine continuous instances of beatitudes introduced by μακάριοι, and in Luke 6:20-22 there are four. Such a collection of beatitudes has no counterpart in the Old Testament. There are, indeed, paired beatitudes in 1 Kgs 10:8; 2 Chr 9:7; Ps 32:1-2 (quoted by Paul in Rom 4:7-8); 84:5-6; 119:1-2; 137:8-9; 144:15.[12] But there is no extended collection of macarisms such as one finds in Matthew 5 or Luke 6.

A collection of beatitudes as a distinct literary form has now turned up in Qumran literature. In the article cited above, in which Puech reconstructed 1QH 6:13, he justified his reconstruction by quoting a Cave 4 text (4QBeatitudes or 4Q525), which he has now published more fully.[13] It is a sapiential text written in Herodian script,[14] which belonged originally to the lot of Hebrew fragments entrusted to Jean Starcky.[15] The beatitudes are part of frg. 2, col. ii and are written continuously in lines of Hebrew but are separated by a blank space (vacat). Thus:

אשרי דובר אמת[ ] 0

בלב טהור ולוא רגל על לשונו (vacat) אשרי תומכי חוקיה ולוא יתמוכו 1

בדרכי עולה (vacat) אש[ר]י הגלים בה ולוא יביעו בדרכי אולת (vacat) 2
אשרי דורשיה

11. E. Puech, "Un hymne essénien en partie retrouvé et les béatitudes: 1QH V 12–VI 18 (= col. XIII-XIV 7) et 4QBeat.," *RevQ* 13 (Mémorial Jean Carmignac, 1988) 59-88, esp. 66.

12. Also Sir 25:8-9. Cf. A. Mattioli, "Identità letteraria e dottrinale delle beatitudini della Bibbia ebraica — classificazione tematica," *Anton* 63 (1988) 189-226, esp. 203; C. H. Dodd, "The Beatitudes," in *Mélanges bibliques rédigés en l'honneur de André Robert* (Travaux de l'Institut Catholique de Paris 4; Paris: Bloud et Gay, 1957) 404-10, esp. 408.

13. E. Puech, "4Q525 et les péricopes des béatitudes en Ben Sira et Matthieu," *RB* 98 (1991) 80-106 (+ pl. 1). Here the photograph of three fragments is supplied, together with a transcription and translation of them.

14. See Puech, "Un hymne," 84-88.

15. See P. Benoit et al., "Editing the Manuscript Fragments from Qumran," *BA* 19 (1956) 75-96, p. 96: "One ms of *sapential* variety contains a series of *beatitudes* directed to those who keep the commandments and a description of torments which await the impious, which are not to be identified with similar passages in I Enoch." Cf. *RB* 63 (1956) 49-67 (the French original).

3 בבור כפים ולוא ישחרנה בלב מרמה *(vacat)* אשרי אדם השיג חוכמה ויתהלך

4 בתורת עליון ויכן לדרכיה לבו *(vacat)* ויתאפק ביסוריה ובנגיעיה ירצה תמ[י]ד

5 ולוא יטושנה בעוני מצר[יו] ובעת צוקה לוא יעוזבנה ולוא ישכחנה] בימי[פחד

6 ובענות נפשו לוא יגעל[נה] כי בה יהגה תמיד ובצרתו ישוחח [בתורה ובכו]ל

7 היותו בה[ישכיל וישיתה]לנגד עיניו לבלתי לכת בדרכי]   [

8 [   ] ה יחד ויתם לבו אליה].   [

9 [ותשית עטרת ? על ראו]שו ועם מלכים תוש]יבנ/הו   [

10 [   ] אחים יפר].   [

11 [   ] [   ]   [

12 [   ] ועתה בנים שמעו לי וא]ל תסור[ו מ . . .   [

13 [   ]ם[   ]

0. [Blessed is the one who speaks truth]

1. with a pure heart and slanders not with his tongue. Blessed are those who cling to her statutes and cling not

2. to paths of iniquity. Bles[s]ed are those who rejoice in her and babble not about paths of foolishness. Blessed are those who search for her

3. with clean hands and seek not after her with a deceitful heart. Blessed is the man who has attained wisdom and walks

4. by the law of the Most High and fixes his heart on her ways, gives heed to her admonishments, delights con[stant]ly in her chastisements,

5. and forsakes her not in the stress of [his] trou[bles]; (who) in time of distress abandons her not and forgets her not [in days of] fear,

6. and in the affliction of his soul rejects [her] not. For on her he meditates constantly, and in his anguish he ponders [the law; and in al]l

7. his existence [he considers] her [and puts her] before his eyes, so as not to walk in the paths of [   ]

8. [   ] his [   ] together, and he perfects his heart for her [   ]

9. [and she will put a crown   upon] his [hea]d and make [him s]it with kings

10. [   ] he will *pr*[   ] brothers [   ]

11. [   ]

12. [And now, children, listen to me, and] turn [n]ot away [from . . .   ]

13. [   ]*m*[   ]

Here in a clearly sapiential text from Qumran, we have a collection of five beatitudes. The text is fragmentary, and no one knows how many beatitudes would have preceded the extant five. The feminine suffix that occurs throughout the text undoubtedly refers to "wisdom" (חוכמה), mentioned in

line 3, but it could conceivably refer to "the law of the Most High" (תורת
עליון), in line 4, since both nouns ("wisdom" and "law") are feminine in Hebrew. In any case, the "wisdom" is the "law of the Most High," and the Mosaic
law is thus being proposed as the wise guide of human conduct for the Essene
community of Qumran.

Such a collection of beatitudes in a pre-Christian Palestinian Jewish
writing thus provides an interesting example of a literary form that until now
was attested only in the Greek New Testament, or in literature dependent on
the beatitudes in Matthew 5 and Luke 6. It shows why Jesus' beatitudes were
gathered into a collection in imitation of such a Palestinian Jewish literary
convention. The utterance of beatitudes in multiple form is now seen as characteristic of that background.

The Qumran beatitudes are different from those of Jesus in that they
are centered on one topic, wisdom or the *tôrāh*, and its influence in human
conduct. There is little of the eschatological nuance that characterizes the
Matthean or Lucan beatitudes, just as there is little of the sapiential content or
formulation in the Matthean or Lucan collection of Jesus' beatitudes.

Another difference is seen in the form of the Qumran beatitudes. The
first four of the five begin with a positive statement (. . . אשרי), which is then
followed by a negative one (. . . ולוא). The fifth one is only positive in formulation and much longer, resembling the ninth Matthean beatitude.

Another element that runs through the Qumran collection of beatitudes and makes it different is the mention of parts of the body, "heart" (lines
1, 3), "tongue" (line 1), and "hands" (line 3). This makes one think of the
catchword bonding used to link Old Testament quotations in the testimonia
list of Rom 3:10-18.[16]

In his fuller presentation of the text, Puech suggests that the beginning
of the collection would have been preceded by three other beatitudes now
lost.[17] This would mean that the Qumran collection had eight beatitudes.
While this is theoretically possible, there is no certainty. Puech seeks to make
this plausible by comparing the Qumran collection with the Matthean, while
recognizing the problem about the number of the latter, whether they should
be reckoned as eight or nine.[18] To make the number eight more acceptable, he

16. See J. A. Fitzmyer, "'4QTestimonia' and the New Testament," in *ESBNT* or *SBNT,*
59-89, esp. 66; cf. idem, *Romans: A New Translation with Introduction and Commentary*
(AB 33; New York: Doubleday, 1993) 333-40.

17. See Puech, "4Q525 et les péricopes," 90.

18. See A. A. Di Lella, "The Structure and Composition of the Matthean Beatitudes," in *To Touch the Text: Biblical and Related Studies in Honor of Joseph A. Fitzmyer, S.J.*
(ed. M. P. Horgan and P. J. Kobelski; New York: Crossroad, 1989) 237-42.

compares the expanded macarism of Sir 14:20-27. Whereas there are, indeed, eight items in Sirach, they are not all introduced by μακάριος or אשרי; in fact, there is only one instance of this introductory formula for the group of eight in Sirach.

George J. Brooke has also compared 4QBeatitudes with the Matthean beatitudes and studied varied similarities in the two passages.[19] Unfortunately, some of his comparisons are overdrawn (e.g., the comparison of 4QBeatitudes with Ps 37:29-31, which is not used in the Qumran text). It may also be questioned whether the Matthean beatitudes are all that concerned with wisdom, as Brooke tries to make out. The Qumran beatitudes are certainly so concerned; but Brooke is reading too much of the sapiential background of the Qumran collection into the Matthean text and has not sufficiently attended to the different kinds of beatitudes that were in use in the Jewish tradition. Jacques Dupont has shown that there are two kinds of beatitudes, sapiential and eschatological.[20] The Matthean beatitudes belong to the latter class, whereas this Qumran collection is clearly an example of the former.

One must also stress the use of Old Testament phrases, which make up the beatitudes, in both instances. For instance, 4QBeatitudes begins with a paraphrase of Ps 15:3, which in the MT reads, ודבר אמת בלבבו לא רגל על לשנו, "who speaks the truth in his heart and scandals not with his tongue." Instead of בלבבו, 4QBeatitudes uses בלב טהור, "with a pure heart," a Hebrew phrase that is closer to the Matthean expression καθαροὶ τῇ καρδίᾳ, "clean of heart" (5:8).[21] The phrase בור כפים, "cleanness of hands," is derived from Job 9:30 or 22:30, where the singular occurs (בר כף).[22] Similarly, two of the phrases can be found elsewhere in Qumran literature: דרכי עולה, "paths of iniquity" (line 2), finds a parallel in כל דרך עולה of 1QH 14:26; and ענות נפשו, "the affliction of his soul" (line 6), may have its counterpart in 1QS 3:8,

---

19. See G. J. Brooke, "The Wisdom of Matthew's Beatitudes (4QBeat and Mt. 5:3-12)," *ScrBull* 19 (1989) 35-41. Strangely enough, though he recognizes the sapiential character of the Qumran beatitudes, Brooke translates תומכי חוקיה as "who hold fast to his statutes," when the suffix on the second word is clearly feminine, "her statutes," that is, the statutes of wisdom.

20. See J. Dupont, "Beatitudine/Beatitudini," in *Nuovo dizionario di teologia biblica* (ed. P. Rossano et al.; Cinisello Balsamo (Milano): Paoline, 1988) 155-61, esp. 156. Also in the Spanish version, "Bienaventuranza/Bienaventuranzas," in *Nuevo diccionario de teología bíblica* (ed. G. Barbaglio and S. Dianich; Madrid: Cristiandad, 1990) 264-72.

21. Brooke ("The Wisdom," 37) rightly points out that this Hebrew phrase, used in a macarism from Qumran, reveals how pointless was M. Black's attempt to regard the Matthean phrase as a mistranslation of an Aramaic expression (דכי לב) in *An Aramaic Approach to the Gospels and Acts* (3d ed.; Oxford: Clarendon, 1967) 158 n. 2.

22. Cf. 2 Sam 22:21; Ps 18:21, 25, where a similar phrase (בר ידי) occurs.

if the meaning is the same. Moreover, the third Matthean beatitude is derived from Ps 37:11.

A similar collection of beatitudes is known from the pseudepigraphon *2 Enoch*,[23] but the date of that composition is quite disputed.[24] In 13:64-70, each of seven macarisms is introduced with the formula, "Blessed the one who . . . ," and in each instance it is paralleled with "Cursed be the one who. . . ." This formulation imitates not only the Palestinian Jewish collection of beatitudes now known from Qumran, but also the Greek Old Testament parallelism of μακάριος and οὐαί in Eccl 10:16-17. Possibly too the collection form in this writing is influenced by the New Testament collections of Matthew and Luke themselves, especially the latter with its parallel macarisms and woes.

Note also the Christian collection of beatitudes in the *Acts of Paul and Thecla* 3:5-6, which may number thirteen.[25]

So once again, a Qumran text has been discovered that sheds light on an important New Testament feature. We have, however, to await the full publication of 4Q525 in order to situate it in its own proper context. Even though Starcky had revealed to the scholarly world in 1956 the kind of text that he had, it is regrettable that New Testament interpreters had to wait more than forty years for the publication of such a text.[26]

23. See H. F. D. Sparks, ed., *The Apocryphal Old Testament* (Oxford: Clarendon, 1984) 348-49.

24. R. H. Charles thought that it was written in Greek by an Alexandrian Jew about the beginning of the Christian era; A. S. D. Maunder attributed it to a Bogomil author sometime between the twelfth and the fifteenth century A.D. A. Vaillant more rightly regards it as the work of a Jewish Christian who sought to compose in Greek a counterpart of the Jewish *1 Enoch* in the second or third century A.D.; see H. F. D. Sparks, ed., *The Apocryphal Old Testament,* 323. See further L. Rost, *Judaism outside the Hebrew Canon: An Introduction to the Documents* (Nashville: Abingdon, 1976) 112: ". . . should probably be dated in the first half of the first century C.E. Its final form is due to a Christian revision in the Eastern church dating from the seventh century."

25. See C. Schmidt, *Acta Pauli aus der Heidelberger koptischen Papyrushandschrift Nr. 1* (2 vols.; 2d ed.; Leipzig: Hinrichs, 1904-5; reprint, Hildesheim: Olms, 1965) 2:29-30; 5*-6*; cf. W. Schneemelcher, *New Testament Apocrypha* (2 vols.; Louisville: Westminster John Knox, 1992) 2:239-40.

26. See now the full publication of 4Q525 in E. Puech, ed., *Qumrân Grotte 4: XVIII. Textes hébreux (4Q521-4Q528, 4Q576-4Q579)* (DJD 25; Oxford: Clarendon, 1998) 115-78.

CHAPTER 7

Aramaic Evidence Affecting the Interpretation of Hōsanna in the New Testament

Three of the evangelists preserve the Semitic word *hōsanna* in their Greek accounts of Jesus' entry into the city of Jerusalem. The earliest occurrence is found in Mark 11:9-10: οἱ προάγοντες καὶ οἱ ἀκολουθοῦντες ἔκραζον· Ὡσαννά· εὐλογημένος ὁ ἐρχόμενος ἐν ὀνόματι κυρίου· εὐλογημένη ἡ ἐρχομένη βασιλεία τοῦ πατρὸς ἡμῶν Δαυίδ· Ὡσαννὰ ἐν τοῖς ὑψίστοις. "Those who went before and those who followed kept crying aloud, 'Hosanna! Blest be he who comes in the name of the Lord! Blest be the kingdom of our Father David that is coming! Hosanna in the highest!'"

Matthew has slightly redacted the same acclamation in 21:9: οἱ δὲ ὄχλοι οἱ προάγοντες αὐτὸν καὶ οἱ ἀκολουθοῦντες ἔκραζον λέγοντες· Ὡσαννὰ τῷ υἱῷ Δαυίδ· Εὐλογημένος ὁ ἐρχόμενος ἐν ὀνόματι κυρίου· Ὡσαννὰ ἐν τοῖς ὑψίστοις, "The crowds that went before him and those following kept crying aloud, saying, 'Hosanna to the son of David! Blest be he who comes in the name of the Lord! Hosanna in the highest!'" Matthew also repeats the first part of the acclamation as he recounts the reaction of the chief priests and the scribes to Jesus' purging of the Temple and the children crying aloud in the Temple precincts (21:15), Ὡσαννὰ τῷ υἱῷ Δαυίδ, "Hosanna to the son of David!"

The third and last evangelist who records the cry is not the Synoptist Luke,[1] but John in his account of Jesus' entry into Jerusalem (12:13): ἔλαβον

---

1. Luke undoubtedly omitted ὡσαννά because its meaning would have been missed

119

τὰ βαΐα τῶν φοινίκων καὶ ἐξῆλθον εἰς ὑπάντησιν αὐτῷ καὶ ἐκραύγαζον·
Ὡσαννά· εὐλογημένος ὁ ἐρχόμενος ἐν ὀνόματι τοῦ κυρίου, καὶ ὁ βασιλεὺς τοῦ
Ἰσραήλ, "They took branches of palm trees and went out to meet him, crying
aloud, 'Hosanna! Blest be he who comes in the name of the Lord, the King of
Israel!'"

Commentators recognize that the acclamation quotes in part the Greek
translation of Ps 118:25-26,[2] ὦ κύριε, σῶσον δή, ὦ κύριε, εὐόδωσον δή.
εὐλογημένος ὁ ἐρχόμενος ἐν ὀνόματι κυρίου, "O Lord, save (us); O Lord,
make prosperous (our) way! Blest be he who comes in the name of the Lord!"
This Greek translation renders well the sense of the Hebrew original, אנא
יהוה הושיעה נא. אנא יהוה הצליחה נא ברוך הבא בשם יהוה, "save (us), we
pray, O LORD! O LORD, we pray, give us success! Blest be the one who comes in
the name of the Lord."[3] The acclamation is derived from that part of Psalm
118 in which thanks are expressed to Yahweh for deliverance from distress, as
the psalmist makes a summons for a procession of gratitude. The acclamation
itself is a cry for help addressed to Yahweh, whose blessing of salvation and
success is being invoked on those who process in his name. The imperative
הושיעה is elsewhere addressed to Yahweh, especially in the Psalter (Ps 12:2;
20:10; 28:9; 60:7; 86:16; 108:7); a shorter form of the imperative הושע is used
of Yahweh in Ps 86:2 and possibly in Jer 31:7.[4] The long imperative הושיעה is
further addressed by a woman of Tekoa to King David (2 Sam 14:4; cf. 2 Kgs
6:26) and by the men of Gibeon to Joshua (Josh 10:6). In every instance the
imperative is translated into Greek in the LXX by σῶσον, "save," except in
Josh 10:6, where ἐξελοῦ, "deliver (us)," is found instead. Nowhere in the Greek

by his predominantly Gentile Christian readers. See F. D. Coggan, "Note on the Word
hōsanna," *ExpTim* 52 (1940-41) 76-77; also E. Lohse, "Hosianna," *NovT* 6 (1963) 113-19,
esp. 114.

2. See A. Rahlfs, *Psalmi cum Odis* (Göttingen Septuaginta 10; Göttingen:
Vandenhoeck & Ruprecht, 1931) 287.

3. Other discussions of this term can be found in L. S. Potvin, "Words in New Testament Greek Borrowed from the Hebrew and Aramaean," *BSac* 33 (1876) 52-62; F. Spitta,
"Der Volksruf beim Einzug Jesu in Jerusalem," *ZWT* 52 (1910) 307-20; F. C. Burkitt, "W
and Θ: Studies in the Western Text of St Mark (Continued): Hosanna," *JTS* 17 (1916) 139-
52; E. F. F. Bishop, "Hosanna: The Word of the Joyful Jerusalem Crowds," *ExpTim* 53
(1941-42) 212-14; J. S. Kennard, Jr. "'Hōsanna' and the Purpose of Jesus," *JBL* 67 (1948)
171-76; T. Lohmann, "Hosianna," *Biblisch-Historisches Handwörterbuch* (4 vols.; ed.
B. Reicke and L. Rost; Göttingen: Vandenhoeck & Ruprecht, 1962-79) 2:752; B. Sandvik,
Das Kommen des Herrn beim Abendmahl im Neuen Testament (ATANT 58; Zurich: Zwingli
Verlag, 1970) 37-51; W. Rebell, "ὡσαννά," *EDNT,* 3:509.

4. In the latter case the LXX (38:7) understood הושע not as an imperative, but as a
perfect, and rendered it ἔσωσεν, "he saved."

version does a transliterated Semitic word occur for הושיעה or הושע, as in the New Testament, and only in Ps 118:25 does the precative particle נא follow the imperative הושיעה, which is translated σῶσον δή, "save, we pray."

Even if one has to recognize that Ps 118:25-26 lies behind the acclamation in the Gospels, it is noteworthy that the Semitic form הושע נא is transcribed here in its earliest attestation in Greek as ὡσαννά; none of the evangelists has used the Greek translation of it from the LXX. It stands, for that reason, a good chance of representing a genuine primitive Christian recollection of what was shouted to Jesus on the occasion of his entry into Jerusalem or at least of what was often shouted to pilgrims like him coming to the city of Jerusalem.

The later rabbinic tradition associated Ps 118:25-26 with the feast of Tabernacles and its liturgy.[5] Indeed, it used the term as a name in Aramaic for the seventh day of that feast, יומא דהושענא, "the day of Hosanna" (*Leviticus Rabbah* 37.2).[6] Moreover, the term was even used of the branches, otherwise called לולב, waved in the rain-making ceremony, which was part of the liturgy (*b. Sukkah* 30b, 37b; cf. *Tg. Esther II* 3:8).[7] By the time these rabbinic texts were written down, roughly in the fifth century A.D.,[8] the sense of the original cry of help to Yahweh had disappeared. The term had undergone a semantic shift and become "a fixed formula in the procession round the altar of burnt offering."[9] How early did this shift in meaning take place? Before we try to answer that question, there are other aspects of the word *hōsanna* that have to be considered.

When Origen (A.D. 185-254) commented on Matt 21:9, he realized that the Gospels were written (copied?) "by Greeks . . . who did not know the lan-

---

5. See Str-B, 1:845-50. Cf. Lohse, "Hosianna," 114-16.

6. See *Midrash Rabbah* (10 vols.; ed. M. Freedman and M. Simon; London: Soncino, 1951) 4:466: "*Hosha'na Rabbah*" as the name of the seventh day of the feast of Tabernacles.

7. See L. Goldschmidt, *Der babylonische Talmud* (9 vols.; Berlin: 1897-1935) 3:83. Also A. Sperber, *The Bible in Aramaic* (4 vols., vol. 4 in two parts; Leiden: Brill, 1959-68) 4a:189; P. de Lagarde, *Hagiographa chaldaice* (Osnabrück: Zeller, 1967) 247. Cf. J. J. Petuchowski, "Hoshi'ah na' in Psalm cxviii 25 — A Prayer for Rain," *VT* 5 (1955) 266-71.

8. The first two of these writings date from about A.D. 450. See M. D. Herr, "Midrash," *Encyclopedia Judaica* (16 vols.; New York: Macmillan; Jerusalem: Keter, 1972) 11:1507-14. Herr dates *Leviticus Rabbah* among the classical Amoraic midrashim of the early period (A.D. 400-640). E. Berkovits dates the *Babylonian Talmud* "from the days of Abba Aricha . . . and Samuel, in the first half of the third century, to the end of the teaching of Ravina in 499" ("Talmud, Babylonian," ibid., 15:755-68, esp. 755). *Tg. Esther II* would come from a still later date. See Y. Komlosh, "Targum Sheni," ibid., 15:811-15: "at the end of the seventh or the beginning of the eighth century."

9. See E. Lohse, "*Hōsanna*," *TDNT*, 9:682.

guage" (ὑπὸ Ἑλλήνων . . . μὴ εἰδότων τὴν διάλεκτον) and were confused by what was written in Psalm 118. He transliterated the Hebrew of verses 25-26 thus: ἀννὰ ἀδοναὶ ὁσιαννά, ἀννὰ ἀδοναὶ ἀσλιάννα· βαροὺκ ἀββὰ βσαῖμ ἀδοναί.[10] Origen understood the psalm correctly but made no attempt to explain the Greek transliteration in the Gospels, ὡσαννά, or how it differed from Hebrew הושיע נא. Eusebius (A.D. 260-340) did not understand ὡσαννά at all, when he wrote about "the great crowd of men and children (who) went before him [Jesus], shouting with joy Ὡσαννὰ τῷ υἱῷ Δαυίδ." He commented that "instead of ὦ κύριε, σῶσον δή, which he found in the (Greek) psalm, they shouted in a more Hebraic (form) ὡς ἀννά," writing the word as two and wrongly dividing it.[11] Later, when Jerome (A.D. 342-420) wrote to Pope Damasus about the term, he cited Hilary's explanation of *hōsanna* as meaning "redemptio domus David" (redemption of the house of David), written *hebraico sermone* and rejected Hilary's explanation, along with that of other unnamed interpreters who said that *hōsanna* was Hebrew for "glory" or "grace."[12] Jerome then cited the Hebrew of what he called Psalm 117 in a form almost identical with Origen's transliteration given above. He further noted that the Hebrew word is *osianna*, which "we in ignorance corruptly pronounce *osanna*," and he further interpreted Hebrew *anna* (with initial *aleph*) as *obsecro*, "I beg, pray," and *osianna* as *salvifica* or *salvum facere*, "save" or "make safe."[13] Jerome also explained the difference between *hosanna* and *osianna* as an elision of a medial vowel.[14]

When E. J. Goodspeed was preparing his English translation of the New Testament, he surveyed older English versions of Matt 21:9 and published a note that gave many of the variant ways in which English translators had handled ὡσαννά: from "Osanna (that is I preye save)" of Wyclif (1382), to "hosaianna" of Tyndale (1525) and Coverdale (1535), to "Hosanna the sonne of Davie" of Geneva (1560), to "Hosanna to the Son of David" of many subsequent versions. Goodspeed himself maintained that the cry had lost its liturgical character and had become a spontaneous outburst like "Vive le roi!" or "God save the King!" He explained, "The pilgrims called down blessings upon

10. Origen, *Comm. in Matth.* 16.19; GCS 40.541-42.

11. Eusebius, *Dem. evang.* 6.8.2; GCS 23.258). E. Lohse analyzes the Eusebian form as Greek ὡς (= εἰς) ἀνά (*TDNT*, 9:683 n. 14).

12. Jerome, *Ep.* 20.1 (Ad Damasum, CSEL 54.104).

13. Jerome, *Ep.* 20.3; CSEL 54.106.

14. Jerome, *Ep.* 20.5; CSEL 54.109: "'*osianna*' sive, ut nos loquimur '*osanna*,' media uocali littera elisa." For other ancient uses of the cry, see A. Resch, *Aussercanonische Paralleltexte zu den Evangelien gesammelt und untersucht* (TU 10/1-5; Leipzig: Hinrichs, 1893-97) 2:533-35.

Jesus as he went by: 'God bless the Son of David! . . . God bless him from on high!'"[15]

When E. Kautzsch discussed the Aramaic words in the New Testament, he recognized that commentators rightly explained the relation of the acclamation in the Gospels to Psalm 118, but that "the form ὡσαννά cannot be identified with הושיעה נא"; he quoted Elias Levita's explanations that the Greek form was a "shortened pronunciation of the prayer cry = *hôšaʿnāʾ* and compared Syriac *ʾawšaʿnāʾ*, citing A. Hilgenfeld's suggestion that Greek ὡσαννά reflected "Aram. *ʾôšaʿnāʾ*."[16]

The problem with this explanation has always been the lack of any evidence that the root *yšʿ* was ever used in Aramaic prior to or contemporary with the New Testament.[17] The root appears abundantly in Hebrew,[18] and it is attested in Moabite,[19] but neither Jean-Hoftijzer,[20] I. N. Vinnikov,[21] nor K. Beyer[22] gives any evidence of its use in Aramaic, apart from the proper name ישעיה (*AP* 5:16; 8:33; 9:21), which is undoubtedly a Hebrew name, identical with that of the famous Old Testament prophet, Isaiah. Because of this situation scholars have at times called attention to the short form of the imperative הושע used in Ps 86:2 and possibly in Jer 31:7.[23] This does not help,

15. See E. J. Goodspeed, *Problems of New Testament Translation* (Chicago: University of Chicago Press, 1945) 34-35. See also *The Complete Bible: An American Translation* (Chicago: University of Chicago Press, 1960), NT, 21.

16. E. Kautzsch, *Grammatik des Biblisch-aramäischen mit einer kritischen Erörterung der aramäischen Wörter im Neuen Testament* (Leipzig: F. C. W. Vogel, 1884) 173. Cf. A. Hilgenfeld, ZWT 27 (1875) 358 (non vidi); also *Evangeliorum secundum Hebraeos . . . quae supersunt* (2d ed.; Leipzig: T. O. Weigel, 1884) 25. He translates Aramaic הושע נא as "serva nos."

17. See P. Joüon, *L'Evangile de Notre-Seigneur Jésus-Christ* (VS 5; Paris: Beauchesne, 1930) 128: "totalement inconnue en araméen." Cf. J. Jeremias, "Die Muttersprache des Evangelisten Matthäus," *ZNW* 50 (1959) 270-74, esp. 274.

18. See *HALAT*, 427-28.

19. See H. Donner and W. Röllig, *Kanaanäische und aramäische Inschriften* (2d ed.; Wiesbaden: Harrassowitz, 1966-69) §181:3-4.

20. C. F. Jean and J. Hoftijzer, *Dictionnaire des inscriptions sémitiques de l'ouest* (Leiden: Brill, 1965) 112. Similarly J. Hoftijzer and K. Jongeling, *Dictionary of the North-West Semitic Inscriptions* (HdO 1/21; 2 vols.; Leiden: Brill, 1995) 476.

21. I. N. Vinnikov, "Slovar arameyskich Nadpisey," *Palestinskii Sbornik* 7/70 (1962) 236.

22. K. Beyer, *Die aramäischen Texte vom Toten Meer samt den Inschriften aus Palästina, dem Testament Levis aus der Kairoer Genisa, der Fastenrolle und den alten talmudischen Zitaten* (Göttingen: Vandenhoeck & Ruprecht, 1984) 601. See now the *Ergänzungsband* (1994) 359, where Beyer lists it as a Hebraism: "(< hebr.) 'retten.'"

23. See n. 4 above for the problem of Jer 31:7.

however, since there is no evidence that the short הושע was ever used with the precative particle נא in Hebrew; it seems to occur only with the long imperative, and then only in Ps 118:25.

Now, however, two instances of the root *yšʿ* have come to light in Aramaic texts, and even though הושע נא has not yet been found, the instances lend support to the interpretation of Greek ὡσαννά as a transcription of Aramaic הושע נא.

The first bit of evidence is found in the recently discovered Old Aramaic inscription from Tell Fakhariyah. In it a "king of Gozan" (מלך גוזן) sets up a statue of himself before the god Hadad of Sikan. The king's name is written as הדיסעי. Line 1 of the Aramaic text reads: דמותא / זי / הדיסעי : זי : שם : קדם : הדדסכן, "The likeness of Hadduyith'i, which he erected before Hadad of Sikan. . . ."[24] Thus begins the long Aramaic inscription from the ninth century B.C., from the phase of Old Aramaic. It is a translation, not exact in all details, of an accompanying Assyrian inscription; the latter is inscribed on the front skirt of the statue of the king, and the Aramaic on the back skirt. The Assyrian text has no counterpart of line 1 of the Aramaic, but in line 8 of the Assyrian text the name of the king is given as *ᴵU-it-ʾi GAR.KUR ᵁᴿᵁgu-za-ni*, that is, *ᴵadad₂-it-ʾi šakin māti ᵃᴵGu-za-ni*, "H., governor of the land of Gozan."[25]

The striking thing about this name is the newly attested preservation of an effort to represent by the consonant *samekh* in the borrowed Phoenician alphabet the interdental t *(tha)*, which was still being so pronounced by the Arameans of this period. In other Old Aramaic inscriptions this interdental was usually represented by *šin* (e.g., in the Sefire inscription: שוב, Sf III 6, 20, 24, 25; ישב, Sf III 7, 17; שם, Sf III 6).[26] In this new inscription, however, it appears as *samekh*.

The king's name appears to be Aramaic; its theophoric element is that of Hadad, the storm god of the Aramean pantheon. His name means "Hadad is my salvation." The second half of the name is a form of the root *ytʿ* and is related to the Hebrew noun ישע (see Mic 7:7; Hab 3:18; Ps 18:47 [for the same suffixal form in Hebrew]). The editors have vocalized the king's Aramaic name as "Hadad-yisʿi" (and the Assyrian form as *Adad-itʾi*). S. A.

24. See A. Abou-Assaf, P. Bordreuil, and A. R. Millard, *La statue de Tell Fekherye et son inscription bilingue assyro-araméenne* (Etudes Assyriologiques, cah. 7; Paris: Editions Recherche sur les civilisations, 1982) 23. Cf. S. A. Kaufman, "Reflections on the Assyrian-Aramaic Bilingual from Tell Fakhariyeh," *Maarav* 3/2 (1982) 137-75.

25. *La statue*, 13, 15; cf. Kaufman, "Reflections," 159.

26. See J. A. Fitzmyer, *The Aramaic Inscriptions from Sefire* (rev. ed.; BibOr 19/A: Rome: Biblical Institute, 1995) 187.

Kaufman vocalizes the Aramaic name as "Had-Yiṯ'i," explaining it as "Had(du) is my help." He notes that the name of the god is otherwise spelled הדד in the Aramaic inscription (lines 1, 15, 17), that *Haddu* is the Amorite form of the name, and that the Akkadian form is sometimes *Ad*.[27] The form Had-Yiṯ'i is strange for an Aramaic name, and I should prefer to read it as Haddu-yiṯ'i. In any case, no matter what the correct form of the name may be, it shows that the Proto-Semitic root *yṯ'*, "save," was used in Aramaic. Kaufman further commented, "The root *yṯ'*, well known in its Hebrew guise of *yš'*, is found in Aramaic only in proper names from this early period."[28] This comment leads to my second instance.

In a fragmentary text from Qumran Cave 4, which J. T. Milik had partially published and provisionally labeled Pseudo-Daniel[a], there is an instance of *yš'* in an Aramaic text written in Herodian script.[29] In fragment 16, line 2 one reads, [בי . . .]דה רבתא ויושע אנ[ון], "[. . . with] his great [ha]nd, and he will save th[em]." Here the root *yš'* clearly appears, and in a form that is again striking. One would have expected it to appear as יותע in the Middle Phase of the Aramaic language, but instead it appears as in Hebrew as יושע. This is, however, not the only instance of *š* instead of *ṯ* in the Aramaic of this period, since אשור, "Asshur, Assyria," appears in 1QapGen 17:8,[30] whereas אתור is regularly the form in Ahiqar (lines 3-5, 8, 10-14, 20, 32, etc.). So it seems that *yš'* was occasionally used in Aramaic, even outside of proper names.

Although הושע נא as such has not yet been found in Aramaic, the two instances noted above show that the root *yṯ'*/*yš'* was not completely unknown in Aramaic, even if only rarely attested. Moreover, the precative particle נא/נג is likewise attested in the Middle Phase of the Aramaic language: 11QtgJob 30:1; 34:3, 6, 7; 37:6 (used after an imperative in each instance); 1QapGen 20:25 (used after a jussive).[31] There is no long form of the imperative in Ara-

---

27. Kaufman, "Reflections," 163-64.

28. Ibid., 164.

29. J. T. Milik, "Prière de Nabonide et autres écrits d'un cycle de Daniel: Fragments araméens de Qumrân 4," *RB* 63 (1956) 407-15, esp. 411-15 (what Milik then called fragment D). See now 4Q243 16:2, as published by J. J. Collins, "**243. 4QPseudo-Daniel**[a]," in *Qumran Cave 4: XVII. Parabiblical Texts, Part 3* (DJD 22; ed. G. Brooke et al.; Oxford: Clarendon, 1996) 97-121, esp. 108 (+ pl. VIII).

30. See N. Avigad and Y. Yadin, *A Genesis Apocryphon: A Scroll from the Wilderness of Judaea* (Jerusalem: Magnes, 1956) 22; and my commentary, *The Genesis Apocryphon of Qumran Cave 1: A Commentary* (2d ed.; BibOr 18A; Rome: Biblical Institute, 1971) 58, 103.

31. See J. P. M. van der Ploeg and A. S. van der Woude, *Le targum de Job de la grotte xi de Qumrân* (Leiden: Brill, 1971) 70, 78, 84; Avigad and Yadin, *A Genesis Apocryphon*, col. 20.

maic; so הושע would be the normally expected form. Indeed, one wonders whether the short Hebrew form in Ps 86:2 and Jer 31:7 (if imperatival) is not really Aramaized.[32]

Such, then, is the Aramaic evidence that affects the interpretation of ὡσαννά in the Greek accounts of Jesus' entry into Jerusalem. It makes it plausible that הושע נא, and not הושיעה נא, was the current Aramaic form of the acclamation shouted to Jesus, as a greeting, the first evidence of which is, strikingly enough, preserved in the Greek text of the Gospels.

The evidence for the relation of הושע נא to the feast of Tabernacles in the later rabbinic tradition has been cited above. The shift in meaning thus attested is clear, but is there any evidence that that shift had already taken place in the first century A.D.? Was it being used then as a cry to greet pilgrims coming to Jerusalem for the feast of Tabernacles, or even some other feast? In other words, had it already lost its original meaning of a cry for help addressed to Yahweh, as in Ps 118:25? No little debate has surrounded this question in modern times. I turn to a review of the explanations, because some of them are farfetched. As far as I can see, the evidence for the shift having taken place in the first century is found in the Greek of the Gospel texts themselves.

If we had only the Johannine form of the tradition about Jesus' entry into Jerusalem, the debate would probably not have arisen, since there (John 12:13) Ps 118:25-26 is quoted and modified only by the addition of [καὶ] ὁ βασιλεὺς τοῦ Ἰσραήλ, "[even] the King of Israel." However, both Mark 11:10 and Matt 21:9 record the cry Ὡσαννὰ ἐν τοῖς ὑψίστοις, "Hosanna in the highest," which suggests that the cry had acquired a stereotyped meaning that no longer corresponded to its original sense in Psalm 118. Otherwise, how could ὡσαννά have been joined to the following phrase, "in the highest"? This meaning is further suggested by the cry twice used in Matthew alone, Ὡσαννὰ τῷ υἱῷ Δαυίδ, "Hosanna to the son of David!" (Matt 21:9, 15). The dative is clear in the Matthean Greek. If ὡσαννά were felt as reflecting the original sense of the transitive הושיעה נא of Ps 118:25 or even of Greek σῶσον δή, why would the dative be used? Hence, it must have carried the sense of "Hail to the son of David," or something like the forms suggested by Goodspeed above.

Attempts have been made to explain the dative by citing Old Testament examples of הושיע followed by -ל (e.g. Ps 72:4, יושיע לבני אביון, "may he save the poor"; Ps 86:16, והושיעה לבן אמתך, "and save the son of your handmaid"; Ps 116:6, ולי יהושיע, "and he saves me"). G. Dalman appealed to such instances to show that Hebrew הושיע could be construed with -ל, and so

<hr>

32. See n. 4 above.

ὡσαννά would not mean "give greeting to."[33] Apparently unaware of Dalman's treatment, C. T. Wood repeated the argument, regarding the examples from the psalms as cases of the "Dative in late Hebrew": "*a fortiori* must the dative follow in Aramaic." Hence Wood translated Matt 21:9: "Oh save the Son of David."[34] If the Hebrew of the psalms cited is, indeed, "late," would not the more logical explanation of -ל in such passages be that it represents Aramaic interference, with -ל being the sign of the accusative, as it is frequently used in Aramaic, and not a mode of expressing a dative?[35] For the LXX has rendered these clauses with the object in the accusative: σώσει τοὺς υἱοὺς τῶν πενήτων (71:4); σῶσον τὸν υἱὸν τῆς παιδίσκης σου (85:16); and καὶ ἔσωσέν με (114:6). If this be correct, one would have to claim either that Matt 21:9 is an overliteral translation of הושע נא ל- or that the Greek ὡσαννά there reflects the semantic shift of הושע נא from a cry for help to a greeting. The reason why the latter is preferred is the form that the cry eventually takes in *Didache* 10:6, where one finds Ὡσαννὰ τῷ Θεῷ Δαυείδ. This hardly means, "Save the God of David." It is rather, "Hosanna (Hail) to the God of David!"

The debate, however, continues in another fashion, since F. D. Coggan tried to insist on the association of ὡσαννά with the meaning of Jesus' own name ('Ιησοῦς = יהושוע / ישוע), related by him to the root *yš*: "Do now that which your name implies — that for which we have been so long waiting, namely, be a modern Joshua and bring about a national deliverance and save us from our enemies. . . . 'Save, we pray thee' goes up the cry. 'Jesus, live up to the honored name "Joshua" and be at once deliverer and King.'"[36] Coggan squirmed, however, in seeking to get around the formulation of Matt 21:9, 15 with its dative, by claiming its originality and suggesting the translation, "Save (us), we pray! (Hither) to the Son of David!"[37] Such an explanation of ὡσαννά may seem to suit the Matthean Gospel, because the evangelist records the *popular* etymology of Jesus' name in 1:21, καλέσεις τὸ ὄνομα αὐτοῦ 'Ιησοῦν· αὐτὸς γὰρ σώσει τὸν λαὸν αὐτοῦ ἀπὸ τῶν ἁμαρτιῶν αὐτῶν, "You shall name him Jesus, for he will save his people from their sins." That the real

33. G. Dalman, *The Words of Jesus Considered in the Light of Post-Biblical Jewish Writings and the Aramaic Language* (Edinburgh: Clark, 1909) 220-23, esp. 221.

34. C. T. Wood, "The Word *hosanna* in Matthew xxi.9," *ExpTim* 52 (1940-41) 357.

35. See GKC §117n; P. Joüon, *Grammaire de l'hébreu biblique* (2d ed.; Rome: Biblical Institute, 1947) §125k. C. C. Torrey (*Documents of the Primitive Church* [New York: Harper & Bros., 1941] 77-78) had recognized this feature earlier.

36. Coggan, "Note," 77.

37. Coggan thinks that the Matthean form is more original, despite the fact that τῷ υἱῷ Δαυίδ is absent from the earlier Marcan form and the independent Johannine tradition.

etymology of the name of Jesus, however, is a form of *yš'* is another matter. I shall not repeat here all the reasons why the form יהושוע (*Yĕhôšûă'*, "Joshua"), of which ישוע (*Yēšûă'*, "Jesus") is an abridgement, is to be related to the root ישוע and why the full name really means "Yahweh, help!"[38] Consequently, I am highly skeptical about Coggan's suggestion. The best explanation of the dative τῷ υἱῷ Δαυίδ remains that הושע נא had lost its original meaning of a cry for help and had become a cry of greeting to pilgrims coming to Jerusalem for feasts.[39] If this be correct, then the other cry, Ὡσαννὰ ἐν τοῖς ὑψίστοις is equally explicable: Let the greeting being given to the Son of David extend even to the heights of heaven (where God Himself dwells)![40]

What had been originally a cry for help in pre-Christian Judaism (Ps 118:25) thus became in first-century Palestine a spontaneous cry of greeting or a cry of homage.[41] That ὡσαννά was a prayer addressed to God for help to be shown to the Messiah, as E. P. Gould once sought to explain it,[42] is unlikely. That the greeting is extended to him who is the Messiah in Christian belief in Mark 11:10 or Matt 21:9 is clear, but there is simply no evidence for the association of the cry הושע נא with a messianic expectation in pre-Christian Judaism. The same has to be said for E. Werner's interpretation of הושע נא as a "messianic supplication," which was later suppressed by both Jews and Christians. Werner tried to show further that "in apostolic times, Ps 118 was considered a direct prophecy of the coming of Christ," and he cited 1 Pet 2:4-7 as an indication of such an interpretation.[43] That it was so considered may be

---

38. See my commentary, *The Gospel according to Luke* (2 vols.; AB 28-28A; Garden City, N.Y.: Doubleday, 1981) 1:347. Cf. W. Baumgartner, *HALAT*, 379-80; M. Noth, *Die israelitischen Personennamen* (Beiträge zur Wissenschaft vom Alten und Neuen Testament 3/10; Stuttgart: Kohlhammer, 1928; reprint, Hildesheim: Olms, 1966) 101-10, 154.

39. See H. Bornhäuser, *Sukka (Laubhüttenfest)* (Die Mischna II/6; Berlin: Töpelmann, 1935) 106-7.

40. Jerome's interpretation: "Denique Matthaeus, qui euangelium Hebraeo sermone conscripsit, ita posuit: 'osianna barrama'. Id est 'osanna in excelsis', quod saluatore nascente salus in caelum usque, id est etiam ad excelsa peruenerit pace facta non solum in terra, sed et in caelo" (*Ep.* 20.5; CSEL 54.110). W. C. Allen interprets it thus: "Let those in the heights of heaven say, 'Hosanna'" (*Critical and Exegetical Commentary on the Gospel according to St. Matthew* [3d ed.; ICC; Edinburgh: Clark, 1912] 221). To what extent has Ps 148:1 affected the interpretation of this phrase?

41. *Pace* E. Werner, "'Hosanna' in the Gospels," *JBL* 65 (1946) 97-122. He claims, "Yet in all Hebrew literature no passage in which *Hosanna* expresses exultation occurs" (p. 99).

42. E. P. Gould, *Critical and Exegetical Commentary on the Gospel According to St. Mark* (ICC: Edinburgh: Clark, 1907) 208-9.

43. Werner, "Hosanna," 114. In Ps 20:7 one reads עתה ידעתי כי הושיע יהוה משיחו, "Now I know that Yahweh has saved His anointed one," where the verb "saved" is used of an

right, but that would be a Christian interpretation of the psalm, and it says nothing about how the Jews of the time or in pre-Christian times would have understood it. Moreover, Werner's evidence for the "messianic" interpretation of Psalm 118, when he cites Jewish sources, is drawn from *b. Pesaḥim* 117b; *j. Megilla* 2.1; and *Midrash Hallel,* rabbinic documents which do not antedate the fifth century A.D., and none of which can be associated with pre-Christian Palestinian Judaism. Similarly, E. Lohse has claimed that Psalm 118 was "sometimes interpreted Messianically," citing *Midr. Psalms* 118:22 (on Ps 118:24-29),[44] but Jewish scholars themselves date this text to the middle period of midrashic literature, between A.D. 640 and 900![45]

The upshot of this discussion is that, although there is now evidence that Greek ὡσαννά could well represent the Aramaic form הושע נא, and although that form would merely be an Aramaized form of the Hebrew imperative in Ps 118:25, the term undoubtedly represents a cry that Jerusalemites used to greet pilgrims coming to Jerusalem for feasts like that of Tabernacles, and perhaps even for Passover, as in the Gospels. That the original sense of the term, a cry for help addressed to Yahweh in Ps 118:25, was in the course of time lost is clear. The Gospel texts of Mark and Matthew themselves suggest that the term was already a cry of greeting or homage, and the New Testament occurrence remains the oldest available evidence for that semantic shift. It is, indeed, confirmed by later Christian usage (*Didache* 10:6) and by still later Jewish usage, but none of the later usage can be used to show that הושע נא was *per se* a "messianic supplication" in pre-Christian Judaism.

---

anointed one delivered by God (in the past tense). To read that deliverance of an anointed one into הושיעה נא of Ps 118:25 and apply it to an awaited Messiah, or even to read it into the Gospel use of ὡσαννά is quite another matter. That is hardly the basis for the interpretation of the latter as a "messianic supplication."

44. E. Lohse, *TDNT,* 9:683; cf. idem, "Hosianna," 116. There is no evidence whatsoever for Lohse's claim that this specifically messianic shift had taken place "in pre-Chr. Judaism . . . when the temple was still standing, i.e. prior to 70 A.D."

45. See Herr, "Midrash," 11:1511-14; W. G. Braude, *The Midrash on Psalms* (2 vols.; New Haven: Yale University, 1959) xi-xxxi. Cf. C. Burger, *Jesus als Davidssohn: Eine traditionsgeschichtliche Untersuchung* (FRLANT 98; Göttingen: Vandenhoeck & Ruprecht, 1970) 48. He recognizes the same defect in Lohse's argument.

CHAPTER 8

The Significance of
the Qumran Tobit Texts
for the Study of Tobit

The fragmentary Aramaic and Hebrew texts of Tobit from Qumran Cave 4 were acquired in 1952 along with many others from the same cave and were assigned for study and publication to Jósef Tadeusz Milik,[1] but they remained unpublished until 1995.[2] Milik was mainly responsible for identifying and piecing together the many tiny fragments that form the Tobit texts, and I am happy to recognize his contribution. Much of what I have to say here about the Qumran Aramaic and Hebrew texts depends on him, and I gladly acknowledge my dependence on his remarkable pioneering work.

1. See the report of J. T. Milik in P. Benoit et al., "Editing the Manuscript Fragments from Qumran," *BA* 19 (1956) 75-96, esp. 88 (French original in *RB* 63 [1956] 49-67, esp. 60). There Milik spoke of only two manuscripts in Aramaic. See also his article, "Le travail d'édition des manuscrits du désert de Juda," in *Volume du Congrès, Strasbourg 1956* (VTSup 4; Leiden: Brill, 1957) 17-26, esp. 23-24, where he mentions "un troisième ms. du Tobie araméen"; and his book, *TYDWJ*, 31-32. Eventually we learned something about the contents of the Aramaic and Hebrew fragments in his article, "La patrie de Tobie," *RB* 73 (1966) 522-30, esp. 522 n. 3.

2. See now J. A. Fitzmyer, "Tobit," in *Qumran Cave 4, XIV: Parabiblical Texts, Part 2* (DJD 19; ed. M. Broshi et al.; Oxford: Clarendon, 1995) 1-76 (pls. I-X): "**196**. 4QpapTobit[a] ar," 7-39; "**197**. 4QTobit[b] ar," 41-56; "**198**. 4QTobit[c] ar," 57-60; "**199**. 4QTobit[d] ar," 61-62; "**200**. 4QTobit[e]," 63-76. The Aramaic and Hebrew texts of Tobit are reprinted in Chapter 9 below. Cf. my article, "Preliminary Publication of pap4QTob[a] ar, Fragment 2," *Bib* 75 (1994) 220-24.

Not long ago a small part of 4QpapTob[a] ar was published in a questionable form,[3] which made the official publication of the Tobit texts all the more urgent.[4]

The Aramaic and Hebrew texts of Tobit were reassigned to me by the Israel Antiquities Authority through Emanuel Tov at the end of 1991,[5] and I had the official photographs of them since the spring of 1992. Earlier I had worked on some of the Tobit texts during the year 1957-1958, when I began the concordance of Cave 4 nonbiblical texts in the Scrollery of what was then called the Palestine Archaeological Museum.[6] At that time only three Aramaic texts of Tobit had been identified (4QTob[a,b,c]), one more than Milik had mentioned in the report on his work on Cave 4 texts published in 1956.[7] There are now four Aramaic texts, with 4QTob[d] being represented by only two small fragments with eight words in all. In addition to these four Aramaic

---

3. See R. H. Eisenman and M. Wise, *The Dead Sea Scrolls Uncovered: The First Complete Translation and Interpretation of 50 Key Documents Withheld for Over 35 Years* (Rockport, Mass.: Element Books, 1992) 97-99. The readings should be checked against the *editio princeps* in DJD 19 (n. 2 above). See n. 32 in Chapter 2 above.

4. A year before my publication appeared, K. Beyer published a form of the Aramaic text in *Die aramäischen Texte vom Toten Meer samt den Inschriften aus Palästina, dem Testament Levis aus der Kairoer Genisa, der Fastenrolle und den alten talmudischen Zitaten* (Göttingen: Vandenhoeck & Ruprecht, 1984) 298-300 (only the readings released by Milik in various earlier publications); and then fully in the *Ergänzungsband* (1994) 134-47. See also B. Z. Wacholder and M. Abegg, *A Preliminary Edition of the Unpublished Dead Sea Scrolls: The Hebrew and Aramaic Texts from Cave Four,* Fascicle Three (Washington, D.C.: Biblical Archaeology Society, 1995) 1-5 (the Hebrew text of 4Q200).

See further C. A. Moore, *Tobit: A New Translation with Introduction and Commentary* (AB 40A; New York: Doubleday, 1996); E. M. Cook, "Our Translated Tobit," in *Essays in Honour of Martin McNamara* (JSOTSup 230; ed. K. J. Cathcart and M. Maher; Sheffield, UK: Sheffield Academic Press, 1996) 153-62; P. Grelot, "Les noms de parenté dans le livre de *Tobie*," *RevQ* 17 (1996) 327-37; G. W. E. Nickelsburg, "The Search for Tobit's Mixed Ancestry: A Historical and Hermeneutical Odyssey," *RevQ* 17 (1996) 339-49.

5. See E. Tov, "The Unpublished Qumran Texts from Caves 4 and 11," *BA* 55 (1992) 94-104, esp. 97.

6. Available only in a limited edition: H.-P. Richter, ed., *Preliminary Concordance to the Hebrew and Aramaic Fragments from Qumran Caves II-X* (5 vols.; Göttingen: Private Publication, 1988). The concordance was based on the tentative readings of texts by the different scholars who provided the texts for the composition of the concordance. They are at times far from the definitive readings.

This concordance was used by B. Z. Wacholder and M. Abegg in their edition of Qumran texts: *A Preliminary Edition of Unpublished Dead Sea Scrolls.* See J. N. Wilford, "Computer Hacker Bootlegs Version of Dead Sea Scrolls," *New York Times,* 5 September 1991, A1.

7. See n. 1 above.

texts, now officially numbered as 4Q196-4Q199, there is also one fragmentary text of Tobit in Hebrew (4QTob[e], 4Q200).[8]

Of the Aramaic texts, the first, 4QpapTob[a] ar, is written on light brown papyrus in a late semiformal Hasmonean script (*ca.* 50-25 B.C.).[9] It uses a looped *taw;* there are no ligatures, and the *yods* are clearly distinguishable from *waws,* as are the *bets* and *kaps.* The second, 4QTob[b] ar, is written on tan skin in a beautiful Herodian formal script (*ca.* 25 B.C.–A.D. 50).[10] The third, 4QTob[c] ar, is also written on skin in an early Herodian book hand (*ca.* 50 B.C.),[11] and the fourth, 4QTob[d] ar, is inscribed on skin in a typical Hasmonean script (dating from *ca.* 100 B.C.).[12] The Hebrew text of Tobit (4QTob[e]) is written on light brown skin in an early Herodian formal hand (*ca.* 30 B.C.–A.D. 20).[13] These dates, roughly 100 B.C. to A.D. 50, are those of the copies, and they tell us little or nothing about the date of the composition of the book. That dating, usually said today to be about the beginning of the second century B.C., is scarcely affected by the discovery of the Aramaic and Hebrew texts from Qumran Cave 4. (A further comment on this matter will be made later.)

My remarks on the Qumran Tobit texts will fall under four headings: the contents of them, the kind of Aramaic and Hebrew in which they are written, new Aramaic words, and references to Aḥiqar.

Contents

For centuries Christians, for whom the book of Tobit was a deuterocanonical writing and part of the Old Testament, had read the story of Tobit mainly in the short form, either that found in the Greek manuscripts Alexandrinus (A), Vaticanus (B), and Venetus (V), or that of the Latin Vulgate.[14] The longer

---

8. For a recent general introduction to the literature on Tobit, see C. A. Moore, "Scholarly Issues in the Book of Tobit before Qumran and After: An Assessment," *JSP* 5 (1989) 65-81; idem, "Tobit, Book of," *ABD,* 6:585-94.

9. Compare F. M. Cross, "The Development of the Jewish Scripts," in *The Bible and the Ancient Near East: Essays in Honor of William Foxwell Albright* (ed. G. E. Wright; Garden City, N.Y.: Doubleday, 1961) 170-264, esp. 190 §4. The dates are my own, but I have been able to check them with Prof. Cross, to whom I express my thanks.

10. Ibid., 176 §5.

11. Ibid., 176 §3.

12. There are so few letters preserved on this text, and none of them very distinctive, that one cannot establish a more precise date for these two fragments.

13. Cross, "The Development of the Jewish Scripts," 176 §5.

14. See J. Gamberoni, *Die Auslegung des Buches Tobias in der griechisch-lateinischen*

Greek text, now known mainly from Sinaiticus (S), came to light only in 1844.[15] Even though the longer form was extant in the Vetus Latina, it was by and large neglected throughout the centuries, once Jerome's shorter version appeared in the Vulgate. Moreover, the ancient story of Aḥiqar, to which allusion is made in the book of Tobit, came to light only in 1907, when the Aramaic form of that story was discovered among the papyri of Elephantine.[16]

Of the 245 verses found in the fourteen chapters of Tobit according to the numbering of S in the Göttingen Septuagint,[17] parts of 103 verses are preserved in the Aramaic texts. In some cases, however, this might mean only one word or part of a word. In any case, about 42 percent of the verses are thus represented in the preserved Aramaic text. Of the Hebrew text, parts of only 32 verses are preserved; by the same count that means about 13 percent of the verses are represented. Would that these figures really represented 42 percent and 13 percent of the whole text! Alas, less than half of that might be a truer estimate.

In Aramaic text a, nineteen fragments or groups of fragments are certainly identified, sometimes with multiple columns, and about thirty hopeless cases, papyrus fragments too tiny and with too few letters on them to permit certain identification. The verses of Tobit identified are: 1:17; 1:19–2:2; 2:3; 2:10-11; 3:5; 3:9-15; 3:17; 4:2, 5, 7; 4:21–5:1; 5:9; 6:6-8; 6:13-18; 6:18–7:6;

Kirche der Antike und der Christenheit des Westens bis zum 1600 (SANT 21; Munich: Kösel, 1969).

15. See C. Tischendorf, *Codice Friderico-Augustanus sive fragmenta Veteris Testamenti e codice graeco* . . . (Leipzig: Koehler, 1846), containing Tob 1:1–2:2 (ἡμῶν); *Bibliorum codex sinaiticus petropolitanus* (St. Petersburg: Publisher unknown, 1862; repr. Hildesheim: Olms, 1969) 2:2-8, containing Tob 2:2–14:15 (with two significant lacunae, 4:7-19b; 13:6h-10b). Related to S are two other fragmentary manuscripts: the important 319 (*Vatopedi* [Βατοπαιδίου] 513, dated 1021) and 910 (Papyrus Oxyrhynchus 1076). The former contains only 3:6–6:16, which fills in the first lacuna of S, and the latter has only 2:2-8. Cf. M. Löhr, "Alexandrinus und Sinaiticus zum Buche Tobit," *ZAW* 20 (1900) 243-63.

16. See E. Sachau, *Aramäische Papyrus und Ostraka aus einer jüdischen Militär-Kolonie zu Elephantine* (2 vols.; Leipzig: Hinrichs, 1911) 147-82. Cf. *AP*, 204-48. The Aḥiqar story was known earlier in expanded translations. See F. C. Conybeare, J. R. Harris, and A. S. Lewis, *The Story of Aḥikar from the Syriac, Arabic, Armenian, Ethiopic, Greek and Slavonic Versions* (London: C. J. Clay, 1898). After the publication of the Elephantine Aramaic text, these authors put out a second edition, in which *Aramaic* was added to the title (Cambridge: Cambridge University, 1913).

17. See R. Hanhart, *Tobit* (Septuaginta: Vetus Testamentum graecum auctoritate Academiae Scientiarum Gottingensis editum 8/5; Göttingen: Vandenhoeck & Ruprecht, 1985). The numbering of chapters and verses of the book of Tobit in this article follows that of G[II] in Hanhart's edition.

7:13; 12:1; 12:18–13:6; 13:6-12; 13:12–14:3; 14:7. There is nothing from chapters 8-11. These figures differ slightly from those already made known by Milik.[18]

In Aramaic text b, five substantial fragments have been identified with certainty, one having parts of three columns; two other tiny fragments are problematic. The following verses are represented: 3:6-8; 4:21–5:1; 5:12-14; 5:19–6:12; 6:12-18; 6:18–7:10; 8:17–9:4.

In Aramaic text c, one fragment is identified with certainty, containing 14:2-6; and another possibly contains part of 14:10. The second fragment was torn in antiquity and stitched together again, making it very difficult to read.

In Aramaic text d, two small fragments contain parts of 7:11 and 14:10.

In the Hebrew text, seven fragments, two of which have double columns, are certainly identified, on which the following verses appear: 3:6; 3:10-11; 4:3-9; 5:2; 10:7-9; 11:10-14; 12:20–13:4; 13:13-14; 13:18–14:2. Two other fragments are not identified with certainty, but one may be part of 3:3-4.

The fact that we now have both Aramaic and Hebrew forms of the book of Tobit reveals something about the book which neither Origen nor Jerome knew. In his *Letter to Africanus,* written *ca.* A.D. 240, Origen cited a form of Tob 2:3, which agrees verbatim with none of the extant Greek versions but does correspond to them in sense, telling of persons "strangled and thrown on the streets unburied." Having thus alluded to the text of Tobit, Origen then added,

> Concerning it, we must recognize that Jews do not use Tobit; nor do they use Judith. They do not have them even among the Apocrypha in Hebrew, as we know, having learned (this) from them. But because the churches use Tobit, one must recognize that some of the captives even in their captivity became rich and well to do.[19]

The Tobit texts from Qumran now show that *some* Jews at least in pre-Christian Palestine did read the Tobit story in Hebrew, and not only in Hebrew, but also in Aramaic. The Qumran texts thus correct the ignorance of

18. Milik, "La patrie de Tobie," 522 n. 3.

19. *Ep. ad Africanum* 19 (SC 302.562). The Greek text runs as follows: Περὶ οὖ ἡμᾶς ἔχρην ἐγνωκέναι ὅτι Ἑβραῖοι τῷ Τωβίᾳ οὐ χρῶνται, οὐδὲ τῇ Ἰουδίθ· οὐδὲ γὰρ ἔχουσιν αὐτὰ κἂν ἐν ἀποκρύφοις ἑβραιστί, ὡς ἀπ' αὐτῶν μαθόντες ἐγνώκαμεν. Ἀλλ' ἐπεὶ χρῶνται τῷ Τωβίᾳ αἱ ἐκκλησίαι, ἰστέον ὅτι καὶ ἐν τῇ αἰχμαλωσίᾳ τινὲς τῶν αἰχμαλώτων ἐπλούτουν καὶ εὖ ἔπραττον. See further J. Ruwet, "Les 'antilegomena' dans les oeuvres d'Origène," *Bib* 24 (1943) 18-58; "Les apocryphes dans les oeuvres d'Origène," *Bib* 25 (1944) 143-66, 311-34; W. Reichardt, *Die Briefe des Sextus Julius Africanus an Aristides und Origenes* (TU 34/3; Leipzig: Hinrichs, 1909) 65.

Origen and reveal that the Greek form of the story with which he was acquainted was a version produced perhaps in Alexandria, along with the rest of the Greek Old Testament.

Nor did Jerome know of a Hebrew form of Tobit, for he seems to have regarded it only as an Aramaic composition. The Qumran Aramaic form of the Tobit story may supply, then, a basis for Jerome's explanation of the way he produced his translation, but certainly not for the translation of it into Latin, known as *Liber Tobiae* or sometimes as *Liber utriusque Tobiae*, which he produced for the Vulgate. In his letter to the bishops Chromatius and Heliodorus, which is used in the Vulgate as the preface to his Latin translation, Jerome tells how the Jews had excised Tobit from their collection of sacred Scripture and relegated the book, written in "Chaldee," to the Apocrypha. Although he was not really interested in translating the Aramaic text of Tobit, he thought it better to yield to episcopal demands for a new Latin translation, even though he knew that that would go against the judgment of contemporary Pharisees about the book. He wrote:

> Because the language of the Chaldeans is related to the Hebrew tongue and since I had found someone who was an expert speaker in both languages, I devoted the work of one day (to the translation): Whatever he rendered for me in Hebrew, I would express in Latin for an engaged secretary.[20]

That is Jerome's own account of the form of the Tobit story that we have in the Vulgate. Modern studies of the Vulgate, however, show that Jerome's version was also heavily dependent on the Vetus Latina, even though his ren-

---

20. The Latin text of Jerome's letter runs as follows:

Cromatio et Heliodoro episcopis Hieronymus presbyter in Domino salutem!

Mirari non desino exactionis vestrae instantiam: Exigitis enim, ut librum Chaldeo sermone conscriptum ad Latinum stylum traham, librum utique Tobiae, quem Hebrei de catalogo divinarum Scripturarum secantes, his, quae Agiografa memorant, manciparunt. Feci satis desiderio vestro, non tamen meo studio. Arguunt enim nos Hebreorum studia et imputant nobis, contra suum canonem latinis auribus ista transferre. Sed melius esse iudicans Phariseorum displicere iudicio et episcoporum iussionibus deservire, institi ut potui, et quia vicina est Chaldeorum lingua sermoni hebraico, utriusque linguae peritissimum loquacem repperiens, unius diei laborem arripui et quicquid ille mihi hebraicis verbis expressit, haec ego accito notario sermonibus latinis exposui. Orationibus vestris mercedem huius operis compensabo, cum gratum vobis didicero me quod iubere estis dignati, complesse.

(*Biblia Sacra iuxta latinam Vulgatam versionem ad codicum fidem ... edita* [17 vols.; Rome: Typis polyglottis Vaticanis, 1926-87] 8:155-56. Cf. *PL* 29.23-26).

dering is a considerable abridgement in comparison with the Vetus Latina, for the Vulgate form of the Tobit story belongs to the short recension.[21] If Jerome's version is indeed based on an Aramaic form of the story, then that must have been considerably different in places from the form now known from the Qumran fragments.

It is customary to relate the short recension of Tobit to the Greek manuscripts A, B, V, and a host of minuscule texts.[22] The long recension of Tobit had been known in the Vetus Latina, but it was neglected until Constantin von Tischendorf discovered the Greek text of Sinaiticus in 1844. Indeed, Robert Hanhart seems even to favor the short recension in his edition of Tobit in the Göttingen Septuagint, where it is printed at the top of the page and is followed by the long recension at the bottom.[23] The discovery of S and its long

21. See G. Dalman, *Grammatik des jüdisch-palästinischen Aramäisch . . . Aramäische Dialektproben* (2d ed.; Leipzig: Hinrichs, 1905 and 1927; reprint, Darmstadt, 1960, 1981) 35-37. According to Dalman (pp. 35-36), "da dieselbe [Jerome's translation of Tobit] sich aber also blosse Überarbeitung der Vetus Latina gibt [in a footnote Dalman refers to Fritzsche, *Libri apocryphi Veteris Testamenti graece*, xviii], lassen sich von daher keine sicheren Schlüsse auf seinen aramäischen Text ziehen, und es muss zweifelhaft bleiben, ob auch nur eine ältere Rezension des uns bekannten aram[äischen] Textes Hieronymus vorgelegen hat."

22. For a list of the minuscule manuscripts, see Hanhart, *Tobit*, 8-10. The text of A, B, V, etc. has been judged to be, in general, the more original Greek version by the following: O. F. Fritzsche, *Die Bücher Tobi und Judith erklärt* (Kurzgefasstes exegetisches Handbuch zu den Apokryphen des Alten Testaments 2; Leipzig: Hirzel, 1853) 8; M. Löhr, "Das Buch Tobit," in *Die Apokryphen und Pseudepigraphen des Alten Testaments* (ed. E. Kautzsch; 2 vols.; Tübingen/Leipzig: Mohr [Siebeck], 1900) 1:135-47, esp. 136; J. Müller, *Beiträge zur Erklärung und Kritik des Buches Tobit* (BZAW 13; Giessen: Töpelmann, 1908) 1-53; T. Nöldeke, "Die Texte des Buches Tobit," *Monatsberichte der königlich preussischen Akademie der Wissenschaften zu Berlin* (1879) 45-69, esp. 61; M. Rosenmann, *Studien zum Buche Tobit* (Berlin: Mayer & Müller, 1894); P. Vetter, "Das Buch Tobias und die Achikar-Sage," *TQ* 96 (1904) 321-64, 512-39; 87 (1905) 321-70, 497-546. They held this despite the fact that Tob 1:6-8 in this Greek form is made to agree with the later custom set forth in the Mishnah. See n. 23 below.

23. Hanhart makes it clear in his other book (*Text und Textgeschichte des Buches Tobit* [Mitteilungen des Septuaginta-Unternehmens 17; Göttingen: Vandenhoeck & Ruprecht, 1984] 21-38) that he considers S to be prior to the A, B, V Greek tradition. Manuscript S has been judged to be, in general, the more original Greek version by the following: H. Grätz, "Das Buch Tobias oder Tobit: Seine Ursprache, seine Abfassungszeit und Tendenz," *MGWJ* 28 (1879) 145-63, 385-408, 433-55, 509-20; J. R. Harris, "The Double Text of Tobit: Contribution toward a Critical Inquiry," *AJT* 3 (1899) 541-54; E. Nestle, "Zum Buche Tobit," in *Septuagintastudien III* (Stuttgart: Maulbronn, 1899) 22-35; F. H. Reusch, *Libellus Tobit e codice Sinaitico editus et recensitus* (Freiburg im B.: Herder, 1870); E. Schürer, "Ein chaldäischer Text des Buches Tobit," *TLZ* 3 (1878) 21-22; Review of A. Neubauer, *The Book of Tobit, TLZ* 3 (1878) 333-35; D. Simonsen, "Tobit-Aphorismen,"

form of Tobit restored the Vetus Latina version to its proper and important place in the history of the transmission of the text of Tobit.

The Qumran Aramaic texts a, c, d and the Hebrew text e contain parts of verses of chapters 13 and 14, that is, parts of Tobit's hymn of praise (13:1-18), of his final counsel to his son Tobiah before he dies (14:1-11), and of the account of Tobiah's move to Ecbatana with his family after his mother's death (14:12-15). These texts reveal, then, that the last two chapters were already part of the book of Tobit in pre-Christian times and thus put an end to the long-standing controversy about whether or not chapters 13 and 14 were a later addition to the original story of Tobit.

As far as I have been able to establish, the first to propose that chapters 13 and 14 were not part of the original composition was G. F. Hitzig in 1860.[24] He was followed by H. Grätz (1866), A. Kohut (1872), A. Neubauer (1878), and M. Rosenthal (1885).[25] As late as 1958 a similar proposal was put forth by F. Zimmermann.[26] The latter maintained that the last two chapters were composed in the Christian period, even after A.D. 70, whereas Grätz and Neubauer dated the book of Tobit itself to the time of Hadrian. Neubauer wrote that it "can scarcely have been composed earlier, since it was not known to Josephus."[27] Now that Hadrianic or post–A.D. 70 date can safely be ruled out.

The Qumran Aramaic text also preserves the narrative in the first person in 1:3–3:15 and continues with that of the third person, beginning at 3:16. In this the Qumran Aramaic text agrees with the Greek versions (of S, A, B, and V) as well as with the Vetus Latina, but it differs from the Vulgate,

---

in *Gedenkbuch zur Erinnerung an David Kaufmann* (ed. M. Braun and F. Rosenthal; Breslau: Schles. Verlagsanstalt, 1900) 106-16. Compare this S version of Tob 1:6-8 with Lev 27:32-33 and *Jub.* 32:15 to see a tradition that is earlier than that of the Mishnah (n. 22 above).

24. See his article, "Zur Kritik der apokryphischen Bücher des Alten Testaments," *ZWT* 3 (1860) 240-73, esp. 250-61.

25. See H. Grätz, *Geschichte der Juden vom Untergang des jüdischen Staates bis zum Abschluss des Talmud* (5 vols.; 2d ed.; Leipzig: Leiner, 1866) 4:465-67; A. Kohut, "Etwas über die Moral und die Abfassungszeit des Buches Tobias," *Jüdische Zeitschrift für Wissenschaft und Leben* 10 (1872) 49-73; A. Neubauer, *The Book of Tobit: A Chaldee Text from a Unique Ms. in the Bodleian Library, with Other Rabbinical Texts, English Translations, and the Itala* (Oxford: Clarendon, 1878) xvii; M. Rosenthal, *Vier apokryphische Bücher aus der Zeit und Schule R. Akiba's* (Leipzig: Schulze, 1885) 104-50.

26. F. Zimmermann, *The Book of Tobit: An English Translation with Introduction and Commentary* (Jewish Apocryphal Literature; New York: Harper & Row, for Dropsie College, 1958) 24-27.

27. Neubauer, *The Book of Tobit*, xvii.

which is a narrative entirely in the third person and which Jerome claimed was based on an Aramaic text. The Qumran text likewise differs in this regard from the medieval Aramaic and Hebrew forms (HL and HG) published by A. Neubauer and M. Gaster.[28]

Milik had already revealed that the Qumran texts "follow the longer recension, which is that attested by the Codex Sinaiticus and by the Vetus Latina" and that sometimes the Qumran texts and the Vetus Latina are "the only witnesses to certain readings, as, e.g. the *seven* sons of the young Tobiah (Tob. 14.3)."[29]

The importance of the Vetus Latina for the study of the Tobit story cannot be underestimated. Unfortunately, there is as yet no critical text of the Vetus Latina of Tobit.[30] One has to begin the study of Old Latin Tobit with the eighteenth-century text of P. Sabatier,[31] which has been reproduced in a slightly improved form in the Septuagint edition of Brooke-McLean-Thackeray.[32] Sabatier's text was based on two manuscripts (known in his day as Codex Regius 3564 [now Paris, Bibl. Nat., lat. 93], often called Q; and Codex Sangermanensis 15 [now Paris, Bibl. Nat. 11553], often called G). In his

28. The medieval Aramaic text (Hebrew ms. Bodleian 2339) was published by Neubauer, *The Book of Tobit*. See also M. Gaster, "Two Unknown Hebrew Versions of the Tobit Legend," *Proceedings of the Society of Biblical Archaeology* 18 (1896) 208-22, 259-71; 19 (1897) 27-38; reprinted in *Studies and Texts in Folklore, Magic, Mediaeval Romance, Hebrew Apocrypha, and Samaritan Archaeology . . .* (3 vols.; London, 1928; reprinted with a prolegomenon by T. Gaster; New York: Ktav, 1971) 1:1-38; 3:1-11, 11-14.

29. *TYDWJ*, 31-32 (his emphasis).

30. Only last year (1998) did I learn that a critical text of the VL of Tobit is being prepared by J.-M. Auwers of Université Catholique de Louvain, Louvain-la-Neuve, Belgium.

In my edition of the Qumran texts of Tobit (see n. 2 above), I had to rely on the VL as given in Brooke-McLean-Thackeray, but I was able to learn of readings in other manuscripts of the VL through the gracious cooperation of P.-M. Bogaert, who has collated many of them. See his article, "La Bible latine des origines au moyen âge: Aperçu historique, état des questions," *RTL* 19 (1988) 137-59, 276-314. Cf. J. R. Busto Saiz, "Algunas aportaciones de la Vetus Latina para una nueva edición crítica del libro de Tobit," *Sef* 38 (1978) 53-69.

31. *Bibliorum sacrorum latinae versiones antiquae, seu Vetus Italica . . .* (Rheims: R. Florentain, 1743; 2d ed.; Paris: Didot, 1751; reprinted in 3 vols.; ed. B. Fischer; Turnhout: Brepols, 1976) 1:706-43.

32. See A. E. Brooke, N. McLean, and H. St J. Thackeray, *The Old Testament in Greek* (3 vols.; Cambridge: Cambridge University Press, 1906-1940) 3.1:85-144 (Codex B, 85-110; Codex S, 111-22; VL, 123-44). The Greek text of R. Hanhart (n. 17 above) supersedes this edition of the Greek today, but Brooke-McLean-Thackeray still has to be consulted for the VL. Cf. H. A. A. Kennedy, "Latin Versions, The Old," in *A Dictionary of the Bible* (5 vols.; ed. J. Hastings; New York: Scribner, 1900-1904) 3:47-62.

apparatus criticus Sabatier also made use of a MS C (Codex Reginensis Latinus [Vatican Library, Regin. lat. 7]), an important manuscript which, for the book of Tobit, has the text of the Vetus Latina up to 6:12 (the rest being that of the Vulgate). Today there are other manuscripts of the Vetus Latina that one can consult, but they are widely scattered. Of easy access are three: MS M (Codex Monacensis [Munich, Bayerische Stadtsbibliothek, Clm. 6239),[33] MS R (Codex Rodensis [Paris, Bibl. Nat. fonds lat. 6]),[34] and MS X (Codex Complutensis 1 [Madrid, Biblioteca de la Universidad Central, 31]).[35] The last-mentioned is, however, very paraphrastic and of little use in text-critical matters.[36]

In citing the example about Tobiah's "seven sons" from Tob 14:3 and its relation to the Vetus Latina, Milik did not tell us that only the *taw* of the construct of some numeral is preserved before בנוהי, "his sons" (4QTobᵃ ar 18:16). That *taw*, of course, could just as easily have been part of שתת, "six." Then שתת would agree with the Greek MSS A and 98 and with the Sahidic version of the short recension, all of which mention "six sons." In this regard, there is no help from S, which does not mention the number of sons.

A better example of the agreement of both the Aramaic texts and the Hebrew text with the Vetus Latina would be Tob 14:1, which mentions Tobit's age as fifty-eight, when he was blinded, שנין חמשין ותמנה (4QTobᵃ ar 18:13), which agrees with the Vetus Latina, *quinquaginta autem et octo annorum erat cum oculis captus est*, whereas S has ἑξήκοντα δύο ἐτῶν ἦν, "he was sixty-two years old."[37] The Qumran Aramaic and Hebrew texts, however, do agree in general with the long recension of S and the Vetus Latina, and

33. See J. Belsheim, *Liber Tobit, Liber Judit, Liber Ester: Tobias, Judits og Esters B ger i gammellatinsk Oversaettelse efter et Haandskrift i der Kgl. Bibliothek i München . . .* (Throndhjem: Interessentskabstrykkeriet, 1893) 31-50 (a publication of the manuscript that is unfortunately not entirely trustworthy).

34. Published by F. Vattioni, "La Vetus Latina di Tobia nella Bibbia di Roda," *Revista catalana de Teologia* 3 (1978) 173-201. Cf. P. Klein, "Date et scriptorium de la Bible de Roda: Etat de recherches," *Cahiers de Saint-Michel de Cuxà* 3 (1972) 91-101.

35. See F. Vattioni, "Tobia nello *Speculum* e nella prima Bibbia di Alcalà," *Aug* 15 (1975) 169-200.

36. See further P.-M. Bogaert, "Bulletin de la Bible Latine," *RBén* 85 (1975) [1]-[28], nos. 1-83; 87 (1977) [29]-[64], nos. 84-181; 88 (1978) [65]-[92], nos. 182-248; 90 (1980) [93]-[116], nos. 249-313; 91 (1981) [117]-[136], nos. 314-372; 93 (1983) [137]-[164], nos. 373-444; 95 (1985) [165]-[196], nos. 445-534; 96 (1986) [197]-[200], nos. 535-601; 98 (1988) [221]-[252], nos. 602-701; 99 (1989) [253]-[280], nos. 702-774; 101 (1991) [281]-[308], nos. 775-861; 105 (1995) 200-236, nos. 81-82; 106 (1996) 386-412. Also his "Fragments de la vieille version latine du livre de Tobit," *RBén* 80 (1970) 166-69.

37. Cf. J. Alonso Díaz, "Tobit curado de su ceguera (Tb 11,7-8)," *CB* 26 (1969) 67-72.

there are times when they are fuller than either of these (with added words and phrases), but also times when they are shorter than either S or VL. The agreement or correspondence still has to be worked out in greater detail.

There are unfortunately no answers in the Qumran Aramaic and Hebrew texts to some of the problematic questions that the diverse forms of the Tobit story in the ancient versions have raised. For instance, Aramaic text b breaks off in 6:2 just where one would look for mention of the dog that goes along on the journey with Tobiah and the angel. The dog is mentioned not only in the Greek short recension (Tob 5:17) and the Vulgate (11:9), but also in the long recension of S and the Vetus Latina (6:2), but it is missing in the medieval Aramaic and Hebrew forms. Yet 4QTob^b ar 4 i 5 has]ך[לה]ו[, "and there went," and the text breaks off just where one looks for the mention of the dog.[38]

Similarly, the text of Tob 13:4 breaks off in the Hebrew version just after "your Lord and your God," where S has καὶ αὐτὸς πατὴρ ὑμῶν and the Vetus Latina has *pater noster*. So we shall never know whether the original text of Tobit referred to God as Father.

Again we are left in the dark by the Aramaic and Hebrew texts of Qumran if we want to know whether Tobiah and Sarah postponed the consummation of their marriage until the third night (see the Vulgate of Tob 8:4) or how the demon we call Asmodeus (Tob 3:8) was named in Aramaic. Nor does the Aramaic text of Tobit solve the problem of the verbs in Tob 7:9, whether two verbs are used, as in S (ἐλούσαντο καὶ ἐνίψαντο, "they washed and bathed") or one verb, as in the Vetus Latina and Vulgate; or whether the verb corresponds to *lauerunt*, "they washed," of the Vetus Latina or to *locuti sunt*, "they spoke," of the Vulgate.[39] Similarly, there is nothing in these Qumran texts that helps in the literary interpretation of the book, nothing about the Grateful Dead, the Monster in the Bridal Chamber, the tractate of Khons, or the Tale of the Two Brothers.[40] The only thing clear is the allusion to the story of Aḥiqar in the Ara-

---

38. In my publication of the text I have restored כלבא, "the dog," on the basis of S and VL, because the angel is already mentioned in an earlier part of the verse. Cf. J. Abrahams, "Tobit's Dog," *JQR* 1/3 (1888-89) 288.

39. For the problem, see L. Rosso, "Un'antica variante del libro di *Tobit* (*Tob.*, VII, 9)," *RSO* 50 (1976) 73-89; B. Couroyer, "Tobie, vii, 9: Problème de critique textuelle," *RB* 91 (1984) 351-61.

40. These folkloric tales have often entered the discussion of the literary sources and motifs of the book of Tobit. See J. Goettsberger, *Einleitung in das Alte Testament* (Herders theologische Grundrisse; Freiburg im Breisgau: Herder, 1928) 173-81; I. Nowell, *The Book of Tobit: Narrative Technique and Theology* (Dissertation, Catholic University of America, Washington, D.C., 1983; Ann Arbor, Mich.: University Microfilms International, 1985 [No. 8314894]); "Irony in the Book of Tobit," *TBT* 33 (1995) 79-83.

maic version, to which I shall return below. Moreover, the biblical background of several chapters of Tobit will now have to be studied anew, for some of the ancient versions have often recast the story, making much or little use of phrases from various books of the Old Testament.

A problem that the Aramaic text does solve is whether the angel ate some of the fish or not. The long recension of S tells of only Tobiah eating of the fish, using ἔφαγεν (in the third singular, "he ate," Tob 6:6), but MS C of the Vetus Latina and the Greek short recension (A, B, etc.) use a plural verb (*manducauerunt,* ἔφαγον, "they ate"), as does the Syriac version (*'klw*). Here 4QTob[b] clearly reads the singular ואכל (4 i 10). Later on, 4QTob[a] 17 i 2 clearly depicts Raphael claiming [ל]א אשתית, "I did not drink" (Tob 12:9), with which S agrees (οὐκ ἔφαγον οὐθέν, "I did not eat anything"), whereas the Vetus Latina has *uidebatis enim me quia manducabam, sed uiso uestro uidebatis,* "for you saw me eating, but you saw with your (faculty of) vision." In this case, the short Greek recension has ὠπτανόμην ὑμῖν, καὶ οὐκ ἔφαγον οὐδὲ ἔπιον, ἀλλὰ ὅρασιν ὑμεῖς ἐθεωρεῖτε, "I appeared to you, and I did not eat or drink, but you beheld a vision."

It is also clear that some of the Qumran Aramaic forms of the Tobit story differ in slight details. In the few instances where there are overlaps, and where one can compare the wording, there are small divergences. Thus, Tob 6:7 is partly preserved in texts a and b, and the first reads מה סם בלבב נונא וכבדה, "what medicine is there in the heart of the fish and its liver" (4QpapTob[a] 13:3), whereas, instead of וכבדה, the second reads ובכבדה, "and in its liver" (4QTob[b] 4 i 12), that is, with the preposition *bĕ-* repeated before *kabdēh.* Again, in Tob 7:1 there is a difference in the clause "and they found Raguel sitting," for 4QpapTob[a] 14 ii 6 has והשכחו לרעואל יתב, whereas 4QTob[b] 4 iii 3 has ואשכחו לרעואל יתב, that is, the latter uses an *aphel* form of שכח, whereas the former has a *haphel.* Again, in Tob 14:12 the words "to bless the Lord and to acknowledge his majesty" appear in 4QpapTob[a] 18:15 as והוסף למדחל . . . ולהודיה רבותה . . . לברכה ל, whereas 4QTob[c] 1:1 has לאלהא ולהודיה רבותה, "and he continued to fear God and to acknowledge his majesty." The Greek text of S and the Vetus Latina agree with the latter using τὸν θεόν and *Deum* instead of a way of representing the tetragrammaton in a nonverbal way (four dots, which appear elsewhere at times in text a). Again, in Tob 14:3 the word "and he ordered him" appears in 4QpapTob[a] 18:16 as ובקדה, with the first radical a *bet,* whereas 4QTob[c] 1:2 has the correct form ופקדה, with the letter *pe.*

Because of these differences we have to recognize that the Aramaic form of the Tobit story may not have been absolutely uniform in all details and that slightly different copies of it circulated.

This raises a further question about the relation of the Vulgate to the Qumran fragments. The Latin text of the Vulgate is so different at times from the Greek long recension and the Qumran forms that one wonders what sort of Aramaic text Jerome was using. A dissertation has been written at the Catholic University of America in Washington, D.C., by one of my students, Vincent Skemp, who has studied this relationship in detail.

Finally, a similar study must be undertaken to investigate the relation of the different forms of Syriac Tobit to the Qumran Aramaic and Hebrew fragments. Here the question is whether the Syriac form is a translation of the Aramaic or Hebrew or even of one of the Greek forms.

The Kind of Aramaic and Hebrew Used in Qumran Tobit

Long before the discovery of the Dead Sea Scrolls, scholars had recognized that Tobit, which was known from ancient versions, Latin, Greek, Syriac, and so forth, must have been originally a Semitic composition. I have already noted that Origen claimed that "Jews do not use Tobit, nor do they use Judith. They do not even have them among the Apocrypha in Hebrew."[41] Jerome too apparently did not know of a Hebrew form of Tobit. Although he was aware that "the language of the Chaldeans is related to the Hebrew tongue," he surprisingly could not read the Aramaic and had to get an expert Jew to translate Aramaic Tobit for him into Hebrew, which he then translated into Latin and dictated to a secretary.[42]

From Jerome's statement scholars knew of an ancient Aramaic form of Tobit, and because of Origen's denial of the existence of a Hebrew Tobit, most of them concluded that the original Semitic form of Tobit was Aramaic.[43]

---

41. See n. 19 above.

42. See n. 20 above.

43. For some of those who espoused this opinion, either in dependence on Jerome's testimony or on Neubauer's publication, see J. H. Moulton, "The Iranian Background of Tobit," *ExpTim* 11 (1899-1900) 257-60; Harris, "The Double Text," 541-54; D. C. Simpson, "The Book of Tobit," in *APOT*, 2:174-241; L. H. Brockington, *A Critical Introduction to the Apocrypha* (Studies in Theology; London: Duckworth, 1961) 33-39; A. P. Wikgren, "Tobit, Book of," *IDB* 4 (1962) 658-62, esp. 661; O. Eissfeldt, *The Old Testament: An Introduction Including the Apocrypha and Pseudepigrapha, and also the Works of Similar Type from Qumran* (New York: Harper and Row, 1965) 583-85, 771; W. Dommershausen, "Tobias," *Bibel Lexikon* (2d ed.; ed. H. Haag; Tübingen: Benziger, 1968) 1759-61; J. M. Fuller, "Tobit," in *The Holy Bible: Apocrypha* (2 vols.; Speaker's Commentary; ed. H. Wace; London: John Murray, 1888) 1:149-240, esp. 152-55; J. C. Greenfield, "Studies in Aramaic Lexicography, I," *JAOS* 82 (1962) 290-99; J. T. Milik, *TYDWJ*, 31; G. W. E. Nickelsburg, "Tobit,"

Now that we have fragments of the book in both Aramaic and Hebrew with clear overlaps, which show that it was used at Qumran in both Semitic languages, the question is posed anew: In which language was Tobit originally composed?

Because there are four fragmentary Aramaic texts of Tobit and only one Hebrew text, the multiple copies of the Aramaic might suggest that it was read more often in Aramaic than in Hebrew. That, however, may be coincidental, and it certainly is no sign that the writing was originally composed in Aramaic. Moreover, although the texts found in Cave 4 may have been copied at Qumran, nothing in them reveals that Tobit was part of Essene sectarian literature or was composed by a member of that community. More than likely both forms of Tobit, Aramaic and Hebrew, were imported to Qumran, having been composed elsewhere. Unfortunately, because the Qumran copies of Tobit are all fragmentary, very little of the Hebrew form overlaps with the Aramaic, and what does overlap scarcely provides a sufficient basis for a judgment about which was the original language.

The overlaps are few. In the following list of them, the words in the first column are the Aramaic words or phrases from 4Q196; in the second the Hebrew correspondents from 4Q200:

	Aramaic (4Q196)			Hebrew (4Q200)
6:6	לק]ב[לן] (Tob 3:11)		1 ii 5	[הח]לון]
9:1	ו]ביומך.] (4:5)		2:3	וכול ימיכה בני
9:2	ולמשטה]מאמרה[(4:5)		2:4	[ ] מאמרו
9:3	ד שקר] [(4:5)		2:5	בדרכ]י שקר
10:1	ידך ברי הוי ע]בד (4:7)		2:6	וכאשר ידכה בני היה]עשה
17 i 4	למחזה ל]ה (12:21)		6:2	ולוא עוד ראו] או]תו
17 i 4-5	והוו]מברכין[(12:22)		6:2	והיו המה מברכים
17 i 5	[אתחזי להון מל]אך ... [.]		6:3	איכה נראה]להמה מלאך
17 i 13	בה]ון ותמן (13:3-4)		6:8	בהמה ושמה ספר]ו
17 i 14	הוא מראכ]ון והוא (13:4)		6:9	כיא הוא אדוניכ]מה] והוא

---

in *Jewish Writings of the Second Temple Period* (CRINT 2/2; ed. M. E. Stone; Assen: Van Gorcum; Philadelphia: Fortress, 1984) 40-46, esp. 45; R. H. Pfeiffer, *History of New Testament Times: With an Introduction to the Apocrypha* (New York: Harper & Bros., 1949) 258-84, esp. 272; L. Rost, *Judaism outside the Hebrew Canon: An Introduction to the Documents* (Nashville: Abingdon, 1976) 60-64; J. D. Thomas, "The Greek Text of Tobit," *JBL* 91 (1972) 463-71; C. C. Torrey, *The Apocryphal Literature: A Brief Introduction* (New Haven: Yale University Press, 1945) 82-88, esp. 86-87; F. Vattioni, "Studi e note sul libro di Tobia," *Aug* 10 (1970) 241-84; Zimmermann, *The Book of Tobit*, 127-49, esp. 139-49 (Greek MS S was more original than others; its *Vorlage* was a Hebrew translation of an Aramaic original).

18:11	עלם] עלמיא דביכי יברכון	7 ii 3	אשר [בכי ברכו את שמו
	ש[מה קדישא (13:18)		הק[דוש ל]
18:12	[וספו מלי תודה טו]בי	7 ii 4	ותמ[ו דברי תודה טובי
	ומית בשלם ב]ר (14:1)		וימ[ות בשלום בן]
18:13	[והוא בר] שנין חמשין	7 ii 5	והו[א בן שמונה וחמש]ים
	ותמ[נה הוה] (14:2)		
18:14	[חזות ע]ינוהי (14:2)	7 ii 6	מ[ראה]

While Milik was still joining fragments of the Tobit texts, he wrote, "a preliminary investigation suggests that Aramaic was the original language of the book."[44] Whether he still holds that view I do not know, but I tend to agree with his estimate.

I find little difference between the kind of Aramaic in which these Qumran Tobit texts are written and the Aramaic otherwise known from Qumran nonbiblical texts, such as the *Genesis Apocryphon, 1 Enoch,* or the *Targum of Job.*[45] In making this judgment, I am following the lead of Kutscher in his study of the *Genesis Apocryphon*[46] and of van der Ploeg and van der Woude in their study of the *Targum of Job.*[47] Kutscher dated the *Genesis Apocryphon* to "the 1st century B.C.E (— 1st century C.E.)," and van der Ploeg and van der Woude maintained that the *Targum of Job* had to be dated between the book of Daniel and the *Genesis Apocryphon.* My own conclusion about the Aramaic Tobit text is that it too should be dated about the same time as the *Targum of Job.*

In support of this judgment, I offer the following brief considerations.

1. The masculine proximal demonstrative pronoun in the Tobit texts is always דן, never the earlier דנא or דנה (not to mention the זנה of Imperial Aramaic).[48]

2. The relative or determinative pronoun is always די (never the earlier זי or the later ד). On one occasion (4QpapTob[a] 18:11) the word דביכי ap-

44. *TYDWJ*, 31.

45. See J. A. Fitzmyer, "The Phases of the Aramaic Language," in *WA*, 57-84, esp. 61-62, 71-74. Cf. E. Y. Kutscher, "Aramaic," in *Linguistics in South West Asia and North Africa* (Current Trends in Linguistics 6; The Hague: Mouton, 1971) 347-412, esp. 347-48; A. Vivian, "Dialetti giudaici dell'Aramaico medio e tardo," *OrAnt* 15 (1976) 56-60.

46. E. Y. Kutscher, "The Language of the 'Genesis Apocryphon': A Preliminary Study," in *Aspects of the Dead Sea Scrolls* (ScrHier 4; ed. C. Rabin and Y. Yadin; Jerusalem: Magnes, 1958) 1-35.

47. J. P. M. van der Ploeg and A. S. van der Woude, *Le targum de Job de la grotte xi de Qumrân* (Koninklijke nederlandse Akademie van Wetenschappen; Leiden: Brill, 1971), 4. They too depend on Kutscher.

48. דן occurs in 4QpapTob[a] 14 i 10; 4QTob[b] 4 ii 3, 6, 13; 4 iii 5.

pears. This is an anomalous form for "for in you" (fem., referring to Jerusalem), and it is undoubtedly an isolated scribal metathesis for די בכי, because the Vetus Latina has *quoniam in te benedicent.*

3. The adverb for "there" is תמן (4QpapTob[a] 17 i 3), as in 4QEnoch texts and the *Genesis Apocryphon,* never the earlier תמה of Biblical or Imperial Aramaic. Similarly, the adverb for "here" is תנא (4QTob[b] 5:9; 4QTob[d] 1), as in Imperial Aramaic, 4QEnoch texts, and the *Genesis Apocryphon.*

4. The third plural masculine pronoun is always אנון (4QTob[a] 2:4; 4QTob[b] 4 iii 4, 5), as in 4QEnoch and the *Genesis Apocryphon,* never המו or המון, which occur earlier in Biblical Aramaic.[49]

5. The causative conjugation of the verb is normally *aphel,* with an initial *aleph* (4QpapTob[a] 2:5, 8, 11; 17 i 2; 4QTob[b] 4 i [7], 8 [bis], [15]; 4 ii 3, [16]; 4 iii 4, [13]; 5:6; 4QTob[c] ar 1:9),[50] but there are nine instances of *haphel* (4QpapTob[a] 2:1, [12]; 12:2; 14 ii 6; 17 ii 3 [bis], [9]; 4QTob[c] 1:1, [1]). In contrast, the *Genesis Apocryphon* has only *aphel* forms. Similarly, the derived conjugations like *ithpeel, ittaphal,* or *ophal* have forms that begin with *aleph,* not with *he;* in this regard they are like the *Genesis Apocryphon* and differ from Biblical Aramaic and the *Targum of Job* (the latter has both *aleph* and *he* as the first letter of derived forms).

6. The letter *nun* at the end of a closed syllable is sometimes assimilated to the first consonant of the following syllable, but there are a number of instances where the *nun* is not assimilated (nine instances of the latter versus four of the former).

7. The sign of the accusative is always -ל (when it is used), never -ית.[51]

My own revered teacher, W. F. Albright, once claimed that the Aramaic of the Tobit texts was "in large part Imperial Aramaic, earlier than Daniel,"[52] but I do not find that to be so. Moreover, if this estimate of mine about the Aramaic in which the Tobit story is preserved in these Qumran fragments is correct, then the form of the language does bear somewhat on the date of the

---

49. The form המון occurs in 11QtgJob 35:2, but in none of the Tobit texts.

50. Numbers enclosed in square brackets mean that a part of the word has been restored. In no case, however, is a word listed that is wholly restored.

51. An anomalous form אתהייתה occurs in 4QpapTob[a] 2:13, which is probably to be understood as an *ittaphal* imperative of אתי, "come," but it seems to have also a pronominal suffix. Since it is all written as one word, it cannot be thought to be a form involving the sign of the accusative -ית, which is found rarely in Imperial and Biblical Aramaic, and also in 4QEnoch and 11QtgJob.

52. *BO* 17 (1960) 242. Albright's opinion seems to have been picked up by others. See J. M. Grintz, פרקים בתולדות בית שני (*Chapters in the History of the Second Temple Times*) (Jerusalem: Marcos, 1969) 66 n. 46 (in Hebrew); D. Flusser, "Prayers in the Book of Tobit," in Stone, ed., *Jewish Writings of the Second Temple Period,* 555-56.

composition of the story. For it would tend to situate the Aramaic Tobit in the period from the end of the second century B.C. until the beginning of the second century A.D.

Even if the Aramaic of these Qumran texts proves to be later than Daniel, it differs considerably from the medieval Aramaic form found in part of the fifteenth-century manuscript (Hebrew MS 2339 of the Bodleian Library), published by A. Neubauer.[53] That medieval Aramaic form of the story agrees with the Vulgate in telling the story of Tobit in the third person in chapters 1–3, but otherwise differs from the Vulgate in many ways. Yet Neubauer thought that "our Chaldee text in a more complete form was the original from which the translation of the Vulgate was made."[54] Moreover, Neubauer even maintained that the medieval Aramaic form "agrees for the greater part with the Sinaitic text,[55] and consequently with the Itala." However, "the Chaldee text has sentences which are to be found sometimes in one, sometimes in another of the above-mentioned texts; others are peculiar to the Chaldee text or the Hebrew translation."[56] Neubauer was convinced, moreover, "that the original composition of the book was in Hebrew, although no such text is mentioned by Origen and his contemporaries."[57]

Neubauer also maintained that the medieval Aramaic text that he was publishing was not a translation of either a Greek or a Latin text. About that, however, I am not so sure. For the name of Ahiqar turns up in the medieval Aramaic text as אקיקר בר חמאל (1:21), not as אחיקר, the form correctly appearing in Qumran Aramaic, which agrees with the form attested in Elephantine papryi. The medieval Aramaic form (with a *qop* instead of a *het*) clearly reflects the Greek Ἀχίχαρον τὸν Ἀναὴλ . . . υἱόν or the Latin *Achicarum* of the Vetus Latina. Again, the "good meal" that is offered to Tobit on the Feast of Weeks is called in the medieval Aramaic text אריסטוון רב (2:1; also 8:19), which is clearly an attempt to render the Greek ἄριστον καλόν, such as one

---

53. Neubauer, *The Book of Tobit*. The manuscript bears the title מעשה טוביה and is actually part of *Midrash Rabbah de Rabbah* on Gen 28:22. Cf. Nöldeke, "Die Texte des Buches Tobit"; G. Bickell, "Der chaldäische Text des Buches Tobias," *ZKT* 2 (1878) 216-22.

54. Neubauer, *The Book of Tobit*, vii; see also p. x.

55. In this view he was joined by E. Schürer, *Geschichte des jüdischen Volkes im Zeitalter Jesu Christi* (3 vols.; 4th ed.; Leipzig: Hinrichs, 1909-11) 3:245.

56. Neubauer, *The Book of Tobit*, xi. By "Hebrew translation," Neubauer meant the medieval Hebrew translation of Tobit ascribed to S. Münster and reproduced in B. Walton's London Polyglot, 4:35-63. Neubauer collated this Hebrew text with the following manuscripts: Paris Hebr. 1251, De Rossi 194, and the Persian Afterversion (Paris Hebr. 130). Brooke-McLean-Thackeray (*The Old Testament in Greek*, ix) mention that Neubauer's reprint of Sabatier's text of the Itala is "not very accurate."

57. Neubauer, *The Book of Tobit*, xiv-xv.

finds in S (2:1). Similarly, the medieval Aramaic text uses ומה סימנא for "what sign" (5:2). This reflects something in a Greek *Vorlage*, such as τί σημεῖον in S. Again, the use of טרפעיקא (5:15) as the name of a coin, the half-denarius, reflects the Greek τροπαϊκός. Another strange form in the medieval Aramaic text is אושפיזא for "guest" (5:6), which can only reflect the Latin *hospes*. Whereas in Qumran Aramaic the name of the Tigris River is דקלת, preserved also in Syriac as *deqlat*, the medieval Aramaic form of the text (6:2) has תיגרין, which is clearly a transcription of the Greek name Τίγρις, in the accusative case. Other examples of this usage could be added,[58] but, in my opinion, they show that the medieval Aramaic form of Tobit that Neubauer published was certainly a translation from Greek.

Moreover, the Aramaic in which the medieval form is written is not Middle Aramaic, in which the Qumran texts of Tobit are composed, but rather Late Aramaic, like the language of the Babylonian Talmud or like Syriac.[59] It was scarcely the *Vorlage* of the Vulgate, as H. B. Swete once maintained,[60] probably in dependence on A. Neubauer. As J. T. Marshall

58. For example, in this medieval Aramaic text the name Ἐκβατάνοις, which occurs in the Greek versions in the dative (3:7; 4:1; 5:5; 6:5), becomes אגבתניס, a strange form with a final *samekh*. Similarly, in this Aramaic text the name Ῥάγοις (5:2) becomes רגיש, again with a final *sin* (see S. J. A. Churchill, "An Origin for the Biblical Name Rhages," *Indian Antiquary* 17 [1888] 329). Greek νυμφῶνα (MSS A, B, S) becomes Aramaic אנדרונא, which really is a transcription of ἀνδρών. Ταμιεῖον (8:1, 4, 12, 13) becomes אידרונא; and μαρσύπιον, "bag, sack," becomes מרצופיה (9:2, 5), where S has χειρόγραφον.

59. Dalman (*Grammatik*, 37) considered the medieval Aramaic Tobit to have been composed not before the seventh century A.D. and listed all the peculiarities of Late Aramaic, which he found to be "vorwiegend dem Targum des Onkelos verwandt." They date from a time even later than Onqelos in reality! Other marks of Late Aramaic are found in such enclitic forms as שלחתנון (10:11), הוינא (5:6), and ידענא (5:6). Whether the Greek version on which the medieval Aramaic form of text depends is that of S or of A or B is debated. For the former see E. Schürer, "Apokryphen des Alten Testaments," in *Realencyklopädie für protestantische Theologie und Kirche* (24 vols.; ed. J. J. Herzog; 3d ed.; Leipzig: Hinrichs, 1896-1913) 1:622-53, esp. 642-44; idem (revised by G. Vermes), "Jewish Literature Composed in Hebrew or Aramaic," in *The History of the Jewish People in the Age of Jesus Christ* (3 vols., vol. 3 in 2 parts; ed. G. Vermes et al.; Edinburgh: Clark, 1973-87) 3.1:177-469, esp. 222-32; Müller, *Beiträge*, 1-53, esp. 28-33.

With these two different forms of Aramaic Tobit (Qumran and medieval), one should compare the two forms of Aramaic Job (11QtgJob and the later targum of Job). See van der Ploeg and van der Woude, *Le targum de Job* and P. de Lagarde, *Hagiographa chaldaice* (Osnabrück: Zeller, 1967) 85-118. For a comparison of the Job targums, see J. A. Fitzmyer, *WA*, 161-82. Compare D. M. Stec, *The Text of the Targum of Job: An Introduction and Critical Edition* (AGAJU 20; Leiden: Brill, 1994).

60. See *The Old Testament in Greek according to the Septuagint* (2 vols.; 3d ed.; Cambridge: Cambridge University Press, 1907) 1:131 n. 2.

long ago rightly concluded, the medieval Aramaic form of Tobit is a translation of a Greek *Vorlage*, probably not of S (as Schürer thought), but of MS B.[61]

The Hebrew in which 4QTob[e] is written is clearly an example of late postexilic Hebrew, which is met at times in some books of the Old Testament. Examples of such late Hebrew are the use of an infinitive absolute to resume the narrative sequence of a finite verb,[62] or in the use of the verb "to be" (היה) with a participle to express an imperative,[63] or in the use of the conjunction אשר to introduce an object clause or even a causal clause, in the sense of "because."[64] In the last instance, one might see a slavish translation of Aramaic די, because this particle functions in Aramaic in all these ways. There are isolated examples of this usage, however, in biblical Hebrew, especially in its late postexilic form.[65] There are also some word formations that seem to be peculiarly Aramaic in this Hebrew text: for example, תשבוחת, "praise" (4QTob[e] 6:4), which is not found in biblical Hebrew, but does occur in 1QM 4:8; 4Q510 1:1 (in the plural); 4Q511 2 i 8; 6Q18 2:8. The more normal Hebrew form is תְּשָׁבָּחָה (Sir 51:12). So this word of the Hebrew Tobit text may be an Aramaic form (cf. Syriac tešbôḥtā').

All these elements make one think that the Hebrew form of Tobit is secondary, a translation from Aramaic. This has also been the opinion of J. T.

61. See J. T. Marshall, "Tobit, Book of," in *A Dictionary of the Bible* (5 vols.; ed. J. Hastings; New York: Scribner, 1900-1904) 4:785-89.

62. The infinitive absolute is so used in 4QTob[e] 2:2; 4:3; 5:2; 7 i 2, and is possibly to be restored in 5:3. It can also be found in Dan 9:5; Hag 1:6. Cf. GKC §113z; *GBH* §123x. Apparently, this usage is almost nonexistent in Qumran Hebrew. In his study of the infinitive absolute, E. Qimron makes mention of it only once, in 4QMMT C 28 (*The Hebrew of the Dead Sea Scrolls* [HSS 29; Atlanta: Scholars Press, 1986] 47-48 [§310.14]).

63. See 4QTob[e] 2:3 (היה זכר); 2:4, 6, 8 ([עושה] היה). According to P. Joüon (*GHB* §121e), there is no example of this usage in the Old Testament, but he cites an example from *m. 'Abot* 1:9, not surprisingly a Mishnaic example. Moreover, E. Qimron (*Hebrew*) gives no instances of such a periphrastic imperative in Qumran Hebrew texts. The periphrastic imperative is found, however, in Aramaic: 4QpapTob[a] 10:1; Hermopolis Letters 2:14 (והוי יהבת עבד לוחפרע), "and give a slave to Wḥpr'"); 1:11; 3:9-10; 7:2-3. (I am indebted to D. Dempsey for these Egyptian Aramaic references.) See further J. C. Greenfield, "The Periphrastic Imperative in Aramaic and Hebrew," *IEJ* 19 (1969) 199-210.

64. The use of אשר in this Hebrew text is somewhat unusual. In addition to the usual relative usage (4QTob[e] 4:2; 6:7, 8; 7 ii [2]), there are times when it introduces a dependent object clause (4:3, 4, 5) and times when it seems to mean "because" (6:5 [bis]; 7 ii 3); at least it has been so understood in the ancient versions.

65. For the object clause, see Esth 3:4; 4:11; Qoh 6:10; 8:12; cf. GKC §157c; Joüon-Muraoka, *GBH* §157a,c. For the causal sense, see Gen 30:18; 31:49; cf. GKC §158b; Joüon-Muraoka, *GBH* §170e.

Milik,[66] and it seems most likely to me, even though there is no real proof for it.

Again, the Qumran Hebrew text of Tobit has nothing to do with the medieval Hebrew forms of the story, of which four are extant:

1. the Hebrew Tobit of Sebastian Münster, said to be a fifth-century version, which was first published in Constantinople in 1516, and again in 1542, and was reproduced in the London Polyglot.[67]

2. the Hebrew Tobit of Paul Fagius, first published in 1517 and reprinted in 1542, which is also found today in the London Polyglot.[68]

3. the Hebrew text of London (HL, British Museum Add. 11,639), dated to the thirteenth century, which was published by Moses Gaster;[69]

4. the Hebrew text of Gaster (HG), another translation that condenses

66. See J. T. Milik, *TYDWJ*, 31-32. Those who have held in the past that Hebrew was the original language in which the book of Tobit was composed are H. Bévenot, "The Primitive Book of Tobit: An Essay in Textual Reconstruction," *BSac* 82 (1926) 55-84, esp. 57; Bickell, "Der chaldäische Text"; J. C. Dancy, *The Shorter Books of the Apocrypha* (Cambridge Bible Commentary on the NEB; Cambridge: Cambridge University Press, 1972) 1-66; A. Dupont-Sommer, "L'Essénisme à la lumière des manuscrits de la Mer Morte: Angélologie et démonologie: Le livre de Tobie," *Annuaire du Collège de France* 68 (1968-69) 411-26, esp. 414-26; Grätz, "Das Buch Tobias oder Tobit"; D. Heller, "ספר טוביה," הספרים החיצונים (ed. A. Kahana; 2d ed.; Tel Aviv: Masada, 1956) 2:291-347; M. Iglesias González and L. Alonso Schökel, *Rut, Tobias, Judit, Ester* (Los Libros Sagradas 8; Madrid: Cristiandad, 1973) 37-98, esp. 42; P. Joüon, "Quelques hébraïsmes du Codex Sinaiticus de Tobie," *Bib* 4 (1923) 168-74; I. Lévi, "La langue originale de Tobit," *REJ* 44 (1902) 288-91; W. O. E. Oesterley, *An Introduction to the Books of the Apocrypha* (London: SPCK, 1935) 161-71; but see Oesterley, *The Books of the Apocrypha: Their Origin, Teaching and Contents* (London: R. Scott, 1914) 349-71; G. Priero, *Il libro di Tobia: Testi e introduzioni: Studio filologico, critico-analitico, esegetico* (Como: Ostinelli, 1924) 12; E. Renan, *Histoire des origines du christianisme* (7 vols.; Paris: Calman Levy, 1879) 6:554-61; P. Saydon, "Some Mistranslations in the Codex Sinaiticus of the Book of Tobit," *Bib* 33 (1952) 363-65.

Some have insisted that the original was written in a Semitic language, but could not decide whether it was Aramaic or Hebrew: A. Clamer, *Tobie* (La Sainte Bible [de Pirot-Clamer] 4; 4th ed.; Paris: Letouzey et Ané, 1949) 385-480, esp. 401; M. M. Schumpp, *Das Buch Tobias übersetzt und erklärt* (EHAT 11; Münster: Aschendorff, 1933) xlvii; D. C. Simpson, "The Book of Tobit," in *APOT*, 1:174-241, esp. 185.

67. See B. Walton, *SS. Biblia Polyglotta complectentia textus originales hebraicos cum Pentat. Samarit: Chaldaicos graecos versionumque antiquarum Samarit. Graec. Sept., Chaldaic., Syriacae Lat. Vulg. Arabicae, Aethiopic. persicae . . .* (6 vols.; London: Roycroft, 1653-57) 4:35-63.

68. Ibid. It is thought to be dependent on the Greek of MS B.

69. See Gaster, "Two Unknown Hebrew Versions." It is written in cento-style Hebrew, imitating many biblical phrases, and, in general, agrees with the Vulgate in its narrative.

in Hebrew the narrative found in the medieval Aramaic text, with which it otherwise largely agrees.[70]

In any case, it is now evident that the original text of Tobit was Semitic, most likely Aramaic. This, then, gives the lie to all those commentators who maintained that the original composition was Greek.[71] It is also evident that the Greek form, especially that of S, was derived from a Semitic *Vorlage*, as many had maintained earlier, because of the multiple Semitisms that S contains in contrast to the more literary form of Greek Tobit found in the short recension of MSS A, B, and V.[72] Despite the recent attempt of P. Deselaers[73] to argue for a Greek original of the type of MS A or B, one has to reject that effort. That theory has been spun out of whole cloth by someone who had not seen the Semitic texts of Tobit.

As many had maintained even before the discovery of the Qumran texts, the original form of the Tobit story must be sought in Aramaic, and in an Aramaic from which neither Jerome's Vulgate nor the medieval Aramaic version has been derived. The Qumran texts now reveal that, of the various Greek forms, S is the one to which one must reckon priority. The process that apparently governed the different Greek forms of the book was one of abridgement. S was the earliest Greek text, then the short recension found in

70. See Gaster, "Two Unknown Hebrew Versions." Cf. M. Rist, "The God of Abraham, Isaac and Jacob: A Liturgical and Magical Formula," *JBL* 57 (1938) 289-303, esp. 295-97.

71. Some of the commentators who so maintained are Fritzsche, *Die Bücher Tobi und Judith*, 8; A. Guillaumont, "Tobit," in *La Bible: Ancien Testament* (Bibliothèque de la Pléiade 120, 139; 2 vols.; Paris: Gallimard, 1956, 1959) 2:1569-97; Schürer, *Geschichte* (3d ed.; Leipzig: Hinrichs, 1898) 3:174-81 (but cf. the 4th ed., 3:240); Löhr, "Das Buch Tobit," 1:135-47, esp. 136; Oesterley, *The Books of the Apocrypha*, 349-71; O. Zöckler, *Die Apokryphen des Alten Testaments nebst einem Anhang über die Pseudepigraphenliteratur* (Kurzgefasster Kommentar . . . zu den Apokryphen 9; Munich: Beck, 1891) 162-84; L. E. T. André, *Les apocryphes de l'Ancien Testament* (Florence: O. Paggi, 1903) 170-89, esp. 181; Nöldeke, "Die Texte des Buches Tobit"; P. Deselaers, *Das Buch Tobit: Studien zu seiner Entstehung, Komposition und Theologie* (OBO 43; Fribourg/Göttingen: Universitätsverlag, 1982).

72. See Joüon, "Quelques hébraïsmes"; Saydon, "Some Mistranslations."

73. See Deselaers, *Das Buch Tobit*. Deselaers claims that the Greek form of Tobit found in MS B was the original, composed in the mid-third century B.C., which was subsequently rendered in Aramaic *ca.* 220 B.C., and then into another, expanded form of Greek, as in S (*ca.* 195 B.C.). His theory has found little support or following. See I. Nowell's review of his book in *CBQ* 46 (1984) 306-7; cf. R. Doran, "Narrative Literature," in *Early Judaism and Its Modern Interpreters* (ed. R. A. Kraft and G. W. E. Nickelsburg; Philadelphia: Fortress; Atlanta: Scholars Press, 1986) 287-310, esp. 296-97; Hanhart, *Text und Textgeschichte*, 21-22 n. 1.

MSS A, B, V, and others. As for the third form of the Greek, that found in MSS 44, 106, 107 and reflected in some of the Syriac version, little can be said about it from the standpoint of the Qumran Aramaic or Hebrew texts. It still seems to be an intermediary Greek form between the long recension of S and the short recension of A, B, and V. It was probably an inner-Greek or Greek-to-Greek production, reflecting neither an Aramaic nor a Hebrew *Vorlage*.

In any case, Klaus Beyer, in his 1984 publication of *Die aramäischen Texte vom Toten Meer,* proposed rather that Hebrew was the original language.[74] In that book he collected eleven Aramaic fragmentary lines or words of Tobit that Milik had revealed at times in various publications. Even before he had seen the Qumran Aramaic and Hebrew fragments of Tobit, Beyer spoke of the Qumran texts as "probably . . . the Hebrew original and the more widely used Aramaic targum, popular because of its story."[75] Consequently, he classified the Aramaic words of Tobit with the "Targums" in his book. In the *Ergänzungsband* of 1994 he repeated the same opinion and treated Tobit along with other Qumran targums:[76] "The original of the Book of Tobit is written in Middle Hebrew . . . and the Aramaic text has been translated from Hebrew."[77]

Beyer regards the original Tobit to have been composed in Hebrew for two main reasons: (1) The Aramaic text uses five Hebrew words: אליל, "idol" (4Q198 1:13 [= Greek 14:6]); ארור, "cursed (be)" (4Q196 17 ii 15-16 [13:12]); תהלי[ן], "psalms" (4Q196 17 ii 7 [13:8]); קרא, "call!" (4Q196 12:1 [5:9]); משפחתי, "my family" (4Q196 2:9 [1:22]). (2) Two features are said to be "un-Aramaic": (a) the use of הא אנה, "Here I am," as an answer to a call (4Q197 4 i 16 [6:11]), which Beyer seems to regard as a clumsy translation of Hebrew הנני, "behold me"; and (b) the use of four dots as a substitute for the tetragrammaton יהוה (4Q196 18:5).

I would agree that אליל, "idol," תהלין, "psalms," and משפחתי, "my family," are Hebrew words; at least I have not been able to find them attested in contemporary Aramaic texts.[78] I find it strange, however, that such a phe-

---

74. See Beyer, *Die aramäischen Texte,* 299.

75. Ibid.: "wahrscheinlich . . . das hebräische Original und das wegen der grossen Beliebtheit dieser Geschichte weiter verbreitete aramäische Targum."

76. See Beyer, *Ergänzungsband,* 137-47.

77. Ibid., 134.

78. The last word, משפחתי, is found in the Late Aramaic form of the Cairo Genizah *Testament of Levi* (copied *ca.* A.D. 1000; Bodleian Library, Ms. Heb. c. 27 fol. 56), column b, line 16. See R. H. Charles and A. Cowley, "An Early Source of the Testaments of the Patriarchs," *JQR* 19 (1906-7) 566-83 (+ photograph). Cf. J. C. Greenfield and M. E. Stone, "Remarks on the Aramaic Testament of Levi from the Geniza," *RB* 86 (1979) 214-30. Unfortunately, the fragments of the Levi Document recovered from Qumran Caves have not preserved the counterpart of this part of the Genizah text.

nomenon is offered as proof that Tobit was originally composed in Hebrew, because it is well known that the Palestinian Aramaic of this period was at times influenced by Hebrew.[79] Moreover, what Beyer reads as אֲרוּר, I have read as אֲרִירִין (4Q196 17 ii 15-16)[80] because of the clear Aramaic ending -ִין. If one should prefer to read אֲרוּרִין, I should not object much, because in this case it is difficult to distinguish the *waw* and *yod*. Though אֲרַר is not otherwise attested in a contemporary Aramaic text, it occurs in 4Q196 three times over, twice in fragmentary form.[81] Perhaps it is a Hebrew loanword, but that scarcely shows that Tobit was composed in Hebrew. Again, that the imperative קְרָא, "call!" is found in 4Q196 12:1 is no proof of original Hebrew composition either. That verb occurs many times in earlier and contemporary Aramaic.[82]

Similarly, the two features that Beyer regards as un-Aramaic provide no proof for his position. הָא אֲנָה is regularly the translation of Hebrew הִנְנִי as an answer to a call in the later targums: *Tg. Onqelos* and *Tg. Pseudo-Jonathan* write it in a contracted form as הָאֲנָה or הָאֲנָא, whereas *Tg. Neofiti 1* has it as two words, הָא אֲנָה (see Gen 27:1; 31:11; 37:13). Since Tobit is here employing an obviously biblical expression, that can scarcely be evidence for an original Hebrew composition.[83] Finally, why should not an Aramaic text of Tobit use four dots as a substitute for the writing of the tetragrammaton? The device is known elsewhere in Qumran texts,[84] and so it may even indicate that Aramaic Tobit was actually copied in the Qumran scrollery.[85] Consequently, I

79. See S. E. Fassberg, "Hebraisms in the Aramaic Documents from Qumran," in *Studies in Qumran Aramaic* (Abr-NSup 3; ed. T. Muraoka; Louvain: Peeters, 1992) 48-69. Cf. my book, *The Genesis Apocryphon of Qumran Cave I: A Commentary* (BibOr 18A; Rome: Biblical Institute, 1971) 26.

80. See *Qumran Cave 4, XIV* (DJD 19), 27.

81. It is used in the later *Tg. Jonathan* of 2 Kgs 9:34: אֲרוּרְתָּא הָדָא, "this accursed woman."

82. See E. Vogt, *Lexicon linguae aramaicae Veteris Testamenti documentis antiquis illustratum* (Rome: Biblical Institute, 1971) 151; J. A. Fitzmyer and D. J. Harrington, *A Manual of Palestinian Aramaic Texts* (BibOr 34; Rome: Biblical Institute, 1978) 336; J. Hoftijzer and K. Jongeling, *DNWSI*, 2:1026.

83. E. M. Cook ("Our Translated Tobit," 160) notes that הָא אֲנָה as used here "suggests that the expression had become natural in Aramaic."

84. See, e.g., 1QS 8:14 (quoting Isa 40:3); 4QTestim (4Q175) 1, 19 (quoting Deut 5:28 and 33:11); 4QTanhumim (4Q176) 1-2 i 6, 7, 9; 1-2 ii 3; 8-11:6, 8, 10. Cf. J. A. Fitzmyer, "The Semitic Background of the New Testament *Kyrios*-Title," in *WA*, 115-42, esp. 127.

85. I mention this only as a remote possibility, because it seems that most of the Aramaic texts of Qumran were imported from elsewhere. Very few, if any, of the sectarian writings seem to have been composed in Aramaic.

find it difficult to go along with Beyer's judgment that the book of Tobit was originally written in Hebrew.[86]

Michael O. Wise has also spoken of Hebrew Tobit as the original, citing its "tendency to use the infinitive absolute in place of finite verbal forms," and considering such usage "surprising if this text is translation Hebrew, not least because one rarely encounters the infinitive absolute at all in Qumran Hebrew."[87] The infinitive absolute with *waw*, consecutive to a finite verb, is found five times in Hebrew Tobit, 4Q200 2:2; 4:3; 5:2; 6:4; 7 i 2. It imitates examples of this use of the infinitive absolute in late postexilic biblical Hebrew (Hag 1:6; Esth 8:8; Neh 9:8, 13; Dan 9:5). Indeed, at least two other instances of it in Qumran texts have been overlooked by Wise: 4QMMT C 26 (ונסלוח) and 4QTNaphtali 2:10 (ונתון). That phenomenon, however, is hardly a probative argument that Tobit was originally composed in Hebrew.[88] Hebrew Tobit is simply using a construction that is otherwise known in the Hebrew language,[89] even though it may not be common in what we call Qumran Hebrew,[90] for there is no reason to think that Hebrew Tobit was written at Qumran.

These, then, are the reasons why I prefer to regard Tobit as an original Aramaic composition, and the Hebrew form of it as a translation of that. In other words, Aramaic Tobit is not a targum (in the normal sense). I have given rea-

---

86. My reaction to Beyer's judgment about "Aramaic words" in the Hebrew form of Tobit (4Q200) is likewise mixed. The word תשבוחת, "praise" (6:4) is an Aramaism, as is שימה, "treasure" (2:9). That כבר, "already" (4:3, 5), is an Aramaism is usually admitted, but it also appears in the Hebrew of Qoh 1:10; 2:12, 16; 3:15 (bis); 4:2; 6:10; 9:6, 7. So too for בכן, "then" (6:4), which is found in Qoh 8:10; Esth 4:16; Sir 13:7; כשר (1 ii 3), which appears in Esth 8:5; Sir 13:4; and perhaps also פצי, "save, rescue" (6:7); הרויח, "widen" (1 i 4). It is far from certain that חך, "stay" (imperative, 4:7), is from Aramaic חכך, as Beyer claims, for it is rather the apocopated piel imperative of חכי; see GKC §75cc.

E. M. Cook also finds Beyer's analysis unconvincing ("Our Translated Tobit," 155-56). He is also skeptical about Beyer's thesis that the Greek versions of Tobit were based on a Hebrew original, an issue that does not concern us here.

87. See M. O. Wise, "A Note on 4Q196 (papTob ar^a) and Tobit i 22," *VT* 53 (1993) 566-70, esp. 569 n. 4.

88. Unfortunately, no instances in 4Q200 are found in passages that overlap with Aramaic texts; so there is no way to be certain about what their counterparts might be in Aramaic. E. M. Cook ("Our Translated Tobit," 156 n. 13) argues: "If the liberal use of the infinitive absolute is otherwise absent in free Hebrew composition at Qumran, then its use in Tobit indicates that it is *not* freely composed Hebrew, but a translation — perhaps an effort to duplicate the nuance of the narrative participle in Aramaic" (his emphasis).

89. See GKC §113z; Joüon-Muraoka, *GBH* §123x; G. Bergsträsser, *Hebräische Grammatik* (Hildesheim: Olms, 1962) 2:§12m.

90. See E. Qimron, *The Hebrew of the Dead Sea Scrolls* (HSS 29; Atlanta: Scholars Press, 1986) 48 §310.14.

sons above for identifying the Aramaic fragments of Tobit as examples of Middle Aramaic, related to other Qumran Aramaic texts such as the *Genesis Apocryphon, 1 Enoch,* and the *Targum of Job.*[91] It seems most likely that Tobit was composed originally in such Aramaic toward the end of the third century or about the beginning of the second century B.C. In this I find myself basically in agreement with Milik, who wrote, "In the Essene *scriptorium* of Ḥirbet Qumrân texts originally composed in Aramaic were occasionally translated into the Hebrew language,"[92] and he cites Tobit as an example. He also mentions the New Jerusalem texts, of which most of the fragments are preserved in Aramaic (1Q32, 2Q24, 4Q554-555, 5Q15, 11Q18), but of which one fragment is in Hebrew (4Q232, as yet unpublished). According to some commentators, the book of Daniel was originally written in Aramaic and then some parts of it were translated into Hebrew (to insure its place in the Jewish biblical canon).

New Aramaic Words

Among a good number of new Aramaic words five may be singled out for special comment:[93]

1. שרו (*šārû*), "dinner, meal" (pap4QTob[a] 2:11), a feminine form modified by טבה, "good." This word for "dinner" is actually known from Elephantine texts (שרתא in Cowley's text, *AP* 72:2, 3, 10, 17, 18), but now appears for the first time in Qumran Aramaic.

2. נפתניא (*niptānayyā'*), "delicacies" (pap4QTob[a] 2:11), a word related to Akkadian *naptanu*, "Mahlzeit" (von Soden, *AHW*, 2:741).

3. המרכלות (*hămarkělût*), "treasury account" (4QpapTob[a] 2:6), translated as διοίκησις in S and as *regio* in the Vetus Latina, an abstract form of המרכל (*hămarkal*), which is also found in 2:7. It is related to the Egyptian Aramaic phrase המרכריא זי במצרין (*AD* 8:1*; 9:1*; 10:1*) and derived from Persian *hamarakara*, "treasury accountant," a word well studied by J. C. Greenfield.[94] It now turns up in a form with an initial *he*, a form which has

---

91. Cf. J. A. Fitzmyer, "The Phases of the Aramaic Language," *WA*, 57-84, esp. 61-62, 71-73.

92. J. T. Milik, *The Books of Enoch: Aramaic Fragments of Qumrân Cave 4* (Oxford: Clarendon, 1976) 56. I am not sure, however, that Tobit was *composed* at Qumran.

93. Others are יצף, "worry, be troubled" (4QTob[b] 4 i 3); סדר, "follow in order" (4QTob[b] 4 i 5); אתן, "smoke" (4QTob[b] 4 i 13); סחר סחרתא, "encounter" (4QTob[b] 4 i 14).

94. J. C. Greenfield, "*Hamarakara > 'Amarkal," in *W. B. Henning Memorial Volume* (Asia Minor Library; ed. M. Boyce and I. Gershevitch; London: Lund Humphries, 1970), 180-86.

been postulated as transitional to that found with an initial *aleph* in rabbinic texts (אמרכל).

4. The most problematic word of all is שיזפן (pap4QTob^a 2:8), of which a related form (שיזפנות) is probably to be restored in 2:5. It corresponds to Greek ἐκλογιστής and ἐκλογιστία in S, terms also found in Oxyrhynchus Papyri, which Liddell-Scott-Jones explain as "accountant" and "accounts." It seems to be a name for an official in a royal court and for the post that he held. The form, however, is strange. I originally thought that it might be an Iranian word, but J. C. Greenfield has more plausibly suggested that it is a *shaphel* formation of the root יזף, "borrow," or in the causative stem, "lend." It would, then, appear with an *-ān* ending for the official, and with *-ānût* for the post.

5. The word for "wood" appears in pap4QTob^a 18:8 as עע, a form often postulated as the intermediary between עק of Elephantine texts and the Biblical Aramaic form אע.[95]

Aḥiqar

Of particular interest in the Tobit text are the passages that refer to Aḥiqar.[96] He is first mentioned in Tob 1:21 in the context of the account of

95. Greenfield has informed me that עע also appears in 4QLevi. See now 4Q214b 2-3:2; 5-6 i 5 (M. E. Stone and J. C. Greenfield, "214b. 4QLevi^f ar," in *Qumran Cave 4: XVII. Parabiblical Texts, Part 3* [DJD 22; ed. G. Brooke et al.; Oxford: Clarendon, 1996] 61-72, esp. 64, 66).

96. See further J. C. Greenfield, "Aḥiqar in the Book of Tobit," in *De la Tôrah au Messie: Etudes d'exégèse et d'herméneutique bibliques offertes à Henri Cazelles . . .* (ed. M. Carrez et al.; Paris: Desclée, 1981) 329-36. Cf. J. M. Lindenberger, *The Aramaic Proverbs of Ahiqar* (Baltimore: Johns Hopkins University Press, 1983); F. Altheim and R. Stiehl, "Aḥīkar und Tobit," in *Die aramäische Sprache unter den Achaimeniden II* (Frankfurt am Main: Klostermann, 1960) 182-95; J. H. Charlesworth, *The Pseudepigrapha and Modern Research: With a Supplement* (SBLSCS 7; Missoula, Mont.: Scholars Press, 1981) 75-77; F. C. Conybeare et al., "The Story of Ahiqar," in *APOT*, 2:715-84; idem, *The Story of Aḥikar from the Aramaic . . .* (n. 16 above); E. Cosquin, "Encore l'"Histoire du sage Ahikar,'" *RB* 8 (1899) 510-31; idem, "Le livre de Tobie et l'"Histoire du sage Ahikar,'" *RB* 8 (1899) 50-82; R. Degen, "Achikar," in *Enzyclopädie des Märchens* (Berlin/New York: de Gruyter, 1977-93) 1:53-59; J. van Dijk, *XVIII vorläufiger Bericht . . . Ausgrabungen in Uruk-Warka, Winter 1959/60* (AbhDOG 7; Berlin: Deutsche Orientgesellschaft, 1962) 43-52; E. J. Dillon, "Ahikar the Wise: An Ancient Hebrew Folk Story," *Contemporary Review* 73 (March 1898) 362-86; M. Gaster, "Contributions to the History of Akikar and Nadan," *JRAS* (1900) 301-19; J. Halévy, "Tobie et Akiakar," *RevSém* 8 (1900) 23-77; F. Nau, *Histoire et sagesse d'Ahikar l'assyrien (Fils d'Anael, neveu de Tobie): Traduction des versions syriaques . . .* (Paris:

the assassination of Sennacherib by two of his sons, who fled to the mountains of Ararat, and of the succession of Esarhaddon as king.

> [Esarhaddon] put Ahiqar, son of ʿAnaʾel, my kinsman, in charge of all the credit accounts of his kingdom; and he had control over all the treasury accounts of the king. And Ahiqar made intercession on my behalf . . . for Ahiqar, my kinsman, had been the chief cupbearer, the keeper of the signet rings, the treasury accountant, and credit officer under Sennacherib, the king of Assyria. Then Esarhaddon put him in charge as Second to himself. Now he was the son of my brother, of my father's house, and of my family. (4QpapTob[a] 2:5-9)

To be noted here are three things:

    1. The form of the name of Tobit's kinsman עַנָאֵל is written with an initial ʿayin and not with a ḥeth, as many have understood the name relying on the Greek Ἀναήλ, with a rough breathing.

    2. The name of Sennacherib is given as אסרחריב (4QpapTob[a] 2:8). In the Old Testament it is usually written as *sanḥērîb* (2 Kgs 18:13; 19:16, 20, 36; Isa 36:1; 37:17, 21, 37; 2 Chr 32:1, 2, 9, 10, 22; defectively in 2 Kgs 19:20) and in the LXX as Σενναχηρ(ε)ίμ or Σεναχείριμος (with many variants in manuscripts) in Josephus, *Ant.* 10.1.1 §1. In the Elephantine text of Aḥiqar it is more correctly given as שנחאריב (line 3) or סנחאריב (lines 50, 51, 55). Here, the scribe of 4QpapTob[a] has confused it with the name of Esarhaddon, starting to write אסר(חדון), but finishing it with the correct final consonants חריב, thus producing an anomalous name.[97] The scribe seems to have been unaware of the Akkadian meaning of either name, either *Sin-aḫḫe-erib(a)*, "Sin has replaced the brothers," or *Aššur-aḫ-iddin*, "Asshur has given a brother."

Letouzey et Ané, 1909) 15-59; E. Nestle, "The Story of Ahikar," *ExpTim* 10 (1898-99) 276-77; J. O'Carroll, "Tobias and Achikar," *Dublin Review* 185 (1929) 252-63; L. Pirot, "Ahikar," *DBSup* 1 (1928) 198-207; T. Reinach, "Un conte babylonien dans la littérature juive: Le roman d'Akhikhar," *REJ* 38 (1899) 1-13; L. Ruppert, "Zur Funktion der Achikar-Notizen im Buch Tobias," *BZ* 20 (1976) 232-37; C. Schmitt, "Der weise Achikar der morgenländischen Sage und der Achikar des Buches Tobias nach der Übersetzung der LXX," *Pastor Bonus* 26 (1913-14) 83-90; P. Termes, "Aḥiqar y el libro de Tobías," in *Enciclopedia de la Biblia* (6 vols.; Barcelona: Garriga, 1963) 1:266-68; P. Vetter, "Das Buch Tobias" (n. 22 above); K.-T. Zauzich, "Demotische Fragmente zum Ahikar-Roman," *Folia rara: Wolfgang Voigt LXV diem natalem celebranti* . . . (Verzeichnis der orientalischen Handschriften in Deutschland Supplementband 19; ed. H. Francke et al.; Wiesbaden: Steiner, 1976) 180-85.

    97. Note the equally anomalous form אסרחאריב in Aḥiqar 19 for Esarhaddon (cf. B. Porten and A. Yardeni, *Textbook of Aramaic Documents from Ancient Egypt. Volume 3: Literature, Accounts, Lists* (Jerusalem: Hebrew University, 1993) 24-25.

3. The status of Aḥiqar at the royal court is given in greater detail in this Aramaic text than in the versions. Here he is said not only to have been put in charge of all the *šayzĕpānût* of the kingdom and to have had control over all the treasury accounts of the king, but also to have been the chief cupbearer, keeper of the signet rings, treasury accountant, and *šayĕzpān* under Sennacherib. Now Esarhaddon has even set him up as "Second to himself" (תנין לה). The last term is important because it clarifies the often-misunderstood sense of the Greek κατέστησεν αὐτὸν . . . ἐκ δευτέρας. For instance, *La Sainte Bible de Jérusalem* translated the Greek phrase merely as "et Assarhaddon l'avait maintenu en fonction."[98] An expression, however, found in the Greek text of Judith 2:4 supplies a more accurate rendering: δεύτερον ὄντα μετὰ αὐτόν, "being second after him." This translates better the Aramaic expression of the Qumran text that describes Aḥiqar's status, as "the Second" to the king, that is, the first man in the court after the sovereign. It can be compared with the Hebrew of Esth 10:3, משנה למלך, or that of Gen 41:43, המשנה אשר לו, and with the Akkadian *turtānu* or *tartānu*, "man in the second place" (von Soden, *AHW*, 3:1332).

Conclusion

All these elements increase our understanding of the story of Tobit, but unfortunately, all the Qumran forms of the Tobit story are fragmentary, preserving for us perhaps not more than a fifth of the original Semitic texts. When they will be fully studied, however, and compared with the ancient versions, they will at times clarify the meaning of the Greek, Latin, or Syriac versions. Yet there is little in them that is radically new or different from the form of the story in either S or the Vetus Latina. Their real value, however, lies in the increase they make to the body of literary Aramaic and Hebrew that is being gradually made known by the publication of Qumran texts.

98. Similarly *The New Jerusalem Bible*: "and Esarhaddon kept him in office" (1:22); *NAB*: "and Esarhaddon reappointed him"; *NRSV*: "and Esarhaddon reappointed him."

CHAPTER 9

The Qumran Texts of Tobit

4Q196-200: 4QpapTobit[a] ar, 4QTobit[b-d] ar, and 4QTobit[e]

Introduction

The identification and assembling of the fragments that make up the Tobit texts 4Q196-200 were the work of Jósef Tadeusz Milik, who worked on them from approximately 1953 to 1960. What I present here is mostly dependent on his pioneering work. Today these fragments are found in their most definitive form on ten photographs, PAM 43.175-84. Specific references will be given below to these photographs, along with the numbers of older ones, which sometimes help in deciphering the fragments. The photographs marked with an asterisk were used for plates I-X of volume 19 of the Discoveries in the Judaean Desert series.

Contents of the Qumran Tobit Texts

Five fragmentary texts of Tobit have been recovered from Qumran. Of these, four (4QTob[a-d] ar) are in Aramaic and one (4QTob[e]) is in Hebrew. The texts are composed of sixty-nine fragments or groups of fragments (a group being defined as joined fragments that belong together or related fragments that cannot be physically joined). 4QpapTob[a] ar has nineteen identified fragments or groups of fragments and thirty tiny unidentified fragments. Tob[b] ar has five fragments or groups of fragments identified and two that are unidentified. Tob^c ar has two fragments that are identified. Tob^d ar has two fragments that are identified. Tob^e has seven fragments that are identified and two that are unidentified.

Table 1 gives an overview of the identified fragments. The numbering of chapters and verses follows that of Sinaiticus or G^{II} in the Hanhart edition (see below).

Table 1: Contents of 4Q196-200

4QpapTob^a ar Frg.	Passage	4QTob^b ar Frg.	Passage	4QTob^c ar Frg.	Passage	4QTob^d ar Frg.	Passage	4QTob^e Frg.	Passage
1	1:17								
2	1:19–2:2								
3	2:3								
4	2:10-11								
5	3:5	1	3:6-8					1 i	3:6
6	3:9-15							1 ii	3:10-11
7	3:17								
8	4:2								
9	4:5							2	4:3-9
10	4:7								
11	4:21–5:1	2	4:21–5:1					3	5:2
12	5:9	3	5:12-14						
13	6:6-8	4 i	5:19–6:12						
14 i	6:13-18	4 ii	6:12-18						
14 ii	6:18–7:6	4 iii	6:18–7:10						
						1	7:11		
15	7:13	5	8:17–9:4						
								4	10:7-9
								5	11:10-14
16	12:1								
17 i	12:18–13:6							6	12:20–13:4
17 ii	13:6-12							7 i	13:13-14
18	13:12–14:3			1	14:2-6			7 ii	13:18–14:2
19	14:7			2	14:10	2	14:10	8	?
20-49	?	6-7	?					9	3:3-4?

Relation of the Qumran Tobit Texts to Ancient Versions

Both the Aramaic and the Hebrew form of the Tobit story agree in general with the long recension of the book found in the fourth-century Greek text of Sinaiticus, which contains the whole text, except for two lacunae: 1:1–4:6; 4:19c–13:6h; 13:10c–14:15 (the lacunae being 4:7-19b and 13:6i-10b). Part of the text of this recension is also found in the eleventh-century minuscule manuscript 319 (Vatopedi 513, dated A.D. 1021); it contains Tob 3:6–6:16 (up to δαιμονίου τούτου). A small portion is also preserved in the sixth-century manuscript 910 (= Papyrus Oxyrhynchus 1076 [B. P. Grenfell and A. S. Hunt (eds.), *The Oxyrhynchus Papyri: Part VIII* (London: Egypt Exploration Society, 1911) 6-9]), which contains Tob 2:2-5, 8. The long recension is also found in manuscripts of the Vetus Latina.

The Greek text of Sinaiticus and of the readings of the manuscripts related to it (319, 910) can be found at the bottom of the pages in the critical edition of the Greek text of Tobit published by Robert Hanhart (*Tobit* [Septuaginta: Vetus Testamentum graecum auctoritate Academiae Scientiarum Gottingensis editum 8/5; Göttingen: Vandenhoeck & Ruprecht, 1983]; the Hanhart edition supersedes that of A. E. Brooke, N. McLean, and H. St J. Thackeray, *The Old Testament in Greek* [Cambridge: Cambridge University Press, 1940] 3.1:85-110 [Vaticanus], 111-22 [Sinaiticus]). The short recension of the book of Tobit is found today in the Greek manuscripts Alexandrinus, Vaticanus, Venetus, 990 (= Papyrus Oxyrhynchus 1594 [Grenfell and Hunt, *The Oxyrhynchus Papyri*, 13:1-6]) and a host of other minuscule manuscripts. The critical text of the short recension (togther with variants from its related manuscripts) can be found at the top of the pages in the Hanhart edition.

In the comments on the individual fragments given below, the long text of Sinaiticus (S) as well as that of the Vetus Latina (La) will be quoted, to the extent that they correspond to the Semitic texts. At times readings will be added from the short recension, when they are considered important. The abbreviation "AB" (= Alexandrinus and Vaticanus) will be used to designate the short recension as a whole, since it is not possible here to present an extensive *apparatus criticus*. For variants within the text tradition of this short recension, the reader can consult the *apparatus criticus* in the Hanhart edition. Especially at the beginning of our edition, the Greek text of the short recension will occasionally be quoted, when it differs from the long recension; this is for the sake of comparison so that readers may see the reason for preferring to cite the long text of S and La.

There is also an intermediate Greek recension found in manuscripts 44 106 107, which may have some pertinence for Tob 6:9–13:8 (for the rest it reproduces the text of B).

Since there is no critical edition of La for the book of Tobit, one must begin the study of the long recension in Latin with the form given by Brooke-McLean (*Old Testament*, 123-44), which essentially reproduces the Latin text of P. Sabatier, *Bibliorum sacrorum latinae versiones antiquae, seu Vetus Italica* . . . [Rheims: Reginald Florentain, 1732; 2d ed.; Paris: Didot, 1751; reprinted in 3 vols.; ed. B. Fischer; Turnhout: Brepols, 1976] 1:706-43). This Latin text was based on two ninth-century manuscripts: Q (Codex Regius, Paris, Bibliothèque Nationale, fonds lat. 93 [what Sabatier called ms. Regius 3564]) and P (Codex Corbeiensis, Paris, Bibliothèque Nationale, fonds lat. 11505 [what Sabatier called ms. Sangermanensis 4]). Sabatier also added readings from G (Codex Sangermanensis, Paris, Bibliothèque Nationale, fonds lat. 11553 [what he called Sangerm. 15]), which contains the text up to Tob 13:2 *(Explicit Tobi iustus);* and from W (Codex Reginensis, Rome, Bibliotheca Apostolica Vaticana, Regin. lat. 7), which contains the text only as far as Tob 6:12 (the rest being a copy of the Vulgate). Of manuscript W, Brooke-McLean say that it is "nearest to that of the Sinaitic Greek Manuscript (S), but it is probably not the earliest form of the Old Latin Version" (p. x). Yet, as Brooke-McLean note, "the manuscripts of the Old Latin Version known to us, complete or incomplete, are not all of one type" (p. ix). In the absence of a critical text of La of Tobit, this difference constitutes a problem which still has to be resolved. Two other manuscripts of La of Tobit have been studied (although the differences between them amply illustrate this lack of 'one type' of La text): the tenth-century manuscript R (Biblia de Rosas r, Paris, Bibliothèque Nationale, fonds lat. 6 [often called the Biblia de Roda]) and the ninth-century manuscript X (Codex Complutensis 1, Madrid, Biblioteca Univers. Centr. 31 [often called the Prima Biblia de Alcalá]). Both have been published by F. Vattioni: "La Vetus Latina di Tobia nella Bibbia di Roda," *Revista catalana de teologia* 3 (1978) 173-200; "Tobia nello *Speculum* e nella prima Bibbia di Alcalà," *Augustinianum* 15 (1975) 169-200 (in this article Vattioni also supplies the numerous readings of the Tobit text found in the second *Speculum,* a work attributed to Augustine [F. Weihrich, *Liber de divinis scripturis sive Speculum quod fertur S. Augustini* (CSEL 12 [1887] 287-725)], to be distinguished from the authentic *Speculum).* The Latin text of the Alcalá Bible is very paraphrastic, representing a much expanded form of the Latin text found in Brooke-McLean; it is of little use in text-critical work.

The short recension of the book of Tobit is also found in the Vulgate (Vg), the critical text of which has been published by the Benedictines of San Girolamo, *Biblia Sacra iuxta Latinam Vulgatam versionem ad codicum fidem . . . edita,* vol. 8, *Libri Ezrae, Tobiae, Iudith* [Rome: Vatican Polyglot Press, 1950] 163-209).

The book of Tobit is also preserved in Syriac, Coptic (Sahidic), Ethiopic, Armenian, and Arabic, but all these versions are secondary derivatives of the different Greek forms of the book and are of little concern here.[1] In general,

---

1. See R. Hanhart, *Tobit,* 15-23.

the same can be said about the medieval Aramaic and (four) Hebrew versions of Tobit.[2]

Although the Aramaic form of Tobit from Qumran frequently agrees with the long recension of S and the La, neither the Greek nor the Latin is a direct translation of such an Aramaic *Vorlage;* the latter contains inverted phrases, expanded expressions, and words not rightly understood by either the Greek or Latin translator of these versions.[3]

Table 2: Manuscripts of the Vetus Latina of Tobit

Conventional Siglum	Beuron Number	Date	Name
D	145	9 cent.	Reginensis (Rome, Vatican Library, Reg. lat. 7)
G	7	beg. 9 cent.	Sangermanensis g' (Paris, B.N. fonds lat. 11553)
H	134	12 cent.	Oscensis, Biblia de Huesca (Madrid, Museo Arqueológico 485)
J	135	9/10 cent.	Bobbiensis (Milan, Bibl. Ambrosiana E. 26 inf.)
L	133	A.D. 960	Gothicus Legionensis (Leon, S. Isidore)
M	130	8/9 cent.	Monacensis (Munich, Bayerische Staatsbibliothek Clm 6239)
P	150	A.D. 822	Corbeiensis (Paris, B.N. fonds lat. 11505)
Q	148	9 cent.	Codex Regius (Paris, B.N. fonds lat. 93)
R	62	10 cent.	Biblia de Rosas (Roda) (Paris, B.N. fonds lat. 6)
V	123	10 cent.	Vercellensis (Vercelli 11 [22])
W	143	9 cent.	Reginensis (Rome, Vatican Library, Regin. lat. 7)
X	109	9 cent.	Complutensis 1, Prima Biblia de Alcalá (Madrid, Bibl. Univers. Centr. 31)

2. See A. Neubauer, *The Book of Tobit: A Chaldee Text from a Unique* MS. *in the Bodleian Library, with Other Rabbinical Texts, English Translations and the Itala* (Oxford: Clarendon, 1878); B. Walton, *SS. Biblia Polyglotta complectentia textus originales . . .* (6 vols.; London: Roycroft, 1653-1657) 4:35-63 (this includes the Hebrew texts of both P. Fagius and S. Münster); and M. Gaster, "Two Unknown Hebrew Versions of the Tobit Legend," *Proceedings of the Society of Biblical Archaeology* 18 (1896) 208-22, 259-71; 19 (1897) 27-38; reprinted in *Studies and Texts in Folklore, Magic, Mediaeval Romance, Hebrew Apocrypha, and Samaritan Archaeology . . .* (3 vols.; London: Maggs, 1928; reprinted with a prolegomenon by T. Gaster; New York: Ktav, 1971) 1:1-38; 3:1-14.

3. I am indebted to Dom P.-M. Bogaert, O.S.B. of Louvain-la-Neuve, Belgium, for help with La readings and to Dr. R. H. Johnson of the Rochester Institute of Technology for the enhancement of some problematic fragments. Permission has been kindly granted by Vandenhoeck & Ruprecht to quote from R. Hanhart, *Tobit* (Septuaginta: Vetus Testamentum graecum 8/5; Göttingen, 1983); and also by Cambridge University Press to quote the Vetus Latina from A. E. Brooke, N. McLean, and H. St J. Thackeray, *The Old Testament in Greek* 3/1 (Cambridge, 1940).

4Q196: 4QpapTobit^a ar

Physical Description

4Q196 is written on papyrus that is light brown in color, with thirteen or sixteen lines to a column; the columns are generally about 15 cm wide.

Palaeography

The text is carefully written in a late semiformal Hasmonean script and dates from *ca.* 50 B.C.[4] There are no ligatures; the *taw* is normally looped. There is usually a clear distinction between *waw* and *yod,* and between *bet* and *kap.* The *bet* has a clearly separate horizontal bar, and the *kap* is usually drawn with a longer vertical shaft on the right.

Frg. 1   Tob 1:17

[שורא די נינוה]   [   ] 1

Mus. Inv. 666
PAM 41.647, 42.212, 43.175*

NOTES ON READINGS

This small papyrus fragment contains three words on one line.
    L. 1 The final *he* has almost disappeared.

TRANSLATION

    1. [   ] the wall of Nineveh [   ]

COMMENTS

    L. 1 Cf. S: ὀπίσω τοῦ τείχους Νινευή. La: post murum Nineue.

---

4. See F. M. Cross, "The Development of the Jewish Scripts," in *The Bible and the Ancient Near East: Essays in Honor of William Foxwell Albright* (ed. G. E. Wright; Garden City, N.Y.: Doubleday, 1961) 133-202, esp. 149 §2; reprinted, Anchor Books (1965) 170-264, esp. 190 §2.

Frg. 2   Tob 1:19–2:2

top margin

1   [חד מ]ן בֿ׳ נינוה והחוי למלכ[א עלי ד]יֿ אנֿה קב[ר אנון ו]אֿחוית וכדי
     ידעת [די] ידע בי

2   [ולי בעה למקט]לֿ .דחלת וערקתֿ[ל 20כ]לֿ דֿ[י]הוה לי ולא שביק {פֿ} לי כל
     מנד[עם]

3   [ל]הן חנ[ה א]נֿתֿ[תי וטוֿבֿיה ברי 21ולֿא הוה יומין א]רבעיֿן   [

4   תרי בנו]הֿי ואנון ערקו לטורי אררט ומלך [ומֿ]לֿך אסרחדו[ן   [

5   והוא [אֿ]שֿלט לאחיקר בר ענאל אחי על כל שֿ[יזפנו]תֿ   [

6   [מ]לכותה   ולה הוה שֿ[לטֿן עֿל] כֿ[ל]ֿ הֿמֿרכלוֿת מלכא 22ובעה אחיקר עֿלֿי   [

7   ואחי[קֿרֿ אֿחֿיֿ הוה רֿבֿ שקה ורב עזֿקֿן והֿמֿרֿכֿל   [

8   [ו]שֿיזפן קדם אסרחריב מלך אתוֿר ואשלטה אסרחדוֿן תנין לה ארי

9   בֿרֿ אֿחֿי   הוה ומן בית אבי ומן משפחתי 2:1וביומי אסרחדוֿן [מל]כֿא כדי
     תבת

10   לבֿיֿתֿי ואתבת לי חנה אנתתי וטובֿיה ברי ביום חג שבֿו[עיֿא הות] לֿ[יֿ]

11   שרו טבה ורבעת ל[מאכ]לֿ 2וֿאֿקרבוֿ פֿתֿ[ו]רֿא לקודמי וחזית נפֿתֿנֿיא די קרבו

12   עלוהי שגיאין ואמרֿ[ת לטו]בֿיה ברי אזל דבר לכל מֿ[ן די ת]ֿהֿשֿכֿח
     באחֿ[ינא]

13   [   ].ֿבֿרי אזל דבר ואתהייתה ויכֿלֿ [כחדא   עֿמֿיֿ והֿא אֿנֿהֿ   [

bottom margin

Mus. Inv. 666
PAM 41.646, 41.648, 42.211, 43.175*

NOTES ON READINGS

Much of this column of thirteen lines is preserved. Line 11 shows the width of the column, even though a few letters in the middle of it are lost. A small fragment found on PAM 41.646 and on PAM 43.179 belongs at the end of lines 4-6.

L. 1 The letters נֿי are written above the line, above the first *bet*. The *nun* of the pronoun אנה has almost disappeared. The upper layer of papyrus at the left leg of *taw* in ידעת has been lost, but the rest is clear.

L. 2 A dot precedes the *dalet* of דחלת, probably the bottom of a *waw* (*waw apodoseos*). Only a dot remains of the upper shaft of the *lamed* of כל, and of the following *dalet* only a trace of its horizontal bar. After שביק a letter resembling a *pe* appears. It may have been a *kap* or a *nun* through which a vertical bar has been drawn, apparently as a sign of deletion. It is to be disregarded in the reading.

L. 3 Only slight traces of the *tet, waw,* and *bet* in Tobiah's name are preserved.

L. 4 After a clear ומלך there appear toward the end of the line traces of ומ, which seem to be dittographical and should be disregarded in the reading. At the end of the added fragment (from PAM 43.179), there is a trace of a final *nun*.

L. 5 Toward the end of the line, after traces of כל, there is a stroke that seems to be the right side of a *šin*, which is more visible on PAM 41.646. With it one should compare the first word of line 8. At the very end there is a trace also of the last letter, probably a *taw* (see PAM 41.646).

L. 6 Of this badly preserved line there is the top of a *lamed*, followed by the top of a *ṭet* and traces of a final *nun* and an *'ayin*. The last word (עלי) is clearly seen on PAM 41.646.

L. 7 The traces of the first letters resemble קר, followed by what seems to be אחי, after which one reads הוה. This is seen more clearly on PAM 41.648 (last fragment on lower left), which preserves the beginning of this line.

L. 8 The first trace seems to be the left side of a *šin*, probably the beginning of a word related to the last on line 5. The *waw* of אתור is lost in a crack of the papyrus, as is also the lower part of the *waw* in אסרחדון. In ארי at the end of the line, the *yod* is clear; it cannot be a *waw* (compare אחוית in line 1 or ביומי in line 9).

L. 9 A faint trace of the crossbar of a *bet* and that of a *reš* remain at the beginning of the line, after which come a doubtful *'alep* and fairly clear traces of a *ḥet* and a *yod*.

L. 10 At the beginning of the line there are faint traces of לבית, which appear more clearly on PAM 41.646. The same is true of the *waw* before Tobiah's name. At the end, after a lacuna, one can see the very top of a *lamed*, under the final *taw* of תבת.

L. 11 After ואקרבו there is a trace of the upper part of a *pe* and a *taw*, part of פתורא, and later of the *pe* and *taw* of נפתניא.

L. 12 There is a space between the ברי and ברי.

L. 13 The slight trace of a *bet* in ברי is clear on PAM 43.175, but it is no longer seen on the papyrus itself.

TRANSLATION

1. [one o]f the Ninevites, and he made known to [the] king [about me th]at I was bury[ing them], and I hid. When I knew [that] he knew about me

2. [and was seeking to kil]l [me], I became afraid and I fled. [20   a]ll th[at] was mine, and noth[ing] was left to me

3. ex[cept Hann]ah, my wife, and Tobiah, my son. 21And there were not f[orty] days

4. [   ] his [two sons   ] and they fled to the mountains of Ararat. Then [Esarhaddo]n began to reign

5. [and he] put Aḥiqar, son of 'Ana'el, my kinsman, in charge of all the c[redit accoun]ts

6. [of his kingdom; and he had c]ontrol over [al]l the treasury accounts of the king. 22And Aḥiqar interceded on my behalf.

7. [Now Aḥi]qar, my kinsman, had been the chief cup-bearer, the keeper of the signet rings, treasury-accountant,

8. [and c]redit accountant under Sennacherib, the king of Assyria. Esarhaddon put him in charge as second to himself. Now

9. he was the [so]n of my brother, of my father's house, and of my family. ²:¹In the days of Esarhaddon, the [ki]ng, when I had returned

10. [to] my house, and Hannah, my wife, and Tobiah, my son, were restored to me, [there was] for [me] on the day of the festival of Wee[ks]

11. a fine dinner, and I reclined to [ea]t. ²And they brought in the t[ab]le before me, and I saw (that) the delicacies that they offered

12. upon it were many. [I] said [to To]biah, my son, "My son, go, get anyone [whom you] will find of [our] kinsfolk

13. [   ] my son, go (and) get (him), and let him be brought in that he may eat [together] with me; and look, I

Comments

L. 1 Cf. S: καὶ ἐπορεύθη εἷς τις (mss A, B omit τις) τῶν ἐκ τῆς Νινευὴ καὶ ὑπέδειξεν τῷ βασιλεῖ περὶ ἐμοῦ ὅτι ἐγὼ θάπτω αὐτούς, καὶ ἐκρύβην. καὶ ὅτε ἐπέγνων (mss AB: ἐπιγνοὺς δὲ ὅτι ζητοῦμαι ἀποθανεῖν) ὅτι ἔγνω περὶ ἐμοῦ ὁ βασιλεύς. La: et renuntiatum est (ms W: indicauit regi) illi (mss GM: regi) quoniam ego sepeliebam illos. For אחית, read אחבית, and for similar consonantal shifts, see 4QEnᵍ 1 iv 17 (בקשוט = וקשוט; but see Milik, *The Books,* 266); 4QpNah 3-4 ii 4 (בגויתם = וגויתם) [cf. MT Nah 3:3]). For the converse shift from *waw* to *bet,* see 1QS 3:3 (ועם = בעין).

L. 2 Cf. S: καὶ ὅτι ζητοῦμαι τοῦ ἀποθανεῖν, ἐφοβήθη καὶ ἀπέδρασα (mss AB: φοβηθεὶς ἀνεχώρησα). καὶ ἡρπάγη πάντα, ὅσα ὑπῆρχέν μοι (mss AB: πάντα τὰ ὑπάρχοντά μοι), καὶ οὐ κατελείφθη μοι οὐδέν. La: et quaerebat me occidere; ego autem fugi. Et direpta est omnis substantia mea; et nihil mihi remansit (ms X: ita ut nicil amplius remaneret mici in domo).

L. 3 Cf. S: πλὴν Ἄννας τῆς γυναικός μου καὶ Τωβία τοῦ υἱοῦ μου. καὶ οὐ διῆλθον ἡμέραι τεσσαράκοντα (mss AB: πεντήκοντα; ms V: πεντήκοντα πέντε). La: plus quam uxor mea Anna et Thobias filius meus. . . . Post dies quadraginta quinque. Since the long recension differs here in S and VL, one could possibly restore [א]רבעין וחמשה to agree with La.

L. 4 Cf. S: οἱ δύο υἱοὶ αὐτοῦ. καὶ ἔφυγον εἰς τὰ ὄρη Ἀραράτ, καὶ ἐβασίλευσεν Σαχερδονός. La: duo filii sui et fugerunt in montem (ms M: montes) Ararath. Et regnauit post eum Archedonassar. אררט is written here as in MT Gen 8:4. Cf. תורדט in 4QCommGen A (4Q252) 1:10, if T. H. Lim's reading is correct (*JJS* 43 [1992] 288-98). Could this be rather הוררט, as in 1QIsaᵃ 31:19 (= MT Isa 37:38 [אררט])? Cf. 1QapGen 10:12: הארדט.

L. 5 The subject of אשלט is Esarhaddon, the new king. Cf. S: καὶ ἔταξεν Ἀχίχαρον τὸν Ἀναὴλ τὸν τοῦ ἀδελφοῦ μου υἱὸν ἐπὶ πᾶσαν τὴν ἐκλογιστίαν τῆς βασιλείας αὐτοῦ. La: Et constituit Achicarum filium fratris mei Annanihel super omnem curam (ms M: actionem; ms W: exactionem) regni. For שיזפנות, compare the first word in line 8. The form is probably an abstract noun, denoting the post, a *Šap'el* form of the root יזף, "borrow," in the *'Ap'el,* "lend." Cf. Syriac *'izep.* The word is translated in S as ἐκλογιστία, a Greek term that is found in Papyrus Oxyrhynchus

1436.23 (ὑποκ[ειμένων] ἐκλογι[στείᾳ], Grenfell and Hunt, 12.103) and is explained there as impost due to the office of the ἐκλογιστής. The *eclogistes* was an Alexandrian official who was appointed one for each nome to inspect revenue accounts (see also Papyrus Oxyrhynchus 1480.12, 15 [12.238-39]). Origen (*Ep. ad Africanum* 19 [13]) used the term τὴν λογιστείαν τῆς βασιλείας (SC 302.564), which is also found on a Greek inscription (H. Henne, "Inscriptions grecques," *BIFAO* 22 [1923] 195), where it seems to mean "la revision des comptes" (oversight of accounts).

L. 6 Cf. S: καὶ αὐτὸς εἶχεν τὴν ἐξουσίαν (mss AB omit αὐτὸς . . . ἐξουσίαν) ἐπὶ πᾶσαν τὴν διοίκησιν. τότε ἠξίωσεν Ἀχίχαρος περὶ ἐμοῦ. La: Et ipse habebat potestatem super omnem regionem. Tunc locutus est (mss DJPV: petiit) Achicarus pro me.

L. 7 Cf. S: Ἀχίχαρος γὰρ ἦν ὁ ἀρχιοινοχόος (mss AB: οἰνοχόος) καὶ ἐπὶ τοῦ δακτυλίου καὶ διοικητής. La: qui erat praepositus super annulis et procurator domus (ms M: et erat amicus meus qui erat super a[]; ms W: et erat amicus meus qui erat propositus super annulus).

L. 8 Cf. S: καὶ ἐκλογιστὴς ἐπὶ Σενναχηρεὶμ βασιλέως Ἀσσυρίων (mss AB omit ἐπὶ . . . Ἀσσυρίων) καὶ κατέστησεν αὐτὸν Σαχερδονὸς ἐκ δευτέρας. ἦν δέ. La: et exactor et suasit regi Assyriorum. . . . Erat enim (ms W: et suasit regi Assyriorum et praestituit me rex Acedonossar iterum. Erat autem). The form אסרחריב for "Sennacherib" is strange. In the Elephantine text of *Aḥiqar* the name is written as either שנחאריב (line 3) or סנחאריב (lines 50, 51, 55); in MT 2 Kgs 19:16, 20, 36; Isa 36:1; 37:17, 21, 37 it is written as סנחריב. These all represent approximations of the Akkadian *Sin-aḫḫē-erib(a)*, "Sin has replaced the brothers." Apparently the scribe started to write the name of Esarhaddon and merely continued with the second part of Sennacherib's name without deleting or changing the first part. In the Elephantine text of *Aḥiqar*, Esarhaddon's name is written as אסרחאדן (lines 5, [7], 10, 11, etc.), which is close to the form used in lines 8 and 9 of this text, אסרחדון, and to that found in the MT 2 Kgs 19:37; Isa 37:38; Ezra 4:2, אסר־חדן. All are approximations of the Akkadian *Aššur-aḫ-iddin*, "Asshur has given a brother." The strange form אסרחריב finds an equally strange counterpart in the story of *Aḥiqar*, where the name of Esarhaddon is written אסרחאריב. See B. Porten and A. Yardeni, *Textbook of Aramaic Documents from Ancient Egypt*, vol. 3: *Literature, Accounts, Lists* (Jerusalem: Hebrew University, Department of the History of the Jewish People, 1993) 24-25. For שיזפן, see the comment on line 5. The form used here, *šayzĕpān*, denotes the person who has the post (cf. H. Bauer and P. Leander, *Grammatik des Biblisch-Aramäischen* [Halle/Salle: Niemeyer, 1927] §51b‴). In S it is translated as ἐκλογιστής, as also in Origen (*Ep. ad Africanum* 19 [13]; SC 302.564).

L. 9 Cf. S: ἦν δὲ ἐξάδελφός μου καὶ ἐκ τῆς συγγενείας μου. Καὶ ἐπὶ Σαρχεδόνος βασιλέως κατῆλθον (mss AB omit καὶ ἐκ . . . βασιλέως). La: Achicarus compatruelis meus et ex cognatione mea et ex cognatione regis. Et sub Sarcedonassar regem descendi (ms J: reversus sum; mss GR: pervenissem; ms X: redissem).

L. 10 Cf. S: εἰς τὸν οἶκόν μου, καὶ ἀπεδόθη μοι ἡ γυνή μου Ἄννα (mss AB: Ἄννα ἡ γυνή μου) καὶ Τωβίας ὁ υἱός μου. Καὶ ἐν τῇ πεντηκοστῇ τῆς ἑορτῆς ἡμῶν, ἥ ἐστιν ἁγία ἑβδομάδων, ἐγενήθη μοι. La: in domum meam, et redita est mihi uxor mea Anna et Thobias filius meus. In Pentecosten die festo nostro, qui est sanctus a septimanis, et factum est mihi.

L. 11 Cf. S: ἄριστον καλόν (mss AB: ἐγενήθη ἄριστον καλόν μοι), καὶ ἀνέπεσα τοῦ ἀριστῆσαι (mss AB: φαγεῖν καὶ ἐθεασάμην ὄψα πολλά). Καὶ παρετέθη μοι ἡ τράπεζα, καὶ παρετέθη μοι ὀψάρια. La: prandium bonum et discubui ut pranderem; et posita est mihi mensa, et uidi pulmentaria.

L. 12 Cf. S: πλείονα, καὶ εἶπα τῷ Τωβίᾳ τῷ υἱῷ μου (mss AB omit the name) Παιδίον, βάδιζε καὶ (ms 910: βάδιζε καὶ ἄγαγε; mss AB: βάδισον καὶ ἄγαγε) ὃν ἂν εὕρῃς πτωχὸν τῶν ἀδελφῶν ἡμῶν (mss AB: τῶν ἀδελφῶν ἡμῶν ἐνδεῆ). La: complura, et dixi Thobiae filio meo Vade (ms R adds: fili) et adduc (ms J adds: fili) quemcunque pauperem inueneris ex fratribus nostris.

L. 13 Cf. S: καὶ ἄγαγε αὐτὸν καὶ φάγεται κοινῶς μετ᾽ ἐμοῦ, καὶ ἴδε προσμενῶ σε, παιδίον (mss AB: καὶ ἰδοὺ μενῶ σε). La: hunc adduc ut manducaret pariter nobiscum prandium hoc; ecce sustineo te, fili, donec uenias. The form אתהייתה is strange. It seems to be an attempt to write the *'Ittap'al* imperative of אתי, "come," which would be *'ittaytî,* "let him be brought," lit. "let him be made to come," but then it seems to have a pronominal suffix as object, and the initial *'alep* has become a *he*. A better form would have been the *'Ap'el* imperative with a suffix, איתיה, "bring him." K. Beyer (*Die aramäischen Texte vom Toten Meer* [Göttingen: Vandenhoeck & Ruprecht, 1994] 136) reads rather דבר יאתה ויתה ויכל, "bring ihn her! Und er möge kommen und essen." The *scriptio plena* of -תי is anomalous, as is the *scriptio defectiva* of יתה from אתי.

Frg. 3   Tob 2:3

[   ] את[חנק]   ] 1

Mus. Inv. 666
PAM 41.648, 42.211, 43.175

NOTES ON READINGS

This small papyrus fragment contains only three letters on one line. It certainly belongs here, because this is the only place in the Tobit story where "strangle" would occur.

TRANSLATION

1. [   ]has been strangled[   ]

COMMENTS

L. 1 Cf. S, AB: πεφόνευται. La: occisus laqueo circumdato (ms R: occisus circumdatus laqueo). Vg: iugulatum.

Frg. 4   Tob 2:10-11

[לעי]לם ¹¹בעד]נא דן   ] 1

Mus. Inv. 808
PAM 41.648, 42.212, 43.179*

NOTES ON READINGS

Five letters are preserved on the middle of one line. A mere trace of the *lamed* in עילם is visible.

TRANSLATION

1. [to E]lam. [11]At [that] tim[e]

COMMENTS

L. 1 Cf. S: εἰς τὴν Ἐλυμαΐδα. Καὶ ἐν τῷ χρόνῳ ἐκείνῳ (MSS AB omit the phrase in v 11). La: in Limaidam (MS C: Elimaida). In illo tempore.

Frg. 5   Tob 3:5

[ל]מֹעבד בֹּי]   ] 1

Mus. Inv. 851
PAM 42.215, 43.176*

NOTES ON READINGS

Six letters are preserved on the middle of one line. What may look like the tip of a *lamed* on a second line (under the *dalet*) is actually a break in the papyrus.

TRANSLATION

1. [   ] to deal with me [   ]

COMMENTS

L. 1 Cf. S, AB: ποιῆσαι ἐξ ἐμοῦ. La: quae de me exigas (MS W: ut facias in me).

Frg. 6   Tob 3:9-15

top margin

אזלי [בתרהון ול]א[נ]חזי לכי בר[או ברה לכל עלמין [	] 1
ובכת וסלק]ת לע̇לית בית [אבוה ¹⁰	] 2
[	] 3
[	] 4
ולא אשמע ח]ס̇ד עוד בחיי ו[ן ¹¹ [	] 5
[לק̇ן ב]ל[	] 6
ובריך [ש̇מ̇ך קדיש̇א [וי]קירא לכל ע̇[למין ו]יברכ̇[ונך כל עובדיך]	] 7
[¹²וכען פנית ע]ליך אנפי עינ̇[י נ]טלת ¹³ ↓ ^{אמר} לאפטרותני מן ע̇[ל ארעא]	] 8
[¹⁴אנתה ⋯ י]דע ד[י]דכיה אנה בגרמי מ[ן כ]ל ט̇מ̇א̇ת̇[גבר]	] 9
[¹⁵ולא ג]ע̇לת ש[מ]י ושם אב]י בכל ארעת שבינ̇א[ן יחי]ד̇א אנה] לאבי]	] 10
[ולא [ב̇ר לה אחרן די יר̇ת̇נ̇[ה]ו̇א̇ח לה ו̇ק̇ר̇י̇ב̇ ל̇[א איתי] ל[ה די]	] 11
[אנטר נ]פ̇שי לבר ד[י אהו]ה לה אנתה כבר א̇ב̇[דו]מ̇ני שב̇ע̇[ת גברין [	] 12
[ל̇[	] 13

Mus. Inv. 851
PAM 41.647, 42.212, 43.176*

NOTES ON READINGS

This group of fragments has traces of eleven out of thirteen lines, with lines 3-4 being completely lost.

L. 1 After a clear בתרהון there is a trace of the top of a *waw*, followed by the upper stroke of a *lamed* and the top of a *nun*.

L. 2 The line begins with the trace of the upper part of a *taw*. The last letter is the upper part of *taw* in בית.

L. 5 At the beginning of the line there are traces of a *samek* and a *dalet*.

L. 6 Only three letters are preserved in the middle of this line.

L. 7 At the beginning of the line there are traces of three letters: שמך. There is only a part of the *'alep* after קדיש. There is the trace of the initial *lamed* of לכל and of the *'ayin* of עלמין.

L. 8 אמר has been written above the line with an inverted half-arrow after the last letter of נטלת, indicating where it is to be inserted. At the end, the letters מן ע are very faintly preserved, but they are clear.

L. 9 At the end of the line there are very faint traces of four letters, now almost illegible; a possible reading is טמאת [גבר].

L. 10 At the end of the line the letters דא אנה are faint, but they are clearly preserved.

L. 11 The first letter is clearly the bottom of a *bet*. Before the first lacuna one can see the traces of the lower parts of ירתנ. After the lacuna the letters ואח are clear, after which come traces of the bottoms of ל וקריב.

L. 12 Toward the end of the line traces are found of an 'alep and possibly a bet; at the very end are the remains of a bet and possibly of an 'ayin.

TRANSLATION

1. [Go] after them! May we ne[ver] see a son [or daughter] of yours!
2. [^{10} and she wept and wen]t up to an upstairs room of [her father's] house
3. [   ]
4. [   ]
5. [and may I no] longer [hear such a re]proach in my lifetime, and [^{11}]
6. [   ]tow[a]rd[   ]
7. [Blest be] your holy and honorable name for[ever!] May [all your deeds] bless [you!]
8. [^{12}And now I have turned] my face [t]o you and [have lif]ted up [my] eyes. ^{13}Bid me depart from up[on the earth.]
9. [^{14}You, O Lord, k]now th[at] I myself am clean fr[om al]l defilement [with a man.]
10. ^{15}I [have not be]smirched [my] na[me or the name of] my [father] in all the land of our captivity. I am [my father's on]ly child,
11. [and] he has [no] other child who will be an heir to [him]; n[or] does he [have] a kinsman or relative,
12. [for whom I should keep my]self, or a son for who[m I shal]l be a wife. Already seve[n husbands] ha[ve] perished on me.

COMMENTS

L. 1 Cf. S: βάδιζε μετ' αὐτῶν, καὶ μὴ ἴδοιμεν υἱόν σου μηδὲ θυγατέρα εἰς τὸν αἰῶνα. La: Vade et tu cum illis, et numquam ex te uideamus filium neque filiam in perpetuum.

L. 2 Cf. S: καὶ ἔκλαυσεν καὶ ἀναβᾶσα εἰς τὸ ὑπερῷον τοῦ πατρὸς αὐτῆς (mss AB: ταῦτα ἀκούσασα ἐλυπήθη σφόδρα). La: et lacrimans ascendit in locum superiorem (mss MR add: domus) patris sui. אבוה is restored as in 4QTob^b ar 4 ii 1; but it could also be אבוהא, as in 4QTob^b 4 ii 2.

L. 5 Cf. S: καὶ μηκέτι ὀνειδισμοὺς ἀκούσω ἐν τῇ ζωῇ μου (mss AB have nothing similar). La: et iam nullum improperium audiam in uita mea, neque ego neque pater meus.

L. 6 See Tob^e 1 ii 5. Cf. S: διαπετάσασα τὰς χεῖρας πρὸς τὴν θυρίδα. La: exporrectis manibus ad fenestram.

L. 7 Cf. S: καὶ εὐλογητὸν τὸ ὄνομά σου (mss AB: καὶ ἔντιμον) εἰς τοὺς αἰῶνας, καὶ εὐλογησάτωσάν σε πάντα τὰ ἔργα σου. La: et benedictum est nomen tuum sanctum et honorabile in omnia saecula. Benedicant tibi (mss GMRW: te) omnia opera tua. עלמין is restored, following 4QEn^g ar 1 iv 25.

L. 8 Cf. S: καὶ νῦν ἐπὶ σὲ τὸ πρόσωπόν μου καὶ τοὺς ὀφθαλμούς μου ἀνέβλεψα (mss AB: τοὺς ὀφθαλμούς μου καὶ τὸ πρόσωπόν μου εἰς σὲ δέδωκα. εἶπον ἀπολυθῆναί με ἀπὸ τῆς γῆς. La: Et nunc, Domine, ad te faciem meam leuo (ms M: conuerto) et oculos meos dirigo. Iube iam me dimitti desuper terra. M. Morgenstern ("Language and Literature in the Second Temple Period," *JJS* 48 [1997] 130-45, esp. 132) would rather read at the end למא[ען מן, which he does not translate. That is hardly right and certainly does not agree with the versions, especially La (desuper terra).

L. 9 Lit., "I am clean in my bones." Cf. S: σὺ γινώσκεις, δέσποτα (mss AB: κύριε), ὅτι καθαρά εἰμι ἀπὸ πάσης ἀκαθαρσίας (mss AB: ἁμαρτίας) ἀνδρός. La: Tu scis, Domine, quia munda sum ab omni immunditia uiri.

L. 10 Cf. S, AB: καὶ οὐχὶ ἐμόλυνά μου τὸ ὄνομα καὶ οὐδὲ τὸ ὄνομα τοῦ πατρός μου ἐν τῇ γῇ αἰχμαλωσίας μου. μονογενής εἰμι τῷ πατρί μου. La: neque dehonestaui (ms R: quoinquinaui) nomen (mss MW: meum nec nomen) patris mei in terra captiuitatis meae. Vnica sum patri meo. For גֿעל, "besmirch," see *Tg. Isa* 6:5.

L. 11 Cf. S: καὶ οὐχ ὑπάρχει αὐτῷ ἕτερον τέκνον, ἵνα κληρονομήσῃ αὐτόν, οὐδὲ ἀδελφὸς αὐτῷ ἐγγὺς οὔτε συγγενὴς αὐτῷ ὑπάρχει. La: et non habet alium filium uel filiam qui possideat haereditatem illius; neque frater est illi quisquam uel proximus aut propinquus.

L. 12 Cf. S: ἵνα συντηρήσω ἐμαυτὴν αὐτῷ γυναῖκα. ἤδη ἀπώλοντό μοι ἑπτά. La: ut custodiat me illi uxorem. Iam perierunt mihi uiri septem.

Frg. 7   Tob 3:17

[לא[ס̇יא ח̇]רריא   ] 1
[נהר]ת ש̇]מיא   ] 2
    [   ]ל[   ] 3

Mus. Inv. 808
PAM 42.215, 43.179*

NOTES ON READINGS

This tiny papyrus fragment is not certainly identified. The letters are fairly clear on the remains of the three lines, which are from the middle of a column.

TRANSLATION

1. [to cu]re [the] whi[te scales   ]
2. [the ligh]t of hea[ven   ]
3. [   ]

COMMENTS

L. 1 Cf. S: ἀπολῦσαι τὰ λευκώματα. La: curare a maculis oculorum (MS R: maculas; MS W: albugines).

L. 2 Cf. S: τὸ φῶς τοῦ θεοῦ (MS 319: τὸ φῶς τοῦ οὐρανοῦ). La: aspectum luminis (MS M: lumen caelorum; MS W: lumen caeli).

Frg. 8   Tob 4:2

[מו[ת ולמא לא] אקרא לטוביה   ] 1
[ע]ל֗ כֿסֿפֿא] דן   ] 2

Mus. Inv. 852
PAM 43.177

NOTES ON READINGS

This small papyrus fragment comes from the middle of two lines.

L. 1 The line begins with part of a letter, possibly a *taw*.

L. 2 The trace of the upper shaft of a *lamed* is faint, but clearer on the papyrus than on the photograph. The traces of *samek* and *pe* are very faint.

TRANSLATION

1. [dea]th, and why [should I] not [call Tobiah   ]
2. [a]bout [this] money [   ]

COMMENTS

1. Cf. S: Ἰδοὺ ἐγὼ ᾐτησάμην θάνατον. τί οὐχὶ καλῶ Τωβίαν. La: Ecce ego postulaui mortem. Cur non uoco Thobian.

2. Cf. S: περὶ τοῦ ἀργυρίου τούτου. La: de hac pecunia.

Frg. 9   Tob 4:5

[בֿיֿוֿמֿר֗ [.]ֿ[   ] 1
[מאמרה] הוי דכר ל⋯ ואל תצבי ל[מֿחֿטא ולמשטה   ] 2
[   ] שֿקֿר֗ [ ]ֿ[   ] 3

Mus. Inv. 852
PAM 42.215, 43.177*

NOTES ON READINGS

The joined papyrus fragments contain the middle parts of three lines.

L. 1 The remains of six letters can be seen, though only the first can be read with certainty.

L. 2 Faint traces reveal the first four letters, two of which are very difficult to read.

TRANSLATION

1. [and] in your day [   ]
2. [Be mindful of the Lord, and seek not to] sin or to transgress [his command   ]
3. [   ] wickedness [   ]

COMMENTS

L. 1 Cf. S: καὶ πάσας τὰς ἡμέρας σου. La: Et omnibus diebus uitae tuae.

L. 2 See 4QTob^e 2:3-4. Cf. S: τοῦ κυρίου μνημόνευε καὶ μὴ θελήσῃς ἁμαρτεῖν (mss 319, AB: ἁμαρτάνειν) καὶ παραβῆναι τὰς ἐντολὰς αὐτοῦ. La: Deum in mente habe et noli uelle peccare uel praeterire praecepta illius. למשטה is the *Pe'al* infinitive of the verb שׂטי, "transgress," spelled in later Aramaic as סטי.

L. 3 See 4QTob^e 2:5. Cf. S, AB: καὶ πορευθῇς ταῖς ὁδοῖς τῆς ἀδικίας. La: et noli ire in uiam iniquitatis (ms R: neque ambulaueris in uia iniquitatis).

Frg. 10   Tob 4:7

[כארך ['י]דך ברי הוי עֹ[בד צדקתא   ]   1

Mus. Inv. 852
PAM 41.647, 42.212, 43.177*

NOTES ON READINGS

This papyrus fragment contains a part of the middle of one line. Of the initial letter there is only a trace, probably the bottom edge of the left stroke of a *yod*.

TRANSLATION

1. [according to what is in] your hand, my son, gi[ve alms   ]

COMMENTS

L. 1 Lit., "according to the length of your hand, my son, be making alms" (see 4QTob^e 2:6). Cf. La: Ex substantia tua, fili, fac eleemosynam. S omits 4:6-19, but mss AB read: ἐκ τῶν ὑπαρχόντων σοι ποίει ἐλεημοσύνην.

Frg. 11   Tob 4:21–5:1

[א[לה]ך ···   ] 1
   [5:1כול די פקד]ת̇ לי אעבד[   ] 2

Mus. Inv. 851
PAM 41.648, 42.213, 43.176*

NOTES ON READINGS

This papyrus fragment contains the remains of the middle of two lines. The first line
may have had four dots for the tetragrammaton preceding אלהך.

TRANSLATION

1. [the Lord, your G]od[   ]
2. [5:1All that] you [have ordered] me I shall do [   ]

COMMENTS

   L. 1 Cf. S: καὶ ποιήσῃς τὰ ἀγαθὰ ἐνώπιον κυρίου τοῦ θεοῦ (MSS AB: ἐνώπιον
αὐτοῦ). La has nothing to correspond to these words.
   L. 2 Cf. S: πάντα, ὅσα ἐντέταλταί μοι, ποιήσω (MSS AB: Πάτερ, ποιήσω πάντα,
ὅσα . . .). La: omnia quaecumque praecepisti mihi, pater, sic faciam.

Frg. 12   Tob 5:9

[קרא̇] לי   1
   [מהי̇]מן   2

bottom margin

Mus. Inv. 851
PAM 42.213, 43.176*

NOTES ON READINGS

This papyrus fragment contains the beginning of two lines from the bottom of a column. There is a clear space between the right side of the letters and what would have
been the preceding column.

   L. 1 There is only a trace of an 'alep after קר.
   L. 2 There is only a trace of a yod after מה.

TRANSLATION

1. Call [for me   ]
2. trustwor[thy   ]

COMMENTS

L. 1 Cf. S: κάλεσόν μοι τὸν ἄνθρωπον. La: Roga mihi hominem.
L. 2 Cf. S: καὶ εἰ πιστός ἐστιν. La: Et an fidelis sit.

Frg. 13   Tob 6:6-8

top margin

נונא ואכ]ל ואף לאורחא שׁוֹהֹ מֹל]יחה שאר]יתֹ{י}א אֹ]זלו תריהון[	1
⁷באדין ש[אֹל עולימא למֹל]אכא[*(vacat)*]עזריה[אֹחי אֹמֹ]ר לי[	2
מה סם ב]לֹבֹבֹ נונא וכֹבֹֹדֹה] [עֹלוהי .] וֹ[	3
[וֹ].לֹ]א יסחרון[⁸]	4
[ ]לֹ[ ]	5

Mus. Inv. 852
PAM 41.647, 42.213, 43.177*, 43.179*

NOTES ON READINGS

These papyrus fragments come from the top of a column (with the margin still in evidence) and contain parts of the middle of five lines. To frg. 13a belongs a second small fragment (frg. 13b), the top line of which continues line 2 of frg. 13a; it also offers letters from lines 3-4. A third fragment (frg. 13c), from PAM 43.179, forms part of lines 3-5.

L. 1 After לאורחא there is the trace of a *šin* that is followed by וה. After the lacuna there are clear traces of ית, followed by a *yod*, which was apparently marked for deletion. It is followed by an *'alep*, a slight space, another *'alep*, and then a space before the break in the papyrus.

L. 2 There is a short *vacat* before עזריה. The inscribed upper level of the papyrus has flaked off after למל. On frg. 13b the first letter is almost certainly an *'alep*, of which the upper right shaft is twisted by a slight tear in the papyrus. The last stroke on this line seems to be the right side of the curve of a *lamed*, a *mem*, or a *qop*. Here the Aramaic text seems to be fuller than either S or La.

Ll. 3-5 The last letter on line 3, a final *nun*, along with the remains of lines 4 and 5, are found on frg. 13c, a small three-lined papyrus fragment from PAM 43.179.

TRANSLATION

1. [the fish and a]te (it); moreover, he sal[ted] the [re]st for the journey. [The two of them] jo[urneyed along]

2. [[7]Then] the youth [a]sked [the] an[gel] *vacat* [Azariah] my brother, tel[l me],

3. [what medicine is in] the heart of the fish and its liver? [   ]about it [   ]

4. [[8]   and] they will no[t] encounter [   ]

5. [   ]

COMMENTS

L. 1 Lit., "moreover, for the journey he made the rest salted"; see 4QTob[b] ar 4 i 10. Cf. S: καὶ ὤπτησεν τοῦ ἰχθύος καὶ ἔφαγεν (mss AB: ἔφαγον) καὶ ἀφῆκεν ἐξ αὐτοῦ ἡλισμένον, καὶ ἐπορεύθησαν ἀμφότεροι κοινῶς. La: et partem piscis assauerunt et tulerunt in uia, cetera autem salierunt (ms. R: partem uero ex eodem pisce assatam sustulerunt, et cetera salierunt); et coeperunt iter agere (ms W: piscem uero assauit et manduauerunt. Reliquum autem eius in uiam reliquit). Syriac: ʾklw. The Aramaic agrees with S in making the verb "to eat" a singular, in contrast to the plural of mss AB and the Syriac, which implies that the angel also ate some of the fish. La ordinarily says nothing about their eating the fish, so the testimony of ms W is extraordinary.

L. 2 Cf. S: καὶ τότε ἠρώτησεν τὸ παιδάριον τὸν ἄγγελον καὶ εἶπεν αὐτῷ Ἀζαρία ἄδελφε. La: Et (ms G: tunc; ms M: et [erased] Tunc) interrogauit puer angelum dicens Azarias frater.

L. 3 See 4QTob[b] ar 4 i 12. Cf. S: τί τὸ φάρμικον ἐν τῇ καρδίᾳ καὶ τῷ ἥπατι τοῦ ἰχθύος καὶ ἐν τῇ χολῇ (mss AB: τί ἐστιν τὸ ἧπαρ καὶ ἡ καρδία καὶ ἡ χολὴ τοῦ ἰχθύος;). La: quod remedium est in hoc felle et corde et iecore piscis? (ms R: quod remedium est in corde isto et in fel et in ieccore; ms W: quod est medicamentum in his quae de pisce seruare iussisti).

L. 4 Cf. S: ᾧ ἀπάντημα δαιμονίου ἢ πνεύματος πονηροῦ. La: qui incursum daemonis aut spiritum immundum habet.

Frg. 14 i   Tob 6:13-18

[ו]כֹֿדי נת]וב מן [	[13]]	1
[	]	2
[	]	3
[15]דחל אנה מן שדא דן] דֹֿי רֹ]חֹ]מֹ לֹה	]	4
[שֹֿדֿ קטל להן	]	5
חי]ֿי אבי ואמי	]	6
לא איתי להון בר אחרן]די יקבר	]	7
הלא תדכר לפק]ודי אֿבוך די פקדך	[16]]אנון[	8

178

וכע]ן שמעֿ לי אחי אֵל ‏[9

בלי]לֿיֿאֿ דֿן ‏[10

ס]ב מן לבב 17 ‏[11

וירי]ֿח שדא וֿ]ֿיֿ[ערק] 18 נ]ונא‏ 12

וכדי תצבי] ל[מהוה עמה] ‏[13

Mus. Inv. 852
PAM 41.647, 42.213, 42.215, 43.177*

Notes on Readings

This group of eight papyrus fragments contains traces of two columns with at least eleven lines on them. On the right are the ends of the lines of one column; on the left are the beginnings of the lines of the following column. It is difficult to determine whether the columns had thirteen or sixteen lines. At least two lines (2-3) have been completely lost. There is no trace of either an upper or a lower margin.

L. 1 There is a slight space between the *yod* and the *nun*, which rules out the reading מדינת.

L. 4 There are traces of the heads of די, a trace of the lower left corner of a final *mem* (just above the *lamed* of קטל in line 5); then after a slight space are the lower tip of a *lamed* and a clear *he*.

L. 5 The traces of שד at the beginning of this line are problematic. A dot is probably part of the upper left head of *dalet*, and another dot is part of its downshaft. To the right of it, on a bit of papyrus, there is what now looks like a horizontal stroke, but its original direction is no longer certain. It could have been part of a *šin*.

L. 6 A vertical break in the papyrus, due to the flaking of its underside, has created two holes after אבי; one extends into the line above (in the space after קטל).

L. 8 Frg. 14b contains traces of four letters belonging to this line: ודי א, but the ʾalep* is not certain. At the end of the line the downshaft of the final *kap* coincides with a crack in the papyrus and ends just to the right of the head of a *lamed* at the end of line 9, which also coincides with the crack.

L. 9 The first letter preserved is clearly a final *nun*, followed by a clear שמ and a partly preserved ʿayin*. After אחי there is a slight trace of an ʾalep*, which is otherwise lost in the holes of the papyrus.

L. 10 On this line traces of five letters are visible. דן is clear, preceded by a doubtful יא and the top of a *lamed*.

L. 11 Preceding the last word (לבב) there is a tear in the papyrus to the lower left of the final *nun* of מן. In PAM 43.177 it looks like the bottom of a *bet*.

L. 12 Two dots on the papyrus fibers, part of the first letters of a word, are probably to be read as וי.

TRANSLATION

1. [and] when we retu[rn from   ].
2. [   ]
3. [   ]
4. [15"I am afraid of this demon] which is [in lo]ve with her.
5. [   ] a demon kills them.
6. [the li]fe of my father and my mother
7. [They do not have another child] who will bury
8. [them." 16"Do you not remember the com]mands of your father, who ordered you
9. [No]w listen to me, my brother; do not
10. [on] this (very) [ni]gh[t
11. [17   t]ake some of the heart of
12. [the fish. 18   and] the demon [will sme]ll (it) and will [flee]
13. [and when you wish] to [be with her]

COMMENTS

L. 1 Cf. S: καὶ ὅταν ἐπιστρέψωμεν ἐκ ῾Ράγων. La: et cum regressi fuerimus ex Rages. Neubauer: וכד נתוב מן ראגיש.

L. 4 S omits the clause preserved here, but MS 319 has: καὶ νῦν φοβοῦμαι ἐγὼ ἀπὸ τοῦ δαιμονίου τούτου ὅτι φίλει αὐτήν. La: timeo hoc daemonium, quoniam diligit illam.

L. 5 Cf. verse 14 of S: δαιμόνιον ἀπεκτέννει αὐτούς, and of La: daemonium est quod illos occidit. This clause, however, precedes what is preserved in the Aramaic text of line 4. Following what is in line 4, verse 15 of La has: eum qui illi adplicitus fuerit ipsum occidit.

L. 6 See 4QTob[b] ar 4 ii 10, which has a *lamed* before אמ׳ and probably had it also before ב[א]. Cf. S: καὶ κατάξω τὴν ζωὴν τοῦ πατρός μου καὶ τῆς μητρός μου. La: deducam patris mei uitam et matris meae cum dolore ad inferos.

L. 7 See 4QTob[b] ar 4 ii 11. Cf. S: καὶ υἱὸς ἕτερος οὐχ ὑπάρχει αὐτοῖς, ἵνα θάψῃ αὐτούς. La: neque habent alium filium qui sepeliat illos.

L. 8 See 4QTob[b] ar 4 ii 12. Cf. S: οὐ μέμνησαι τὰς ἐντολὰς (MSS AB: τῶν λόγων) τοῦ πατρός σου. La: Memor esto mandatorum patris tui quoniam (MS M: qui) praecepit tibi.

L. 9 Cf. S: καὶ νῦν ἄκουσόν μου, ἄδελφε, καὶ μὴ λόγον ἔχε τοῦ διαμονίου τούτου (MSS AB transpose the last clauses). La: et nunc audi me, frater, noli computare (MS H: timere).

L. 10 Cf. S: γινώσκω ἐγὼ ὅτι τὴν νύκτα ταύτην δοθήσεταί σοι γυνή. La: Scio enim quoniam dabitur tibi hac nocte uxor.

L. 11 Cf. S: λάβε ἐκ τοῦ ἥπατος τοῦ ἰχθύος καὶ τὴν καρδίαν. La: tolle iecor et cor piscis illius (MS R: tolle de iecore et corde piscis illius).

L. 12 Cf. S: καὶ ὀσφρανθήσεται τὸ δαιμόνιον καὶ φεύξεται. La: et odorabitur illud daemonium et fugiet.

L. 13 Cf. S: ὅταν μέλλῃς γίνεσθαι μετ' αὐτῆς. La: et cum coeperis uelle esse cum illa. Neubauer: וכד תצבי למיעל לותה.

Frg. 14 ii   Tob 6:18–7:6

4   שׄגׄיא ר[חמה   [
5   ⁷:¹עזרׄיׄה אחׄ[י   [
6   וה[ש]כׄחו לרׄעואל יתב ק[דם תרע]דׄרׄתׄ[ה ושאלו שלמה לקדמין ואמר]
7   להון לשׄלׄםׄ אתיתׄון ועׄל[ו ב]שלם[אחי ואעל אנון לביתה ²ואמר לעדנא
       אנתתה]
8   כמה ד[נה עלימא דן לטובי בר דדי] ³ושאל[ת אנון עדנא   [
9   ואמר[ו לה מן בני נפתלי] דׄי שׄבׄי[ן בנינוה ⁴   [
10   וא[מרין לה די]יׄדׄעין אנח[נא נא לה   [
11   [⁵ואמר טוביה די] אבי הׄוׄא ⁶יש[ור רעואל   [
12   [   ]
13   [   ].

Mus. Inv. 852
PAM 41.647, 41.648, 42.213, 43.177*, 43.179*

NOTES ON READINGS

See NOTES ON READINGS of frg. 14 i. The first three (?) lines of this column are lost. The fifth line here corresponds to what is line 8 of the preceding column. Frgs. 14b, d, e, g, h are separated by lacunae from the main fragment, 14c. A small fragment on PAM 43.179 (frg. 2 on line 5) belongs above שלם in line 7 of this column, and has been identified as frg. 14f on pl. III. It preserves the bottom of some letters belonging in line 6 as well.

L. 5 Faint traces of ריה in Azariah's name are visible, followed by a faint but clear 'alep and the trace of a ḥet.

L. 6 Faint but clear traces of כחו can be seen near the beginning of this line. The line is restored as in 4QTobb ar 4 iii 3.

Ll. 6-7 Frg. 14f from PAM 43.179 contains parts of these two lines. On its first line, the bottoms of three letters are visible, and probably represent דרת. On the second line can be seen the tops of שלם.

L. 8 The certain כמה at the beginning of the line is followed by a dalet. On frg. 14g, a dot is preserved before the šin, as is a bit of the lamed.

L. 9 After the first three letters a slight vertical stroke is found, probably of a reš. On frg. 14g there are the clear tops of די שבי.

L. 10 On frg. 14h there are faint but clear letters דעין אנ, preceded by the trace of an initial yod and followed by that of a ḥet.

L. 11 Faint but clear traces exist for אבי, followed by fainter traces of הוא and *waw*, as well as that of a *šin* (at the end).

L. 13 At the beginning of this line there is a clear dot (visible on PAM 41.647), the trace of some letter.

TRANSLATION

4. he fell very much [in love with her]
5. 7:1Azariah, [my] brother[   ]
6. and they fo[u]nd [R]aguel sitting be[fore the gate of his] dwelling, [and they greeted him first. And he said]
7. to them, "In peace have you come! Now enter [in] peace, [my brothers." And he brought them into his house. 2He said to Edna, his wife,]
8. "How [this youth] re[sembles Tobi, the son of my uncle."] 3So [Edna] ask[ed them,   ]
9. and [they] said [to her, "We are of the Naphtalites], who are captive[s in Nineveh." 4   ]
10. and [they] sa[id to her], "W[e] do know [him,   "]
11. [5and Tobiah said], "He is my father!" 6Then [Raguel] jum[ped up].
12. [   ]
13. .[   ]

COMMENTS

L. 4 See 4QTob^b ar 4 iii 1. Cf. S: λίαν ἠγάπησεν αὐτήν. Most of the manuscripts of the La omit the clause, but MS X has: direxit in eam animum suum.

L. 5 See 4QTob^b ar 4 iii 2. Cf. S: Ἀζαρία ἄδελφε. La: Azarias frater.

L. 6 See 4QTob^b ar 4 iii 3. Cf. S: καὶ εὗρον αὐτὸν καθήμενον παρὰ τὴν θύραν τῆς αὐλῆς. La: et inuenerunt illum sedentem in atrio, circa ostium domus suae.

L. 7 See 4QTob^b ar 4 iii 3-4. Cf. S: καὶ εἶπεν αὐτοῖς Χαίρετε πολλά (MSS 106, 107: ἐν εἰρήνῃ), ἀδελφοί, καὶ καλῶς ἤλθατε ὑγιαίνοντες. La: et dixit Raguel, Bene ualeatis, fratres, intrate salui et sani.

L. 8 See 4QTob^b ar 4 iii 4-5, following which Edna is restored as in S and La. Cf. S: Ὡς ὅμοιος ὁ νεανίσκος οὗτος Τωβεῖ (MSS AB: Τωβίτ) τῷ ἀδελφῷ μου. καὶ ἠρώτησεν αὐτοὺς Ἔδνα (MSS AB: Ῥαγουήλ). La: Quam similis est hic iuuenis Thobi consobrino meo. Et interrogauit illos Anna (MS X: respiciens Ethna ad illos interrogabit eos). Vg: Dixit illis Raguhel. Syriac: *wš'l 'nwn r'w'l*. Noteworthy is the difference of the name of the inquirer, Raguel or his wife (Edna or Anna), in the various forms of the Tobit story.

L. 9 See 4QTob^b ar 4 iii 6. Cf. S: καὶ εἶπαν αὐτῇ Ἐκ τῶν υἱῶν Νεφθαλεὶμ ἡμεῖς τῶν αἰχμαλωτισθέντων ἐν Νινευή. La: et illi dixerunt Ex filiis Nepthalim nos sumus, ex captiuis Niniue.

L. 10 See 4QTob^b ar 4 iii 7. Cf. S: καὶ εἶπαν αὐτῇ Γινώσκομεν ἡμεῖς αὐτόν. La: et dixerunt Nouimus.

L. 11 See 4QTob^b ar 4 iii 7-8. Cf. S: καὶ εἶπεν Τωβίας Ὁ πατήρ μού ἐστιν. καὶ ἀνεπήδησεν Ῥαγουήλ. La: tunc Thobias dixit Pater meus est de quo quaeris. Et exsiliit Raguhel.

Frg. 15   Tob 7:13

[   ]וחתם[   ]   1

Mus. Inv. 822
PAM 42.215, 43.178*

NOTES ON READINGS

This small papyrus fragment has only four letters on one line, without any margins. Only cracks in the papyrus represent what may seem to be part of the second line. Even though the fragment contains only four letters, it is identified with certainty, because Tob 7:13 is the only place in the book of Tobit that mentions the "sealing" of a document.

TRANSLATION

1. [   ] and he sealed (it). [   ]

COMMENTS

L. 1 Cf. VL: ille scripsit et signauit. S omits the clause, but MSS AB have: ἔγραψεν συγγραφήν, καὶ ἐσφραγίσαντο.

Frg. 16   Tob 12:1

[   ]די הוה עמ[ך ונתן לה אגרה]   1

Mus. Inv. 851
PAM 41.647, 42.213, 43.176*

NOTES ON READINGS

On this fragment only one line is visible. The papyrus is damaged above it, but there may have been an upper margin.

TRANSLATION

1. [who was with] you, and we shall give him his wages [   ]

COMMENTS

L. 1 Cf. S: τῷ ἀνθρώπῳ τῷ πορευθέντι μετὰ σοῦ (mss AB: συνελθόντι σοι) καὶ προσθεῖναι αὐτῷ εἰς τὸν μισθόν. La: Homini illi qui tecum fuit (mss GM: ierat) reddamus honorem suum, et adiiciamus illi ad mercedem. Neubauer: ונתן ליה אגריה.

Frg. 17 i   Tob 12:18–13:6

top margin

18כדי ה] וית עמכון		] 1
ל]א אשתית	19	] 2
הא אנ]ה סלק	20	] 3
למחזה ל]ה22והוו	21	] 4
אתחזי להון מל]אך ·[·]	מברכין]	5
[		] 6-12
בה]ון 4ותמן	13:3	] 13
הוא מראכ]ון והוא		] 14
על כל הט]איכון 5		] 15
ע]לוהי בכל 6		] 16

bottom margin

Mus. Inv. 822
PAM 41.648, 42.213, 42.215, 43.178*

NOTES ON READINGS

Both an upper and a lower margin are preserved in this group of nine fragments. Three narrow pieces of papyrus (frgs. 17a-c) preserve parts of nine lines, the upper five and the lower four. They seem to be the ends of lines of a column (col. i). The column that follows must have had sixteen lines, to some of which these nine correspond, but there is no certainty that they have been lined up correctly.

L. 1 A dot is all that is left of the first letter, probably a *waw*.
L. 2 The last letter is probably a *taw*.
L. 3 The last letter is probably a *qop*.
L. 5 The end of the line has the first three of the four dots that stand for the tetragrammaton.
L. 14 Traces of ון begin the line on frg. 17c.

184

L. 15 The line begins with the trace of an *'alep,* followed by יכון in various stages of preservation.

TRANSLATION

1. [		[18]When] I [w]as with you,
2. [	19	] I did [n]ot drink
3. [		20 Look, I] am ascending
4. [		21 to see h]im. [22]And they were
5. [blessing		there had appeared to them the an]gel of the Lor[d.]
6-12. [		]
13. [		[13:3]among t]hem. [4]And there
14. [		he is y]our Lord, and he is
15. [	5	because of all] your [si]ns,
16. [	6	t]o him with all

COMMENTS

L. 1 Cf. S: ἐγὼ ὅτε ἤμην μεθ' ὑμῶν (ms 990: ἐγὼ μεθ' ὑμῶν οὐχ ὅτι). La: cum essem uobiscum.

L. 2 Cf. S: ἐθεωρεῖτέ με ὅτι οὐκ ἔφαγον οὐθέν (ms 990: οὐ[κ] ἔφαγον ... []; mss AB: ὠπτανόμην ὑμῖν, καὶ οὐκ ἔφαγον οὐδὲ ἔπιον, ἀλλὰ ὅρασιν ὑμεῖς ἐθεωρεῖτε). La: uidebatis enim me quia manducabam, sed uisu uestro uidebatis (ms M: uisui uestro uidebatis me quia bibebam). Vg: uidebar quidem uobiscum manducare et bibere sed ego cibo inuisibili et potu qui ab hominibus uideri non potest utor. Noteworthy is the coincidence of the Aramaic text with S in that the angel asserts that he did not eat, whereas some of the versions try to explain the phenomenon as a vision.

L. 3 Cf. S: ἰδοὺ ἐγὼ ἀναβαίνω πρὸς τὸν ἀποστείλαντά με. La: ecce ego ascendo ad eum qui me misit.

L. 4 Cf. S: οὐκέτι ἠδύναντο ἰδεῖν αὐτόν (mss AB: καὶ οὐκέτι εἶδον αὐτόν), καὶ ηὐλόγουν. La: non potuerunt illum uidere. Et benedicebant.

L. 5 Three dots are preserved in the text. There undoubtedly were four, representing the tetragrammaton, as in 4QpapTob[a] ar 18:15, and in some other Qumran texts (1QS 8:14 [quoting Isa 40:3]; 4QTestim [4Q175] 1, 19 [quoting Deut 5:28 and 33:11]; 4QTanh [4Q176] 1-2 i 6, 7, 9; 1-2 ii 3; 8-11:6, 8, 10). Cf. S: ὡς ὤφθη αὐτοῖς ἄγγελος θεοῦ (mss AB: κυρίου). La: quia apparuit illis angelus Dei.

L. 13 Cf. S: διέσπειρεν ὑμᾶς ἐν αὐτοῖς. καὶ ἐκεῖ. La: dispersit uos in illis; et ibi.

L. 14 Cf. S: αὐτὸς ἡμῶν κύριός ἐστιν, καὶ αὐτὸς θεὸς ἡμῶν. La: ipse est Dominus Deus noster (ms P [correctio manus primae]: uester), et ipse pater noster (ms X: quod ipse est Deus et rex in omnia secula).

L. 15 Cf. S: μαστιγώσει ὑμᾶς (mss AB: ἡμᾶς) ἐπὶ ταῖς ἀδικίαις ὑμῶν. La: Flagellauit uos ob iniquitates uestras (Mozarabic Psalter and Vg: nos ... nostras).

L. 16 Cf. S: ὅταν ἐπιστρέψητε πρὸς αὐτὸν ἐν ὅλῃ τῇ καρδίᾳ ὑμῶν. La: Cum conuersi fueritis ad illum ex toto corde uestro.

Frg. 17 ii   Tob 13:6-12

top margin

לבכון ו[בכל נ[פְּשכון ל[מעבד קושטא אדין י[תְּפנה עליכון	1
ולא [יְסתר אנפו[הְי מנכון עֹ[וד והודו [לה בכל פמכון	2
ובר[כו למרה [קושטא ורוממו לה אנה בארעא[שביא מהודה לה	3
ומחֹ[וה אנה לג[בְּורתה ורבו[תה קדם עם חט[אין על לבבֹכֹוֹן	4
קֹו[שטא עבדו[קְדמוה[י מן[יֹד[ע הן תהוה ס[ליחא[לכון ֺ[ולאלהי	5
[מרומם אנה ונ[פֹּשי למ[לך שמיא [כל יומֹ[י חיי	6
] וכ[ל] ישב[חו רבותה ⁸ימללון בתהלי[ן [	7
] ⁹ירושלם [קְרית קדשא ֺ[כת[שֹנֹבֹ[י על [	8
] 10 בקו[שטא הוד[י [	9
] יתבנ[ה לֹכֹ[י [	10
] 11 [	11-13
] מן ד[רֹין לדרין ינתנון בכֹ[י [	14
[ו]שֹם רב [יהוה לד[רי עלמא ¹²ארי[רין כ]לֹ [די[בֹזיין ו[כל די עלי[כי	15
[ו]אריריN בֹ[ל שנאי[כֹי ו[כל [ממ]לֹ[לין ע[לֹיכי אֹרֹיֹרֹי[ן [	16

bottom margin

Mus. Inv. 822
PAM 41.648, 42.214, 42.215, 43.178*

NOTES ON READINGS

See NOTES ON READINGS of frg. 17 i. This column is made of six groups of joined fragments (frgs. 17d-i), with the remains of an upper and lower margin. The first word of it is a continuation of the last phrase in col. i, line 16. The space between the columns is clearly shown on the first fragment (frg. 17d), with the beginnings of lines 1-5.

L. 2 There is a trace of a *he* before the *yod* just under the hole in the papyrus.

L. 4 The third letter is preserved only as the right shaft of what is probably a *het*. After the lacuna there is the bottom stroke of a *bet*, followed by a *waw* and a *reš*.

L. 5 The second letter is preserved only at the top; it is probably a *waw*. After the lacuna a dot precedes the clear *dalet*, but it is impossible to say whether it is part of a *waw* or a *qop*.

L. 6 The first stroke is clearly the end of a *pe*. At the end of the line, after a *yod* and a *waw*, there is the trace of a letter, probably a *mem*.

L. 7 The last two letters are *lamed* and probably *yod*. What seems to be the tail of a final *nun* on the photograph is only the edge of the upper layer of the papyrus.

L. 8 Only two dots are preserved of the top of קר at the beginning of what

186

remains of the line. After קדשא only the lower end of *yod* is visible. At the very end only the top of letters can be seen, probably שנב.

L. 10 Only the left stroke of a letter is preserved at the beginning, possibly a *he*.

L. 14 The first two letters are preserved only at the bottom, probably a *reš* and a *yod*. The last letter in the line seems to be a *yod*.

L. 15 Only dots are preserved for the top of a *bet* and a *yod* toward the end of the line. The *kap* of וכל is written above the line.

L. 16 At the beginning of the line, only the left side of an *'alep* can be seen. Again, *kap* is written above the line. The upper tip of a *lamed* can be seen under a *reš* in line 15, part of ממללין. Before the final אררין there are traces of the upper part of three or four letters, of which the last could be a *yod*.

TRANSLATION

1. your heart and [with all] your [s]oul to [do what is righteous. Then he] will turn to you

2. and will no lon[ger hide hi]s [face] from you. [Now acknowledge] him with all your mouth,

3. and bl[ess the Lord of] righteousness, and ex[alt him. In the land of] captivity [I] acknowledge him,

4. and [I] make kn[own] his [po]wer and [his] maj[esty before a sin]ful [people]. According to your heart

5. [do what is] right[eous] before hi[m. Who] know[s whether p]ardon[will be yours. 7I exalt my]

6. [God, and] my [s]oul (exalts) the ki[ng of heaven . . .] all the day[s of my life]

7. [and let al]l [prai]se his majesty. 8Let them speak with psalm[s   ]

8. [9Jerusalem,] holy city, he will [affl]ict yo[u, concerning]

9. [10   with righ]teousness acknowle[dge   ]

10. [shall be bui]lt for yo[u

11. [   ]

12. [   ]

13. [11]

14. [from ge]nerations to generations they will present in you [   ]

15. [and] a great name [it will be for] everlasting [gene]rations. 12Cur[sed be al]l [who] despise (you) and all who [inveigh] against [you]

16. [and] cursed be al[l who hate] you and all [who sp]e[ak again]st you. Curs[ed be]

COMMENTS

L. 1 This line continues directly from line 16 of the preceding column. Cf. S: ἐν ὅλῃ τῇ καρδίᾳ ὑμῶν καὶ ἐν ὅλῃ τῇ ψυχῇ ὑμῶν ποιῆσαι ἐνώπιον αὐτοῦ ἀλήθειαν, τότε ἐπιστρέψει πρὸς ὑμᾶς. La: ex toto corde uestro, ut faciatis coram illo ueritatem. Tunc reuertetur ad uos.

187

L. 2 Cf. S: καὶ οὐ μὴ κρύψῃ τὸ πρόσωπον αὐτοῦ ἀφ' ὑμῶν οὐκέτι . . . ἐξομολογήσασθε αὐτῷ ἐν ὅλῳ τῷ στόματι ὑμῶν. La: et non auertet (mss MRX: nec abscondet) faciem suam a uobis amplius. . . . confitemini illi ex toto corde uestro.

L. 3 Cf. S: καὶ εὐλογήσατε τὸν κύριον τῆς δικαιοσύνης καὶ ὑψώσατε τὸν βασιλέα τῶν αἰώνων. At this point ms S breaks off until verse 10. mss AB continue: ἐγὼ ἐν τῇ γῇ τῆς αἰχμαλωσίας μου ἐξομολογοῦμαι αὐτῷ. La: Benedicite Domino in iustitia (mss MX: Dominum iustitiae) et exaltate regem saeculorum. Ego in terra captiuitatis meae confiteor illi. ארעת is restored as in frg. 6:10 above.

L. 4 This may also be translated: "before a people of sinners." Cf. AB: καὶ δεικνύω τὴν ἰσχὺν καὶ τὴν μεγαλωσύνην αὐτοῦ ἔθνει ἁμαρτωλῶν. La: et ostendam uirtutem ipsius, et maiestatem eius coram natione peccatrice. Nothing in the Greek or Latin versions corresponds to the last two words on this line.

L. 5 Cf. AB: ἐπιστρέψατε, ἁμαρτωλοί, καὶ ποιήσατε δικαιοσύνην ἐνώπιον αὐτοῦ. τίς γινώσκει εἰ θελήσει ὑμᾶς καὶ ποιήσει ἐλεημοσύνην ὑμῖν; La: et facite iustitiam coram illo; quis scit si uelit uos ut faciat uobiscum misericordiam?

L. 6 Cf. AB: τὸν θεόν μου ὑψῶ καὶ ἡ ψυχή μου τὸν βασιλέα τοῦ οὐρανοῦ. La: Ego et anima mea regi caeli laetationem dicimus, et anima mea laetabitur omnibus diebus uitae meae.

L. 7 Cf. AB: καὶ ἀγαλλιάσεται τὴν μεγαλωσύνην αὐτοῦ. Λεγέτωσαν πάντες καὶ ἐξομολογείσθωσαν αὐτῷ ἐν Ἱεροσολύμοις. La: et omnes laudate maiestatem eius. Agite dies laetitae et confitemini illi.

L. 8 Cf. AB: Ἱεροσόλυμα πόλις ἁγία, μαστιγώσει ἐπὶ τὰ ἔργα τῶν υἱῶν σου. La: Hierusalem, ciuitas sancta, flagellauit te in operibus manuum tuarum.

L. 9 Cf. AB: ἐξομολογοῦ τῷ κυρίῳ ἀγαθῶς καὶ εὐλόγει. La: Confitere (ms M: confitemini) Domino in bono, et benedic (ms M: benedicite) Domino saeculorum.

L. 10 Cf. S: καὶ πάλιν ἡ σκηνή σου οἰκοδομηθήσεταί σοι. La: ut iterum tabernaculum tuum aedificetur in te.

L. 14 Cf. S: γενεαὶ γενεῶν δώσουσιν ἐν σοί. La has no real equivalent.

L. 15 Cf. S: καὶ ὄνομα τῆς ἐκλεκτῆς εἰς τὰς γενεὰς τοῦ αἰῶνος (mss AB omit the last clause). Ἐπικατάρατοι πάντες, οἳ ἐροῦσιν λόγον σκληρόν, ἐπικατάρατοι ἔσονται πάντες οἱ καθαιροῦντές σε. La: et nomen magnum erit in saecula saeculorum (ms R: et nomen sanctum eius in secula seculorum; ms X: et magnum erit nomen tuum in secula seculorum).

L. 16 Cf. La: maledicti erunt omnes qui oderunt te, et omnes qui dixerint uerbum durum. S has no equivalent, but mss AB read: ἐπικατάρατοι πάντες οἱ μισοῦντές σε at the beginning of the verse, which otherwise differs.

Frg. 18   Tob 13:12–14:3

top margin

[	שורי[כֹּ וכל ממגרֹ[ן מגדליכי	] 1
[	13אדין [חדי ובועי בב[ני קשיטיא	] 2

188

[טובי כ]ל¹⁴ רחמיכי וטוב]י כל   ]   3

[ע]ל [כ]ל מכתשיכי ד]י   ]   4

[ברכי ל⸱⸱⸱] למלכא רבא ¹⁶ד]י   ]¹⁵   5

[שארי]תא מן זרעי ל]מחזה   ]   6

[תרעי ירושלם ברקת ו]ספׄיׄר תתבנין[   ]   7

[מגדלי ירושלם ד]הב תתבנין ועי]תא   ¹⁷   ]   8

[י]ׄן ובאבן די י[¹⁸   ]   9

[י]מׄ]ל]לׄו] להׄל]לויה   ]   10

[עלם עלמיא]   בריך עד עלם]עלמיא דביכי יברכון שׄ]מה קדישא עד עלם עלמיא[11

[עשרה וקביר] וספו מלי תודת טו]בי ומית בשלם ב]ר שנין מאה תרתי⸗עשרה וקביר[^{14:1}   12

[²והוא בר]שנין חמשין ותמנ]נה הוה   ]   13

[חזות ע]נׄוׄהי חי בטב ובכ]ל עבד   ]   14

קרא[לברכה ל]⸱⸱⸱ ולהודיה רב]ותה ³   ]   15

[לטוביה ברה ושבע]ת בנוהי ובקדה ואׄמׄ]ר ברי   ]   16

bottom margin

Mus. Inv. 808
PAM 41.648, 42.214, 43.179*

Notes on Readings

This column is represented by a narrow strip of joined papyrus fragments, which form the centre of a column that had sixteen lines. The upper and lower margins are preserved.

     L. 1 What might seem to be a medial *waw* written above the line and belonging to וכל is a break in the papyrus.

     L. 2 What may appear in the photograph as part of a *nun* at the end of the line after בב is only a break in the layers of the papyrus.

     L. 3 The top of a *lamed* at the beginning of the line can be seen under the *ḥet* in line 2.

     L. 4 Only a dot remains from the upper stroke of the first *lamed*.

     L. 5 The tetragrammaton may have preceded למלכא רבא.

     L. 9 The letters before ובאבן seem to be ין (compare the final *nun*s in lines 7 and 8). They are probably the ending of a verb. The last letter may be a *yod, gimel,* or *'alep,* beginning a word describing the stone. יקר (= τίμιος), or [ופיר]א, if the letter is an *'alep,* is a possibility.

     L. 10 There is the trace of a letter before the first *lamed,* which could be part of the right side of a *mem.* What is not certain is how much space should be left between the upper and lower fragments for this line. The upper stroke of a *lamed* seems to have disappeared in the lacuna. To the left of the heads of the three *lameds* there might seem to be another in the photograph, but that is only a crack in the papyrus.

     L. 12 The last letter is undoubtedly a *bet.* Perhaps the first fragment of the last

189

line of PAM 42.215 belongs here: [ר]קיב ר[יקב], followed by [בנינוה] at the beginning of the next line, "and was buried with honor at Nineveh."

L. 15 The tetragrammaton was written with four dots. Not visible in the photograph is the tiny part of a dot to the right of the three preserved; it is still visible on the fragment itself. Before it is a small space of the same width as those between the first and second and the second and third dots. At the end of the line there is a dot, corresponding to the right edge of the crossbar of a *bet*.

L. 16 The reading ובקדה is certain; it is to be understood as ופקדה, as in 4QTob^c ar 1:2.

Translation

1. [ ] your [walls], and all who overthr[ow your towers]
2. [¹³Then] rejoice and exult over the child[ren of the righteous]
3. [¹⁴Blessed are al]l those who love you, and bles[sed are all]
4. [a]t [al]l your afflictions, becau[se]
5. [¹⁵ bless the Lord], the great king, ¹⁶becau[se]
6. [there is] the [remna]nt of my offspring to [see]
7. [the gates of Jerusalem] will be built (with) [beryl and] sapphire,
8. [and the towers of Jerusalem] will be built (with) [g]old, and wood[¹⁷]
9. [ ] and with stone of [¹⁸]
10. [ ]and let them s[a]y, 'Hal[lelujah,']
11. [blessed be he for ever] and ever, because in you they will bless [his holy] na[me for ever and ever."]
12. [^{14:1}T]obit's [words came to an end], and he died in peace, at the ag[e of one hundred and twelve, and he was buried]
13. [²He was] fifty-eight years [old, when]
14. [the sight of] his [e]yes. He lived in goodness, and in al[l he gave alms]
15. [to bless] the Lord and to acknowledge [his] majes[ty. ³ he summoned]
16. [Tobiah his son and] his [sev]en sons and ordered him, saying, "My son,

Comments

L. 1 This line continues 4QpapTob^a ar 17 ii 16. Cf. S: κατασπῶντες τὰ τείχη σου καὶ πάντες οἱ ἀνατρέποντες τοὺς πύργους σου. La: et destruunt muros tuos, et omnes qui subuertunt turres tuas.

L. 2 Cf. S: τότε πορεύθητι (mss AB: χάρηθι) καὶ ἀγαλλίασαι πρὸς τοὺς υἱοὺς τῶν δικαίων. La: Tunc gaude et laetare in filiis iustorum.

L. 3 Cf. S: μακάριοι οἱ ἀγαπῶντές σε, καὶ μακάριοι οἳ χαρήσονται ἐπὶ τῇ εἰρήνῃ σου. La: felices (mss JM: beati) qui diligunt te, et qui (ms M: et beati qui; ms X: et felices qui) gaudent in pace tua.

L. 4 Cf. S: ἐπὶ πάσαις ταῖς μάστιξίν σου, ὅτι. La: contristabuntur in omnibus flagellis tuis, quoniam.

L. 5 Cf. S: ἡ ψυχή μου, εὐλόγει τὸν κύριον (mss AB: θεόν) τὸν βασιλέα τὸν μέγαν, ὅτι. La: benedic Domino regi magno, quia (ms R: qui liberabit [Spanish Latin pronunciation for liberauit]).

L. 6 Cf. S: ἂν γένηται τὸ κατάλειμμα τοῦ σπέρματός μου ἰδεῖν (mss AB omit the clause). La: si fuerint reliquiae de semine meo ad uidendam.

L. 7 S: αἱ θύραι Ἰερουσαλὴμ σαπφείρῳ καὶ σμαράγδῳ οἰκοδομηθήσονται. La: ostia Hierusalem sapphiro et zmaragdo aedificabuntur. The two precious stones mentioned are found together (with many others) in Ezek 28:13.

L. 8 Cf. S: οἱ πύργοι Ἰερουσαλὴμ χρυσίῳ οἰκοδομηθήσονται. La: et turres Hierusalem auro aedificabuntur.

L. 9 Cf. S: αἱ πλατεῖαι Ἰερουσαλὴμ ἄνθρακι ψηφολογηθήσονται καὶ λίθῳ (mss AB: ἐκ) Σουφίρ. La: Et plateae Hierusalem carbunculo lapide sternentur.

L. 10 Cf. S: πᾶσαι αἱ οἰκίαι (mss AB: ῥῦμαι) αὐτῆς ἐροῦσιν Ἀλληλουιά. La: ostia illius canticum laetitiae dicent, et omnes uici eius loquentur. Vg: et per uicos eius alleluia cantabitur.

L. 11 Cf. S: καὶ εὐλογητοὶ εὐλογήσουσιν τὸ ὄνομα τὸ ἅγιον εἰς τὸν αἰῶνα καὶ ἔτι. La: benedictus in omnia saecula saeculorum: quoniam in te benedicent nomen sanctum suum (mss MR: sanctum) in aeternum. For דביכי, which is undoubtedly a scribal metathesis, read די בכי. For the restored phrase, see Dan 2:4, 44; 7:18.

L. 12 See 4QTob^e 7 ii 4. Cf. S: καὶ συνετελέσθησαν οἱ λόγοι τῆς ἐξομολογήσεως Τωβίθ. Καὶ ἀπέθανεν ἐν εἰρήνῃ ἐτῶν ἑκατὸν δώδεκα καὶ ἐτάφη ἐνδόξως ἐν Νινευῆ. La: et ut consummati sunt sermones confessionis Thobi, mortuus est in pace, annorum centum duodecim, et sepultus est praeclare in Niniue.

L. 13 See 4QTob^e 7 ii 5. Cf. S: ἑξήκοντα δύο ἐτῶν ἦν (mss AB: καὶ ἦν ἐτῶν πεντήκοντα ὀκτὼ) ὅτε ἐγένετο ἀνάπειρος τοῖς ὀφθαλμοῖς. La: quinquaginta autem et octo annorum erat cum oculis captus est. Vg: quinquaginta namque et sex annorum oculorum lumen amisit, sexagenarius uero recepit.

L. 14 Cf. S: μετὰ τὸ ἀναβλέψαι αὐτὸν ἔζησεν ἐν ἀγαθοῖς καὶ ἐλεημοσύνας ἐποίησεν. La: postquam lucem recepit uixit, in omnibus faciens (mss MX: uixit in bonis omnibus et faciens eleemosinas) eleemosynas.

L. 15 Compare 4QTob^c ar 1:1, where the text at first sight is similar to what is preserved here: [והוסף למדחל לאלהא ולה[ודיה רבותה, "he continued to fear God and acknowledge his majesty." Instead of אלהא, this text has the tetragrammaton written with four dots. One may debate, then, whether it would be better to restore the lacuna before the tetragrammaton with לברכה, as I have done, following the version of S, or use למדחל of 4QTob^c, which would be closer to Greek mss AB; see M. Morgenstern, "Language," 131. Given the length of the following lacuna, one may hesitate whether the form of Aramaic text in 4QpapTob^a 18 was identical to that of 4QTob^c. Cf. S: ἔτι προσέθετο εὐλογεῖν τὸν θεὸν (mss AB: προσέθετο φοβεῖσθαι κύριον τὸν θεὸν) καὶ ἐξομολογεῖσθαι τὴν μεγαλωσύνην τοῦ θεοῦ. La: proposuit magis Deum colere et confiteri magnitudinem eius.

L. 16 Cf. S: ἐκάλεσεν Τωβίαν τὸν υἱὸν αὐτοῦ καὶ ἐντείλατο αὐτῷ λέγων Παιδίον. But ms A reads: τὸν υἱὸν αὐτοῦ καὶ τοὺς ἐξ υἱοὺς τοῦ υἱοῦ (also ms 98 and the Sahidic version). La: accersiit Thobiam filium suum et septem filios eius, et praecepit illis (ms M: illi; ms R: ad illum; ms X: ei) dicens. All manuscripts of La read: septem filios. Cf. J. T. Milik, *TYDWJ*, 32; see pp. 139-40 above.

Frg. 19   Tob 14:7

[	באר̇ע אברה]ם̇ ב̇ת̇[	] 1
[	ר̇חמי [אלהא	] 2
[	]ל̇[	] 3

Mus. Inv. 808
PAM 43.179

TRANSLATION

1. [in the land of Abraha]m in [   ]
2. [   ]those who [truly] love [God   ]
3. [.   ]

COMMENTS

L. 1 Cf. S: καὶ οἰκήσουσιν τὸν αἰῶνα ἐν τῇ γῇ Ἀβραὰμ μετὰ ἀσφαλείας. Neither the Greek mss AB nor La have anything to correspond to these words.

L. 2 Cf. S: καὶ χαρήσονται οἱ ἀγαπῶντες τὸν θεὸν (mss AB: κύριον τὸν θεὸν) ἐπ' ἀληθείας. La: et gaudebunt qui diligunt Deum uerum (mss MR: uere).

Unidentified Fragments

Frg. 20   Tob 7:?

[	]ו̇[	] 1
[	[להון כ]	] 2
[	[סוכ]	] 3
[	[ויבר.]	] 4
[	]ל̇[	] 5

Mus. Inv. 822
PAM 41.648, 42.215, 43.178*

192

NOTES ON READINGS

On this papyrus fragment there are traces of five lines. The first is marked only by the tail of a final *nun*, and the last by the tip of a *lamed*.

TRANSLATION

1. [   ]
2. [   ] to them [   ]

Frg. 21-49

Mus. Inv. 808
PAM 43.179

Frg. 21

[   ]גבי ו[   ] 1
[   ].[   ] 2

Frg. 22

[   ]יב א[   ] 1
[   ]ותר[   ] 2

Frg. 23

[   ]כד]י[   ] 1

TRANSLATION

1. [   ] whe[n   ]

Frg. 24

[   ]לרחצנ[   ] 1

TRANSLATION

1. [   ]for confiden[ce   ]

Frg. 25

[   ]ל קום[   ] 1
[   ].בֹשֹרֹ[   ] 2

Frg. 26

[.ארע]א[   ] 1

TRANSLATION

1. [the] land[   ]

Frg. 27

[   ]ג מֹייֹא[   ] 1
[   ]אֹ יכֹל[   ] 2

NOTES ON READINGS

L. 2 The *waw* in וכל is written above the line.

TRANSLATION

1. [   ]the water [   ]
2. [   ]and all[   ]

Frg. 28

[   ]ה.[   ] 1
[   ].ע.[   ] 2

Frg. 29

[   ].[   ] 1
[   ]כֹדי יפלג.[   ] 2

TRANSLATION

1. [   ].[   ]
2. [   ] when he/they will divide

Frg. 30

1 [ ]בֿת ו.ת[[

2 [ ]ל[[

Frg. 31

1 [ ]וברא לע.[[

TRANSLATION

1. [   ] and the son [

Frg. 32

1 [ ]עֿלמיא.[[

TRANSLATION

1. [   ] the ages [   ]

Frg. 33

1 [ ]א עד ד.[[

TRANSLATION

1. [   ] until [   ]

Frg. 34

1 [ ]י למר[[

2 [ ]עֿל[[

Frg. 35

1 [ ]בח.[[

Frg. 36

1 [ ]א ת[[

Frg. 37

[	לם] [	] 1
[	ל][	] 2

Frg. 38

[	א..[	] 1
[	אל][	2
[	ל][	] 3

Frg. 39

[	לה תתו][	] 1

Frg. 40

[	שגיא][	] 1

TRANSLATION

1. [   ]much [   ]

Frg. 41

[	]...[	] 1

Frg. 42

[	].[	] 1
[	ש.[	] 2
[	ל][	] 3

Frg. 43

[	בריך][	] 1

TRANSLATION

1. [   ] blest be [   ]

Frg. 44

[[בחר]   ] 1

TRANSLATION

1. [   ] he chose [   ]

Frg. 45

[   ]דא[   ] 1

TRANSLATION

1. [   ] this [   ]

Frg. 46

[   ]בא[   ] 1

Frg. 47

[   ]ל.[   ] 1

Frg. 48

[   ]עה ל[   ] 1

Frg. 49

[   ]שׁית ל.[   ] 1

4Q197: 4QTobit[b] ar

Physical Description

The second copy of the Aramaic text of Tobit is written on skin fragments which are brown in color. There are several columns of text, usually of nineteen lines each.

Palaeography

This copy of Tobit has been written in a beautiful early formal Herodian script and can be dated *ca.* 25 B.C.–A.D. 25 (Cross, "Scripts," 138 §5; Anchor Books edition, 176 §5).

Frg. 1   Tob 3:6-8

```
[              מ[ן די למ[ן]חזה              ]  1
 [             חסדי[ן] מן חדה]              7  ]  2
[         שדא באי[שא קטל] אנון              8]  3
```

Mus. Inv. 132
PAM 41.353, 42.216, 43.180*

NOTES ON READINGS

This small fragment contains the remains of three lines.

L. 1 The dot before די belongs to a final *nun.*
L. 2 The first letter that is partly visible is a final *nun.*
L. 3 The final letter is a *lamed,* the upper stroke of which can be seen at the very edge of the left side of the fragment.

TRANSLATION

1. [th]an to se[e   ]
2. [7   repro]aches from one [   ]
3. [8   ] the [ev]il [demon] killed [them   ]

COMMENTS

L. 1 It might be possible to fill out the last word as למחוה, "to live"; cf. S: μᾶλλον ἢ βλέπειν ἀνάγκην πολλήν. Earlier in the verse, however, one finds μᾶλλον ἢ ζῆν, and the La has in both places: expedit mihi mori magis quam uiuere (MS R: mori quam paciar tantas necessitates).

L. 2 Cf. S: αὐτὴν ἀκοῦσαι ὀνειδισμοὺς ὑπὸ μιᾶς τῶν παιδισκῶν τοῦ πατρὸς ἑαυτῆς. La: ut et ipsa audiret improperium (MSS MW: improperia) ab una ex ancillis patris sui.

L. 3 Cf. S: Ἀσμοδαῖος τὸ δαιμόνιον τὸ πονηρὸν ἀπέκτεννεν αὐτούς. La: Asmodaeus daemonium nequissimum occidebat eos.

Frg. 2   Tob 4:21–5:1

[מסכנא ⁰⁰[ח   21   ] 1
[לכלהון][.][5:1   ] 2

Mus. Inv. 132
PAM 42.217, 43.180*

NOTES ON READINGS

This small fragment contains the remains of two lines from the middle of the column that followed frg. 1.

L. 1 Before מסכנא are the remains of two letters, not easily identified. The second letter looks like a *yod*, although a faint tail resembling a final *nun* seems to be present on the photograph. Examination of the fragment itself, however, reveals that the faint stroke is deceptive, since it does not end with the dot on line 2.

TRANSLATION

1. [the li]fe of the poor[   ]
2. [   ]all of them[   ]

COMMENTS

L. 1 Cf. S: ὅτι ἐπτωχεύσαμεν. La: quia pauperem uitam gessimus.
L. 2 Cf. S: πάντα, ὅσα ἐντέταλσαί μοι, ποιήσω. La: Omnia quaecumque praecepisti mihi, pater, sic faciam.

Frg. 3   Tob 5:12-14

[צ]רויך לך[.][   ] 1
[למנדע[.]   ] 2
[אנה עזר]יה בר   13] 3
[¹⁴ואמר לה[   ] 4
[למנדע בק]שטא   ] 5

Mus. Inv. 132
PAM 41.353, 42.216, 43.180*

NOTES ON READINGS

These joined fragments contain the remains of five lines in the middle of the column that must have followed frg. 2 (PAM 41.353 shows two separate fragments of this group).

L. 1 At the end of the first word the down-shaft of a final *kap* is clear; it is preceded by a dot that could be part of a *yod* and is followed by a dot that is part of the curve of a *lamed*.

L. 5 The stroke at the end of the line, after the *bet*, resembles the curve of a *qop*.

TRANSLATION

1. [ne]cessary [for] you[   ]
2. [   ]to know [   ]
3. [13   ]I am Azar[iah, son of]
4. [   ] [14]And he said to him[   ]
5. [   ]to know in tr[uth   ]

COMMENTS

L. 1 Cf. S: τί χρείαν ἔχεις φυλῆς. La: quid necesse est te scire genus meum?

L. 2 Cf. S: βούλομαι γνῶναι τὰ κατ᾽ ἀλήθειαν τίνος εἶ (MSS AB: ἐπιγνῶναι τὸ γένος σου καὶ τὸ ὄνομα). La (MS W): scire uolo nomen tuum ex ueritate.

L. 3 Cf. S: καὶ εἶπεν αὐτῷ Ἐγὼ Ἀζαρίας Ἀνανίου τοῦ μεγάλου. La: ego sum Azarias Annaniae magni filius.

L. 4 Cf. S: καὶ εἶπεν αὐτῷ. La: et dixit illi Thobis.

L. 5 Cf. S: τὴν ἀλήθειαν ἐβουλόμην γνῶναι. La: quod uoluerim uere scire de genere tuo.

Frg. 4 i   Tob 5:19–6:12

top margin

1   ]   [19]   [אֹל ידבק [בכס]ף ברי וכא.]
2   [20]   [21]ו]אמר לה אל תדחלי בשלם יהך ברי
3   ]   בש]לֹֹם אל תדחלי ואל תצפי לה אחתי
4   [22]]הֹ אר]חה   [6:1]ושתק]הֹ עוד ולא בכת *vacat*
5   [2]   ומלא]כֹא עמה ו]הל]ךֹ [כלבא   ואזלו]כֹחדא וסדר להון
6   [לילה והכו ע]דֹ דלקת [3]ונחת עלימֹ]א   ושור נו]ןֹ חד רב מן
7   [מיא למב]לֹע רגל עלימֹ]א   [4]   א]תֹקֹף נֹ]ונא וג]בֹר עלימא
8   לנונא ואנפ]קֹה ליבשא וא]מר לה מלאכא [5]פר]קֹהי ואנפקֹ] למררתא ולבב]הֹ
9   [וכבדה שים ב]ֹידך ומעוֹה]י טרד סם הוא מררתה ולבב]הֹ וכבדה
10   [[6]ו]פרק
11   [[מררתה ול]בֹבֹה ו]כבדה   מן נ]וֹנא ואכל ואֹף]
12   [[שארית]א אזלין תריֹהֹ]וֹ]ן [כ]חדו [עד] קֹ]רבו ל]הון למדי[7] *vacat*
13   [הו]ן   [8]   [וא]מר לה עזריה אחי מה סם בלבב נונא ו]בֹ]בֹדה ובמררתה
14   [[ת]אֹתנה קדם גבר או אנתא נגיעי שד או רוח] באישא
15   [[לא] יסֹחרון סחרתהוֹ]ן] לעלם [9]ומררתא למכחל עֹ]ני אנש

200

15 ‏[ ].[ ] ‏[חֹרריא וﬠֹחﬞין ‏10‏[וֹבﬞ]דﬞ‏ﬠֹלו לגו מדי וכבר הוא מﬞ]דבק לאחמתא
‏[אמר רפאל]‏11

16 ‏[לﬠלי]מﬞﬡ טֹﬠﬞ]בﬞ'ה אחי ואמרﬠ ‏[לﬠ הא אנה ואמר לה אﬞבﬞ'ﬠﬞ] רﬠואל נבﬠﬠ [

17 ‏[וגﬠבﬞרﬡ מן בﬠﬡ אבונא הוא ואﬠﬠﬠ לﬠ ברﬡ שפﬠרﬠ]‏12‏[ואחרﬠ]

18 ‏[לﬡ אﬠﬠﬠ לﬠ להﬠז] שרﬠ ‏[ב]ל[חודﬠﬠ]ﬠ ואנﬠﬠ קﬠרﬠﬠ]בﬞ להﬠ ﬠל כל אנש
‏למﬠﬠﬠﬠﬠ

19 ‏[וכול דﬠ לאבוﬠ סבﬠ]לﬞﬥ ל[אנﬠﬠ]א[ן ו]דﬠﬠﬠ לﬞ[ﬥ   ﬠלﬠﬠﬠﬡ]

bottom margin

Mus. Inv. 132
PAM 40.625, 41.353, 42.216*, 43.180*

Notes on Readings

This group of joined fragments (frgs. 4a, b) on PAM 43.180 lacks a fragment (frg. 4c) that appears on both PAM 42.216 and on PAM 40.625 and is now lost. It contains the first preserved words of lines 4-9. It has been added to the rest on pl. VI. There is a clear upper margin and a bit of the lower margin visible under דינא of line 19. The space between this column and the following one can be seen at the ends of lines 2-7.

L. 1 The first letter is poorly preserved, being probably an 'alep. At the end of the line, after a clear וכא there is the trace of a vertical shaft that could belong to one of several letters.

L. 3 Faint traces are preserved of the tops of a final *mem* and an 'alep.

L. 4 The first stroke is the end of a word because it is followed by a space; it is possibly a *he,* the end of some verb that governs the following word, which begins with a clear אר. After the lacuna the line begins again with what seems to be a *he.* At the end of the line is a *vacat.*

L. 5 The first trace of a letter may be that of a *kap,* or less likely of a *bet.* After עמה there is the trace of a letter, probably a *waw,* and then a little further on the bottom tip of a final *kap* is visible. After the lacuna the line begins again with a trace of a letter that may be a *kap.*

L. 6 The line begins with the trace of a letter that could be the left side of the head of a *dalet.* After the lacuna the line begins again with the head of a final *nun.*

L. 7 After the first lacuna, a clear final *pe* is preceded by the down-shaft of a *qop* and the tail end of a *taw.* It is followed by a space and a *nun.* After the second lacuna the line begins again with a dot, the top of some letter, probably a *bet,* and a *reš.*

L. 8 A dot is visible before a clear *he,* which could be part of a *qop.* After the lacuna the traces of the first letter could be the remains of a *qop.* At the end of frg. 4b there are faint traces of another *qop.* At the very end of the line, the final character is almost surely a *he.*

L. 9 The first trace of a letter is probably a *yod.* After the lacuna the line begins with a trace of a *he.* The last letter preserved is undoubtedly a *waw.*

201

L. 10 Traces are found of four letters: the bottom strokes of two *bets*, followed by the upper right side of a *he* and perhaps a *waw*. After a space, the down-stroke of some letter, probably a *waw*, is apparent, followed by a *nun* and an *'alep*.

L. 11 Before the first lacuna there is the trace of a *he*, and in the middle of the line before the last lacuna a trace of the down-shaft of a *qop*. There was probably a short *vacat* at the end, before the text resumed.

L. 13 The line begins with a trace of an *'alep*. In the middle, the lower part of an *'alep* and a *nun* can be seen. The line ends with the right stroke of a *ḥet*.

L. 14 The line begins with a dot and the top of a *samek*. At the lacuna there is still the trace of a letter after *he*, probably a *waw*.

L. 15 The line begins with the trace of the bottom of a letter *(bet* or *mem)*, then a lacuna of one space, and the left side of a *ḥet*. In the second word there is a dot after the initial *waw*, which is probably what is left of a *yod*. The beginning of the next word is probably a *waw* and a *kap*. After the lacuna are the remains of a *yod*. The last letter preserved on the line is probably a *mem*, not a *qop*.

L. 16 The line begins with a broken *mem* on a tiny fragment twisted out of position. It is followed by an *'alep* and the remains of a *ṭet*; after a lacuna are the remains of a *bet* and a *yod*, part of the name of Tobiah. At the end of the line after a clear אבי, the right side of a *taw* is barely visible.

L. 17 The first two letters (בר) are lowered because of a tear in the skin.

L. 18 The *śin* and the *he* of Sarah's name are broken because of a tear in the skin.

L. 19 The first letters preserved are a *lamed* and the top bar of a final *kap*, followed by a space and another *lamed*.

TRANSLATION

1. [19   ]Let my son not cling [to mon]ey, but (let it be for him) like [   ]
2. [20   21And] he said to her, "Do not fear! My son will go safely,
3. [safe]ly. Do not fear and do not become anxious about him, my sister.
4. [22   his] journ[ey 6:1And becoming sile]nt, she wept no more. *vacat*
5. [2   and] the [ange]l (was) with him, and [the dog wen]t [along, and] together [they travelled]. And there followed for them
6. [a night, and they came t]o the Tigris. 3[The] you[th went down [to   and] a big [fis]h [leaped up] from
7. [the water to swal]low the foot of [the] youth. [4   "O]verpower [the] fi[sh!" And] the youth [grab]bed
8. [the fish and brou]ght it to dry land. And [the angel] s[aid to him, 5"Sl]it it open and take out [its gall], its [heart,
9. [and its liver. Keep them w]ith you, but [throw away] it[s] inwards. [A medicine is its gall], its [heart], and its liver." And [he slit open   ]
10. [its gall,] its [he]art, and [its liver.   6   some of] the [f]ish, and he ate (it). Moreover, [   ]

11. the [rest]. The two of t[h]em went along together [until they] dr[ew near] to Me-
    dia. *vacat* [7   ]

12. [and s]aid to him, "Azariah, my brother, what medicine is in the heart of the fish,
    [its] liv[er, and its gall?" 8   "If]

13. [you] smoke it in the presence of a man or a woman afflicted by a demon or an
    [evil] spirit,

14. [and] thei[r] encounters will [nev]er occur again. 9And the gall is for anointing
    the ey[es of a human being]

15. [   ] white scales, and they will get well." 10When they entered Media, and he
    was already ap[proaching Ecbatana, 11Raphael said]

16. to the [you]th, "Tobiah, my brother." And he said to him, "Here I am." He said to
    him, "In the house of [Raguel we shall pass the night,]

17. [and] the [m]an is from the house of our father. He has a beautiful daughter[
    12and]

18. he has [no one else] bu[t] Sarah a[lone.] You are re[lat]ed to her [more than any-
    one else, to inherit her]

19. [and all that belongs to her father. Take her] to yourself as [a wif]e; to [you] be-
    longs the right. [This young girl   ]

COMMENTS

L. 1 Cf. S: ἀργύριον τῷ ἀργυρίῳ μὴ φθάσαι, ἀλλὰ περίψημα τοῦ παιδίου ἡμῶν
γένοιτο. La: nunquam esset pecunia illa, sed purgamentum sit (MS G adds: filio meo; MS
R: illa pecunia quam purgamento essem sine filio meo). No Latin version
corresponds exactly to the Aramaic.

L. 2 Cf. S: καὶ εἶπεν αὐτῇ Μὴ λόγον ἔχει (MSS AB add: ἀδελφή). ὑγιαίνων
πορεύσεται τὸ παιδίον ἡμῶν. La: et dixit illi Thobis Noli uereri, saluus ibit filius
noster.

L. 3 Cf. S: ᾗ ἂν ἔλθῃ πρὸς σὲ ὑγιαίνων. μὴ λόγον ἔχε, μὴ φοβοῦ περὶ αὐτῶν,
ἀδελφή. La: et saluus reuertetur ad nos, et oculi tui uidebunt illum illa die qua uenerit.
Nihil timueris de illo, soror (MS M: ne timueris pro illo [omitting soror]). *Pace*
M. Morgenstern ("Language," 132), תצפי (ואל) cannot mean "(Don't) fear"; that
negative is already expressed in אל תדחלי. The verb תצפי is undoubtedly a *Pa'el*
imperfect of יצף, "be concerned."

L. 4 Cf. S: καὶ εὐοδωθήσεται ἡ ὁδὸς αὐτοῦ. . . . καὶ ἐσίγησεν κλαίουσα. La: bene
disponet uiam illius. . . . Et cessauit plorare. Cf. 4QLevi^a ar 1: 19 ושתק עוד ולא צלה,
καὶ ἐσίωπα ἔτι δεόμενος; Dan 9:20.

L. 5 Cf. S: καὶ ὁ ἄγγελος μετ᾽ αὐτοῦ, καὶ ὁ κύων ἐξῆλθεν μετ᾽ αὐτοῦ . . . καὶ
ἐπορεύθησαν ἀμφότεροι, καὶ ἔτυχεν αὐτοῖς νὺξ μία. La: et angelus cum illo, et canis
secutus est eos; et ibant pariter, et comprehendit illos proxima nox (MSS GMR: prima
nox). The verb סדר normally means "put in order," but Akkadian *sadāru* has also the
meaning "occur regularly, follow regularly" (*AHW* 2:1001), which seems to be the
sense here.

L. 6 Cf. S: καὶ ηὐλίσθησαν ἐπὶ τοῦ Τίγριδος ποταμοῦ. καὶ κατέβη τὸ παιδίον περινίψασθαι τοὺς πόδας εἰς τὸν Τίγριν ποταμοῦ, καὶ ἀναπηδήσας ἰχθὺς μέγας ἐκ τοῦ ὕδατος. La: et manserunt super flumen Tigrim. Et descendit Thobias lauare pedes suos in flumine, et exsiliuit piscis de aqua magnus (MS M: immanis). Neubauer: נפק נון חד מן נהרא. The numeral חד is used here as the indefinite article; cf. 1QapGen 19:14, 15.

L. 7 Cf. S: ἐβούλετο καταπιεῖν τὸν πόδα τοῦ παιδαρίου καὶ ἔκραξεν. καὶ ὁ ἄγγελος τῷ παιδαρίῳ εἶπεν Ἐπιλαβοῦ καὶ ἐγκρατὴς τοῦ ἰχθύος γενοῦ. Καὶ ἐκράτησεν τὸ παιδάριον τοῦ ἰχθύος. La: Et circumplexus est pedes eius; pene puerum deuorauerat et exclamauit puer. Et dixit illi angelus Comprehende et tene illum (MS R: adprehende et exsupera illum) et comprehendit puer piscem et eduxit illum in terram. Neubauer: ואפקיה ליבשתא.

L. 8 Cf. S: καὶ ἀνήνεγκεν αὐτὸν ἐπὶ τὴν γῆν. Καὶ εἶπεν αὐτῷ ὁ ἄγγελος, ἀνάσχισον τὸν ἰχθὺν καὶ ἔξελε τὴν χολὴν καὶ τὴν καρδίαν καὶ τὸ ἧπαρ αὐτοῦ. La: Et dixit angelus puero, Exintera hunc piscem, et tolle fel et cor et iecor illius.

L. 9 Cf. S: καὶ ἀπόθες αὐτὰ μετὰ σεαυτοῦ καὶ τὰ ἔγκατα ἔκβαλε. ἔστιν γὰρ εἰς φάρμακον χρήσιμον ἡ χολὴ καὶ ἡ καρδία καὶ τὸ ἧπαρ αὐτοῦ. Καὶ ἀνασχίσας τὸ παιδάριον τὸν ἰχθὺν συνήγαγεν. La: Et repone et habe tecum . . . et cetera interanea proice. Et exinterauit puer piscem illum, et abstulit fel et cor et iecor.

L. 10 Cf. S: τὴν χολὴν καὶ τὴν καρδίαν καὶ τὸ ἧπαρ καὶ ὤπτησεν τοῦ ἰχθύος καὶ ἔφαγεν καὶ ἀφῆκεν ἐξ αὐτοῦ ἡλισμένον. La: et partem piscis assauerunt et tulerunt in uia (MS W: et manducauerunt) cetera autem salierunt. Note how MS W of the La uses a plural verb for eating, whereas S follows the Aramaic in using the singular. Cf. 4QpapTob[a] ar 13:1.

L. 11 Cf. S: καὶ ἐπορεύθησαν ἀμφότεροι κοινῶς, ἕως ἤγγισαν εἰς Μηδίαν (MSS AB: ἐν Ἐκβατάνοις). La: et coeperunt iter agere donec peruenirent in regionem Medorum (MS W: in Mediam). If להון is the correct reading, then it is an ethical dative.

L. 12 Cf. S: καὶ εἶπεν αὐτῷ Ἀζαρία ἄδελφε, τί τὸ φάρμακον ἐν τῇ καρδίᾳ καὶ τῷ ἥπατι τοῦ ἰχθύος καὶ ἐν τῇ χολῇ; (MSS AB: τί ἔστιν τὸ ἧπαρ καὶ ἡ καρδία καὶ ἡ χολὴ τοῦ ἰχθύος;). La: interrogauit puer angelum dicens Azarias frater, quod remedium est in hoc felle et corde et iecore piscis? (MS R: est in corde isto et in fel et in iecore?).

L. 13 Cf. S: κάπνισον ἐνώπιον ἀνθρώπου ἢ γυναικός, ᾧ ἀπάντημα δαιμονίου ἢ πνεύματος πονηροῦ. La: cor et iecor fumigatur coram uiro et muliere, qui incursum daemonis aut spiritum immundum habet; et fugiet ab illo omnis incursus. [ת]אתנה is the 2d sg. ʾApʿel imperfect of תנן, "cause to go up in smoke," with a suffix.

L. 14 Lit., "and they will never encounter their encounters." The verb סחר actually means "go around, about, travel (as a tradesman)," but here it has the connotation of "encounter, attack." Cf. S: καὶ φεύξεται ἀπ᾽ αὐτοῦ πᾶν ἀπάντημα καὶ οὐ μὴ μείνωσιν μετ᾽ αὐτοῦ εἰς τὸν αἰῶνα. Καὶ ἡ χολή, ἐγχρῖσαι ἀνθρώπου ὀφθαλμοὺς οὗ λευκώματα ἀνέβησαν ἐπ᾽ αὐτῶν, ἐμφυσῆσαι ἐπ᾽ αὐτούς. La: et non apparebit in aeternum. Et fel facit ad unguendos oculos homini.

L. 15 Lit., "and they will live." Cf. S: ἐπὶ τῶν λευκωμάτων, καὶ ὑγιαίνουσιν. Καὶ ὅτε εἰσῆλθεν εἰς Μηδίαν (mss AB: ὡς δὲ προσήγγισαν τῇ Ῥάγῃ) καὶ ἤδη ἤγγιζεν εἰς Ἐκβάτανα, λέγει Ῥαφαήλ. La: cui fuerint albugines, uel ad flandum in ipsis oculorum maculis, ut ad sanitatem perueniat. Et postquam intrauerunt in regionem Medorum adpropinquauerunt ciuitati Ecbathanis; et dixit Raphahel angelus (ms W omits name).

L. 16 Cf. S: τῷ παιδαρίῳ Τωβίᾳ ἄδελφε. Καὶ εἶπεν αὐτῷ Ἰδοὺ ἐγώ. Καὶ εἶπεν αὐτῷ Ἐν τοῖς Ῥαγουήλου τὴν νύκτα ταύτην δεῖ ἡμᾶς αὐλισθῆναι. La: et dixit Raphahel angelus (ms M: Rafael angelus Tobia frater, et ille respondit), Raguhel, penes quem hac nocte manere nos oportet. The form אבית (= בבית), "in the house of," is also found in Hebrew in 1QpHab 11:6; Mur 42:4. See further E. Y. Kutscher, "כנענית-עברית-פניקית-ארמית — לשון חז״ל-פונית," *Lešonenu* 33 (1969) 83-110, esp. 108; H. Yalon, "הערות לשוניות לפשר חבקוק," *Kirjath Sepher* 27 (1951) 173-75. Cf. E. Qimron, *The Hebrew of the Dead Sea Scrolls* (HSS 29; Atlanta: Scholars Press, 1986) 39.

L. 17 Cf. S: καὶ ὁ ἄνθρωπος συγγενής σού ἐστιν, καὶ ἔστιν αὐτῷ θυγάτηρ (ms 319 adds: καλή), ᾗ ὄνομα Σάρρα. La: homo est propinquus tuus et habet filiam speciosam nomine Sarram.

L. 18 Cf. S: καὶ υἱὸς ἄρσην οὐδὲ θυγάτηρ ὑπάρχει αὐτῷ πλὴν Σάρρας μόνης, καὶ σὺ ἔγγιστα αὐτῆς εἶ παρὰ πάντας ἀνθρώπους κληρονομῆσαι αὐτήν. La: sed neque masculum ullum neque feminam aliam praeter illam habet. Et tu proximus es illius super omnes homines ut possideas eam (ms R: tu illi proximus es preter omnes, ut possideat hereditatem). On the comparative use of the preposition על, see Dan 3:19; 6:4; 1QapGen 20:6.

L. 19 Cf. S: καὶ τὰ ὄντα τῷ πατρὶ αὐτῆς (ms 319: τὰ ὑπάρχοντα τοῦ πατρός) σοὶ δικαιοῦται κληρονομῆσαι (ms 319: δικαιοῦται καὶ ταύτην λαβεῖν γυναῖκα). La: et omnem substantiam patris eius. Accipe illam uxorem.

Frg. 4 ii   Tob 6:12-18

1	[דא היא חכימא ותקיפ]א ושפירא לחדא ואבוה רחם[לה וכל די לה יהב לה]
2	[ול]ך [גזיר למירת ל]אבוהא ועליך דין קשטא 13גזר למ[סבה וכען שמע לי]
3	[אחי תמלל בעל[מ]תא דא בליליא דן תקימנה ותסבנה לך לאנת[ה [
4	[נעבד לה]מ̇ש̇תותא וידע א̇נה די לא יכול רעואל למכליה מנך בדיל ד̇י̇ הוא ידע
5	[ ]ולמסב ברתה מן כל אנ[ש ארי ה]וא י̇ד[ע] די הן ינתננה לגבר
6	[אחרן ספר]מ̇ו̇שה וכע̇[ן נמלל בעלי]מ̇ת[א]דא ליליא דן ונק̇מנה
7	[לך 14אדין ענה טוביה ואמר לרפ]א̇ל עזריה̇ אחי שמעת
8	[ ]ד̇י עלי̇ין עליה הוו ומיתו כ[
9	[ ]ן שדא די 15וכען ד[ה̇ל אנה [מ]
10	[רחמה לא[בי ולאמי
11	[לקברא ובר א[ח̇רן לא
12	[איתי להון די יקבר אנון 16 לפקודי אבוך]ד̇י̇ פקדך
13	[ש[ד̇א דן וסב̇ה

205

14] 17 [
15] 18 [
16] למהוה ע]מה עׄוׄ[רו מן [
17] וא]ל תדחלׄ[די ל]ךׄ היא חליקא ולך[דינא גזר למסבה[
18]]תׄשזבׄ[ה ו]מדמה אנה די להוון לך [מנה בנין ול]הׄוון
19] לך כאחין וכדי ש]מע טוביה מלי רפא[ל די היא ל]הׄ אחא ומן

Mus. Inv. 133
PAM 40.625, 41.353, 42.217, 43.181*

Notes on Readings

The first line of this column follows directly on frg. 4 i 19, even though the upper margin has been lost. The ends of lines 4-13 can be seen, with a space separating them from the following column. Three small independent fragments (4e, f, g) contain the remains of lines 16-19.

L. 2 The bottom tail of a letter, probably belonging to a *kap,* is discernible at the very beginning of the line. At the end of the line there is the trace of the right side of a *mem.*

L. 3 The reading of תמלל and of תקימנה is not certain. The initial letter in each case could rather be ונ, which might correspond to the 1st pl. verbs of some of the versions at this point. Because the third verb (ותסבנה) begins with a *taw,* however, that is preferred also in the first two instances. The final letter on the line is probably a *taw.*

L. 5 The last letter is a *reš,* even though a crack in the skin makes it look like a final *mem.*

L. 6 The verb forms of the versions (in the 1st pl.) agree here with the Aramaic. In the case of ונקימנה, there is a hole in the skin above the initial *waw,* which makes it look as though תקימנה would be preferable. Moreover, both S and La have a conjunction (καί, et) before the verb in the 1st pl.

L. 8 The trace of a letter at the beginning of the line is undoubtedly that of a *yod,* preceded by what may be a *dalet.* A *lamed* is written above the line in עללין.

L. 9 The *lamed* is preceded by a dot, probably the top of a *ḥet.* After the lacuna there is an upper dot, probably the head of a final *nun.*

L. 13 The traces of the first two letters are probably those of a *dalet* and an *'alep.*

L. 16 After the *'ayin* there is a small stroke, not visible on the photograph, but clear on the fragment itself; it is probably part of a *waw.*

L. 17 Parts of this line are preserved on frgs. 4e, f. Before the lacuna there is a trace of a *lamed.* After the lacuna the line resumes with the bottom of a final *kap.*

L. 18. Parts of this line are on frgs. 4e, f, g. The first letter is probably a *taw.*

L. 19. Parts of this line are on frgs. 4f, g. After the lacuna the line begins again with the remains of a *he.*

Translation

1. [is wise, strong,] and very beautiful, and her father loves [her. All that he has he gives to her];

2. [and for] you [the inheritance of] her father [is determined]; and a right decision [13]has been determined on your behalf, to t[ake her. Now listen to me,]

3. [my brother.] You will speak about this [you]ng girl tonight; you will engage her and take her for your wif[e.   ]

4. [And we shall make] the wedding-feast [for her]. I know that Raguel will not be able to withhold her from you, becaus[e] he knows

5. [that you have more right   ] to take his daughter than anyone el[se. For h]e kno[ws] that, if he were to give her to

6. [another] man, [the book of] Moses. And now [we shall speak about] this [you]ng gir[l] tonight, and we shall engage her

7. [for you." [14]Then Tobias said in reply to Raph]ael, "Azariah, my brother, I have heard

8. [and they died, wh]en they went into her.

9. [[15]Now] I am [a]fraid [o]f the demon who

10. [loves her   ] my [fa]ther and my mother

11. [to the grave   an]other [son they] do not

12. [have to bury them." [16]"   the commands of your father] who ordered you

13. [   ]this [de]mon, but take her

14. [   ] [17]

15. [   ]. [18]

16. [to be w]ith her, get up [from   ].

17. [do no]t fear [because] she has been destined for [you], and for you [the decision has been made to take her]

18. [   ]you will save [her,   and] I am sure that there will be [children from her] for you. [And t]hey will be

19. [to you like brothers." When] Tobiah [h]eard the words of Rapha[el that she was h]is kinswoman and of [   ]

Comments

L. 1 Cf. S: καὶ τὸ κοράσιον φρόνιμον καὶ ἀνδρεῖον καὶ καλὸν λίαν, καὶ ἡ πατὴρ αὐτῆς καλὸς (ms 319 reads instead of καλός: ἀγαπᾷ αὐτήν, after which it adds: καὶ ὅσα κέκτηται αὐτῇ δίδωσιν καὶ σοί). La: est autem haec puella sapiens fortis et bona ualde et constabilita; et pater ipsius diligit illam, et quaecumque possedit (mss PGM: possidet) illi tradet.

L. 2 Lit., "and for you it is decided to inherit her father, and on your behalf there is a decision of righteousness," that is, because he is her kin. Cf. S: καὶ εἶπεν Δεδικαίωταί σοι λαβεῖν αὐτήν (mss 106 107: καί σοι δικαίωμα) καὶ ἄκουσόν μου. La: tibi ergo destinata est haereditas (ms W: aequitas est eius ut possedeat haereditatem) patris eius, et te oportet accipere illam. Et nunc audi me. Compare line 18 below. I stick to the interpretation of this line, despite the objections of M. Morgenstern ("Language," 133). There is no correspondence in the Greek or Latin versions for the interpretation of ועליך דין קשטא גזר as meaning "and the Righteous Judge decreed for you."

L. 3 Cf. S: ἀδελφε, καὶ λαλήσω τῷ πατρὶ περὶ τοῦ κορασίου τὴν νύκτα ταύτην, ἵνα λημφόμεθά σοι αὐτὴν νύμφην. But ms 319 reads rather the imperative: λάλησον περὶ αὐτῆς. La: et nunc audi me, frater, et loquere de illa hac nocte, et accipiemus (ms R: accipiamus; ms M: accipe) tibi illam uxorem. *Pace* M. Morgenstern ("Language," 134), "speak about" is the correct translation of -ב תמלל, as the Greek and Latin versions show (λαλήσω, loquere); his reference to a "request" formula in the Elephantine Aramaic papyri is irrelevant, since it does not use מלל, but rather שאל, which admittedly does mean "ask," but that verb is not used in this Tobit text. Morgenstern, however, notes an interesting parallel to the verb תקימנה in *Tg. Onqelos* of Exod 21:8. He also notes the possible alternate restoration of the last word as לאנת[ו], "for marriage," which I too had considered, but I chose to follow the ancient versions, which read νύμφην and uxorem.

L. 4 The order of some of the sentences preserved in the versions clearly differs from that of the Aramaic. For this reason the full text of S and La will be given here. S: ποιήσομεν τὸν γάμον αὐτῆς. Καὶ ἐπίσταμαι ὅτι οὐ μὴ δυνηθῇ Ραγουὴλ κωλῦσαι αὐτὴν ἀπὸ σοῦ ἢ ἐγγυᾶσθαι ἑτέρῳ, ὀφειλήσειν θάνατον κατὰ τὴν κρίσιν τῆς βίβλου Μωυσέως καὶ διὰ τὸ γινώσκειν ὅτι σοὶ κληρονομία καθήκει λαβεῖν τὴν θυγατέρα αὐτοῦ παρὰ πάντα ἄνθρωπον. But ms 319 reads: ὅτι γινώσκει ἐὰν δώσει αὐτὴν ἀνδρί. La: faciemus nuptias eius. Scio autem (ms R: Scito enim) quia Raguhel non negabit illam tibi; nouit enim quia si dederit illam uiro alio morte periet secundum iudicium libri Moysi: et quia scit tibi maxime aptam esse haereditatem illius magis quam alicui homini.

L. 5 See the quotation of S for the previous line. Nothing in S corresponds to the last clause in this line, but ms 319 has its equivalent. The La is also fuller than the Aramaic.

L. 6 For the first three words, see the versions quoted in the comment on line 4. S continues: καὶ νῦν ἄκουσόν μου, ἄδελφε, καὶ λαλήσομεν περὶ τοῦ κορασίου τὴν νύκτα ταύτην καὶ μνηστευσόμεθά σοι αὐτήν, which echoes what Raphael said to Tobiah in the verse quoted in the comment on line 3. La: secundum iudicium libri Moysi. These words in La, however, immediately precede a clause quoted in the comment on line 4 (et quia . . . homini); afterward it continues: nunc ergo, frater, audi me, et loquamur de hac puella et desponsemus illam tibi.

L. 7 Cf. S: τότε ἀποκριθεὶς Τωβίας εἶπεν τῷ Ραφαὴλ Ἀζαρία ἄδελφε, ἤκουσα (mss AB: ἀκήκοα ἐγώ). La: tunc respondit Thobias Raphahel angelo et dixit Azarias frater, audiui.

L. 8 Cf. S: ὁπότε εἰσεπορεύοντο πρὸς αὐτήν, καὶ ἀπέθνησκον. La: mortui sunt in cubiculo nocte, ea hora qua cum illa fuerunt.

L. 9 Cf. S: καὶ νῦν φοβοῦμαι ἐγώ (ms 319: ἀπὸ τοῦ δαιμονίου τούτου) — ὅτι αὐτὴν οὐκ ἀδικεῖ, ἀλλ' ὃς ἂν θελήσῃ ἐγγίσαι αὐτῆς, ἀποκτέννει αὐτόν. La: et nunc timeo hoc daemonium, quoniam diligit illam.

L. 10 See 4QpapTob^a ar 14 i 6, which has no *lamed* before אמי, but has the final *yod* of [חיי]. Cf. S: κατάξω τὴν ζωὴν τοῦ πατρός μου καὶ τῆς μητρός μου μετ' ὀδύνης ἐπ' ἐμοὶ εἰς τὸν τάφον αὐτῶν. La: deducam patris mei uitam et matris meae cum dolore ad inferos.

L. 11 Cf. S: καὶ υἱὸς ἕτερος οὐχ ὑπάρχει αὐτοῖς, ἵνα θάψῃ αὐτούς. La: neque habent alium filium qui sepeliat illos.

L. 12 See 4QpapTob^a ar 14 i 7-8. Cf. S: οὐ μέμνησαι τὰς ἐντολὰς τοῦ πατρός σου, ὅτι ἐνετείλατό σοι; La: memor esto (mss MR: non es memor?) mandatorum patris tui quoniam praecepit tibi.

L. 13 Cf. S: μὴ λόγον ἔχε τοῦ δαιμονίου τούτου καὶ λάβε (without an object). La: noli computare (mss GM: timere) daemonium illud: sed postula illam.

L. 16 Only four letters are preserved from Tob 6:18. They may correspond to S: καὶ ὅταν μέλλῃς γίνεσθαι μετ' αὐτῆς, ἐξεγέρθητε πρῶτον ἀμφότεροι καὶ προσεύξασθε. La: Et cum coeperis uelle esse cum illa, surgite primo ambo et deprecamini Dominum.

L. 17 חליקא. This is the feminine singular passive participle of חֲלַק, "דענתףטרתפפא .סכ ס. καὶ μὴ φοβοῦ, σοὶ γάρ ἐστιν μεμερισμένη (mss AB: σοὶ αὐτὴ ἡτοιμασμένη) πρὸ τοῦ αἰῶνος, καὶ σὺ αὐτὴν σώσεις. La: noli timere, tibi enim destinata est ante saecula; et tu illam sanabis. Cf. J. T. Milik, *The Books of Enoch: Aramaic Fragments of Qumrân Cave 4* (Oxford: Clarendon, 1976) 197.

L. 18 Cf. S: καὶ ὑπολαμβάνω ὅτι ἔσονταί σοι ἐξ αὐτῆς παιδία καὶ ἔσονταί σοι ὡς ἀδελφοί. La: credo quoniam habebis ex illa filios, et erunt tibi sicut fratres.

L. 19 Cf. S: καὶ ὅτε ἤκουσεν Τωβίας τῶν λόγων 'Ραφαὴλ καὶ ὅτι ἔστιν αὐτῷ ἀδελφὴ ἐκ τοῦ σπέρματος τοῦ οἴκου τοῦ πατρὸς αὐτοῦ. La: cum audisset Thobias sermones Raphahel angeli quoniam soror est illius, et de domo seminis patris illius.

Frg. 4 iii   Tob 6:18–7:10

top margin

1 [זרע בית אבוהי ש]גיא רחמה ולבה <דבק> בה [לחדא 7:1 וכדי עלו לגוא אהﬦ[תא אמר]

2 לה טוביה עֿזֿ[ריה אחי ד]ברני קשיטא לבית רעואל אחונא ודברה ואזל[ו לבית]

3 רעוֿאל ואשכחﬢ[ו ל]רֿעֿוֿאֿ[ל י]ﬨב קדם תרע ﬢרﬨה ושאלו שלמה לקדמין ואמר להון

4 לשלם אתיתון ועלו בשל[ם] אחי ואעל אנון לביתה ²ואמר לעדנא אנתתה כמא

5 דמה עלימא דן לטובי בר ددי ³ושאלת אנון עדנא ואמרת להון מנאן אנתון אחי

209

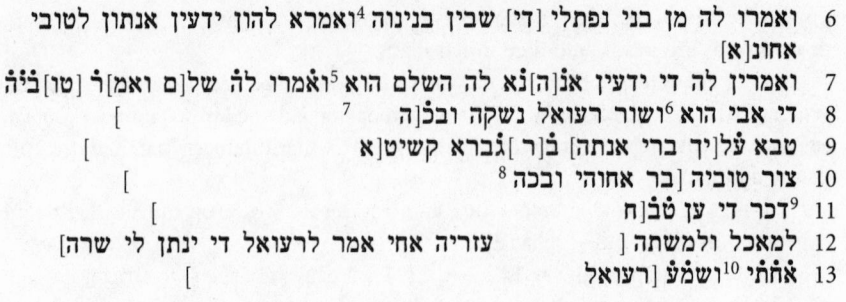

6 ואמרו לה מן בני נפתלי [די] שבין בנינוה⁴ואמרא להון ידעין אנתון לטובי
אחונ[א]

7 ואמרין לה די ידעין אנ[ח]נָֿא לה השלם הוא⁵ואמרו לה של[ם ואמ]רֿ [טו]בִֿֿיֿהֿ

8 די אבי הוא ⁶וישור רעואל נשקה ובכֿ[ה]   ⁷   [

9 טבא עֿל[ו]יך ברי אנתה] בֿ[ר]גֿֿבֿרא קשיטֿ[א   [

10 צור טוביה [בר אחוהי ובכה ⁸   [

11 ⁹דכר די עו טֿבֿ[ח   [

12 למאכל ולמשתה [ ]   עזריה אחי אמר לרעואל די ינתן לי שרה]

13 אֿחֿתֿי ¹⁰ושמֿעֿ [רעואל   [

Mus. Inv. 133
PAM 41.353, 42.217, 43.181*

NOTES ON READINGS

The upper margin of column iii is partly visible above the center of line 1. That is, there is some blank surface, but only the fact that the text of line 1 follows directly on that of col. ii 19 indicates that it is the top margin. Parts of thirteen lines are preserved in this column, which begins after the space following column ii. Despite the lacuna, line 1 continues the text from col. ii 19. This line too seems to be the widest in the column but an omitted word has been supplied in angular brackets. Line 6 would be a better gauge of the width of the column. It measures about 12.3 cm.

L. 1 At the beginning of the line is the trace of the foot of a *gimel* to the right of the *yod*. The scribe omitted a verb after ולבה, probably דבק (see the versions). The last letter preserved is the right bottom curve of a *mem*.

L. 2 Just before the lacuna are traces of two letters, probably *ʿayin* and *zayin*. The upper part of the *reš* of רעואל is clear; the rest of the letter is also faintly visible.

L. 3 The bottoms of four letters can be seen after the first lacuna, probably representing רעוא. Two letters (דר) have been added above the line.

L. 7 After the first lacuna there is the bottom of a *nun*. After the second lacuna is a trace of the top of a *reš*, and then, after another lacuna, are traces of the last three letters of Tobiah's name.

L. 9 There is the trace of the top of a *bet* on the edge of the skin below the *reš* in רעואל of line 8.

L. 11 The last letter is the bottom curve of a *bet*.

L. 13 The traces of the first two letters seem to be of an *ʾalep* and a *ḥet*. The last two strokes belong to the top of a *mem* and an *ʿayin*.

TRANSLATION

1. [the lineage of his father's house,] he fell [ve]ry much in love with her, and his heart <clung> to her [exceeding]ly. 7:1When they entered Ecba[tana], Tobiah [said]

210

2. to him, "Aza[riah, my brother, t]ake me straight to the house of Raguel, our kinsman." He took him, and [they] went [to the house of]

3. Raguel and foun[d] Rague[l s]itting before the gate of his dwelling. They greeted
him first, and he said to them,

4. "In peace have you come! Enter in peac[e], my brothers," and he brought them
into his house. ²Then he said to Edna, his wife, "How

5. this youth resembles Tobit, the son of my uncle!' ³Edna asked them and said,
"Where are you from, my brothers?"

6. They said to her, "We are of the Naphtalites, [who] are captives in Nineveh." ⁴She
said to them, "Do you know Tobit, ou[r] kinsman?"

7. They said to her, "W[e] do know him." "Is he well?" ⁵They said to her, "He is
we[ll]." [And To]biah [sa]id,

8. "He is my father." ⁶Then Raguel jumped up, kissed him, and broke into
tea[rs. ⁷   ]

9. "Blessings upon [you, my son; you are the] so[n of] a righteo[us] man." [He fell
upon]

10. the neck of Tobiah, [the son of his kinsman, and wept ⁸   ]

11. ⁹He slaugh[tered] a ram of the flock [   ]

12. to eat and to drink   ["Azariah, my brother, tell Raguel that he should give
me Sarah],

13. my kinswoman." [¹⁰Raguel] heard [   ]

COMMENTS

L. 1 Lit., "the seed of his father's house." See 4QpapTob^a ar 14 ii 4. Cf. S: ἐκ τοῦ
σπέρματος τοῦ οἴκου τοῦ πατρὸς αὐτοῦ, λίαν ἠγάπησεν αὐτήν, καὶ ἡ καρδία αὐτοῦ
ἐκολλήθη εἰς αὐτήν. καὶ ὅτε εἰσῆλθεν εἰς Ἐκβάτανα, λέγει αὐτῷ. La: haesit cordi eius.
Et cum uenissent in ciuitatem Ecbatanan dixit.

L. 2 See 4QpapTob^a ar 14 ii 5. Cf. S: Ἀζαρία ἄδελφε, ἀπάγαγέ με εὐθεῖαν πρὸς
Ῥαγουὴλ τὸν ἀδελφὸν ἡμῶν. Καὶ ἀπήγαγεν αὐτὸν εἰς τὸν οἶκον Ῥαγουήλου. La:
Thobias angelo Azarias frater, duc me uiam rectam (ms R: recte) ad Raguhelem. Et
uenerunt (ms M: ad domum Raguelis; ms G: in domum Raguel) et. . . .

L. 3 Lit., "They asked his peace first." See 4QpapTob^a ar 14 ii 6. Cf. S: καὶ εὗρον
αὐτὸν καθήμενον παρὰ τὴν θύραν τῆς αὐλῆς καὶ ἐχαιρέτισαν αὐτὸν πρῶτοι, καὶ εἶπεν
αὐτοῖς. La: et inuenerunt illum sedentem in atrio, circa ostium domus suae, et
salutauerunt illum priores. Et dixit Raguhel.

L. 4 See 4QpapTob^a ar 14 ii 7. Cf. S: Χαίρετε πολλά, ἀδελφοί, καὶ καλῶς ἤλθατε
ὑγιαίνοντες. Καὶ ἤγαγεν αὐτοὺς εἰς τὸν οἶκον αὐτοῦ. Καὶ εἶπεν Ἔδνα τῇ γυναικὶ αὐτοῦ
Ὡς. La: Bene ualeatis, fratres, intrate salui et sani; et induxit illos in domum suam. Et
dixit Annae (ms M: Haedna[?]; ms X: Ethne) uxori suae, Quam.

L. 5 See 4QpapTob^a ar 14 ii 8. Cf. S: ὅμοιος ὁ νεανίσκος οὗτος Τωβεῖ τῷ ἀδελφῷ
μου (mss AB: Τωβὶτ τῷ ἀνεψιῷ μου). Καὶ ἐρώτησεν αὐτοὺς Ἔδνα καὶ εἶπεν αὐτοῖς
(mss AB: ἠρώτησεν αὐτοὺς Ῥαγουήλ) Πόθεν ἐστέ, ἀδελφοί; La: similis est hic iuuenis

Thobi (mss PR: Thobis) consobrino meo. Et interrogauit illos Anna (ms M: Haedna; ms X: Ethna) dicens Unde uos estis, fratres? Apart from the different forms of the names of Raguel's wife, one should note how the questioner differs in the versions and in the Aramaic and S.

L. 6 See 4QpapTob^a ar 14 ii 9. Cf. S: καὶ εἶπαν αὐτῇ (mss AB: αὐτῷ) Ἐκ τῶν υἱῶν Νεφθαλεὶμ ἡμεῖς τῶν αἰχμαλωτισθέντων ἐν Νινευή. Καὶ εἶπεν αὐτοῖς Γινώσκετε Τωβὶν τὸν ἀδελφὸν ἡμῶν; La: et illi dixerunt Ex filiis Nepthalim nos sumus, ex captiuis Niniue (ms R: in Ninniue). Tunc illa dixit Nostis Thobin fratrem nostrum?

L. 7 See 4QpapTob^a ar 14 ii 10-11. Cf. S: καὶ εἶπαν αὐτῇ Γινώσκομεν ἡμεῖς αὐτόν. Καὶ εἶπεν αὐτοῖς Ὑγιαίνει; καὶ εἶπαν αὐτῇ Ὑγιαίνει καὶ ζῇ. Καὶ εἶπεν Τωβίας. La: et dixerunt Nouimus. Et illa dixit Fortis est? et illi dixerunt, Fortis est et uiuit. Tunc Thobias dixit.

L. 8 See 4QpapTob^a ar 14 ii 11. Cf. S: Ὁ πατήρ μού ἐστιν. Καὶ ἀνεπήδησεν Ῥαγουὴλ καὶ κατεφίλησεν αὐτὸν καὶ ἔκλαυσεν. La: pater meus est de quo quaeris. Et exsiliit Raguhel et osculatus est illum lacrimans.

L. 9 Lit., "Goodness (be) upon you." Cf. S: εὐλογία σοι γένοιτο, παιδίον, ὁ τοῦ καλοῦ καὶ ἀγαθοῦ πατρός (mss AB: ἀνθρώπου). La: Benedictio tibi sit, fili, quoniam boni et optimi uiri filius es tu.

L. 10 Cf. S: καὶ ἐπιπεσὼν ἐπὶ τὸν τράχηλον Τωβία τοῦ ἀδελφοῦ αὐτοῦ ἔκλαυσεν. La: et incubuit lacrimans super collum Thobiae filii fratris sui.

L. 11 Cf. S: καὶ ἔθυσεν (mss AB: ἔθυσαν) κριὸν ἐκ προβάτων. La: et occiderunt arietem.

L. 12 Cf. S: ὅτε ἐλούσαντο καὶ ἐνίψαντο καὶ ἀνέπεσαν δειπνῆσαι, εἶπεν Τωβίας τῷ Ῥαφαήλ, Ἀζαρία ἄδελφε, εἶπον Ῥαγουὴλ ὅπως δῷ μοι Σάρραν. La: discubuerunt ad cenandum, et dixit Thobias ad Raphahel angelum Azarias frater, dic Raguheli ut det mihi Sarram.

L. 13 Cf. S: τὴν ἀδελφήν μου. καὶ ἤκουσεν Ῥαγουὴλ τὸν λόγον. La: sororem meam. Et audiuit Raguhel hunc sermonem.

Frg. 5   Tob 8:17–9:4

[	חייהון לרחמי]ן ולחדֿוֿהֿ[	] 1
[	¹⁸ופקד לעבדוהי ד[ⁱ יטממו]ן פחתא	] 2
[	¹⁹ דבר תרי [תֿוֿרֿ]ין	] 3
[		] 4
[		] 5
[	אוב]ⁱל עמך לבית א[בוך	²¹ 6
[	בֿרי אנה אבוך ועדנא א[מך	] 7
[	אל ת]דֿחל ברי [⁹:¹ vacat	] 8
[	ואמר ל]הֿ ²עזריה אחי דבר עמך מן תנא אר[בעת עבדין	] 9
[אנתה]⁴/³	תֿאתה בי<תֿ> גֿבֿ]אֿ]ל וֿהֿב כתב וֿסֿ[ב כספא	] 10
[	ידע די מנה [לֿהֿוֿ]ה אבי יו[מֿיא והן	] 11
[	מֿוֿמֿהֿ]ת.[	] 12

Mus. Inv. 133
PAM 41.353, 42.217, 43.181*

Notes on Readings

The remains of this column are found on two fragments (frgs. 5a, b), the second of which is quite twisted, but for the most part legible. The fragments preserve parts of ten lines, but correspondence with the Greek and Latin versions reveals that at least two lines are missing between the two fragments.

L. 2 A trace of a letter begins the line, probably a *yod*.

L. 3 Only the tops of three letters are preserved; they are probably *taw, waw, reš.*

L. 6 At the end of this line only a trace remains of the right side of an *'alep*.

L. 7 The line begins with the trace of a letter, probably the bottom of a *bet*.

L. 8 The first trace is that of the head of a *dalet*. A long *vacat* occupies the rest of the line.

L. 9 The first letter is the remains of a *he*. Despite the twisted skin the rest of the letters are legible.

L. 10 The initial letter seems to be a *taw*. The second word is clearly ב׳ with a space after it. Though this form of the word for "house" is found at times in Aramaic (see Bar Rakkab 16; *AP* 3:18; 8:35; 9:3; 10:9; 82:8; *BMAP* 4:8, 25; 9:12, 27; 10:2, 21; 11:11; 12:12, 13, 35; *Aḥiqar* 125; 1QapGen 21:6), it is otherwise attested only in the absolute state. Hence the restoration of the final *taw* for the construct state needed here. The word is followed by two raised strokes, probably of a *gimel* and a *bet*. After the lacuna of one letter, the top of a *lamed* is preserved, and the traces of והב can be seen in the shrunken and twisted second last line of this part of the fragment. At the end there is the top of a letter, probably of a *waw*, and the top of another letter, probably a *samek*.

L. 11 Toward the end of the line י א are fairly clear, preceded probably by a *mem*.

L. 12 The tops of five letters are preserved, the last four of which are possibly מומת.

Translation

1. [their lives with mer]cy and with joy[ ]
2. [18Then he ordered his servants th]at they should fill up[the hole.]
3. [19 take two]steer[s]
4. [ ]
5. [ ]
6. [21 car]ry (it) with you to the house of [your] fa[ther]
7. [ ] my son, I am your father, and Edna [is your] mot[her.]
8. [Do not f]ear, my son. *vacat* 9:1[ ]
9. [and he said to] him, 2"Azariah, my brother, take with you from here fo[ur slaves]

213

10. [and you will come (to) the hou<se of> Gaba[e]l. Give him the bond, and
g[et the money. ³/⁴[You]
11. [know that my father] will b[e counting] the [d]ays; and if [   ]
12. [   ] oath of [   ]

COMMENTS

L. 1 Cf. S: καὶ συντέλεσον τὴν ζωὴν αὐτῶν μετ᾽ εὐφροσύνης καὶ ἐλέου. La: et
consumma uitam eorum cum misericordia et laetitia.

L. 2 Lit., "then he ordered his slaves that they should fill up." Cf. S: τότε εἶπεν
τοῖς οἰκέταις αὐτοῦ χῶσαι τὸν τάφον. La: et praecepit seruis suis, ut replerent fossam
quam fecerant.

L. 3 Cf. S: ἤγαγεν βόας δύο. La: adduxit uaccas duas.

L. 6 Cf. S: λάμβανε αὐτόθεν τὸ ἥμισυ καὶ ὕπαγε ὑγιαίνων πρὸς τὸν πατέρα σου.
La: ex eo quod possideo accipe partem dimidiam, et uade saluus et sanus cum pace ad
patrem tuum.

L. 7 Cf. S: θάρσει, παιδίον, ἐγώ σου ὁ πατὴρ καὶ Ἔδνα ἡ μήτηρ σου. La: forti
animo esto, fili, ego pater tuus sum, et Anna (ms M: Haedna; ms X: Etna) mater tua.

L. 8 Cf. S: θάρσει, παιδίον. La omits the repeated encouragement.

L. 9 Cf. S: καὶ εἶπεν αὐτῷ, Ἀζαρία ἄδελφε, παράλαβε (mss 106 107: λάβε
ἐντεῦθεν) μετὰ σεαυτοῦ τέσσαρας οἰκέτας. La: tunc accersiuit Thobias Raphahel
angelum dicens, Azarias frater, adsume tecum hinc seruos quattuor et camelos duos.

L. 10 Cf. S: πορεύθητι εἰς Ῥάγας καὶ ἦκε παρὰ Γαβαήλῳ καὶ δὸς αὐτῷ τὸ
χειρόγραφον καὶ κόμισαι (mss 106 107: λαβέ) τὸ ἀργύριον. La: perueni in ciuitatem
Rages ad Gabelum: et redde illi chirographum suum et recipe pecuniam.

L. 11 Cf. S: σὺ γὰρ γινώσκεις ὅτι ἔσται ἀριθμῶν ὁ πατὴρ τὰς ἡμέρας, καὶ ἐὰν
χρονίσω ἡμέραν μίαν. La: scis enim quoniam numerat dies pater meus; et si tardauero
una plus die.

L. 12 Cf. S: καὶ θεωρεῖς τί ὤμοσεν Ῥαγουήλ. La: uides quomodo Raguhel
iurauerit, cuius iusiurandum spernere non possumus.

Frg. 6   Tob ?

[‎ו[כדי מפיגין]   ] 1
[‎]הֿי.[   ] 2

Mus. Inv. 133
PAM 42.217, 43.181*

NOTES ON READINGS

This small fragment contains the remains of two lines from the middle of a column. It
has not yet been possible to identify the part of Tobit to which this fragment belongs.

L. 1 The first letter seems to be a *kap*. It is followed by a clear *dalet* and a *yod*. The next letter is doubtful, apparently a *mem*. It is followed by a clear *pe, yod, gimel*. Is מפיגין possibly the *'Ap'el* participle of פוג?

TRANSLATION

1. [and] when they are (?) [   ]
2. [and [   ]

Frg. 7   Tob ?

[כֹלהוֹן]‬[   ] 1

Mus. Inv. 133
PAM 41.353, 42.217, 43.181*

NOTES ON READINGS

A small fragment with the remains of four letters, the first of which may be a *kaph*. The last could be a *waw*.

TRANSLATION

[   ]all of the[m   ]

4Q198: 4QTobit^c ar

Physical Description

This copy of Aramaic Tobit is found on two fragments of light tan skin. Several parts of the first fragment reveal an upper margin as well as a space at the right, showing that this fragment contains the right side of a column of text. Fourteen lines are preserved in this first fragment; the last line has only the tip of two *lamed*s. The second fragment contains the beginnings of five lines, which are difficult to read.

Palaeography

The script is a late Hasmonean or early Herodian book hand with some semicursive features. It dates from roughly 50 B.C. (see F. M. Cross, "Scripts," 138 §3; Anchor Books edition, 176 §3).

Frg. 1   Tob 14:2-6

top margin

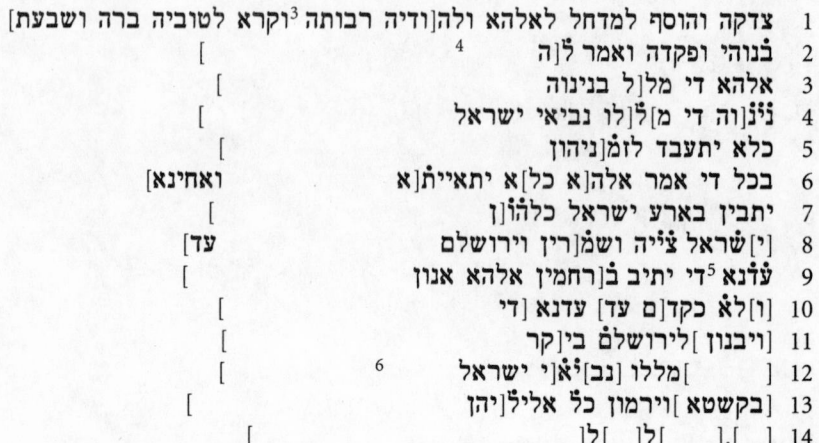

צדקה והוסף למדחל לאלהא ולה[ודיה רבותה ³וקרא לטוביה ברה ושבעת]   1

בְּנוהי ופקדה ואמר לֹ[ה ⁴   [2

אלהא די מל[ל בנינוה   [3

נֹיֹ֗נֹ[ו]ה די מ[ל]לו נביאי ישראל   [4

כלא יתעבד לזמֹ[ניהון   [5

בכל די אמר אלה[א כל]א יתאייתֹ[א   ואחינא]   6

יתבין בארע ישראל כלהֹוֹ]ן   [7

[י]שראל צֹיֹיה ושמֹ[רין וירושלם   עד]   8

עֹדֹנא ⁵די יתיב בֹ[ר]חמין אלהא אנון   [9

[ו]לֹא כקד[ם עד] עדנא [די   [10

[ויבנון]לירושלם בֹין קר   [11

[   ]מללו [נב]יֹאֹי ישראל   ⁶   [12

[בקשטא]וירמון כל אליל[י]הן   [13

[ל]ל [ ].[ ].[ ]   [14

Mus. Inv. 231
PAM 41.595, 42.325, 43.182*

NOTES ON READINGS

L. 2 The first letter seems to be the foot of a *bet*.

L. 4 The line begins on the second group of fragments with a clear *nun*, a *yod*, and a *nun* and is continued with the top of a *lamed* on the bottom edge of the first group.

L. 6 The last letter is represented only by the down-shaft on the right. It could be a *taw*, but not even that is certain.

L. 7 At the end of the line one can see the right side of a *he*, followed by a dot of the next letter on the edge of the skin (most visible on PAM 42.325), possibly the top of a *waw*.

L. 9 A mere trace of the initial *ʿayin* of the first word is visible. The last letter seems to be the right side of a *bet*.

L. 11 The last letter seems to be the remains of a *yod*.

L. 12 Traces are visible of two letters after the second lacuna, which may be a *yod* and an *ʾalep*.

L. 13 The last letter is represented only by a dot, perhaps the bottom of a *lamed*.

TRANSLATION

1. [and gave] alms, and he continued to fear God and ack[nowledge his majesty. ³He summoned his son, Tobiah, and] his [seven]

216

2. sons, and ordered him, saying to [him,   4   ]
3. God, which he uttered about Nineveh.   and]
4. Nine[veh; what the prophets of Israel ut]ter[ed   ]
5. all of those things will be done in [their] tim[es.   ]
6. in all that Go[d] has said. [Al]l of it will be brough[t to pass.   and as for our kinsfolk]
7. dwelling in the land of Israel, all of the[m   ]
8. [I]srael (will become) arid; Samar[ia and Jerusalem   until]
9. the time ⁵when [God] will bring [them] back in [mercy   ]
10. [but] not as it was befo[re, until] the time [that   ]
11. [they rebuild] Jerusalem with hon[or   ]
12. [as the proph]et[s of Israel] have spoken [⁶   ]
13. [in truth], and they shall cast away all [their] idol[s   ]
14. [   ]

COMMENTS

L. 1 Cf. S: καὶ ἐλεημοσύνας ἐποίησεν. καὶ ἔτι προσέθετο εὐλογεῖν τὸν θεὸν (mss AB: φοβεῖσθαι κύριον τὸν θεόν) καὶ ἐξομολογεῖσθαι τὴν μεγαλωσύνην τοῦ θεοῦ. La: faciens eleemosynas (ms R: magis fecit helemosinas), et proposuit magis Deum colere (ms R: et adiecit timorem ad colendum Deum) et confiteri magnitudinem eius.

L. 2 Cf. S: ἐκάλεσεν Τωβίαν τὸν υἱὸν αὐτοῦ (mss AB: τὸν υἱὸν αὐτοῦ καὶ τοὺς ἒξ υἱοὺς τοῦ υἱοῦ αὐτοῦ) καὶ ἐνετείλατο αὐτῷ λέγων. La: accersiit Thobiam filium suum et septem filios eius, et praecepit illis (ms M: illi; ms R: ad illum; ms X: ei) dicens. See pp. 139-40.

L. 3 Cf. S: πιστεύω ἐγὼ τῷ ῥήματι τοῦ θεοῦ ἐπὶ Νινευή. La: credo ego uerbo Dei, quod locutus est in Niniuen.

L. 4 Cf. S: ἐπὶ Ἀθοὺρ καὶ Νινευή, καὶ ὅσα ἐλάλησεν οἱ προφῆται τοῦ Ἰσραήλ. La: super Assur et Niniuen, quae locuti sunt prophetae Israel.

L. 5 Cf. S: καὶ πάντα συμβήσεται τοῖς καιροῖς αὐτῶν. La: sed omnia contingent temporibus suis.

L. 6 Cf. S: πιστεύω ὅτι πάντα, ἃ εἶπεν ὁ θεός, συντελεσθήσεται καὶ ἔσται. La: credo quoniam omnia, quae dicit Dominus, erunt et perficientur.

L. 7 Cf. S: καὶ οἱ ἀδελφοὶ ἡμῶν οἱ κατοικοῦντες ἐν τῇ γῇ Ἰσραήλ πάντες διασκορπισθήσονται. La: et fratres nostri, qui habitant in terra Israel, omnes dispergentur.

L. 8 Cf. S: καὶ ἔσται πᾶσα ἡ γῆ τοῦ Ἰσραήλ ἔρημος, καὶ Σαμάρεια καὶ Ἰερουσαλὴμ ἔσται ἔρημος. La: et erit omnis terra Israel deserta.

L. 9 Cf. S: καὶ καυθήσεται μέχρι χρόνου, καὶ πάλιν ἐλεήσει αὐτοὺς ὁ θεός, καὶ ἐπιστρέψει αὐτοὺς ὁ θεὸς εἰς τὴν γῆν τοῦ Ἰσραήλ. La: et erit deserta usque in tempus. Et iterum miserebitur illorum Deus in terra Israel.

L. 10 Cf. S: καὶ οὐχ ὡς τὸν πρῶτον, ἕως τοῦ χρόνου, οὗ ἂν πληρωθῇ ὁ χρόνος τῶν καιρῶν. La: sed non ut prius; quoadusque repleatur tempus maledictionum.

L. 11 בי]קר or בי]קרא. Cf. S: καὶ οἰκοδομήσουσιν Ἰερουσαλὴμ ἐντίμως. La: et omnes aedificabunt Hierusalem honorifice.

L. 12 Cf. S: καθὼς ἐλάλησαν περὶ αὐτῆς οἱ προφῆται τοῦ Ἰσραήλ. La: sicut locuti sunt de illa omnes prophetae Israel.

L. 13 Cf. S: φοβηθήσονται τὸν θεὸν ἀληθινῶς, καὶ ἀφήσουσιν (mss AB: κατορύξουσιν) πάντες τὰ εἴδωλα αὐτῶν. La: ad timendum Deum uere, et relinquent omnia idola sua.

Frg. 2   Tob 14:10(?)

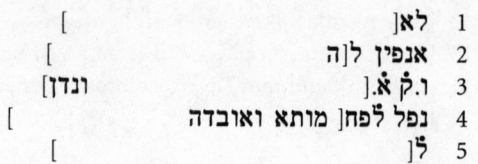

Mus. Inv. 231
PAM 43.182

Notes on Readings

This part of the text was torn in antiquity and repaired then by threads that are still visible as horizontal bars between lines 2 and 3. Part of the thread is also seen after לא at the left end of the first line.

L. 3 Except for the first letter, a *waw,* none of the letters are read with certainty.

L. 4 The first word seems to be נפל. After that comes perhaps לפח.

L. 5 The only letter left on the line is the curved right side of a *lamed,* or possibly of a *qop.*

Translation

1. not [   ]
2. face to [him/her
3.   [and Nadin]
4. fell into the trap of [death, and it destroyed him.   ]
5. [   ]

Comments

L. 4 Cf. S: καὶ Ναδὰβ ἔπεσεν εἰς τὴν παγίδα τοῦ θανάτου, καὶ ἀπώλεσεν αὐτόν (mss AB: Ἀμὰν δὲ ἐνέπεσεν εἰς τὴν παγίδα καὶ ἀπώλετο). La has nothing that corresponds to these words.

4Q199: 4QTobit^d ar

Physical Description

This copy of Aramaic Tobit is represented by only two fragments of brown skin. Frg. 1 preserves the beginning of a column, showing two lines of text with an upper margin. Frg. 2 preserves parts of two words.

Palaeography

The text is written in a Hasmonean script, dating roughly to 100 B.C. (Cross, "Scripts," 138 §4; Anchor Books edition, 176 §4). Not enough distinctive letters are extant on this text to date it more precisely.

Frg. 1   Tob 7:11

top margin

| [| ואמר טו]ביה די לא אכול תנא ול[א אשתה |] 1 |
| |]ל[|] 2 |

Mus. Inv. 231
PAM 41.945, 43.182*

NOTES ON READINGS

L. 1 Before the final *lamed* there is the tip of a letter, probably a *waw*.

TRANSLATION

1. [and To]biah [said], "I shall not eat (anything) here, and I shall no[t drink]

COMMENTS

L. 1 Cf. S: καὶ εἶπεν Τωβίας Οὐ μὴ φάγω ἐντεῦθεν οὐδὲ μὴ πίω. La: et dixit Thobias Hic ego non edam quicquam neque bibam.

Frg. 2   Tob 14:10

| [| ע]ובדי נדן[|] 1 |

Mus. Inv. 231
IAA 363566

This fragment is not found on any PAM photograph. It was newly photographed in 1994.

NOTES ON READINGS

L. 1 The first letters preserved seem to be *waw* and *beth*.

TRANSLATION

1. [the de]eds of Nadin[   ]

COMMENTS

L. 1 Cf. S: ἴδε, παιδίον, ὅσα Ναδὰβ ἐποίησεν Ἀχικάρῳ. La: Ecce filius Nabad, quid fecit Achicaro.

4Q200: 4QTobit^e

Physical Description

The Hebrew text of Tobit is found on nine fragments or groups of joined fragments of light brown skin. The columns are not as wide as in the Aramaic Tobit texts.

Palaeography

The script is an early Herodian formal hand, dating from *ca.* 30 B.C. to A.D. 20 (Cross, "Scripts," 138 §5; Anchor Book edition, 176 §5). *Waw* and *yod* are hardly distinguishable.

Frg. 1 i   Tob 3:6

.[		] 1
עֹפר ...[		] 2
מאש]ֿר לחיות כי חרפות		] 3
ועצבת]רבה עמי אמור להרויח	[שקר שמעתי	4
עו]לֹמים וא]ל תֹסֿתֹֿר	[מן	5
[	את פניך ממני	6

Mus. Inv. 848
PAM 41.368, 42.218, 43.183*

NOTES ON READINGS

This fragment contains parts of lines on two columns. From the additional line at the top of col. ii, it becomes clear that a line preceded the first line preserved on col. i; only the trace of a letter belonging to it remains. The ends of four lines are preserved on this column.

L. 2 Traces of four letters are visible. After the dots representing the first three, there is a space; then the trace of an *'ayin*. Finally, פ‍ר is clear.

L. 3 A dot remains of the foot of a *reš* at the beginning of the line.

TRANSLATION

1. [   ]
2. [·   d]ust.
3. [than] to live, for [false] reproaches
4. [I have heard   and] much [grief] is mine. Give command to move
   (me) far
5. [from   for the] everlas[ting abode. Do no]t hide
6. [your face from me.   ]

COMMENTS

L. 2 Cf. S: καὶ γένωμαι γῆ. La: ut iam dimittar desuper terra (MS X: ut dimittar a conuersatione terre).

L. 3 Cf. S: διὸ λυσιτελεῖ μοι ἀποθανεῖν μᾶλλον ἢ ζῆν ὅτι ὀνειδισμούς. La: expedit mihi mori magis quam uiuere, quoniam improperia.

L. 4 Cf. S: ψευδεῖς ἤκουσα καὶ λύπη πολλὴ μετ' ἐμοῦ. Κύριε, ἐπίταξον ὅπως ἀπολυθῶ. La: falsa audio, et in magno sum taedio. Praecipe ergo, Domine, ut dimittar.

L. 5 Cf. S: ἀπὸ τῆς ἀνάγκης ταύτης. ἀπόλυσόν με εἰς τὸν τόπον τὸν αἰώνιον καὶ μὴ ἀποστρέψῃς τὸ πρόσωπόν σου, κύριε, ἀπ' ἐμοῦ. La: ab hac necessitate (MS M adds: anima mea). Da mihi refrigerium in loco aeterno, et noli auertere a me faciem tuam. Hebr. Fagii: ‏ואל תסתר פניך ממני‎.

Frg. 1 ii   Tob 3:10-11

	[	1 יחרפו א]ת אבי
	[	2 חיה לכה בת]ן יחידה
[לוא עוד]		3 עלי אין כשר לה]תלות
[11		4 אשמע ולוא ישמ‍ע]אבי
	[	5]הח]לון ות]ת]חנן]

221

Mus. Inv. 848
PAM 41.368, 42.218, 43.183*

NOTES ON READINGS

The second column contains the beginnings of five lines, corresponding to the first five of col. i.

L. 1 Only a trace at the bottom of the last letter is preserved; it is probably an 'alep.

L. 2 Only traces of the last four letters remain.

L. 3 The last letter is possibly a *he*.

L. 4 The *lamed* is partly lost in a tear in the skin.

TRANSLATION

1. Let them [not] reproach [my father   ]
2. you have had alive an [only] daughter [   ]
3. For me it is not right to h[ang myself;   that no longer]
4. may I hear, and [my father] may not hear (them either)[11   ]
5. [the w]indow, and she [im]plored favor, [   ]

COMMENTS

L. 1 Cf. S: μήποτε ὀνειδίσωσιν τὸν πατέρα μου. La: ne forte improperent patri meo.

L. 2 Cf. S: μία σοι ὑπῆρχεν θυγάτηρ ἀγαπητή. La: unicam habuisti filiam carissimam.

L. 3 Cf. S: χρησιμώτερόν μοί ἐστιν μὴ (MS 319: οὐ χρήσιμόν μοι) ἀπάγξασθαι. La: non est utile animam laqueo fugare (MS W: non est hoc mihi bonum ut).

L. 4 Cf. S: μηκέτι ὀνειδισμοὺς ἀκούσω ἐν τῇ ζωῇ μου (MS 319: ἐγὼ καὶ ὁ πατήρ μου). La: et iam nullum improperium audiam in uita mea (MSS MRWX omit these last three words), neque ego neque pater meus.

L. 5 Cf. S: διαπετάσασα τὰς χεῖρας πρὸς τὴν θυρίδα ἐδεήθη καὶ εἶπεν. La: exporrectis manibus ad fenestram deprecata est (MSS JW: et deprecata est) Dominum et dixit. See 4QpapTob[a] ar 6:6.

Frg. 2   Tob 4:3-9

[	⁴ רֹצֹוֹנ̇]ה ו[אל ת]וגה רוחה	]	1
[	וסבול אותכה במֹעֹי̇]ה	]	2
	בני		
[	⁵וכול ימיכה לאלהים הי̇]ה ז[כֹ̇ר̇]	vacat	3
[	מֹאמרו̇]	מֹאמרו̇] vacat אמת היֹה̇] עושה כ]ֹל ימי ח̇]ייכה]	4

222

5]בדרכ[י שקר ⁶כי בעשות ה[ן]אמת   יה[ן]ה עמך[.⁷   [

6] [ ]וֹבֿאארך ידכה בני היה[ן עושה   צֿדקות ואל תסן]תר פניך מן כול[

7]ע[נֿוֹ אף ממֿכֿה לוא יסֿ[תרו פני אלהי]ֿם ⁸אם יהיה לכה בנ[י רוב כרוב היה[

8]עוש[ה]ֿ ממנו צֿד[קו]ֿת [vacat] אם יהיה לך מעט כמעטֿ[[

9] [בעש[ו]ֿתֿך צדקה ⁹שימה טוֹבֿהֿ [[

Mus. Inv. 848
PAM 41.368, 42.218, 43.183*

Notes on Readings

This partial column is preserved on three fragments, the first two of which (frgs. 2a, b) almost join each other. Parts of nine lines are extant.

L. 1 Only the bottoms of the first four letters are discernible.

L. 2 Only traces of the last two letters are found, probably *'ayin* and *yod.*

L. 3. A *vacat* appears at the beginning of the line. The vocative בני is written above the line. Just before the lacuna there is a clear *he* and a trace of a *yod.* On the top of frg. 2c there are traces of the bottoms of *kap* and *reš.*

L. 4. After the first preserved word there is a *vacat.*

L. 5 Just before the lacuna there is the trace of a *he.*

L. 6 At the beginning of the line the head of a letter before the *kap* can be seen, probably a *waw.*

L. 7 The line begins with the trace of a *nun,* and then of a *waw,* or less likely a *yod.* After the lacuna the line resumes with the trace of a final *mem.*

L. 8 There may have been a *vacat* in what is now a lacuna.

L. 9 The line begins with the trace of three letters, probably *waw, taw,* and final *kap.*

Translation

1. [her] good pleasure, [and] do not [grieve her spirit   4   ]
2. [and (she) bore you in [her] womb [   ]
3.   *vacat*   ⁵And all your days, my son, [remem]ber God [   ]
4. [   ] his command. *vacat* B[e] honest [a]ll the days of [your] li[fe   ]
5. [in the path]s of wickedness. ⁶For in doing wh[at is honest   will] be with you. ⁷[   ]
6. [   ]According to your ability, my son, gi[ve] alms, and hi[de] not [your face from any]
7. [p]oor person. Then [Go]d[’s face] will not h[idden] from you. ⁸If you have [much, my] son, [according to (your) bounty]
8. [giv]e al[m]s from it [*vacat?*]. If you have little, according to the little (you have) [   ]
9. [By] your [giv]ing alms, ⁹a good deposit [you   ]

COMMENTS

L. 1 Cf. S: ποίει τὸ ἀρεστὸν ἐνώπιον αὐτῆς καὶ μὴ λυπήσῃς τὸ πνεῦμα αὐτῆς ἐν παντὶ πράγματι. La: quod illi placet hoc fac in conspectu eius, et noli contristare spiritum eius in ulla re (ms X: nec contristes uel in modico spiritum eius).

L. 2 Cf. S: κινδύνους πολλοὺς ἑώρακεν ἐπὶ σοὶ ἐν τῇ κοιλίᾳ αὐτῆς. La: quanta pericula passa sit (ms R: uiderit) pro te (mss MR add: et sustinuerit; ms X adds: in utero portauerit te) in utero suo. סבול is the infinitive absolute, resuming some finite verb form that is now missing because of the lacuna. See 4QTobᵉ 4:3; 5:2; 6:4; 7 i 2 and cf. Hag 1:6; Dan 9:5. It is a usage found in late postexilic biblical writings. See GKC §113z; Joüon-Muraoka, *GBH* §123x

L. 3 See 4QpapTobᵃ ar 9:2. Cf. S: καὶ πάσας τὰς ἡμέρας σου, παιδίον, τοῦ κυρίου μνημόνευε. La: et omnibus diebus uitae tuae, fili, Deum in mente habe. For the *lamed* before the direct object, see GKC §117n. It is used especially with participles when the object precedes in late postbiblical Hebrew. Hebr. Fagii: וכל ימי חייך בני זכור את יהוה אלהינו.

L. 4 אמת היה עושה. Lit., "be doing the truth." Cf. S: καὶ μὴ θελήσῃς ἁμαρτεῖν (ms 319: ἁμαρτάνειν) καὶ παραβῆναι τὰς ἐντολὰς αὐτοῦ. δικαιοσύνας ποίει πάσας τὰς ἡμέρας τῆς ζωῆς σου. La: noli uelle peccare uel praeterire praecepta illius. Iustitiam fac omnibus diebus uitae tuae.

L. 5 בעשות ה]אמת. Lit., "in doing the truth." Cf. S: καὶ μὴ πορευθῇς ταῖς ὁδοῖς τῆς ἀδικίας. διότι οἱ ποιοῦντες (ms 319: ποιοῦντος σου, which is closer to the Hebrew) ἀλήθειαν εὐοδωθήσεται ἐν τοῖς ἔργοις αὐτῶν. La: et noli ire in uiam iniquitatis, quoniam agente te ex ueritate (mss WM: ueritatem) erit respectus in operibus tuis (ms W: bene tibi erit) et omnibus qui faciunt iustitiam.

L. 6 כארך ידכה בני היה] עושה [צדקות. Lit., "according to the length of your hand, my son, be doing righteous deeds," that is, giving alms. Cf. 4QpapTobᵃ ar 10:1. S omits Tob 4:7-18, but ms 319 reads: καὶ τὰ ὑπάρχοντά σου and ποίει ἐλεημοσύνην καὶ μὴ ἀποστρέψεις τὸ πρόσωπόν σου. mss AB: ἐκ τῶν ὑπαρχόντων σου ποίει ἐλεημοσύνην. La: ex substantia tua, fili, fac eleemosynam, et noli auertere faciem tuam.

L. 7 נ[ע]. Possibly one should read נ[ע]. Cf. ms 319: ἀπὸ παντὸς πτωχοῦ. mss AB: ἀπὸ παντὸς πτωχοῦ. Καὶ ἀπὸ σοῦ οὐ μὴ ἀποστραφῇ τὸ πρόσωπον τοῦ θεοῦ. Ὡς σοὶ ὑπάρχει, κατὰ τὸ πλῆθος. La: ab ullo paupere, et ita fiet ut nec auertatur a te facies Dei. Quomodo habueris, fili, sic fac eleemosynam. Si tibi largior fuerit substantia, plus.

L. 8 Cf. AB: ποίησον ἐξ αὐτῶν ἐλεημοσύνην. ἐὰν ὀλίγον σοι ὑπάρχῃ, κατὰ τὸ ὀλίγον. La: ex illa fac eleemosynam; si exiguum habueris, ex hoc ipso exiguo communica.

L. 9 Cf. AB: θέμα γὰρ ἀγαθὸν θησαυρίζεις σεαυτῷ εἰς ἡμέραν ἀνάγκης. La: praemium bonum repones tibi in die necessitatis. It is sometimes thought that this saying is echoed in 1 Tim 6:19. Compare Prov 10:2.

Frg. 3   Tob 5:2

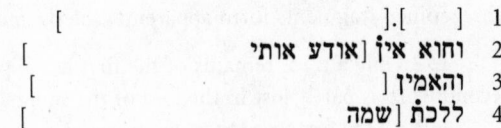

[	].[ ]	1
[	וחוא אי‬ן [אודע אותי	2
[	והאמי‬ן]	3
[	ללכ‬ת [שמה	4

Mus. Inv. 850
PAM 41.368, 42.218, 43.184*

NOTES ON READINGS

This fragment preserves the beginnings of four lines, with only a trace of the first.

L. 2 The bottom of the final *nun* is preserved at the end of the line.
L. 4 Only the top of the last letter is visible, probably a *taw*.

TRANSLATION

1. [   ]
2. since he does not [know me   ]
3. and believe [   ]
4. to go [there   ]

COMMENTS

L. 2 Cf. S: καὶ αὐτὸς οὐ γινώσκει με. La: neque enim me ille nouit.
L. 3 Cf. S: καὶ πιστεύει μοι. La: ut me cognoscat et credat.
L. 4 Cf. S: τοῦ πορευθῆναι ἐκεῖ. La: neque uias regionis illius noui.

Frg. 4   Tob 10:7-9

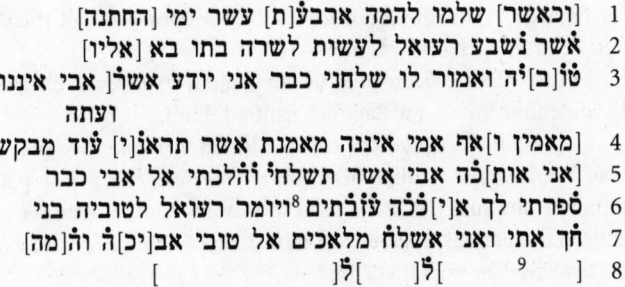

[וכאשר] שלמו להמה ארבﬠ[ת] עשר ימי [החתנה]	1
אשר נשבע רעואל לעשות לשרה בתו בא [אליו]	2
טו[ב]י֯ה ואמור לו שלחני כבר אני יודע אשר֗[אבי איננו] ועתה	3
[מאמין ו]אף אמי איננה מאמנת אשר תראﬠנ[י] ﬠ֗וד מבקש	4
[אני אות]כ֯ה אבי אשר תשלח֗י ו֗ה֯לכתי אל אבי כבר	5
ספרתי לך א[י]כ֯כ֯ה ﬠ֗ז֗בתים 8ויומר רעואל לטוביה בני	6
ח֗ך אתי ואני אשלח֗ מלאכים אל טובי אב[יכ]ה֯ וה֯[מה]	7
[9]ל֯[ ]ל֯[ ]ל֯[	8

Mus. Inv. 850
PAM 41.368 (in part), 42.218, 43.184*

Notes on Readings

Three joined fragments form apparently the beginnings of eight lines of a column.

L. 2 Only a trace remains of the first letter, probably an *'alep*. The *nun* of the second word is partly lost in the fold of the skin.

L. 3. Of the first word there are traces of a *ṭet* and *waw* and then of a *yod* (before the *he*); at the end there is a trace of a *reš*.

L. 4 The adverb ועתה is written above the line.

L. 5 The line begins with the trace of a *kap*.

L. 6. The first letter is probably a *samek*. Only the tops of the letters of the third word are preserved; the same is true for the first three letters of the fourth word.

L. 7 The first letter is undoubtedly a *ḥet*.

L. 8 Only the tips of two *lamed*s are preserved.

Translation

1. [and when] the four[t]een days [of the wedding] were over for them,
2. which Raguel had sworn to make for Sarah, his daughter, [T]o[b]iah came [to him]
3. and said to him, "Send me off; I know already that [my father does not]
4. believe, and] also my mother does not believe that she will see [me] again. Now [I] beg
5. yo[u], my father, that you send me off so that I may go to my father. I have already
6. told you h[o]w I have left them behind." 8Raguel then said to Tobiah, "My son,
7. stay with me, and I shall send messengers to Tobit, yo[u]r father, and th[ey]
8. [   ]

Comments

L. 1 Cf. S: καὶ ὅτε συνετελέσθησαν αἱ δέκα τέσσαρες ἡμέραι τοῦ γάμου. La: et ut consummati sunt quattuordecim (ms X: illi) dies nuptiarum. M. Morgenstern ("Language," 138) calls attention to the temporal sense of the verb שלם in Isa 60:20 and in Aramaic in 1QapGen 6:9-10.

L. 2 Cf. S: ἃς ὤμοσεν Ῥαγουὴλ ποιῆσαι τῇ θυγατρὶ αὐτοῦ, εἰσῆλθεν πρὸς αὐτόν. La: de quibus iurauerat Raguhel, exiit ad illum.

L. 3 Cf. S: Τωβίας καὶ εἶπεν Ἐξαπόστειλόν με, γινώσκω γὰρ ἐγὼ ὅτι ὁ πατήρ μου. La: Thobias et dixit illi Dimitte me, scio enim quia pater meus. Again, the infinitive absolute (אמור) is used to resume a finite verb; see comment on 4QTob[e] 2:2. On the use of כבב, see Qoh 1:10; 2:12-16; 3:15; 4:2; 6:10; 9:6-7; cf. 4QpapTob[a] ar 6:12; 4QTob[b] ar 4 i 15; 4QTob[e] 4:5.

L. 4 Cf. S: καὶ ἡ μήτηρ μου οὐ πιστεύουσιν ὅτι ὄψονταί με ἔτι. καὶ νῦν ἀξιῶ. La: et mater mea non credunt se uisuros me. Nunc itaque peto.

L. 5 Cf. S: σε, πάτερ, ὅπως ἐξαποστείλῃς με καὶ πορευθῶ πρὸς τὸν πατέρα μου. ἤδη. La: pater, dimittas me ut eam ad patrem meum. Iam.

L. 6 Cf. S: ὑπέδειξά σοι ὡς ἀφῆκα αὐτόν. Καὶ εἶπεν Ῥαγουὴλ τῷ Τωβίᾳ. La: tibi indicaui quomodo illum reliquerim. Et dixit Raguhel Thobiae.

L. 7 Cf. S: μεῖνον, παιδίον, μεῖνον μετ' ἐμοῦ. καὶ ἐγὼ ἀποστέλλω ἀγγέλους πρὸς Τωβὶν τὸν πατέρα σου καὶ ὑποδείξουσιν αὐτῷ. La: remane hic penes me (ms R: penes me, fili); et ego nuntios mittam patri tuo, et indicabunt illi de te.

Frg. 5   Tob 11:10-14

[ל[קֹרֹת בנֹו עד .]] 1	
[ומר]ורה הדג בידו ונפוץ [בעיניו ¹¹] 2	
[ויאמר]לו אל תירא אבי [ושם הסם] 3	
[ע]ל̇ עׄיניו וחרוק[¹²] 4	
[חוריו]ת̇ עיני̇ו ¹³וירא את̇] בנו] 5	
[ ].בֹנֹי̇[¹⁴] 6	

Mus. Inv. 850
PAM 41.368, 42.218, 43.184*

Notes on Readings

This small fragment contains parts of six lines of the middle of a column. It has shrunk somewhat, and the beginning of the lines, especially the lower ones, have become twisted.

L. 1 The line begins with the traces of two letters, probably *qop* and *reš*.

L. 4 A small dot precedes עיני, probably the remains of a *lamed*. It cannot be a *bet*.

L. 5 What is left of the first letter seems to be the tail of a *taw*, possibly the end of a feminine noun in the construct state, representing either τὰ λευκώματα, "white scales," or κάνθων, "corners" (of the eyes).

L. 6 Only the tops of three letters are preserved.

Translation

1. [to] meet his son as far as [   ]
2. [¹¹   and the g]all of the fish (was) in his hand, and he scattered (some of it) [on his eyes]
3. [and he said] to him, "Do not be afraid, my father," [and he put the medicine]
4. [o]n his eyes, and it smarted[¹²   ]
5. [the white scal]es of his eyes. ¹³And he saw [his son   ]
6. [¹⁴"   my] son[   ]

Comments

L. 1 Cf. S: καὶ ἐβάδισεν Τωβίας πρὸς αὐτόν. La: et occurrit illi Thobias. Vg: occurrit in obviam filio suo. Hebr. Münsterii: לקראת בנו. Note the defective writing of לקרת, and also the change of subject in the versions. In the Hebrew the elderly Tobit makes his way to meet his son, as also in the Vg and Hebr. Münsterii, but in S and the La Tobiah meets "him," that is, his father.

L. 2 Cf. S: καὶ χολὴ τοῦ ἰχθύος ἐν τῇ χειρὶ αὐτοῦ, καὶ ἐνεφύσησεν εἰς τοὺς ὀφθαλμοὺς αὐτοῦ. La: ferens fel piscis in manibus suis. Et insufflauit (ms R: aspersit illud; ms M: asparsit in; ms G: iniecit oculis) in oculis Thobis patris sui. נפוץ is undoubtedly the infinitive absolute of נפץ, resuming a preceding finite verb; see note on 4QTob^e 2:2. It is unlikely the Nip'al perfect of פוץ, because the waw would not be conversive, and an active form is called for in the context.

L. 3 Cf. S: καὶ εἶπεν Θάρσει, πάτερ, καὶ ἐπέβαλεν τὸ φάρμακον ἐπ' αὐτόν. La: et dixit illi Forti animo esto, pater, et iniecit medicamentum. Possibly one should restore the infinitive absolute ושום.

L. 4 Cf. S: καὶ ἐπέδωκεν, which makes little sense in this context. Hanhart suspects it is a scribal error for ἐπέδακη, "it bit, smarted." La: in oculis eius, et morsum illi praebebat (ms G: momordit eum). חרוק is clearly a form of חרק, but is it a noun form or an infinitive absolute? It is probably the latter. Hebr. Münsterii: ויאמר אל תירא אבי.

L. 5 S lacks verse 12; for 11:13 S reads: καὶ ἀπελέπισεν ἑκατέραις ταῖς χερσὶν αὐτοῦ ἀπὸ τῶν κάνθων τῶν ὀφθαλμῶν αὐτοῦ (no object of the verb is expressed). mss AB: (verse 12) διέτριψεν τοὺς ὀφθαλμοὺς αὐτοῦ. (verse 13) καὶ ἐλεπίσθη ἀπὸ τῶν κανθῶν τῶν ὀφθαλμῶν αὐτοῦ τὰ λευκώματα, καὶ ἰδὼν τὸν υἱὸν αὐτοῦ. La: et decoriauit duabus manibus albugines oculorum illius, et uidit filium suum.

L. 6 Cf. S: εἶδόν σε, τέκνον. La: video te, fili.

Frg. 6   Tob 12:20–13:4

top margin

כתבו את כול [המעשה הזה והעלהו]	*vacat?*	]²¹ [	1
[ולוא עוד ראו] א[ו]תו ²²והיו המה ותומהים מברכים ו[מהללים את אלהים]			2
ומודים אותו על מע[שׂו הגדול ותומהים איכה נרא֯ה [להמה מלאך]			3
אלהים] ¹³:¹בכן דבר טובי וכתוב תהלה בתשבוחֿת וא֯[מור]			4
[ברוך אלהים]ח֯י אשר לכול העולמים היאה מלכותו ²אשר הואֿה] מכה]			5
והוא[ה מרחם מוריד עד שאולה תחתית והואה מעלה מתהֿו[ם]			6
ג[ד֯ו֯ל]ה ומה אשר יפצה מידו ³הודו לו בני ישר[אל לפני]			7
[הגוים] אשר אתֿמה נדחים בהמה ⁴ושמה ספר]ו את גודלו ורוממו]			8
[אותו לפני כו]ל֯ חי כיא הוא אד'ניכֿ[מה] והוא אלה[יכמה]			9
לכו]ל֯ [עולמים [			10

Mus. Inv. 850
PAM 41.368, 42.324, 43.184*

Notes on Readings

This fragment contains the center of ten lines at the top of a column, the upper margin of which is preserved.

L. 1 Above the first preserved word are very faint traces of something that was added in the upper margin, but the traces are not legible. The upper layer of skin of part of this line has been lost. There probably was a short *vacat* after the last preserved word. What would correspond to S at the beginning of verse 21 probably began at the end of this line.

L. 2 The word after המה has been struck out. The scribe's eye had skipped to the line below, and he copied here the word found under it in line 3 and then crossed it out. Only a trace remains of the last letter on the line, probably a *waw*.

L. 3 The first two letters are either שו or שי. The skin has flaked off later in the line, but there are clear traces of a *he*, and then of a *nun*.

L. 4 There may have been a *vacat* before the first preserved word.

L. 5 The last preserved letter is clearly a *he*, despite the photograph, which makes the edge of the skin below the right shaft of the *he* look like that of a final *kap*.

L. 6 The scribe first wrote שאולה, the locative form, but the *he* was later scratched out, making it look somewhat like an *'alep*. The top layer of the skin has flaked off the *waw* in הואה.

L. 7 Only two dots remain at the beginning of the line, the tops of a *dalet* and a *waw*.

L. 8 In the second preserved word a break in the skin has caused the loss of a *mem*. At the end of the line, the trace of the bottom of a letter is probably that of a *reš*.

L. 9 The *waw* of אדוניכ[מה] is written above the line. After the lacuna the line resumes with the trace of a *waw*.

L. 10 Only the tip of a *lamed* is visible.

Translation

1. ["Write down all] that has happened." [21]And he ascended *vacat*? [21   ]
2. [and they saw] h[i]m [no more.] [22]But they were blessing and [praising God],
3. [and acknowledging him because of] his great [de]ed and the amazing fact that [an angel of God] had appeared [to them.]
4. [13:1]Then Tobit spoke up and composed a song in praise, sayi[ng,]
5. ["Blest be the] living [God], because his kingship is for all the ages; [2]because he [afflicts]
6. [and] shows mercy; he brings down to lowest Sheol, and he raises up from the [gr]eat abys[s.]

229

7. What is there that can snatch from his hand? ³Acknowledge him, O children of Isra[el, [before]

8. [the nations], because you are banished among them. ⁴Recoun[t] there [his greatness, and exalt him]

9. [before al]l that lives. For he is your Lord; he is [your] God [   ]

10. [for al]l[ages!"   ]

Comments

L. 1 Cf. Lit., "'[Write] all this deed.' And he caused him to go up." The form והעלהו is strange; it seems to be a *Hip'il* form of עלי, with a pronominal suffix used in a reflexive sense. This sense is also found in Sir 7:7, 16, and possibly in Ezek 29:3. See A. Abronim, "הערות," *Lešonenu* 1 (1928-29) 206-10, esp. 207-8; Joüon-Muraoka, *GBH* §146k. S: γράψατε πάντα ταῦτα τὰ συμβάντα ὑμῖν. Καὶ ἀνέβη. La: scribite ergo omnia quae contigerunt uobis. Et ascendit (ms R: ego enim ascendo ad eum qui me misit). There was probably a *vacat* at the end of this sentence.

L. 2 Cf. S: καὶ οὐκέτι ἠδύναντο ἰδεῖν (mss AB: οὐκέτι εἶδον) αὐτόν, καὶ ηὐλόγουν καὶ ὕμνουν τὸν θεόν. La: et non potuerunt illum uidere. Et benedicebant et decantabant Deo.

L. 3 Perhaps one should reconstruct [מע]ש<ה>ו, since the traces of שו are clear and a singular הגדול follows, which is different from the versions. If one should read שי, one might interpret it as = מעשה, again a singular. The versions, however, show that a pronominal suffix was present in their *Vorlage*, even if the noun for "deed" is plural. Cf. S: καὶ ἐξωμολογοῦντο αὐτῷ ἐπὶ τὰ ἔργα αὐτοῦ τὰ μεγάλα ταῦτα (mss AB: τὰ ἔργα τὰ μεγάλα καὶ θαυμαστὰ τοῦ θεοῦ), ὡς ὤφθη αὐτοῖς ἄγγελος θεοῦ. La: et confitebantur illi in omnibus operibus magnis illius, quia apparuit illis angelus Dei (ms X: propter quod apparuerat illis sanctus angelus Dei). Nothing corresponds to ותומהים in the Latin versions. Being a plural, it does not agree with the preceding noun; so it must be taken as a coordinate substantive.

L. 4 Cf. S: καὶ εἶπεν (mss AB: καὶ Τωβὶτ ἔγραψεν προσευχὴν εἰς ἀγαλλίασιν καὶ εἶπεν). La: tunc locutus est Thobis, et scripsit orationem in laetitia, et dixit. The form תשבוחת is not found in Biblical Hebrew, but occurs in 1QM 4:8; 4Q510 1:1 (plural); 4Q511 2 i 8; 6Q18 2:8. The more normal Hebrew form is תשבחה (*tušbāḥāh*), as in Sir 51:12. The form here may be an Aramaism.

L. 5 One could also translate, "Blest be the living God, whose kingdom is for all ages." The sense of אשר debatable. S and the VL have taken it in a causal sense. Cf. S: εὐλογητὸς ὁ θεὸς ὁ ζῶν εἰς τὸν αἰῶνα καὶ ἡ βασιλεία αὐτοῦ, ὅτι αὐτὸς μαστιγοῖ. La: Benedictus es, Deus, quia magnus es, et uiuis in aeternum. Quoniam in omnia saecula regnum est illius; quia ipse flagellat. אלהים, not אל, is restored, as in Tobᵉ 2:3; 6:9.

L. 6 Cf. S: καὶ ἐλεᾷ, κατάγει ἕως ᾅδου κατωτάτω τῆς γῆς, καὶ αὐτὸς ἀνάγει ἐκ τῆς ἀπωλείας. La: et miseretur; deducit usque ad inferos deorsum et reducit a perditione.

L. 7 Cf. S: τῆς μεγάλης, καὶ οὐκ ἔστιν οὐδέν, ὃ ἐκφεύξεται (mss AB: οὐκ ἔστιν ὃς ἐκφεύξεται) τὴν χεῖρα αὐτοῦ. ἐξομολογεῖσθε αὐτῷ, οἱ υἱοὶ Ἰσραήλ, ἐνώπιον. La: maiestate sua, et non est qui effugiat manum eius. Confitemini illi filii Israel coram. Possibly יפצה is to be read as a *Nip'al*, "that will be snatched from his hand?" The verb פצה is found in the more usual sense, "open (the mouth)," in 4Q511 42:4, as in Gen 4:11.

L. 8 Cf. S: τῶν ἐθνῶν, ὅτι αὐτὸς διέσπειρεν ὑμᾶς ἐν αὐτοῖς. Καὶ ἐκεῖ ὑπέδειξεν ὑμῖν τὴν μεγαλωσύνην αὐτοῦ, καὶ ὑψοῦτε. La: nationibus, quia ipse dispersit uos (MS X: disparsit nos) in illis; et ibi ostendit (MS P: adnuntiate) misericordiam eius, et exaltate (MS X: ut hostendatur ibidem misericordia eius et exaltetur).

L. 9 The last letter before the break has clearly the head of *kap* or *bet*; it cannot be *nun* (to agree with S or VL, ἡμῶν or noster). Cf. S: αὐτὸν ἐνώπιον παντὸς ζῶντος, καθότι αὐτὸς ἡμῶν κύριός ἐστιν. καὶ αὐτὸς θεὸς ἡμῶν. La: illum coram omni uiuente, quoniam ipse est Dominus Deus noster.

L. 10 Cf. S: καὶ αὐτὸς πατὴρ ἡμῶν καὶ αὐτὸς θεὸς εἰς πάντας τοὺς αἰῶνας. La: et ipse pater noster et Deus in omnia saecula saeculorum. Cf. Ps 145:13.

Frg. 7 i   Tob 13:13-14

top margin

	אֹז שמחי ודוֹצי[	] 1
[וּבָרֵךְ את	] על בני הצדיקים	2
] כֹּל	14]אלהי עולם	3
ואשרי השמחים בשלומ[ךָ	] 4

Mus. Inv. 850
PAM 41.368, 42.218, 43.184*

Notes on Readings

This fragment contains the ends of four lines at the top of one column and the beginnings of four lines at the top of the following column. To the second column belongs another fragment (7b) with parts of four lines, the top line of which corresponds to frg. 7a, line 3. The margin above line 1 shows that the lines here belong to the top of a column.

L. 1 Only a trace remains of the first letter, probably an *'alep*.

L. 2 Loose flakes of the skin, still visible in PAM 43.184, covered the first two letters. They were removed on 15 June 1993, and so the *bet* and the final *kap* can now be seen clearly. The verb is in the singular, not the plural, as in the versions.

L. 4 Only the trace of a final letter remains, part of a final *kap*.

TRANSLATION

1. [　　　　　]then rejoice and exult
2. [over the children of the righteous　　　　　　　　　] and bless the
3. [eternal God　　　　　　14　　　] all [　　　　]
4. [　　　　and blessed are those who rejoice in] your [peace.]

COMMENTS

L. 1 The feminine imperatives are addressed to Jerusalem. See 4QpapTob^a ar 18:2. Cf. S: τότε πορεύθητι (mss AB: χάρηθι) καὶ ἀγαλλίασαι πρὸς τοὺς υἱοὺς τῶν δικαίων. La: tunc gaude et laetare in filiis iustorum.

L. 2 The form וברך is probably the infinitive construct used as an infinitive absolute (see Joüon-Muraoka, *GBH* §52c); cf. the comment on 4QTob^e 2:2. Cf. S: καὶ εὐλογήσουσιν τὸν κύριον τοῦ αἰῶνος. La: et benedicent Domino aeterno (mss PR: benedicent Dominum in aeternum). Four dots or some form of the tetragrammaton should undoubtedly be restored in line 3.

L. 3 Cf. S: μακάριοι οἱ ἀγαπῶντές σε. La: felices qui diligunt te.

L. 4 Cf. S: καὶ μακάριοι οἳ χαρήσονται ἐπὶ τῇ εἰρήνῃ σου (mss AB: ὅσοι ἐλυπήθησαν ἐπὶ πάσαις ταῖς μάστιξίν σου). La: et qui (mss RX: felices qui) gaudent in pace tua.

Frg. 7 ii　　　Tob 13:18–14:2

top margin

ברוך]	ירושלים תהלת] שמחה ישירו 1
[	האלהים אש]ר מרים אותך וברוך 2
[	אשר] בכי יברכו את שמו הק]דוש ל]עולם 3
[	14:1ותמ]ו דברי תודת טובי וימ]ות בשלום בן] 4
[	2והו]א בן שמונה וחמש]ים [5
[	מ]ראה] ו]אחר אר]בע וחמשים חיה [6

Mus. Inv. 850
PAM 42.218, 43.184*

NOTES ON READINGS

See NOTES ON READINGS of frg. 7 i. The beginnings of four lines are preserved on frg. 7a, and parts of four lines, the uppermost of which belongs to line 3, are preserved on frg. 7b. In all there are parts of six lines.

L. 1 Toward the end of the line one can see the bottom of a *he*, followed by traces of two letters.

L. 2 The right side of a *šin* is preserved at the end of the line.

232

L. 4 Just before the lacuna there is the trace of a letter, probably of a *mem*. After the lacuna the line resumes with traces of a *waw* and a *taw*. At the very end there are traces of two letters, probably *bet* and final *nun*.

L. 5 The line begins with the remains of an *'alep* and ends with the remains of a *šin*.

L. 6 The line begins with the traces of *reš, 'alep, he*. After the lacuna there is the left tip of an *'alep*; at the end of the lines are traces of an *'alep* and a *reš*.

TRANSLATION

1. [Jerusalem [shall sing] a psalm of [exultation   Blest be]
2. the God wh[o exalts you, and blest   ]
3. because [in you they will bless his h]oly [name] for[ever.]
4. 14:1So [were] completed [the words of Tobit's thanksgiving, and he d]ied in peace at the age of [   ]
5. [2H]e was fif[ty]-eight years old [when   ]
6. [his s]ight, [and] afterwards [he lived fifty-]fo[ur years.]

COMMENTS

L. 1 תהלת, or possibly the plural תהלו[ת, "psalms of." The subject of the sentence is plural; the construct שערי has been lost before ירושלים. Cf. S: καὶ αἱ θύραι Ἰερουσαλὴμ (mss AB: αἱ ῥῦμαι αὐτῆς) ᾠδὰς ἀγαλλιάματος ἐροῦσιν. La: et ostia illius (ms R: plateae tuae; ms M: plateae Hierusalem) canticum laetitiae dicent.

L. 2 Cf. S: εὐλογητὸς ὁ θεὸς τοῦ Ἰσραήλ. La: benedictus Dominus (mss MRX: Deus) qui exaltat te, et benedictus (ms X: benedicetur in omnia saecula saeculorum).

L. 3 Cf. S: καὶ εὐλογητοὶ εὐλογήσουσιν τὸ ὄνομα τὸ ἅγιον εἰς τὸν αἰῶνα καὶ ἔτι. La: quoniam in te benedicent nomen sanctum suum (ms R: sanctum) in aeternum.

L. 4 See 4QpapTob[a] ar 18:12. Cf. S: καὶ συνετελέσθησαν οἱ λόγοι τῆς ἐξομολογήσεως Τώβιθ. Καὶ ἀπέθανεν ἐν εἰρήνῃ ἐτῶν ἑκατὸν δώδεκα. La: et ut consummati sunt sermones confessionis Thobi, mortuus est in pace, annorum centum duodecim.

L. 5 See 4QpapTob[a] ar 18:13. Cf. S: καὶ ἑξήκοντα δύο ἐτῶν ἦν, ὅτε ἐγένετο ἀνάπειρος τοῖς ὀφθαλμοῖς (mss AB: καὶ ἦν ἐτῶν πεντήκοντα ὀκτώ, ὅτε ἀπώλεσεν τὰς ὄψεις). La: quinquaginta autem et octo annorum erat cum oculis captus est.

L. 6 Cf. S: καὶ μετὰ τὸ ἀναβλέψαι αὐτὸν (mss AB: καὶ μετὰ ἔτη ὀκτὼ ἀνέβλεψεν) ἔζησεν ἐν ἀγαθοῖς καὶ ἐλεημοσύνας ἐποίησεν. La: quinquaginta quattuor (ms R: quadraginta quattuor) annis postquam lucem recepit uixit.

233

Unidentified Fragments

Frg. 8

[	‏[ך היום]‏	]	1
[	‏[.רה נפל ג̇]‏	]	2
[	‏[ו̇ב̇י̇ד̇כה]‏	]	3
[	‏[ל̇]‏	]	4

Mus. Inv. 850
PAM 42.324, 43.184*

NOTES ON READINGS

Parts of four lines are preserved on this small fragment. The letters are very difficult to read, although they appear a little more clearly on PAM 42.324.

L. 1 The line begins with the remains of a final *kap*.

L. 2 The trace of the first letter seems to be a *reš*, and that of the last may be a *gimel*.

L. 3 At the beginning of this line one can see the tops of four letters, probably *waw, bet, yod, dalet*.

L. 4 Only the tip of a *lamed* is preserved here.

TRANSLATION

1. [   ] today [   ]
2. [   ] fell [   ]
3. [   ]and in your hand [   ]
4. [   ]   [   ]

Frg. 9   Tob 3:3-4?

[	‏ואל [תשפט]‏	]	1
[	‏[ותטר לשל̇ל̇]‏	]	2
[	‏[ל̇]‏	]	3

Mus. Inv. 850
PAM 43.184*

NOTES ON READINGS

This small fragment contains the remains of three lines.

L. 2 There is the trace of a letter after the second *lamed* of the second word.

L. 3 Only the tip of a *lamed* remains on this line.

Translation

1. [and do not] judge [   ]
2. [   ] and you have kept for despoilment [   ]
3. [   ]   [   ]

Comments

If this fragment does correspond to Tob 3:3-4, then the following quotations may help.

L. 1 Cf. S: καὶ μή με ἐκδικήσῃς ταῖς ἁμαρτίαις μου. La: ne uindictam sumas de peccatis meis.

L. 2 Cf. S: καὶ ἔδωκας ἡμᾶς εἰς ἁρπαγήν. La: et tradidisti nos in direptionem.

CHAPTER 10

The Aramaic Levi Document

The Aramaic Levi Document (ALD) is known from several fragments of the Dead Sea Scrolls that have been published in different places and by different persons. Since these fragments are related to the Aramaic Genizah *Testament of Levi* (GenTL), which was retrieved from the Cairo Genizah at the end of the nineteenth century, and to the Greek Testament of Levi (GkTL) in the *Testaments of the Twelve Patriarchs,* which had been known for a long time, they are clearly important Qumran texts. The Qumran fragments of the Levi Document have been doled out in a fashion that was measured in part by the time-consuming process of identification and piecing together of the jigsaw puzzle of Cave 4 fragments and in part by the subsequent delay in publication known to everybody. The result has been that it has not been easy to keep track of these important Qumran texts or to come to any clarity about the interpretation of them or of the Aramaic in which they have been written. My purpose now is to survey the progress of the study of these Qumran texts and to comment on the language in which they have been composed. This I shall do under two headings: the Qumran Aramaic Levi Document, and the Aramaic of the Levi Document.

The Qumran Aramaic Levi Document

I begin, first, with a few words about the Aramaic Genizah *Testament of Levi.* Discovered in the Genizah of the Ezra Synagogue in Old Cairo in 1896, GenTL is known today from a two-part fragmentary text housed, one part in the Library of Cambridge University (T-S 16.94), and the other part in the Bodleian

Library of Oxford University (Ms. Heb. c. 27 fol. 56). They have proved to be two pieces of a parchment manuscript dated about A.D. 1000 and were duly published in the first decade of this century. H. L. Pass and J. Arendzen published the Cambridge fragment in 1900, and R. H. Charles and A. Cowley the Bodleian fragment in 1907.[1] The Cambridge fragment contains six columns; the Bodleian, four columns. The order of these columns is the following:

Cambridge a
Cambridge b
Bodleian a
Bodleian b
Bodleian c
Bodleian d
Cambridge c
Cambridge d
Cambridge e
Cambridge f

In his further study of the *Testaments of the Twelve Patriarchs,* Charles subsequently reprinted (1908) and translated (1913) the text of GenTL.[2] Important further work was done on GenTL by I. Lévi,[3] P. Grelot,[4] M. de

---

1. See H. L. Pass and J. Arendzen, "Fragment of an Aramaic Text of the Testament of Levi," *JQR* 12 (1890-1900) 651-61 (without a photograph); and R. H. Charles and A. Cowley, "An Early Source of the Testaments of the Patriarchs," *JQR* 19 (1906-7) 566-83 (with a photograph of the Bodleian text).

Prior to the publication of the Qumran fragments, the Genizah fragments were further discussed by W. Bousset, "Ein aramäisches Fragment des Testamentum Levi," *ZNW* 1 (1900) 344-46; I. Lévi, "Notes sur le texte araméen du Testament de Lévi récemment découvert," *REJ* 54 (1907) 166-80; idem, "Encore un mot sur le texte araméen du Testament de Lévi récemment découvert," *REJ* 55 (1908) 285-87; M. de Jonge, *The Testaments of the Twelve Patriarchs: A Study of Their Text, Composition and Origin* (Assen: Van Gorcum, 1953) 129-31, 168-19 (part of the appendix of this book incorporates comments of P. R. Weis).

2. R. H. Charles, *The Greek Versions of the Testaments of the Twelve Patriarchs: Edited from Nine MSS together with the Variants of the Armenian and Slavonic Versions and Some Hebrew Fragments* (Oxford: Oxford University Press, 1908; reprint, Hildesheim: Olms, 1960) 245-56. For his English translation of the Cambridge and Bodleian fragments, see *APOT,* 2:364-67.

3. See n. 1 above.

4. P. Grelot, "Le Testament araméen de Lévi est-il traduit de l'hébreu: A propos du fragment de Cambridge, col. c à d 1," *REJ* ns 14 (1955) 91-99; idem, "Notes sur le Testament araméen de Lévi (fragment de la Bodleian Library, colonne a)," *RB* 63 (1956) 391-406.

Since the publication of some of the Qumran fragments of ALD, Grelot has published

Jonge,[5] R. A. Kugler,[6] J. C. Greenfield and M. E. Stone. The last two have especially studied the text anew with emended readings.[7]

The first news of a Qumran text related to the GenTL was given out by J. T. Milik in 1955, when he published 1Q21 and called it "Testament de Lévi."[8] Later Milik published a fragmentary text of two columns from Cave 4, which he identified as a "Prayer of Levi."[9] In the latter article Milik mentioned that there were two other fragmentary texts of the same document. He said that the first of these, represented by only one fragment, was identical with the Bodleian fragment a 7-21 (= TL §6-9); and that the other, represented by several fragments, corresponded partly to Bodleian fragment d 1-15,[10] partly to Cambridge fragment e 4–f 19 (= TL §82-95), and partly to

---

still other studies: "Quatre cents trente ans (Ex 12,40)," in *Homenaje a Juan Prado: Miscelánea de estudios bíblicos y hebráicos* (ed. L. Alvarez Verdes y E. J. Alonso Hernández; Madrid: Consejo Superior de Investigaciones Científicas, 1975) 559-70; "Le livre des Jubilés et le Testament de Lévi," in *Mélanges Dominique Barthélemy: Etudes bibliques offertes à l'occasion de son 60ᵉ anniversaire* (OBO 38; ed. P. Casetti et al.; Fribourg: Editions Universitaires; Göttingen: Vandenhoeck & Ruprecht, 1981) 110-33; "Une mention inaperçue de 'Abba' dans le *Testament araméen de Lévi*," *Sem* 33 (1983) 101-8; "Le coutumier sacerdotal ancien dans le *Testament araméen de Lévi*," *RevQ* 15 (1991-92) 253-63.

5. M. de Jonge, "The Testament of Levi and 'Aramaic Levi,'" *RevQ* 13 (1988-89) 367-85.

6. R. A. Kugler, *From Patriarch to Priest: The Levi-Priestly Tradition from* Aramaic Levi *to* Testament of Levi (SBLEJL 9; Atlanta: Scholars Press, 1996).

7. See J. C. Greenfield and M. E. Stone, "Remarks on the Aramaic Testament of Levi from the Geniza," *RB* 86 (1979) 214-30. Especially important in this article are the previously unpublished photo of the Cambridge fragment and the list of revised readings of both Cambridge and Bodleian texts (pp. 229-30). This article is reprinted in M. E. Stone, *Selected Studies in Pseudepigrapha and Apocrypha: With Special Reference to the Armenian Tradition* (SVTP 9; Leiden: Brill, 1991) 228-46 (with 2 plates; note errata on 244). See also their article, "Two Notes on the Aramaic Levi Document," in *Of Scribes and Scrolls: Studies on the Hebrew Bible, Intertestamental Judaism, and Christian Origins Presented to John Strugnell* . . . (College Theology Society Resources in Religion 5; ed. H. W. Attridge et al.; Lanham, Md.: University Press of America, 1990) 153-61, esp. 154-58. Also the article of J. C. Greenfield, "The Words of Levi Son of Jacob in Damascus Document iv, 15-19," *RevQ* 13 (1988-89) 319-22. Some pertinent remarks can also be found in E. Puech, "Le Testament de Qahat en araméen de la grotte 4 *(4QTQah)*," *RevQ* 15 (1991-92) 23-54, esp. 39-40 nn. 12-13.

8. See D. Barthélemy and J. T. Milik, *Qumran Cave 1* (DJD 1; Oxford: Clarendon, 1955) 87-91.

9. J. T. Milik, "Le Testament de Lévi en araméen," *RB* 62 (1955) 398-406.

10. Also to the addition to the GkTL 2:3 and 18:2 from MS e (Mount Athos, Koutloumous, Cod. 39 [catal. no. 3108] from the eleventh c. AD), vv. 25-30. The Greek text of this addition can be found in M. de Jonge, *The Testaments of the Twelve Patriarchs: A Critical Edition of the Greek Text* (PVTG 1/2; Leiden: Brill, 1978) 25, 46-48; cf. xvii.

nothing in either GenTL or GkTL. There Milik called the two-columned Prayer of Levi "4QLevi[b]." Then eleven years later he tucked away in a footnote of an article, which was devoted to entirely different Qumran texts, the following admission:

> The "remains of three mss." described on that page [meaning RB 62 (1955) 399] really belong to one scroll alone: 4Q 213 Test Levi[a]. In the meantime I have identified a few pieces of a second ms: 4Q 214 Test Levi[b].[11]

Thus the alleged three fragmentary Qumran texts of Levi, about which Milik wrote in 1955, became one, and he changed its name to "Testament of Levi[a]," identifying it as 4Q213. In a way, it was unfortunate that Milik changed the original name, "4QLevi," to "4Q Testament of Levi." Although the name "Testament of Levi" suits the Genizah fragments, Milik was fully aware in the 1955 article on the two-columned Prayer of Levi from Qumran Cave 4 that he had published a text related, indeed, to GenTL, and that the Greek *Testaments of the Twelve Patriarchs* had built upon such preliminary texts. He also realized, however, that GkTL was not identical to either the GenTL or the 4QTestLevi[a].[12] Nevertheless, Milik continued to speak of the "Prayer of Levi" as 4QTestLevi[a] in 1971 and 1976, and apparently so regards it still.[13]

The two-columned text, "Prayer of Levi," has been more comprehensively studied by Stone and Greenfield,[14] where they still call it 4QTLevi[a], but in their 1993 article they say nothing of its relation to the rest of 4Q213.

In 1994 Stone and Greenfield published five fragments of 4Q213 in an article entitled "The First Manuscript of *Aramaic Levi Document* from Qumran (4QLevi[a] aram)."[15] In this article they rightly refer to the Qumran

---

11. See J. T. Milik, "Fragment d'une source du Psautier (4Q Ps 89) et fragments des Jubilés, du Document de Damas, d'un phylactère dans la grotte 4 de Qumran," *RB* 73 (1966) 94-106, esp. 95 n. 2 (where one should read LXII instead of LXXI).

12. See Milik, "Le Testament de Lévi," 405-6.

13. See J. T. Milik, "Problèmes de la littérature hénochique à la lumière des fragments araméens de Qumrân," *HTR* 64 (1971) 333-78, esp. 344. This designation he repeats in his book, *The Books of Enoch: Aramaic Fragments of Qumrân Cave 4* (Oxford: Clarendon, 1976) 23-24: he claims that a reference to the Enochic Book of Watchers is found in lines 6-7 of what he calls "Test Levi[a] 8 iii." Of that text he publishes there lines 2-8 (without a photograph).

14. See M. E. Stone and J. C. Greenfield, "The Prayer of Levi," *JBL* 112 (1993) 247-66 (with plate reproducing PAM 43.242). Cf. *A Facsimile Edition of the Dead Sea Scrolls Prepared with an Introduction and Index* (2 vols.; ed. R. H. Eisenman and J. M. Robinson; Washington, D.C.: Biblical Archaeology Society, 1991) §1278.

15. M. E. Stone and J. C. Greenfield, "The First Manuscript of *Aramaic Levi Document* from Qumran (4QLevi[a] aram)," *Le Muséon* 107 (1994) 257-81 (with photograph of

Levi texts simply as 4QLevi, "since there are no characteristics within this document which mark it as a testament."[16] This is the reason why I regretted above that Milik had changed the name that he had originally used for the two-column Prayer of Levi. In this 1994 article, Stone and Greenfield indicate that frg. 1, col. 1 of 4Q213 corresponds to GenTL (= TL §82-95), whereas in their 1993 article on "The Prayer of Levi" they had mentioned that the prayer was related to an early part of GenTL. This should have meant that an earlier fragment number was to be assigned to the two-columned prayer, revealing that it would precede what is now called frg. 1, col. i.

Moreover, in their *Le Muséon* article on 4Q213 Stone and Greenfield mention that ALD is "extant in six copies from Qumran, five from Cave 4 and one from Cave 1."[17] The last mentioned is 1Q21, which Milik had published and entitled "Testament de Lévi."[18] It is comprised of sixty tiny fragments, of which only frgs. 3 and 4 certainly correspond to GenTL (Bodleian a 1-9 [= TL §4-6]; Bodleian a 15 [= TL §9]). Milik noted that nine other tiny fragments "perhaps" correspond.

When one seeks to find out what the five texts of ALD from Cave 4 are, it is not easy. One of them is 4Q213, already noted; another is 4Q214, which Milik himself called "TestLevi[b]," as I have already mentioned.[19] At the time this paper was being first written, it was not yet officially published.[20]

PAM 43.241). Cf. *Facsimile Edition*, §1277. From Stone and Greenfield (275 n. 22) we learn that Milik joined frgs. 3 and 4 of 4Q213 (in Milik, *Books of Enoch*, 23) in a way with which they do not agree.

16. They note that this aspect of the Qumran text had been pointed out earlier by H. W. Hollander and M. de Jonge in *The Testaments of the Twelve Patriarchs: A Commentary* (SVTP 8; Leiden: Brill, 1985) 21.

17. Stone and Greenfield, "The First Manuscript," 257. Milik himself counted only five Levi texts from Qumran; see "Ecrits préesséniens de Qumrân: d'Hénoch à Amram," in *Qumrân: Sa piété, sa théologie et son milieu* (BETL 46; ed. M. Delcor; Gembloux: Duculot; Louvain: Leuven University, 1978) 91-106, esp. 95 ("assez nombreux fragments de cinq rouleaux provenant du scriptorium qumranien"). That should have meant 1Q21 and four from Cave 4.

18. See n. 8 above.

19. A photograph of the fragments of 4Q214 is said to be in *Facsimile Edition*, §1296; cf. §525.

20. See now M. E. Stone and J. C. Greenfield, "Aramaic Levi Document," in *Qumran Cave 4: XVII. Parabiblical Texts, Part 3* (DJD 22; ed. G. Brooke et al.; Oxford: Clarendon, 1996) 1-72: "213. 4QLevi[a] ar," 1-24; "213a. 4QLevi[b] ar," 25-36; "213b. 4QLevi[c]," 37-41; "214. 4QLevi[d] ar," 43-51; "214a. 4QLevi[e] ar," 53-60; "214b. 4QLevi[f] ar," 61-72.

A transcription of fragment 1 of 4Q214 is presented in R. H. Eisenman and M. Wise, *The Dead Sea Scrolls Uncovered: The First Complete Translation and Interpretation of 50 Key Documents Withheld for Over 35 Years* (Rockport, Mass.: Element, 1992) 139; and

Two texts, labeled 4QLevi[c] and 4QLevi[d] with a question-mark behind the title, were published by Emile Puech.[21] Both of them once belonged to the lot assigned for publication to Jean Starcky, who had labeled them respectively 4QAh(aronique) Abis and 4QAh(aronique) A.[22] The first, now named by Puech "4QTestLevi[c](?)," is made up of three fragments; and the other, now named "4QTestLevi[d](?)," is comprised of twenty-four fragments. Starcky claimed that they mentioned a figure who resembled a suffering Messiah, something like that of the Isaian Servant Songs. Now that the fragments have been published, one sees that there is no mention in them of a "Messiah," much less of a "suffering Messiah." The texts speak about an eschatological figure, probably a priest, and of opposition to him. One cannot without further ado describe that figure with Christian (and specifically Lucan) terminology as a "suffering Messiah."

One wonders, consequently, whether the two texts, which Puech has published, have been rightly renamed. Starcky spoke of them as Aaronic, even though he toyed with the idea that Levi was the person concerned. Levi himself, however, is not mentioned in either of them. That may, of course, be sheer coincidence because of their fragmentary state, but the absence of the name is a warning. Moreover, whereas the Levi text from Cave 1 and 4QLevi[a] and 4QLevi[b] have clear words and phrases that are also found in the GenTL, this is not true of either 4QLevi[c](?) or 4QLevi[d](?). Puech related some Aramaic phrases in these fragmentary texts to the GkTL, yet none of the phrases corresponds exactly. The phrases in the GkTL merely contain generic echoes of similar Jewish "testamentary" literature, to which Puech's Qumran Aramaic texts may have to be remotely related, but none of them is close enough to identify these Aramaic texts as part of the Levi literature. So the names that Starcky originally used should be retained for these Qumran Aaronic fragments, that is, 4QAh A and 4QAh Abis. Both the ALD from Qumran and these texts refer to an

---

also in K. Beyer, *Die aramäischen Texte vom Toten Meer . . . : Ergänzungsband* (Göttingen: Vandenhoeck & Ruprecht, 1994) 73, where the transcription is unfortunately heavily influenced by the Genizah Testament text.

21. See E. Puech, "Fragments d'un apocryphe de Lévi et le personnage eschatologique: 4QTest Lévi[c-d](?) et 4QAJa," in *The Madrid Qumran Congress: Proceedings of the International Congress on the Dead Sea Scrolls Madrid 18-21 March, 1991* (STDJ 11/1-2; ed. J. Trebolle Barrera and L. Vegas Montaner; Leiden: Brill; Madrid: Editorial Complutense, 1992) 449-501 (+ plates 16-22).

22. A preliminary description of the fragmentary texts was given by Starcky in "Les quatre étapes du messianisme à Qumran," *RB* 70 (1963) 481-505, esp. 492, where he claimed that the fragments "nous paraissent évoquer un messie souffrant, dans la perspective ouverte par les poèmes du Serviteur" (seem to us to speak of a suffering messiah, in the perspective opened by the Servant Songs).

eschatological figure who is priestly and even Aaronic. Even if they refer to the same figure, there is no guarantee that 4QAh A or 4QAh Abis is part of ALD.

At this point in my study I turned to M. E. Stone, who together with the late J. C. Greenfield had been designated the editors of the Cave 4 fragments of ALD for the DJD series. Stone informed me that neither Greenfield nor he considered the fragmentary texts published by Puech to be part of the Qumran ALD. Hence these texts labeled by Puech as 4QTestLévi[c](?) and 4QTestLévi[d](?) have to disappear from the Levi dossier of Qumran.

Stone has also informed me that the Prayer of Levi is now part of 4QLevi[b], as Milik had labeled it initially.[23] That explains why there was no mention of this prayer in the *Le Muséon* article of 1994 devoted to 4QLevi[a] (4Q213). The fragments of 4QLevi[b] have appeared in *Le Muséon*,[24] and the Prayer of Levi is part of it. The further fragmentary texts of ALD have now appeared: 4QLevi[c],[25] 4QLevi[d],[26] 4QLevi[e],[27] and 4QLevi[f].[28]

If I am right, then, this is more or less the state of the question regarding the ALD: one text from Cave 1 (1Q21) and six texts from Cave 4, among which are 4Q213, 4Q213a, 4Q213b, 4Q214, 4Q214a, 4Q214b.[29] This means that seven Qumran texts belong to ALD.

The Aramaic of the Levi Document

In general, one can say that the Aramaic language found in the Levi fragments from Caves 1 and 4 published so far is similar to the Aramaic that we have

---

23. See Milik, "Le Testament de Lévi."

24. M. E. Stone and J. C. Greenfield, "The Second Manuscript of *Aramaic Levi Document from Qumran* (4QLevi[b] aram)," *Le Muséon* 109 (1996) 1-15. See now the *editio princeps* mentioned in n. 20 above. Stone tells me that these fragments are found on PAM 43.242 (five fragments) and 43.243 (one fragment). Cf. *Facsimile Edition*, §1278, 1279.

25. See Stone and Greenfield, "Aramaic Levi Document," in *Qumran Cave 4: XVII*. On PAM 43.242 (one fragment, corresponding to Genizah TL §7-9).

26. On PAM 43.243 (four fragments); cf. *Le Muséon* 109 (1996) 245-59.

27. On PAM 43.260 (three fragments).

28. On PAM 43.260 (remaining eight fragments).

29. In the official listing of the Qumran documents according to photographs and museum plates published by Stephen A. Reed, one still finds the designation "T" (= Testament) for these texts. See *Dead Sea Scroll Inventory Project: Lists of Documents, Photographs and Museum Plates*. Fascicle 10 (Claremont, Calif.: Ancient Biblical Manuscript Center, 1992) 15. No mention is made there of the photograph, which Milik published in *RB* 62 (1955) pl. IV and mentioned in 399 n. 1 (PAM 41.405). On p. 44, however, Reed mentions 4Q213 as TLevi ar[a], appearing on PAM 41.405.

otherwise learned about from other Qumran discoveries. They are good examples of what I have called "Middle Aramaic,"[30] the form of Aramaic in use between 200 B.C. and A.D. 200, or the period when local dialects clearly emerged from the foregoing "Official" or "Standard Aramaic" of 700-200 B.C. Those dialects were the Palestinian or Judean (including Qumran and Murabbaʿat), Nabatean, Palmyrene, Hatran, and Edessene (or Old Syriac). The Qumran form of Aramaic is thus a slight development from the Official or Standard form found in the book of Daniel; it is not yet the form found in the classical targums (*Targum Onqelos* and *Targum Jonathan*) and other rabbinic literature (often called Jewish Palestinian Aramaic or sometimes Galilean Aramaic).

There are now over 120 Aramaic texts from Qumran, many of them fragmentary, which constitute a body of Palestinian Aramaic texts and reveal the creative literary production in that language in the last two centuries B.C. and the first Christian century.[31] They fill in a gap in our knowledge about Aramaic that previously existed, before the discovery of the Dead Sea Scrolls, between the final redaction of the book of Daniel and the earliest of Aramaic rabbinic writings, *Megillat Taʿanit*. For this reason they bear precious testimony to the kind of Aramaic spoken and written in Judea at the turn of the era, as Christianity was emerging.

The reason for discussing the form of Aramaic in which the Qumran ALD appears is to distinguish it from that of the GenTL. In their 1979 article on the GenTL, Greenfield and Stone discussed its language.[32] Earlier P. R. Weis and M. de Jonge had dealt with it,[33] as had P. Grelot.[34] Greenfield and Stone mention that E. Y. Kutscher had refrained from comparing the language of the *Genesis Apocryphon* with that of the GenTL, because he recog-

---

30. See my *The Genesis Apocryphon of Qumran Cave I: A Commentary* (BibOr 18; Rome: Biblical Institute, 1966) 19-20; (2d rev. ed.; BibOr 18A, 1971) 22-23. Cf. my article "The Phases of the Aramaic Language," in *WA* or *SBNT*, 57-84. My classification of the phases of Aramaic has been adopted by no less an Aramaist than E. Y. Kutscher, "Aramaic," in *Current Trends in Linguistics 6: Linguistics in South West Asia and North Africa* (The Hague: Mouton, 1971) 347-412, esp. 347-48.

31. These Qumran texts include copies of biblical texts (Jeremiah, Ezra, Daniel, Tobit), targums (Leviticus, Job), and over a hundred parabiblical writings. The list of them will be found in my article, "Aramaic," in the forthcoming *Encyclopedia of the Dead Sea Scrolls* (New York: Oxford University Press).

32. See Greenfield and Stone, "Remarks," 227-29.

33. "The Fragments of a Jewish Testament of Levi," an appendix to de Jonge's *Testaments of the Twelve Patriarchs*, 129-31, 168-69.

34. P. Grelot, "Le Testament araméen de Lévi"; idem, "Notes sur le Testament araméen de Lévi."

nized that "it was not transmitted in it's [sic] original form."[35] With Kutscher's judgment I readily agree, and I should have no difficulty with the general admission of Greenfield and Stone that "the Aramaic of the Qumran texts is Standard Literary Aramaic,"[36] even though that is not very specific.

Standard Literary Aramaic, however, is a category of the language that Greenfield had proposed earlier,[37] partly in reaction to my own attempt to set forth the phases of the Aramaic language.[38] Greenfield, however, extended the limits of his "Standard Literary Aramaic" to include texts that I would relegate either to "Standard/Official" Aramaic (700-200 B.C.) or to "Late" Aramaic (A.D. 200 on). Whereas Greenfield readily speaks of many dialects in Old Aramaic (900-700 B.C.) and in Official/Standard Aramaic (700-200), he sees "Standard Literary Aramaic" emerging in the latter period. Under this heading he includes the language of the framework story of the Proverbs of Aḥiqar, the Bar Punesh fragment (*AP* 71), the narratives in Ezra and Daniel, the literary works found at Qumran (*Tobit, 1 Enoch, Genesis Apocryphon, Targum of Job*), *Targum Onqelos, Targum Jonathan,* and *Megillat Taʿanit.*[39] In their treatment of the language of the medieval GenTL, Greenfield and Stone include, along with the Qumran texts and the *Targum of Onqelos* and *Targum Jonathan,* even "the Aramaic of the Geniza Testament of Levi"[40] as an example of Standard Literary Aramaic.

Greenfield and Stone cite a number of phrases or expressions found in the GenTL as "typical of Standard Literary Aramaic," even though they admit that the medieval copyist has introduced some "late forms" and "the many first person sg. perfect [forms] which end in *yod.*"[41]

It is, however, just such "late forms" found in the GenTL that clearly distinguish the language in which it has been written from that of the

---

35. See E. Y. Kutscher, "The Language of the 'Genesis Apocryphon': A Preliminary Study," in *Aspects of the Dead Sea Scrolls* (ScrHier 4; ed. C. Rabin and Y. Yadin; Jerusalem: Magnes, 1958) 34.

36. Greenfield and Stone, "Remarks," 227.

37. See J. C. Greenfield, "Standard Literary Aramaic," in *Actes du premier congrès international de linguistique sémitique et chamito-sémitique: Paris 16-19 juillet 1969* (Janua linguarum, series practica 159; ed. A. Caquot and D. Cohen; The Hague/Paris: Mouton, 1974) 280-89. Cf. also his articles, "The Dialects of Early Aramaic," *JNES* 37 (1978) 93-99; "Aramaic and Its Dialects," in *Jewish Languages: Theme and Variations* (ed. H. H. Paper; Cambridge, Mass.: Association for Jewish Studies, 1978) 29-43; "The Languages of Palestine, 200 B.C.E.–200 C.E.," ibid., 143-54.

38. He mentions my attempt in "Standard Literary Aramaic," 281.

39. See "Aramaic and Its Dialects," 34-36.

40. Greenfield and Stone, "Remarks," 228.

41. Ibid., 228-29.

Qumran texts, and these are not merely instances of spelling differences (שׁ replaced by ס, or *aphels* replacing *haphels*) or *scriptio plena* over against earlier *scriptio defectiva*, for there are often genuine morphological differences. There is, of course, an abundance of the characteristic *scriptio plena* of Late Aramaic.[42]

We know today that the Qumran ALD was a writing that does not agree verbatim with the GkTL, or with the important addition to the GkTL from Mount Athos (Koutloumous, Cod. 39), or even with the GenTL. All these texts are seen rather to have been at least revisions of, if not completely new compositions based on, the ancient Jewish Levi text now known to us from the Qumran caves. Consequently, there is no reason to lump the language of the Qumran Levi texts together with that of the medieval GenTL as representatives of a so-called Standard Literary Aramaic. To do so would be to acknowledge that the standard form did not develop in almost a thousand years. The Qumran ALD is for me an example of Middle Aramaic, and the GenTL an example of Late Aramaic, heavily influenced at times even by Late Hebrew, as medieval Aramaic often was.

I shall end this discussion by listing the forms in the Genizah text that differ notably from Qumran Aramaic. Unfortunately, one does not always have exact counterparts in the Qumran ALD, because they are either not extant in the Qumran fragments or occur in the medieval text for the first time, but the GenTL has many words that are examples of Late Aramaic morphology.

First of all, I note the use of the emphatic state of the noun in instances where in Official, Biblical, and Middle Aramaic one would employ the absolute state. Normally, the distinction between the absolute and emphatic states of the noun is still operative in Qumran Aramaic, but the use of the emphatic in the medieval *Testament of Levi* reminds one of its use in Syriac and Jewish Palestinian or Babylonian Talmudic Aramaic.[43] The examples in GenTL are:

---

42. Some examples: קרבית, "I offered" (Bodl a 21); אשלמית, "I finished" (Bodl a 23); בישרא, "flesh" (Bodl b 11); היזדהר, "be on your guard" (Bodl b 14); מיזדהר, "guarding himself" (Bodl c 12); קודם, "before" (= *qŏdām*, Bodl d 16); ביירחה, "in the month" (Camb c 17); טאב, "good" (Camb e 15); רתיכין, "chariots" (= *rětikkîn*, Camb f 19); שׁארי, "he began" (Bodl b 6); זניאן, "harlots" (Bodl b 17); מילי, "words of" (= *millê*, Camb f 15), in contrast to the Qumran מלי (4Q213 5 i 19); מאת, "country" (Camb f 6 [cf. Camb a 15?]), in contrast to מת (4Q213 5 i 15).

43. See T. Nöldeke, *Compendious Syriac Grammar* (London: Williams & Norgate, 1904) 151-52 §202; A. Ungnad, *Syrische Grammatik: Mit Übungsbuch* (2d ed.; Munich: Beck, 1932) 39 §o; C. Levias, *A Grammar of the Aramaic Idiom Contained in the Babylonian Talmud* (Cincinnati: Bloch, 1900) 227 §987; M. L. Margolis, *A Manual of the Aramaic Language of the Babylonian Talmud* (Clavis linguarum semiticarum 3; Munich: Beck, 1910) 62 §43b.

ואנת אנתתא מן משפחתי, "Do take a wife for yourself from my family" (Bodl b 16).[44]

וילידת לי ברתא, "and she bore me a daughter" (Camb c 19);

ותהוי חוכמתא עמכון ליקר עלם, "and let wisdom be with you for ever-lasting glory" (Camb e 19 [similarly e 20,21]). The last instance stands in contrast to the absolute state in מוסר חוכמה, "the instruction of wisdom," where the construct chain would have tolerated the emphatic state.

די אליף חוכמתא, "whoever studies wisdom" (Camb e 20), which stands in contrast to its Qumran counterpart, די אלף חכמה (4Q213 1 i 10).

Second, even though the normal Aramaic form of the first singular perfect form is found in GenTL (e.g., אמרת, "I said" [Bodl a 10]; ענית ואמרת, "I spoke up and said" [Camb e 7]), the use of a Hebraic form, ending in *yod*, as a substitute is striking and noteworthy:

חזיתי, "I saw," instead of חזית (Bodl c 12; cf. Camb c [5]; e 2);

וקריתי, "and I called" (Camb d 10; e 5; cf. Camb c [5]);

הויתי, "I was" (Camb d 21,23);

שריתי, "I began" (Camb e 6);

שויתי, "I put" (Camb c 19).

Such Hebraic forms are found in the Late Aramaic of the Babylonian Talmud and elsewhere.[45]

Third, the usual verb "to see" in Late Aramaic, which is חמא instead of חזא, appears in והתחמיון כו[אתן], "and be seen like us" (Camb a 22).

Fourth, though the following forms may seem at first sight to be merely instances of late *scriptio plena*, they are in reality morphologically different. They are forms with an initial *'alep*, which in earlier stages of the Aramaic language were vocalized with a reduced vowel or *shewa*, so that the entire first

---

44. It has often been thought that משפחה, "family," was a borrowed Hebraism in this medieval text; but it has turned up in the Aramaic of 4QTob[a] 2:9 (see DJD, 19:8).

45. See Levias, *Grammar of the Aramaic Idiom*, 62 §203. The examples cited are all third-weak verbs. Forms of this sort are also found at times in *Targum Onqelos* (e.g., Gen 32:30), but that is merely a sign that this targum also belongs to the phase of Late Aramaic. See G. Dalman, *Grammatik des jüdisch-palästinischen Aramäisch* (Darmstadt: Wissenschaftliche Buchgesellschaft, 1960) 343. Such an ending (תי-) is to be regarded as a Hebraism even in *Targum Onqelos;* it is a sign of the invasion of Hebraic forms into normal Aramaic in this late stage.

syllable was in time syncopated. Thus the well-known instance of אֱנָשׁ, "human being, man," which in Late Aramaic became simply נָשׁ, or in Syriac, where the 'alep was still written, it was fitted with a *linea occultans* and not pronounced. There was, however, another treatment of the initial aleph in Late Aramaic: the fitting it out with a full vowel, in order to preserve the 'alep and the first syllable. Thus אֱנָשׁ, which was then written fully with an added *yodh:* אֵינָשׁ. This form occurs in GenTL (Bodl a 13) and stands in contrast to its Qumran counterpart אֱנָשׁ (4Q213 3:3). Related to it in this regard are the following words: אינון, "they" ('ênûn or 'ênôn, Camb a 20, b 20; Bodl c 10,16,20), instead of earlier 'innûn, which developed in time a secondary 'ĕnôn.

Fifth, in GenTL one finds the use of the late pronominal suffix of the first plural, -*nan* (developed from the enclitic *ḥănan* and the full form *'ănaḥnan*), instead of the earlier -*nā'*, which is also at times retained in this medieval text. Thus אברהם אבונן, "Abraham, our ancestor," alongside the earlier form, יצחק אבונה, "Isaac, our father" (Bodl b 2-3); cf. אחונן, "our brother" (Camb b 22).

The same phenomenon is also found on a verb: אמרנן, "we said" (Camb a 19).

Lastly, there are clear Hebraisms that have been introduced into the medieval Aramaic text, a further well-known feature in the late form of the language that Aramaic had become in the Middle Ages. Thus:

זנות, "harlotry, fornication" (Bodl b 16), instead of absolute זנו;
כבוד, "glory, honor" (Camb c 21);
חודשא, "month" (with an Aramaic ending, Camb c 23);
והיה, "and there was" (Camb c 16);
כילי, "villain, scoundrel" (Camb f 10)

CHAPTER 11

The Qumran Community: Essene or Sadducean?

Ever since the first days of the discovery of the scrolls in Qumran Cave 1 in 1947 and especially since the publication of its rule book, the *Manual of Discipline,* in 1951 and of other sectarian writings, the identification of the Qumran community with the Essenes has been in vogue. In fact, it is the identification most often encountered among scholars even today. Eleazar Lipa Sukenik, professor at the Hebrew University in Jerusalem, who had acquired three of the seven scrolls discovered in Qumran Cave 1, was apparently the first to propose this identification, as far as one can ascertain today.[1] The French scholar André Dupont-Sommer seems to have made the same identification independently of Sukenik,[2] and many other reputable scholars engaged in the study of the Qumran texts have since espoused this identification.

Once, however, fuller knowledge of the Cave 4 text called *miqṣāt ma'ăśê hattôrāh,* "Some Deeds of the Law" (4QMMT), was revealed in the last decade,[3] some scholars sought to challenge the Essene identification of the

---

1. See Y. Yadin, *The Message of the Scrolls* (ed. J. H. Charlesworth; New York: Crossroad, 1992; originally published 1957) 176.

2. J. Dupont-Sommer, *Aperçus préliminaires sur les manuscrits de la Mer Morte* (L'Orient Ancien Illustré 4; Paris: Maisonneuve, 1950) 106-17. Cf. H. H. Rowley, *The Zadokite Fragments and the Dead Sea Scrolls* (Oxford: Blackwell, 1952) 78-79.

3. It had been called by J. T. Milik in earlier times 4QMišnique[a-f] (M. Baillet, J. T. Milik, and R. de Vaux, *Les 'Petites grottes' de Qumrân* [DJD 3; Oxford: Clarendon, 1962] 222). Eventually, more detailed preliminary reports were published in E. Qimron and J. Strugnell, "An Unpublished Halakhic Letter from Qumran," in *Biblical Archaeology To-*

Qumran community and to propose that it was, rather, Sadducean. In order to discuss this matter adequately, I have to treat the following five topics: (1) the new Qumran text 4QMMT; (2) the Zadokite character of the Qumran community; (3) the Mishnaic צדוקים and the Sadducees; (4) the Qumran community and the Sadducees; (5) and the Qumran community and the Essenes.

The New Qumran Text 4QMMT

4QMMT is a text reconstructed from six fragmentary documents (4Q394-4Q399), the beginning of which seems to have been calendaric but is almost completely lost and the end of which, the epilogue, contains the phrase that is used as its title. It was written by a group of Jews who spoke in the first plural and addressed their communication to an opponent, a leader of their adversaries: אנחנו כתבנו עליך, "we have written to you [sg.]. . . ." The writers of the letter also incorporated into it some twenty specific instances of "deeds of the law," or halakhic interpretations of certain prescriptions of Mosaic legislation, which, they insisted, were necessary in the pursuit of righteousness in God's sight, but which, they implied, their adversaries were disregarding. The epilogue of the halakhic letter runs as follows:

> Remember David, who was a man of pious deeds and who was also delivered from many afflictions, and pardon was granted him. Moreover, we have written to you (about) some of the precepts of the law (מקצת מעשי התורה), which we consider for your welfare and that of your people, because w[e recognize] (that) you have prudence and knowledge of the law. Consider well all these (things) and seek from Him good counsel that He may keep you far from evil plots and the scheming of Belial, so that you

---

day: *Proceedings of the International Congress on Biblical Archaeology Jerusalem, April 1984* (Jerusalem: Israel Exploration Society, 1985) 400-27, 429-31. A shorter form of that report, with the same title, can be found in *Israel Museum Journal* 4 (1985) 9-12. A transcription of the text of 4QMMT along with an English translation was published as "An Anonymously Received Pre-Publication of 4QMMT," *QC* 2 (1990), Appendix A (pp. 1-9). That transcription and translation were reproduced in the "Publisher's Foreword" (written by H. Shanks) in R. H. Eisenman and J. M. Robinson, eds., *A Facsimile Edition of the Dead Sea Scrolls Prepared with an Introduction and Index* (2 vols.; Washington, D.C.: Biblical Archaeology Society, 1991) xxxi. The official publication of the text has now appeared: E. Qimron and J. Strugnell, *Qumran Cave 4: V. Miqsat ma'aśe ha-torah* (DJD 10; Oxford: Clarendon, 1994). Cf. Z. J. Kapera, "A Preliminary Bibliography of 4QMMT: 1956-1990," *QC* 2 (1990), Appendix (pp. 10-12).

may rejoice at the end of time, as you find that some of our words (are) right. It will be reckoned to you as righteousness, as you do what is upright and good before Him for your welfare and (that) of Israel. (C 25-32)[4]

What is noteworthy in this paragraph is the relation of "deeds of the law" to the pursuit of "righteousness." On the one hand, the authors of this letter were not mincing words in the criticism of their opponents' failure to carry out the requisite deeds. On the other hand, the letter provides an important pre-Christian Judean background for Paul's criticism of ἔργα νόμου, "deeds/ works of the law," and his view of their relation to the pursuit of righteousness in God's sight among contemporary Jews (or among Christians who might be inclined to adopt such a view).[5] It shows that Paul knew whereof he spoke when he criticized fellow Christian Jews for their attempts to insist on the pursuit of righteousness by carrying out deeds of the law.

Since six fragmentary copies of 4QMMT were found in Qumran Cave 4, that is a good sign that the composition of it was sectarian and reflected the thinking of the Qumran community itself about Jews who did not agree with them and were not part of their number. Just who the adversary leader addressed was or who the opponents were is not evident from the fragmentary document itself, but they seem to have been contemporary influential Jews. They could have been priests serving in the Jerusalem Temple,[6] or they could have been leaders of the Pharisees.

In fact, they have been identified specifically with the Pharisees, because Pharisees have been understood in other Qumran texts as adversaries of the community. Such opponents are often called in Qumran texts *dôrĕšê haḥălāqôt*, "Seekers after Smooth Things" (דורשי החלקות, 1QH 2:15, 32, 4:10; 4QpNah 3-4 i 2, 7; 3-4 ii 2; 3-4 iii 3, 6-7; cf. CD 1:18). This epithet seems to have been a derisive term, used by members of the Qumran community for Pharisees because of their alleged insistence on *hălākôt*, "regulations" (of conduct). Now the writers of 4QMMT would be insisting on the observance of still other מעשי התורה, "deeds of the law," which they deemed necessary in the pursuit of righteousness.

The identification of the opponents addressed in 4QMMT with the Pharisees has also been suggested by scholars who think that the controversy reflected in 4QMMT is the same as, or at least similar to, that which explicitly involves Pharisees in later rabbinic literature. Some of the items recom-

---

4. Qimron and Strugnell, *Qumran Cave 4: V,* 62.

5. Rom 2:15; 3:20, 27-28; Gal 2:16; 3:2, 5, 10. See further J. A. Fitzmyer, *According to Paul: Studies in the Theology of the Apostle* (New York/Mahwah, N.J.: Paulist, 1993) 18-35.

6. See 1QpHab 9:4 for criticism of "the last priests of Jerusalem."

mended in 4QMMT for observance are similar to those in the controversy recorded in various Mishnaic tractates. For instance, one finds in the Mishnah such sentences as אומרים צדוקים קובלים אנו עליכם פרושים, "The Ṣdwqym say, 'We protest against you, Pharisees, . . .'" (*m. Yadaim* 4:6; cf. 4:8).

This rabbinic evidence concerning the Pharisees has become, in fact, the main argument used today by scholars who advocate the Sadducean identification of the Qumran community. It is important because it reveals that the same sort of halakhic dispute which is recorded in rabbinic literature of the third and fourth centuries A.D. was already taking place among Palestinian Jews of the second-first centuries B.C. or the first century A.D. Such debate over differing interpretations of prescriptions of the Mosaic law and of conduct regulated by it is clearly attested in 4QMMT and is shown to have existed in the days before the destruction of Jerusalem and its Temple and well before the codification of halakhic regulations under Rabbi Judah the Prince in the early years of the third century A.D. So 4QMMT may well be aimed at the contemporary precursors of the rabbinic tradition, the Pharisaic Sages, mentioned in such Mishnaic texts. There is little that one can deny in this identification, for it is not only plausible, given the evidence that one has in both the Qumran and rabbinic literature, but also because it identifies the adversaries of 4QMMT with one of the main contemporary groups of Palestinian Jews described by Josephus.[7]

That the Qumran Jewish community would have differed with contemporary Pharisees is not surprising. Whether one explains the origin of the Qumran community as a development of Hasideans, who were originally associated with the Maccabees but broke off from them and who are mentioned in 1 Macc 2:42,[8] or as a group of Jews who returned from the Babylonian Captivity in mid-second century B.C., having heard about the Maccabean revolt and been disappointed at the kind of Jewish life that they encountered in Palestine on their return,[9] makes little difference, as far as the present question is concerned. The Qumran community apparently attached greater importance to the strict observance of the Mosaic law than did their contemporary Jewish colleagues in Judea, and 4QMMT bears testimony to that conviction.

---

7. Josephus describes the rise of the Pharisees in his *Jewish War* (1.5.2 §110) first in the time of Queen Alexandra (78-69 B.C.), but in his *Antiquities* (13.5.9 §171) he speaks of them flourishing already in the time of King Jonathan (160-143 B.C.). The latter seems to be more correct. Cf. G. Stemberger, *Pharisäer, Sadduzäer, Essener* (SBS 144; Stuttgart: Katholisches Bibelwerk, 1991).

8. As explained by F. M. Cross, *The Ancient Library of Qumran* (3d ed.; Minneapolis: Fortress; Sheffield: Sheffield Academic Press, 1995) chap. 3.

9. As explained by J. Murphy-O'Connor, "The Essenes and Their History," *RB* 81 (1974) 215-44; idem, "The Essenes in Palestine," *BA* 40 (1977) 100-124.

The Zadokite Character of the Qumran Community

The Jews who wrote the sectarian literature found in the Qumran caves often refer to themselves as (הכוהנים) בני צדוק, "sons of Zadok (the priests)" (1QS 5:2, 9; 1QSa 1:2, 24; 2:3; 1QSb 3:22; 4QFlorilegium [4Q174] 1-2 i 17; CD 3:21; 4:3; 4QpIsa^c [4Q163] 22:3).[10] The title בני צדוק, "sons of Zadok," indicates that at least some of the members of the Qumran community came from priestly families descended from Zadok, but the problem is, Which Zadok?

The Old Testament knows of a צדוק who was a priest in the time of David (2 Sam 8:17; 15:24, 27, 29, 35; 17:15; 19:12; 1 Chr 12:29; 29:22). He supported Solomon in the strife over the succession of David, and when Solomon became king, Zadok became the chief priest in Jerusalem, and his rival Abiathar was banished (see 1 Kgs 1:32, 34; 2:35). From Zadok was established the priestly line that served in the Jerusalem Temple for generations and that supported the reforms of Josiah (cf. Ezek 40:46; 43:19; 44:10-15). The Zadokite Joshua ben Josedech became the high priest after the Babylonian Captivity (cf. 1 Chr 5:29-34 for Zadokites who trace their lineage to Aaron via Phinehas; Sir 45:25; 51:12). Such sons of Zadok continued their hierocratic rule in Jerusalem until the time of the Maccabees.

Then the Seleucid ruler Alexander I Balas appointed Jonathan as high priest, and from him stemmed the Hasmonean priestly dynasty, which supplanted the Zadokite line. Apparently members of the Zadokite priestly families were among those who founded the Qumran community, the "sons of Zadok," who were "the elect of Israel, called by name, who arose in the latter days" (CD 4:3). They seem to have considered the Hasmonean dynasty serving in Jerusalem as tainted: "the last priests of Jerusalem who pile up for themselves wealth and gain from the booty of the nations" (1QpHab 9:4-5). The Qumran texts give the impression that such Zadokite priests formed the nucleus of the community that settled at Qumran. They were the "the sons of Zadok, the priests that keep the covenant" (1QS 5:2, 9).

The rabbinic tradition, however, traces the Sadducees to a Zadok, the pupil of Antigonus of Socoh (*Abot de-Rabbi Nathan* 5). If that tradition were correct, then one would wonder whether the Sadducees of the first centuries B.C. and A.D. were so called because of any connection with Zadok, priest in the time of David, to which the Zadokite line traced its affinity. This ambiguity has to be reckoned with.

Since some instances of the title "sons of Zadok" occur in the *Damascus Document*, which was found in the Cairo Genizah in 1896, one is not sur-

10. Possibly also 1QS 9:14, depending on how it is read.

prised at early attempts to identify the community mentioned in that text with Judaeo-Christians,[11] or Dositheans,[12] or Pharisees,[13] or even the medieval Karaites.[14] Most of these attempts antedated the discovery of the Qumran scrolls, but even in 1955 R. North toyed with the idea that possibly the Qumran community might have been Sadducean.[15] Now Joseph M. Baumgarten has raised the question again,[16] and Lawrence H. Schiffman has espoused that identification explicitly.[17]

There are, however, many problems with this proposal, and that leads me to my third point.

11. So G. Margoliouth, "The Sadducean Christians of Damascus," *Athenaeum* (London) 4335 (26 November 1910) 657-59.

12. So S. Schechter, who first published the text in *Documents of Jewish Sectaries* (2 vols.; Cambridge: Cambridge University Press, 1910; reprinted in one volume, New York: Ktav, 1970) xxvi (or p. 58). Cf. J. Schousboe, *La secte juive de l'Alliance Nouvelle au pays de Damas et le christianisme naissant* (Copenhagen: Munksgaard, 1942) 52-68.

13. So W. H. Ward, "The 'Zadokite Document,'" *BSac* 68 (1911) 429-56, esp. 449; C. Rabin, *Qumran Studies* (Scripta Judaica 2; Oxford: Oxford University Press, 1957) passim. Rabin also ascribes this interpretation to L. Ginzberg (see *Monatsschrift zur Geschichte und Wissenschaft des Judentums* 47 [1913] 289), but cf. L. Ginzberg, *An Unknown Jewish Sect* (New York: Jewish Theological Seminary of America, 1976) 407-8.

14. So A. Büchler, "Schechter's 'Jewish Sectaries,'" *JQR* ns 3 (1912-13) 429-85; S. Zeitlin, "'A Commentary on the Book of Habakkuk': Important Discovery or Hoax?" *JQR* 39 (1948-49) 234-47, esp. 238. For a refutation of Büchler's views, see Ginzberg, *An Unknown Jewish Sect*, 338-408.

15. He did not reject the then commonly acknowledged Essene identification, but studied "The Qumran 'Sadducees,'" *CBQ* 17 (1955) 44-68 (164-88). That Sadducean identification of the Jews mentioned in the *Damascus Document* was actually used earlier by R. Leszynsky, *Die Sadduzäer* (Berlin: Mayer und Müller, 1912) 142-67; cf. the review of this book by F. Perles, *OLZ* 16 (1913) 417-19.

16. See J. M. Baumgarten, "The Pharisaic-Sadducean Controversies about Purity and the Qumran Texts," *JJS* 31 (1980) 157-70; idem, "Sadducean Elements in Qumran Law," in *The Community of the Renewed Covenant: The Notre Dame Symposium on the Dead Sea Scrolls* (ed. E. Ulrich and J. VanderKam; Notre Dame: University of Notre Dame Press, 1994) 27-36.

17. See L. H. Schiffman, "*Miqṣat maʿaśeh ha-torah* and the *Temple Scroll*," *RevQ* 14 (1989-90) 435-57, esp. 457; idem, "The New Halakhic Letter (4QMMT) and the Origins of the Dead Sea Sect," *BA* 53 (1990) 64-73, esp. 69; idem, "The Temple Scroll and the Systems of Jewish Law of the Second Temple Period," in *Temple Scroll Studies: Papers Presented at the International Symposium on the Temple Scroll, Manchester, December 1987* (JSPSup 7; ed. G. J. Brooke; Sheffield: JSOT Press, 1989) 239-55; idem, "The Temple Scroll and the Nature of Its Law: The Status of the Question," in Ulrich and VanderKam, eds., *The Community of the Renewed Covenant*, 37-55, esp. p. 54. Cf. H. Burgmann, "11QT: The Sadducean Torah," in Brooke, ed., *Temple Scroll Studies*, 257-63.

The Mishnaic צדוקים and the Sadducees

There is, first of all, the problem in rabbinic literature itself, whether those who were in controversy with the Pharisees or the Sages of the Mishnah were indeed "Sadducees." This is taken for granted in many modern editions of the Mishnah and in discussions of this rabbinic controversy. It is, however, far from clear.

Second, there is no doubt that צדוקים or צדוקין occurs in Mishnaic tractates. It is found in *m. Erubin* 6:2; *m. Makkoth* 1:6; *m. Niddah* 4:2; *m. Parah* 3:3, 7; *m. Yadaim* 4:6, 7. It is also found in some texts of the Mishnah (*m. Berakoth* 9:5 and *m. Yadaim* 4:8), where variants occur.[18]

Third, the occurrence of the name is problematic, because in the original tradition the name would have been unvocalized, appearing merely in the consonants צדוקים or צדוקין. Yet how were those consonants pronounced?

a. Some manuscripts and modern editions of the Mishnah simply vocalize them as צְדוּקִים or צְדוּקִין, *Ṣaddûqîm* or *Ṣaddûqîn,* understanding the name as "Sadducees," without questioning the correctness of such a vocalization. So the important Kaufmann manuscript of the Mishnah; also the editions of the Mishnah published by H. Albeck, P. Blackman, and others.[19] This

---

18. In the last two texts mentioned, one finds at times מינים or מינין, "heretics." The צדוקים or צדוקין are also mentioned in the later Talmuds and midrashim, but those later references depend on the Mishnaic occurrences and hardly supply any additional material relevant to the discussion about the meaning of the name in relation to the Qumran community.

19. See G. Beer, *Faksimile-Ausgabe des Mischnacodex Kaufmann A 50* (2 vols.; Jerusalem: [no publisher], 1968) 1:106; 2:305, 511, 542, 568 (bis). In one instance (*m. Yadaim* 4:6 [2:567]) this manuscript has the vocalization צְדוּקִים. Also H. Albeck, *Shishah Sidre Mishnah* (6 vols.; 4th ed.; Tel Aviv/Jerusalem: Bialik Institute, 1957-58) 2:107; 4:221; 6:262, 264, 386, 485, 486 (bis); P. Blackman, *Mishnayoth* (7 vols.; New York: Judaica Press, 1964) 1:72; 2:130; 4:306-7; 6:416, 418, 612, 771-72. With this view agree H. Danby, *The Mishnah Translated from the Hebrew with Introduction and Brief Explanatory Notes* (Oxford: Oxford University Press, 1993) 10, 129, 213, 402, 700, 748, 784; D. A. DeSola and M. J. Raphall, *Eighteen Treatises from the Mishna* (2d ed.; London: Sherwood, Gilbert, and Piper, 1845) 366-67; W. Nowack, *'Erubin* (Die Mischna 2/2; Giessen: Töpelmann, 1926) 58-59; S. Kraus, *Sanhedrin-Makkôt* (Die Mischna 4/4-5; Giessen: Töpelmann, 1933) 320-21; H. L. Strack, *Sanhedrin-Makkoth: Die Mišnatraktate über Strafrecht und Gerichtsverfahren* (Leipzig: Hinrichs, 1910) 33*, 46; D. Hoffmann, *Mischnaiot: Die sechs Ordnungen der Mischna . . . Theil IV Seder Nesikin* (Berlin: Itzkowski, 1898) 202; B. Z. Barslai, *Nidda* (Die Mischna 6/7; Berlin: de Gruyter, 1980) 68-69; G. Mayer, *Para* (Die Mischna 6/4; Berlin: Töpelmann, 1964) 50-51 (but contrast pp. 46-47 on 3:3). Similarly a Parma manuscript of the Mishna: *Mishna Codex Parma (De Rossi 138): An Early Vowelized Manuscript of the Complete Mishna Text* (2 vols.; Jerusalem: Kedem Publishing, 1970) passim, even though it some-

is a vestige of the interpretation of the Mishnah that antedates the discovery in 1896 of the *Damascus Document* in the Cairo Genizah. Before that discovery it was natural to understand צדוקים or צדוקין as צְּדּוּקִים, "Sadducees," because that was the only Jewish group whose name was known from either the New Testament or the writings of Josephus and suited the consonants in the Mishnaic tractates. It has been argued that, because the vocalization צְדּוּקִים is found also in the Yemenite Jewish tradition,[20] it would be independent either of Christian influence or of Josephus's Greek writings. That argument sounds plausible at first, but the manuscript is not of early date, and Yemenite tradition of vocalization really cannot be traced.

b. Other editions merely leave the consonants unvocalized, such as manuscript Parma C and the editions of G. Surenhusius and W. H. Lowe.[21] These texts bear witness to the original unvocalized character of the Mishnaic text.

c. Still others vocalize it, perhaps anomalously, as צָדוֹקִים or צָדוֹקִין.[22] One may debate whether this form of vocalization is meant as a substitute for *Ṣaddûqîm(n)* or testimony to a different way of understanding the consonants, that is, not Sadducean.

d. Significantly enough, it is also vocalized as צָדוֹקִים or צָדוֹקִין in the Paris manuscript of the Mishnah.[23] This may be a way of writing "Zadokites."

What, then, would have been the correct original vocalization of the name? This review of different manuscripts and editions of the Mishnah points up the problem. It reveals that it is far from certain that the controversy of the צדוקים or צדוקין with the Pharisees in rabbinic literature actually concerned Saducees.

---

times leaves the name unvocalized (p. 185ᵛ); J. Neusner, *The Mishnah: A New Translation* (New Haven/London: Yale University Press, 1988) 218, 611, 1016, 1017, 1082, 1130 (bis).

20. See *Sidre ha-Mishnah Nezikin, Kodashim, Tohorot: Ketav-yad Yerushalayim 4 Heb. 1336: Ketav-yad be-nikud lefi masorot Teman (The Mishnah Tractates Neziqin Qodashim Teharoth: Codex Jerusalem Heb 4° 1336: A Manuscript Vocalized according to the Yemenite Tradition)* (ed. S. Morag; Jerusalem: Makor, 1970).

21. *Mishna Codex Parma 'C'- De Rossi 984: Sedarim Nashim Nezikin with the Hebrew Version of Maimonides' Commentary* (Jerusalem: Makor, 1971) 362; G. Surenhusius (Willem Surenhuys), *Mischna sive totius Hebraeorum iuris, rituum, antiquitatum, ac legum oralium systema . . .* (6 vols.; Amsterdam: G. & J. Borstius, 1698-1703) 2:108; 4:272; 6:275, 277, 399, 490, 491 (bis); W. H. Lowe, *The Mishnah on Which the Palestinian Talmud Rests* (2 vols.; Cambridge: Cambridge University Press, 1883), passim; *Šsh sdry mšnh* (2 vols.; Brooklyn: Moriah, 1976), passim; *Mšnywt* (Tipheret Yisrael edition; 6 vols.; New York: Om, 1947 [reprint of Wilna edition of 1891]).

22. See G. Lisowsky, *Jadaim* (Die Mischna 6/11; Berlin: Töpelmann, 1956) 72-77.

23. See *Mšnh ktb yd p'rys (p'rys 328-329): Mishna — Codex Paris (Paris 328-329)* (ed. M. Bar Asher; 3 vols.; Jerusalem: Makor, 1973) 212, 558, 1071, 1073, 1152, 1209-10.

Fourth, if this is so, then *a fortiori* there is no certainty either that the controversy reflected in 4QMMT had anything to do with Sadducees. The Qumran community, which was almost certainly behind the composition of 4QMMT, which addressed its observations about "deeds of the law" in the pursuit of righteousness to opponents who were undoubtedly Pharisees, and which called itself "sons of Zadok, the priests," was most likely the Jewish group to which the Sages of the Mishnah were referring, when they wrote about צדוקים or צדוקין, i.e., צְדוֹקִים! In other words, the title that Solomon Schechter originally put on what we call the *Damascus Document* today was undoubtedly correct, "Fragments of a Zadokite Work."[24] That title rightly labeled the community that we now know from the Qumran scrolls and that referred to itself as "sons of Zadok," or Zadokites.

If there is any validity to these observations, then it follows that the identification proposed by Lawrence H. Schiffman that the Qumran community was Sadducean cannot be correct. Joseph M. Baumgarten, who was reluctant to support that identification outright, was right when in his hesitation he queried, "Could it be that the צְדוֹקִים who are portrayed in the Mishnah as complaining about Pharisaic laxities in the sphere of purity were not the aristocratic Sadducees but heterodox rigorists of the 'Zadokite' type?"[25] My answer to that query is, "Of course!" The צְדוֹקִים mentioned in the Mishnah were the Qumran community, and that form of the name was merely the Mishnaic sages' way of referring to the בני צדוק, the name used by the Qumran community in its own sectarian writings. Possibly, too, Albert Baumgarten was also right when he wrote that the Rabbis were no longer aware of the distinction between the Qumran Zadokites and the Sadducees,[26] but that seems somewhat farfetched in my opinion. It appears more likely that the sages of the Mishnah simply transposed the Qumran name בני צדוק into a more contemporary Hebrew form, צְדוֹקִים or צְדוֹקִים. So the question of Sadducees in controversy with Pharisees in the Mishnaic and later rabbinic writings must simply disappear. The controversy was rather between the sages of the Mishnah (the descendants of the Pharisees) and the צְדוֹקִים, that is, בני צדוק of the Qumran community, the Zadokites, or possibly their descendants.

---

24. See Schechter, *Documents of Jewish Sectaries.*

25. See J. M. Baumgarten, "Pharisaic-Sadducean Controversies," 167.

26. A. Baumgarten, "Qumran and Jewish Sectarianism during the Second Temple Period," in *The Scrolls of the Judaean Desert: Forty Years of Research* (ed. M. Broshi et al.; Jerusalem: Bialik Institute and the Israel Exploration Society, 1992) 139-51.

The Qumran Community and the Sadducees

Evidence for the Qumran community being Sadducean, apart from the above considerations, is, moreover, simply not forthcoming. There are many other difficulties with which one would have to cope in trying to identify the Qumran community with what little is known of the contemporary Sadducees and their tenets. No one would deny that there were Sadducees around at that time, since both Josephus and the New Testament attest their existence and tell us a bit about their differing tenets. There would be problems, however, in trying to predicate of the Qumran community some of the ideas that these sources attribute to Sadducees.

For example, the New Testament ascribes to Sadducees a denial of the resurrection of the dead (Mark 12:18; Matt 22:23; Luke 20:27; Acts 4:2; 23:8), and perhaps a denial of the existence of spirits or angels (Acts 23:8). Josephus concurs in the denial of the resurrection (*Ant.* 18.1.4 §16; *J.W.* 2.8.14 §165). How such Sadducean tenets would fit in with ideas about spirits and angels found in Qumran writings (e.g., 1QS 3:20-24; 4:12; 1QM 1:15; 7:6; 10:11; 12:1, 4, 8; 13:11) or even with Qumran teaching about the afterlife and resurrection is hard to say.[27] The latter would be a special problem in view of the recently published Qumran fragment, the so-called Messianic Apocalypse (4Q521), which speaks of the Lord curing the wounded, raising to life the dead, and evangelizing the poor.[28]

Again, Josephus maintained that the Sadducees "claimed no observance whatsoever of anything but the laws" (i.e., the written laws of the Pentateuch, *Ant.* 18.1.4 §16). How that detail would be squared with the Qumran community's laws and elaborate rulebooks is problematic indeed.

Moreover, Josephus stated that the Sadducees would have nothing to do with the idea of fate (ἡ εἱμαρμένη, *Ant.* 13.5.9 §173). That is a Greek term that he uses to make intelligible for his non-Jewish readers what Jews of his day would have understood as predestination. Yet how such a denial would be consonant with the Qumran community's insistence in God's foreknowledge and predetermination of all things in the conduct of their lives (1QS 3:13–4:1; 1QH 15:13-20) is not evident.

Furthermore, in view of the Qumran community's insistence on the ob-

---

27. See E. Puech, *La croyance des Esséniens en la vie future: Immortalité, résurrection, vie éternelle? Histoire d'une croyance dans le judaïsme ancien* (2 vols.; Etudes bibliques ns 21-22; Paris: Gabalda, 1993) 202-9. Cf. G. G. Stroumsa, "Le couple de l'ange et de l'esprit: Traditions juives et chrétiennes," *RB* 88 (1981) 42-61, esp. 51-52, 57-60.

28. See E. Puech, "Une apocalypse messianique," *RevQ* 15 (1991-92) 475-522 (+ pls. 1-3), esp. 485 (frg. 2 ii + 4, line 12); see pp. 36-37 above.

servance of the Sabbath and feasts according to the solar calendar, as it is used in the *Book of Jubilees*, 11QPsalms^a 27:6-7, and other Qumran writings, it is difficult to reconcile such calendric observance with Sadducean practice.

Years ago Louis Ginzberg, in his discussion of the *Damascus Document*, thoroughly refuted the idea that the sect that composed its text could have been Sadducean. He went so far as to state: "There is not to be found in our document [i.e., in CD] *a single Halakah that we are justified in pronouncing Sadducean.*"[29] As far as I can see, that judgment still holds true after the publication of all the other Qumran sectarian texts, which now have to be related to the *Damascus Document.*

It is one thing to say that the Qumran community and the Sadducees held certain views or interpretations of Scripture in common, but quite another to say that the Jews of Qumran were Sadducees. For instance, both groups held to the same interpretation of Lev 23:11, 15, in determining when "the day after the Sabbath" would occur, as Joseph M. Baumgarten has noted,[30] but that does not mean that the Jews of Qumran were Sadducees.

The Qumran Community and the Essenes

The evidence of the Qumran writings is such that it supports and agrees with, by and large, the description of the Essenes provided by the contemporary Jewish writer, Flavius Josephus.[31] His testimony has been well studied and presented by Todd S. Beall, who compared it in detail with the firsthand Qumran evidence now available in the Scrolls about the Jews of Qumran.[32]

---

29. Ginzberg, *An Unknown Jewish Sect,* 134 (his emphasis).

30. See J. M. Baumgarten, "Sadducean Elements," 34.

31. See esp. *J.W.* 2.8.2 §119-61; *Ant.* 18.1.2, 5 §11, 18-22; *Life* 1.2 §10-12, and other passages of lesser moment. Cf. G. Vermes and M. D. Goodman, *The Essenes according to the Classical Sources* (Oxford Centre Textbooks 1; Sheffield: JSOT Press, 1989) passim.

32. T. S. Beall, *Josephus' Description of the Essenes Illustrated by the Dead Sea Scrolls* (SNTSMS 58; Cambridge: Cambridge University Press, 1988). Beall admits that the identification is not 100 percent certain, but he shows that the vast majority (close to 90 percent) of the details mentioned by Josephus can be documented in the Qumran texts. The result is that there can be little doubt that the Qumran community was related to the Essenes about whom Josephus wrote, even if Josephus himself never hints that they had settled at a spot in the Judean desert on the northwest shore of the Dead Sea, where their community center and cemetery have been found. About that we know from the testimony of Pliny the Elder (*Natural History* 5.15.73). Cf. J. M. Baumgarten's final conclusions in "Sadducean Elements," 35-36; also his article, "The Disqualifications of Priests in 4Q Fragments of the 'Damascus Document,' a Specimen of the Recovery of pre-Rabbinic Halakha," in *The Ma-*

The upshot of his discussion is that the best identification of the Qumran community is still that which early students of the Dead Sea Scrolls have always proposed, namely, the Essene identification.[33]

Consequently, one simply has to forget about the Sadducean identification of the Qumran community suggested in recent times, since the evidence for it is simply not forthcoming. We know so little about the Sadducees that it is useless to try to impose their name on the Jews of Qumran.[34]

---

drid Qumran Congress: Proceedings of the International Congress on the Dead Sea Scrolls, Madrid 18-21 March, 1991 (STDJ 11/1-2; ed. J. Trebolle Barrera and L. Vegas Montaner; Madrid: Editorial Complutense; Leiden: Brill, 1992) 2:503-13, esp. 513.

33. This identification has recently been called in question by L. Cansdale, Qumran and the Essenes: A Re-Evaluation of the Evidence (TSAJ 60; Tübingen: Mohr Siebeck, 1997). The book, however, is a classic example of a petitio principii and has scarcely coped with the arguments of Beall mentioned above. See the reviews of Cansdale's book by E. Puech, RevQ 18 (1997-99) 437-41; J. Magness, DSD 5/1 (1998) 99-104; and my review in JBL 118 (1999) 731-33.

34. See further D. R. Schwartz, "Law and Truth: On Qumran-Sadducean and Rabbinic Views of Law," in The Dead Sea Scrolls: Forty Years of Research (STDJ 10; ed. D. Dimant and U. Rappaport; Leiden: Brill, 1992) 229-40.

CHAPTER 12

The Gathering In of the Teacher of the Community

Two passages in the *Damascus Document* have normally been interpreted as referring to the "gathering in," that is, the death, of the Teacher of the Qumran community. The first, CD 19:33–20:1, reads as follows:

כן כל האנשים אשר באו בברית [34]החדשה בארץ דמשק ושבו ויבגדו
ויסורו מבאר מים החיים: [35]לא יחשבו בסוד עם ובכתבם לא יכתבו
מיום האסף {. . .} [20:1]מורה היחיד עד עמוד משיח מאהרון ומישראל

This passage is usually translated thus:

So all the men who entered the new covenant [34]in the land of Damascus and (then) returned and (who) acted faithlessly, by turning away from the well of living waters, shall not be reckoned in the assembly of (the) people or recorded in their book from the day of the gathering in {erasures} of the Teacher of the Community until the rising of a Messiah from Aaron and from Israel.[1]

---

1. See M. Broshi, ed., *The Damascus Document Reconsidered* (Jerusalem: Israel Exploration Society and the Shrine of the Book, 1992) 45-47. Cf. the *editio princeps*: S. Schechter, *Documents of Jewish Sectaries: Volume I, Fragments of a Zadokite Work; Volume II, Fragments of the Book of Commandments by Anan* (Cambridge: Cambridge University Press, 1910; reprinted in one volume with a prolegomenon by J. A. Fitzmyer; New York: Ktav, 1970) 1:101-2. There in CD 19:35 one should read ובכתבם instead of ובכתבו (see p. 23). See also C. Rabin, *The Zadokite Documents* (Oxford: Clarendon, 1954; 2d ed., 1958) 36-41. In CD 20:1 one should also read היחד instead of היחיד; compare CD 19:33 with 8:21.

The second passage, CD 20:13-15, reads thus:

ומיום ¹⁴האסף יורה היחיד עד תם כל אנשי המלחמה אשר שבו ¹⁵עם
איש הכזב כשנים ארבעים.

This passage is usually translated thus:

> And from the day on which the Teacher of the Community was gathered in until the extermination of the men of war who returned with the Man of the Lie (there will be) about forty years.

In both passages the *Nip'al* infinitive of אסף is used in a construct chain: מיום האסף יורה היחיד or מיום האסף מורה היחיד, literally, "from the day of the gathering in of the Teacher (Instructor) of the Community." The sense of האסף has usually been explained by reference to the biblical use of the *Nip'al* of אסף with prepositional phrases such as אל אבותיו (Judg 2:10), "gathered to his fathers," or אל עמיו (Gen 25:8, 17), "to his people" (where the phrase is parallel to ויגוע וימת, "he breathed his last and died"), or אל קברתיך (2 Kgs 22:20), "to your grave."[2]

Recently, however, Ben Zion Wacholder has contested this interpretation of האסף.[3] He maintains that, since האסף in CD 19:35 and 20:14 is not modified by the usual prepositional phrases, "to one's fathers," "to one's people," "to one's grave," the infinitive does not necessarily bear that figurative meaning of death in these passages. He claims further that, though the *Nip'al* of אסף occurs eighty-one times in the Hebrew Scriptures, of these only seven-

---

2. See J. T. Milik, *TYDWJ*, 79. Other commentators who have understood האסף as referring to death are F. F. Bruce, *The Teacher of Righteousness in the Qumran Texts* (London: Tyndale, 1956); M. Burrows, *The Dead Sea Scrolls* (New York: Viking, 1955) 194; R. H. Charles, "Fragments of a Zadokite Work," *APOT*, 2:820; E. Cothenet, "Le Document de Damas," *TQTA*, 2.178-79; F. M. Cross, *The Ancient Library of Qumran* (3d ed.; Minneapolis: Fortress, 1994) 118 n. 2; P. R. Davies, *The Damascus Covenant: An Interpretation of the "Damascus Document"* (JSOTSup 25; Sheffield: JSOT Press, 1983) 180-81; A. Dupont-Sommer, *The Essene Writings from Qumran* (Oxford: Blackwell, 1961) 140; T. H. Gaster, *The Dead Sea Scriptures in English Translation* (3d ed.; Garden City, N.Y.: Doubleday, 1976) 77-78; J. Murphy-O'Connor, "A Literary Analysis of Damascus Document XIX.33–XX.34," *RB* 79 (1972) 544-64, esp. 546; P. Riessler, *Altjüdisches Schrifttum ausserhalb der Bibel* (2d ed.; Heidelberg: Kerle, 1966) 931; H. Ringgren, *The Faith of Qumran: Theology of the Dead Sea Scrolls* (Philadelphia: Fortress, 1963) 184; G. Vermes, *The Complete Dead Sea Scrolls in English* (New York: Allen Lane/Penguin, 1997) 54.

3. B. Z. Wacholder, "Does Qumran Record the Death of the *Moreh*? The Meaning of *he'aseph* in Damascus Document XIX.35, XX,14," *RevQ* 13 (*Mémorial Jean Carmignac*, 1988) 323-30.

teen are figurative expressions for death, and only fourteen of them have the accompanying prepositional phrase.

Among the three instances that mean "to die" and that lack the accompanying prepositional phrase are Isa 57:1 and Num 20:26. The first reads thus: "The righteous one perishes (אבד), but no one is concerned; the devout are swept away (נאספים) with no one giving it a thought; for the righteous one is removed (נאסף) from evil."[4] Apropos of this verse, Wacholder says:

> If "perish" is the acceptable translation it is so because of the surrounding context (the parallel *'abad*). This usage probably illustrates ellipsis of the idiomatic prepositional phrase which commonly follows. Such ellipsis can also be seen in the only other exception, *Numbers 20.26 (w'aharon ye'aseph umet)*. In any case, it is the context which has determined the meaning "perish" in *Isaiah 57.1*. Thus, while the customary syntagm *he'aseph 'el ammaw (qibrotaw, 'abotaw!)* refers to death there is no reason necessarily to assume that *he'aseph* without such qualification is equivalent.[5]

Again, as Wacholder notes, the prepositional phrase is absent in Num 20:26, but a parallelism with death is clear: אהרון יאסף ומת שם, "and there let Aaron be gathered and die."

Yet because in the majority of cases in the Hebrew Scriptures the *Nip'al* of אסף is used in the sense of "be gathered, be assembled" and denotes "the gathering together by persons,"[6] Wacholder maintains that there is little reason to think that this is not also the sense in CD 19:35 and 20:14. "In none of the dozen or so Qumranic usages outside of our texts does *he'aseph* denote death."[7]

Consequently, Wacholder proposes to translate CD 19:33-34 thus:

> . . . all the people who entered into the new covenant in the land of Damascus, but deviated and deserted and turned away from the spring of living water, they (the apostates) shall not be counted among the council of the people and in their book they shall not be recorded from the day of

---

4. The translations of all biblical texts are my own. Apropos of Isa 57:1, J. L. McKenzie writes, "The lines are obscure, but the sense seems to be that the death of the righteous brings them to security" (*Second Isaiah: Introduction, Translation, and Notes* [AB 20; Garden City, N.Y.: Doubleday, 1968] 154).

5. Wacholder, "Does Qumran," 324-25.

6. Ibid., 325. Wacholder says that this is the sense of אסף even in Qumran texts (1QM 3:4; 18:4; 1QH 6:7; 1QSa 1:1; 1QS 5:7).

7. Wacholder, "Does Qumran," 325.

he'aseph of the *Moreh* of the community until the anointed arises from Aaron and from Israel.[8]

Wacholder insists that הֵאָסֵף "is best understood as the assembling of the community by the Moreh at the inception of the sect in Damascus." He admits that מוֹרֵה would be a subjective genitive following the infinitive.[9] That מוֹרֵה is a subjective genitive is indeed correct, but the problem with his interpretation is grammatical. If הֵאָסֵף is actually a *Nip'al* infinitive, and Wacholder so understands it throughout his discussion, then the clause מִיּוֹם הֵאָסֵף מוֹרֵה הַיָּחִיד cannot mean "from the day of the Moreh's gathering (or assembling) the community." There is no reason to understand the *Nip'al* of אסף as governing a direct object. If that were intended, one would expect the *Qal,* or possibly the *Hip'il* of that root, but then the question arises whether אסף is used in the *Hip'il.* BDB, HALAT, and GesR record no instance of the *Hip'il* of אסף in Biblical Hebrew; nor is there any instance of it in Qumran Hebrew, according to *DCH.*

Again, Wacholder would translate CD 20:13b-15 thus:

And from the day of *he'aseph* of the *Moreh* of the community until the consuming of all the men of war who went after the man of falsehood will be about forty years.[10]

Wacholder comments, "Here again *he'aseph* is best understood as the assembling of the community by the Moreh at the inception of the sect in Damascus."[11] But the *Nip'al* of אסף cannot be given such an active meaning without further ado. As *Nip'al,* it is a reflexive or a passive and cannot govern a direct object.

Wacholder appeals to Num 11:30 as the primary biblical verse that has inspired the statements in CD 19:35 und 20:14. The verse reads: וַיֵּאָסֵף מֹשֶׁה אֶל הַמַּחֲנֶה הוּא וְזִקְנֵי יִשְׂרָאֵל, "Moses gathered himself (i.e., retired) to the camp, he and the elders of Israel." The *Nip'al* is indeed used here, but the sense of it is not active, but rather reflexive. A permutative is used, the subject

8. Ibid., 326. The verb וְשָׁבוּ hardly means "deviated." It refers to the "return" of the Jews from "Damascus" to the land of Israel. See S. Iwry, "Was There a Migration to Damascus? The Problem of שְׁבִי יִשְׂרָאֵל," in *W. F. Albright Volume* (ErIsr 9; ed. A. Malamat; Jerusalem: Israel Exploration Society, 1969) 80-88; Cf. J. Murphy-O'Connor, "The Essenes and Their History," *RB* 81 (1974) 215-44.

9. Wacholder, "Does Qumran," 327 n. 16. For examples of the infinitive followed by a subjective genitive in Biblical Hebrew, see Gen 16:3, 16; Exod 17:1.

10. Wacholder, "Does Qumran," 327.

11. Ibid.

of the singular verb, which is at first "Moses," but it is corrected to include the elders. All together they are the subject of a reflexive verb. It does not mean that Moses "gathered" the elders to the camp, but that they all gathered themselves to the camp.

Genesis 49:1, which according to Wacholder may also have inspired these two passages in CD, reads: ויקרא יעקב אל בניו ויאמר האספו ואגידה לכם, "Jacob called his sons and said, 'Gather round and I shall tell you. . . .'" Here Wacholder correctly translates the reflexive, "Gather yourselves." Again, in Deut 33:5, which reads: ויהי בישרון מלך בהתאסף ראשי עם יחד שבטי ישראל, "And he became king in Yeshurun, when the chiefs of the people assembled together (with) the tribes of Israel." This verse Wacholder discusses as a possible source for the expression מיום האסף מורה היחיד, but the phrase בהתאסף, a *Hitpaʿel* infinitive governed by a preposition, really means "in gathering themselves." It is true, as Wacholder points out, that the *Hitpaʿel* has no apparent difference of meaning from the *Nipʿal,* since both mean "to gather oneself." Moreover, all the instances of the *Nipʿal* of אסף that Wacholder cites from Qumran texts have this reflexive or passive meaning.

Now there are in the Hebrew Scriptures instances of reflexive conjugations *(Nipʿal, Hitpaʿel)* governing a direct object.[12] Wacholder, however, has not justified his interpretation of the *Nipʿal* of אסף in the instances noted above as examples of such a usage. The verb אסף does not appear among any of the examples of this usage in the Bible.

The real trouble is Wacholder's translation: he does not actually translate האסף; he merely transcribes it in his translation of the rest of the passages, thus glossing over the problem of making a *Nipʿal* function as a *Qal* and making it govern a direct object. That, however, is inadmissible. Similarly, he fails to distinguish in English the transitive and intransitive senses of "gather." So his attempt to interpret the *Nipʿal* infinitive of אסף as not referring to the death of the Teacher is simply incorrect.[13]

The best interpretation of האסף in CD 19:35 and 20:14 remains, therefore, the figurative expression for the death of the Teacher of the Community: "from the day of the gathering in of the Teacher of the Community" or "from the day on which the Teacher of the Community was gathered in."

---

12. See Gen 4:18; 21:5; Lev 6:13; Num 7:10. Cf. GKC §117w and §57 n. 2; also P. Joüon, *Grammaire de l'hébreu biblique* (2d ed.; Rome: Biblical Institute, 1947) §128.

13. See further E. Qimron, *The Hebrew of the Dead Sea Scrolls* (HSS 29; Atlanta: Scholars Press, 1986) 48: "The passive is expressed mainly by the *nifʿal.*"

Index of Ancient Writings

271

Index of Modern Authors

Index of Subjects